JEWISH AND CHRISTIAN TEXTS IN CONTEXTS AND RELATED STUDIES

Executive Editor
James H. Charlesworth

JESUS, AN EMERGING JEWISH MOSAIC

JEWISH PERSPECTIVES, POST-HOLOCAUST

JEWISH AND CHRISTIAN TEXTS IN CONTEXTS AND RELATED STUDIES
Volume 2

Daniel F. Moore, S.S.

t&t clark

2008

T & T Clark International, 80 Maiden Lane, New York, NY 10038

T & T Clark International, The Tower Building, 11 York Road, London SE1 7NX

T & T Clark International is a Continuum imprint.

www.continuumbooks.com

tandtclarkblog.com

Printed in the United States of America

ISBN 9780567027382

Library of Congress Cataloging-in-Publication Data

Moore, Daniel F.
    Jesus, an emerging Jewish mosaic : Jewish perspectives, post-Holocaust / Daniel F. Moore.
        p. cm. — (Jewish and Christian texts in contexts and related studies ; v. 2)
    Includes bibliographical references and index.
    ISBN-13: 978-0-567-02738-2 (hardcover : alk. paper)
    ISBN-10: 0-567-02738-4 (hardcover : alk. paper) 1. Jesus Christ—Jewish interpretations. 2. Jesus Christ—Jewishness. 3. Bible. N.T.—Criticism, interpretation, etc., Jewish. 4. Judaism—Relations—Christianity. 5. Christianity and other religions—Judaism. I. Title. II. Series.
    BM620.M66 2008
    232.9'06—dc22
                    2007046069

To

Raymond E. Brown, S.S.

In Memoriam

and

Frederick J. Cwiekowski, S.S.

Both of whom

first introduced me

to the Galilean of Nazareth

Contents

Acknowledgments ix

Introduction: Convergence 1

1. "From a Different Angle" 7

2. Of Glass and Stone: Sources and Inquiry 31

3. Creative Variations: Intuition and Imagination 70

4. Jesus within Judaism: A Triptych 83

5. Jesus, Jewish Brother: Varying Motifs 154

6. "Novelty and Originality" 204

Conclusion: "Theology's Masquerade" 236

Notes 249

Select Bibliography 307

Related Bibliography 315

Index 323

Acknowledgments

First, I would like to express my gratitude to *The Society of Saint Sulpice, The United States Province*, for providing me the opportunity to pursue doctoral studies. I am deeply appreciative of the fraternal encouragement and the advice given me by numerous *confreres* in the society. Their affirmation and prayers sustained me through the rigors of writing. I am obviously grateful to the late John O'Donnell, S.J., and Gerald O'Collins, S.J. for suggesting the topic and directing the thesis. I am deeply indebted to Father O'Collins who guided the thesis to completion at the untimely death of Father O'Donnell, in April 2005.

I am grateful also to my Sulpician *confreres* and faculty colleagues at Theological College, the university seminary at The Catholic University of America, Washington, D.C., for their patience and kind encouragement while I completed the thesis. Among the community at Theological College, I am indebted to the former rector, Thomas R. Hurst, S.S., for his fraternal advice and flexibility given the awkward, often inconvenient, demands of thesis completion. I am equally appreciative of the sustained enthusiasm provided to me by *confreres* Melvin C. Blanchette, S.S.—the current rector, Daniel J. Doherty, S.S., Anthony J. Pogorelc, S.S., David D. Thayer, S.S. and Robert P. Maloney, C.M.

I would be remiss not to mention the contribution and encouragement of various colleagues in this endeavor. I would like to express my gratitude to Dr. Géza Vermès, with whom I met in Oxford and who provided sustained conversation and insight as the thesis drew to completion, Rabbi Jacob Neusner, with whom I exchanged numerous emails, and Rabbi Eugene Borowitz for his kind responses to my inquiry. I would like also to acknowledge the generous encouragement afforded me by James H. Charlesworth of Princeton Theological Seminary. I am grateful to both Jim and Geza not only for their encouragement but also their mutual endorsement of the thesis for publication.

Here, too, I would also like to thank the editorial staff at Continuum, first, for accepting the manuscript for publication and, then, for the kind collaboration of Burke Gerstenschlager and Max Novick in the formatting and editing of the text. In this regard, I would like to mention also the apt assistance of David Garber, the copy editor for the manuscript.

On a more personal note, I would like to acknowledge the enthusiasm and encouragement of my family and friends. Among them, I include Joe Reynolds, David Carter, Judy Ryan, Paul Zilonka, Terry Hogan, Arturo Cepeda, Joe Jarmoluk, and

John Giovannetti, each of whom, in some measure, accompanied and affirmed, cajoled and challenged me during the rigors of research and writing, not to mention the defense of this thesis.

Finally, with a student's gratitude, this book is dedicated to Raymond E. Brown, S.S., *in memoriam*, and to Frederick J. Cwiekowski, S.S., both of whom first introduced me to the Galilean of Nazareth.

Vivere summe Deo in Christo Jesu.
Daniel F. Moore, S.S.
November 21, 2007

Whoever meets Jesus Christ meets Judaism.

John Paul II, Mainz, Germany, November 1980

Introduction

Convergence

In the shadow of the chimneys of the death-camps, anti-Judaism, even academic anti-Judaism, has become not only unfashionable but obscene. For the moment at least, it has largely disappeared, and we have now a more open, positive and constructive approach by New Testament scholars toward post-biblical Judaism.

> Géza Vermès, *Jesus in His Jewish Context,* 61

All honest theology is a theology of catastrophe, a theology that receives its impulse from the misery and the nobility of our human nature.

> Pinchas Lapide, *The Resurrection of Jesus,* 148

"We started with *Jesus the Jew*."[1] Thus concludes James D. G. Dunn in *Jesus Remembered,* the latest entry of scholarly historiography seeking to capture, magisterially, a definitive portrait of the elusive Jesus of Nazareth. Plainly stated, an obvious starting point: the Jewishness of Jesus. Such was not the case for either Jews or Christians when, in the aftermath of the Holocaust, various Jewish scholars with varying motives and goals—scholarly and irenic—sought to discern the face of Jesus from a decidedly and distinctively Jewish perspective.

In 1973, with the publication of *Jesus the Jew: A Historian's Reading of the Gospels*, Géza Vermès, the distinguished Qumran scholar, set the question and facilitated a defining motif, a motif which, some suggest, became the vehicle of a third quest for the historical Jesus during the late twentieth century. In a subsequent book, *Jesus in His Jewish Context,* Vermès recalls the initial response to his thesis:

> *Jesus the Jew*—which is the title of a book that I have written—is an emotionally charged synonym for the Jesus of history as opposed to the divine Christ of the Christian faith that simply re-states the obvious fact, still hard for many Christians and even some Jews to accept, that Jesus was a Jew and not a Christian. It implies a new quest for the historical figure reputed to be the founder of Christianity.[2]

Vermès's was not the first or the only Jewish voice that articulated a position concerning the Jewishness of Jesus—though he states clearly that his inquiry is not written from a denominational perspective, but rather from that of a historian. Previous voices were not always benign. Nor were their efforts clearly objective. Often their perspectives, which mirrored prevalent trends in scholarly inquiry, lacked, in some measure,

1

historical reliability. This, however, would change with the rising influence of the Enlightenment and its embrace of scientific method.

Initially, emboldened by the German Enlightenment and its quest for historical objectivity, German Jewish intellectuals began offering informed opinions and crafting descriptions of Jesus based upon their scrutiny of both Jewish and Christian sources. Though their fledging efforts and expertise in biblical scholarship and hermeneutics were uneven, their voices were not easily dismissed. Nor did Jew or Christian receive them eagerly. Undeterred by Jewish accusations of betrayal or Christian cries of blasphemy, Jewish intellectuals explored more deftly both Jewish and Christian sources and continued to speculate upon the person and life of Jesus.

Their motives varied and so too did their perspectives and influence. It is not the intention of this inquiry to provide a thorough history of the Jewish scholarship pertaining to Jesus, its varying motives, diverse perspectives, and subsequent influence. It is, however, the intention of this inquiry to probe the significance of twentieth-century Jewish scholarship, emerging in the aftermath of the Holocaust, which embraced as an expansive goal a scholarly assessment of Jesus, specifically from a Jewish perspective. This assessment evolved from an inquiry into the person of Jesus by select Jews into a thesis, argued most aptly, as we shall discover, by David Flusser and Géza Vermès, that holds as a prerequisite benchmark for all subsequent Jesus study the Jewish milieu of first-century Palestine in which Jesus was immersed and from which he emerges. Flusser captures their efforts succinctly: "All that we have done in the present study is but a survey of the issues connected with the historical person of Jesus in the framework of his Jewish environment. I claim that this is what one means when one speaks about Jesus from a Jewish perspective."[3] Not surprising, concomitantly with an inquiry into the Jewishness of Jesus arose an inquiry and assessment of the Jewish origins of Christianity as well.

In the latter part of the twentieth century, a convergence occurred that facilitated this conversation, one in which Jews felt compelled to join. Vermès, as our opening citation indicates, views "the impact on the Christian world of the horror of the Holocaust"[4] as integral to the convergence. This, coupled with significant information gleaned from the Dead Sea Scrolls, which powerfully influenced biblical scholarship, formed the two main causes for the surge of interest in Jesus and Judaism.

Carl E. Braaten, in his introduction to Pinchas Lapide's *The Resurrection of Jesus*, paraphrases Jürgen Moltmann's description of the period, as cited by Lapide:

> A Jewish-Christian dialogue is possible today as never before. There is a "Hebrew wave" passing through Christianity in the search for roots of spiritual identity, as Jürgen Moltmann has observed, and currently from the Jewish side there is a "Jesus wave" passing through Judaism. . . . As evidence of a "Jesus wave," Lapide cites "the 187 Hebrew books, research articles, poems, plays, monographs, dissertations, and essays that have been written about Jesus in the last twenty-seven years since the foundation of the state of Israel."[5]

In 1967, Raymond E. Brown, SS, captured the period from a Christian perspective. Writing in the preface of his book *Jesus, God and Man*, Brown stresses "the unfortunate side effect" caused by the church's defense of the divinity of Jesus—given the opposition, by some, to the affirmation of Jesus as true God and true man. Continuing in this vein, he asserts:

> Yet there is also widespread opposition to the humanity of Jesus, an opposition that is often neglected because it is unconscious or not formally articulated. Many Christian believers do not sufficiently appreciate the humanity of Jesus. They transfer the picture of the glorious Jesus back into his public ministry, imagining him to have walked through Galilee with an aura and a halo about him. They cannot imagine him as being like other men; and they are embarrassed by the Gospel vignettes of Jesus as sometimes tired and dirty, annoyed and tempted, indistinguishable in a crowd, treated as a fanatic and a rabble-rouser. How pervasive is this attitude toward the humanity of Jesus becomes evident in the vociferous opposition to any new translation of the Gospels that strips away the hallowed jargon of "Bible English" and has Jesus speak in an everyday manner.[6]

In 1997, Larry W. Hurtado, in an essay entitled "A Taxonomy of Recent Historical-Jesus Work," succinctly describes the larger post-World War II period as the context for Jesus research:

> Early on, there was the theological course-modification regarding the importance of the historical Jesus among leading members of the Bultmann school, then taken up by North American Bultmannians such as James Robinson and Robert Funk. In addition, there were major archaeological finds, in particular the Nag Hammadi codex cache, the Qumran Scrolls and the burgeoning of Israeli-sponsored archaeological work at various sites, all of which contributed to a renewed effort at setting Jesus in a more richly-informed historical context. The last forty years have also witnessed a changing demography of scholars in biblical criticism, once almost entirely a liberal Protestant enterprise, but since 1945 increasingly characterized by the participation of major Catholic and Jewish scholars—still more recently by others such as "Evangelicals," and even those who profess to live outside religiousness of any kind. Finally, with the eclipse of the biblical theology movement, we have seen a broad renewal of a historical investigation of the New Testament that resembles somewhat the history-of-religions endeavour of the early part of this century, and current historical-Jesus work is surely a reflection of this wider tidal change in the field.[7]

Schalom Ben-Chorin speaks of the "great silence"[8] among Jews before this postwar period, which Lapide, given our "mutual curiosity,"[9] currently finds brimming with hopeful possibilities for better relations between Christians and Jews: "Let us study with one another."[10]

Since Martin Buber in *Two Types of Faith* acknowledges Jesus as his "great brother," other Jewish writers have sought to ascertain a place for Jesus within the larger context of Jewish history. The seven diverse Jewish intellectuals—Samuel Sandmel, Schalom Ben-Chorin, David Flusser, Pinchas Lapide, Géza Vermès, Jacob Neusner, and Eugene Borowitz—selected for consideration are representative of this scholarly endeavor and in some measure provide the chronology of its development. It would, however, be misleading to suggest that these scholars have worked in tandem. Yet this is not to suggest that they were unaware of the others' efforts.

Our initial task is to present each author's assessment of Jesus. Their efforts are presented chronologically. The analogy for this effort is an emerging mosaic. Using a grid of questions as a framework in which to place the author's opinions, as if placing squared bits of colored glass and stone within a designated space, permits us to construct the emerging Jewish portrait of Jesus. Several authors, such as Schalom Ben-Chorin and Samuel Sandmel and others, have likened the Synoptic Jesus—and, to some extent, the Jesus quest—to a painting or icon from which one must recover the face of Jesus. Comments about layers of paint or brushstrokes and the necessity of digging beneath the Synoptic overlay convey a sense of discovery, of revealing something previously hidden, obscured, yet now poised to emerge. In an attempt to indicate the complexity of design, meaning the various methodologies employed, and the choice of sources, meaning the sources and the evidence selected to support the design, I have chosen the analogy of mosaic. The value and durability of the mosaic will depend upon the choice and quality of materials as well as the imagination and technique of the craftsman.

Why an *emerging* mosaic? I have chosen the adjective *emerging* in an effort to recapture for the reader what is currently presumed: the Jewishness of Jesus. It may be difficult for some in the twenty-first century to comprehend the significance of what has become commonplace for many. At the dawn of the third millennium, Vermès's synonym, *Jesus the Jew*, lacks its initial emotional, visceral response but not its significance. Both the critical and popular acceptance of Jesus' Jewishness and the subsequent, perhaps less well-known, influence of Judaism upon early Christianity attest to the enduring interest and influence of intertestamental scholarship and Jesus research. Both the interest and influence emerged gradually.

The quest for historical objectivity vis-à-vis Jesus and the Gospels, facilitated initially by nineteenth-century liberal Christian scholarship; then German Jewish scholarship; and the subsequent twentieth-century Jewish and Christian scholarship—these were the watershed. The implications of that quest and scholarship, as obvious among too few or vehemently denied and detested by others, stressed the Jewish heritage of Jesus, gradually gained wider appreciation and critical acceptance, and emerged (if you will) after centuries of lying dormant beneath a kerygmatic overlay. The effort, yet unfinished, gained momentum when viewed from a Jewish perspective.

As to the task at hand, chapter 1 introduces each author and provides a précis of his distinct portrait of Jesus. The group is comprised of three North Americans, one Hungarian, and three Israelis—all of whom emigrated to Palestine from Austria, Czechoslovakia, and Germany, respectively. Having suffered persecution, the latter four fled Nazi occupation, escaping the death camps. Vermès, though not an emigrant to Palestine, avoided capture in occupied Hungary. He currently resides in England. All lost family members and friends in the flames of the Shoah.

I describe these latter authors purposefully. While these authors seek to situate Jesus securely within Judaism, none do so explicitly as an apologia of Judaism. Nor are they motivated by hatred or retribution. Rather, as all seven seek to present Jesus objectively from a Jewish perspective—as defined by Flusser—each has a specific motivation, such as irenical or academic. It remains our task to introduce and explore their perspectives.

The sources constitute the resources from which an author may select the "bits of glass and stone" that inform and comprise the essential portrait; so also, various sources, methodologies, and positions will be identified and explored in chapters 2 and 3. During the course of this inquiry, it will become evident that these Jewish authors represent diverse approaches, both in methodologies and motive, in their quest to bring to light a mosaic of Jesus the Jew of Nazareth. For example, both Flusser and Vermès, writing as exegete and historian, respectively, assert persuasively that their approaches are not one dimensional, not restricted to a "Jewish" perspective in the sense of the scholarly opinion of a Jew. Rather, while not denying their unique Jewishness, their objective is an exploration of the question at hand precisely as experts in the fields of intertestamental comparative literature and history.

The authors chosen for this inquiry are not blended homogeneously, nor should they be. Given the diversity, it became evident that the authors could best be considered in two groupings: critical and creative approaches. The reason for the distinction is self-evident. Though most, if not all, of the seven authors would be considered scholars in their respective fields of endeavor—Lapide, for example, is arguably a controversialist, though irenical—all do not employ scholarly technique or historical-critical hermeneutics critically or objectively. Some, while acknowledging the normative criteria of historical inquiry, set the standards aside in favor of intuition (Ben-Chorin) or imaginative debate (Neusner), or have abandoned the scholarly endeavor in despair of the probable success (Sandmel). These categories, critical or creative, have facilitated the division of material into chapters 2 and 3 for better cohesion and comprehension.

Each author's contribution to what emerges essentially as the third quest for the historical Jesus is distinct and, in some measure, unique to the author, though one could suggest that all are indebted somewhat to previous efforts of both Christian and Jewish intellectuals. Including Eugene Borowitz, an American Jewish theologian and specialist in contemporary Jewish thought and ethics, may seem enigmatic given his limited participation in the historical Jesus debate.[11] His voice, unconventional among the seven—which accounts for the brevity accorded to him—is nonetheless viable, given its ecumenical tenor. That being said, among the Jewish authors selected for our inquiry, one can observe trailblazers, pioneers, and bridge builders, such as Lapide and Vermès, in both dialogical ecumenism and critical scholarship, though the motives for their inquiry are equally diverse and distinct. Their respective perspectives will be presented in chapters 4 and 5.

Early in the investigation, it became clear that the authors varied in their objectives and understanding of their quarry. An essential question to be asked is this: *Which* Jesus is the individual author seeking? The Jesus *of* history, meaning the real Jesus? The *historical* Jesus, meaning the figure who emerges from a critical inquiry into and assessment of Jewish and Christian comparative history and literature? The authors, themselves, are not always in agreement as to the quarry they seek or to the possibility of a successful capture. This apparent disparity and latter distinction also contributes to and parallels, unsurprisingly, similar development and controversy in the expansive field of historical Jesus inquiry and historiography. This may be observed in the explosion of articles pertaining to Jesus and first-century Judaism, as characterized by Jesus research—which is distinguished from a quest for the historical Jesus—emerging in the last two decades of the twentieth century.

After presenting the select authors' mosaics of Jesus, the task remains to compare and contrast critically the validity of their perspectives. The questions to be asked are these: What difference does a Jewish perspective on Jesus make? What has been the contribution (1) to the historical Jesus quest? (2) to Jewish and Christian relations, specifically ecumenically? (3) to contemporary Jewish theology and Christian theology, respectively? In an effort to respond to these questions, various reviews and critiques of the select authors' efforts will be offered in chapter 6. Pertinent evidence and perspectives assimilated from both critical scholarship and irenical dialogue converge into a mosaic of Jesus the Jew. The conclusion comments upon the retrospective.

Our inquiry will conclude with some brief commentary upon the state of the question vis-à-vis the quest for the historical Jesus and Jesus research—as described by J. H. Charlesworth. Necessarily this will involve questions pertaining to viable objectivity and continuity of discipline. For example, is Jacob Neusner correct when asserting vis-à-vis historical Jesus scholarship that what has emerged in Jesus scholarship less resembles history, but more so theology masquerading as history?

This introduction began by observing that in the aftermath of World War II, specifically in the afflicted consciousness of humanity, Jew and Christian alike began to ask how this tragedy could have happened, especially among and against people of faith. Some began to work to bridge the chasm separating these two historic communities of faith—one of which has its origins in the other—from which suspicion, antagonism, and hatred arose, culminating in the murderous twentieth-century genocide of the European Jewry. In an effort to assure that such a tragedy never happens again, the focus of some fell upon Jesus, previously the obstacle to reconciliation, but now perceived as the obvious and most viable bridge to span the chasm and assuage the wound of anti-Jewish and anti-Christian sentiments. Others chose to join and expand the academic quest for the historical Jesus, adding Jewish voices to the effort to explore more rigorously and objectively the figure of Jesus in historical writing. In doing so, they secured for him, a "Jewish brother," a distinguished place within Jewish history. They also brought to both communities of faith initial knowledge of, or renewed appreciation for, their common origins, distinctive traditions, and historic figures.

We begin with Jesus the Jew.

1

"From a Different Angle"

I do not think that it was ever my assumption that my Jewish eyes would see better than Christian eyes, but only that they would see from a different angle.

Samuel Sandmel, *The First Christian Century in Judaism and Christianity*, 144

Samuel Sandmel, 1911–1979

Samuel Sandmel, born in Dayton, Ohio, on September 23, 1911, received his rabbinical training at Hebrew Union College in Cincinnati, receiving an MHL degree. He was ordained a rabbi in 1937. After completing his PhD in New Testament at Yale in 1949, Sandmel accepted a professorship in Jewish studies offered to him by Dr. Harvie Branscomb, the Chancellor of Vanderbilt University and former Chairman of Biblical Studies at Duke University.[12] At Vanderbilt University from 1949–1952, Sandmel held the Hillel Chair of Jewish Religion and Thought. Returning to Hebrew Union College in 1952, Sandmel was named Provost of the College in 1956, a position that he held until 1965. He was a member of the Society of Biblical Literature, serving as its president in 1961. In 1966, Sandmel was named Distinguished Service Professor of Bible and Hellenistic Literature at Hebrew Union College-Jewish Institute of Religion. In 1968–69, he was Visiting Honorary Principal of the Leo Baeck College in London. He was awarded honorary degrees from the University of Vermont, Xavier University in Cincinnati, and Rosary College in River Forest, Illinois. In 1979, Sandmel was honored as the Helena Regenstein Professor of Religion at the University of Chicago, Divinity School. He is the author of twenty books; among them are *A Jewish Understanding of the New Testament, We Jews and Jesus,* and *Judaism and Christian Beginnings.* Sandmel's most influential work concerning the New Testament was his SBL (Society of Biblical Literature and Exegesis) presidential address (1961), published as "Parallelomania" in *Journal of Biblical Literature* (1962).

On occasion Samuel Sandmel has described himself as both "a specialist in the literature of early Christianity and Judaism of the age, and hence, a professional, not an amateur"; and as "an apologist for Jew and Judaism."[13] It is within these parameters, as a Jewish New Testament scholar, that Sandmel engages in a discussion of Jesus of

Nazareth and an appropriate Jewish grasp of him and Christianity. *We Jews and Jesus* is the hallmark of his endeavor.

In *We Jews and Jesus,* Sandmel seeks to provide "a calm and balanced understanding of where Jews can reasonably stand with respect to Jesus."[14] Positioning the German Enlightenment's quest for historical objectivity and the subsequent *Die Wissenschaft des Judentums*[15] among German Jewish intellectuals as the hinge pin upon which the "reversal of historic attitudes"[16] between Jews and Christians turn, Sandmel broadly yet deftly traces the historical development of these attitudes as they relate specifically to Jesus. He reviews the attitudes, first among the Jews, who before this watershed, viewed Jesus either negatively or not at all. Sandmel then focuses on the body of Christian scholarship that captures, or attempts to capture, modern attitudes concerning Jesus. In this latter section, Sandmel acquaints his Jewish readers with the New Testament sources, especially the Gospels and the Letters of Paul, which provide the memories, albeit redacted memories, from which various portraits of Jesus are sketched. He necessarily introduces and discusses the methodologies employed by Christian and, since the Enlightenment, Jewish scholars, himself included, to weigh the historical validity of those memories. Remarkably, he offers to his Jewish reader a nontechnical distillation of a vast body of technical scholarship. Sandmel provides "a reasoned and reasonable approach by a modern Jew,"[17] introducing the body of Jewish and Christian scholarship from the nineteenth century and early twentieth century on the quest for the historical Jesus. Sandmel concludes *We Jews and Jesus* with comments on the implications inherent therein for Jewish-Christian relations.

Jesus, Jewish Nazir, Icon of Western Culture

> I once spoke, on the spur of the moment, of likening the portrait of Jesus to an oil painting rather than a photograph; if one stands too near an oil painting, he sees the brush marks rather than the portrait.
>
> Samuel Sandmel, *We Jews and Jesus,* 108

This portrait of Jesus, of which Sandmel speaks, is captured primarily upon an uncommon canvas: the Gospels. To apprehend the historical Jesus who emerges from the Gospel texts is somewhat complicated for both the Christian and the Jew. Having presented a concise summary of pertinent Jesus research, Sandmel admits to the futility of a continued quest for the Jesus of history given both the nature of the Gospels as primary sources, though redacted sources, and the demonstrated difficulties at arriving at scholarly objectivity. He asserts:

> There is, then, no unmistakable agreement on the Jesus of history to be found in the labors and written works of New Testament scholars. What Schweitzer said almost sixty years ago is just as true now, that the Jesus of history is beyond recovery, and that the Jesus of Gospel scholars of the nineteenth century, and of the twentieth, never existed,

for that Jesus emerges more from the intuition and from the anachronisms of the scholars than from the pages of the Gospels.[18]

Even so, Sandmel admits that he, like his predecessors, could offer some clever portrait of Jesus, such as Jesus as an Essene or a Pharisee or a prophet or even a rabbi. However, he refrains from doing so, not wanting to add to the multiplicity of diverse and contradictory images, which abound as the fruit of previous Christian and Jewish scholarship. This multiplicity of images highlights the essential problem for Sandmel: the Gospels.[19]

Sandmel cannot conceive of a way to get to Jesus beneath these texts, which stand at such a distance from the Jesus of history. Though skilled in critical analysis and exegesis, he despairs of the effort: "I know of no way to separate the strands and to end up with some secure and quantitatively adequate body of material. I simply do not know enough about him [Jesus] to have an opinion, and I surely do not have enough to set him, as it were, in some single category."[20]

Conclusively, he asserts: "But beyond this, it is my conviction that the Gospels are not telling about the man that scholarship seeks, but about the human career of a divine being. To search the Gospels for the man seems to me to involve a distortion of what is in the Gospels. New Testament scholarship has not succeeded in isolating the man Jesus, Jesus the Jew."[21] The Jesus of history is beyond recovery. "We cannot be precise about Jesus. We can know what the Gospels say, but we cannot know Jesus."[22]

Sandmel, frustrated by the inability to retrieve from the tangled matrix of the Gospel fabric the Jesus of history, suggests that, if asked, one could suspend the debate concerning historical reliability and consider the Jesus who emerges from "the essence of the Gospels."[23] This is what Sandmel does.

To appreciate Sandmel's Jesus, recall his earlier distinction between a photograph of Jesus and an oil painting. We, with Sandmel, are invited to step back from the portrait, lest we become too preoccupied with the brushstrokes and painter's technique, and observe the painting from a different perspective: a Jewish perspective.

A Reform Jew, a rabbi, and New Testament scholar,[24] Sandmel broadly describes Jesus as a gifted leader, teacher, and loyal Jew.[25] He asserts that Jesus felt that the end of the world was imminent and that he himself was the Messiah. Sandmel asserts that scholars who disagree with him are incorrect.[26] But here too precision eludes him. He echoes what he previously asserted: "Precisely what kind of man Jesus was—a teacher, a leader, a wonder-worker, a prophet, a social reformer, a political rebel—cannot be ascertained. But that Jesus was a Jew, a son of the Synagogue, is beyond doubt."[27] Sandmel can ascribe to the historical Jesus no originality or uniqueness either in his teaching or his martyrdom.

Sandmel disallows that Jesus should be regarded by Jews as one who has religious significance for them. Any void or religious incompleteness that a Jew might experience would not be filled by the figure of Jesus.[28] However, he does allow and encourage Jews to embrace Jesus as, if you will, an unavoidable icon of Western culture. This would be especially relevant for Jews who participate in Western culture. Sandmel explains: "The figure of Jesus is part of Western culture, and I hold myself in all truth to be a legatee of and a participant in Western culture. In this sense, the figure of Jesus comes into my ken inevitably, just as he comes into the ken of all Western Jews. I cannot value him above the martyr Socrates, but I cannot conceive of myself as unaware of him or isolated from him."[29]

He compares the inevitability of encountering Jesus to that of encountering the music of Bach, and he notes that many Jews do not hesitate to embrace Bach.[30] That Jews may find some aspect of Jesus—his person, life, or influence—to admire should not be feared, least of all by Jews.

Schalom Ben-Chorin, 1913–1999

Schalom Ben-Chorin, born Friedrich (Fritz) Rosenthal in Munich on July 20, 1913, studied philosophy, history of art, and the science of comparative religions while in Munich. Having experienced Nazi brutality at the hands of the Gestapo, the twenty-one-year-old Rosenthal fled Germany in 1935 for Palestine. In Jerusalem, the city that was to become his permanent home, Rosenthal adopted his preferred name, Schalom Ben-Chorin (peace son of liberty), his pseudonym since 1931. The Israeli Ben-Chorin distinguished himself as an author, lecturer, journalist, philosopher, and theologian, publishing more than thirty books on Jewish historical and cultural themes. He was one of the founders of Har-El Synagogue in Jerusalem in 1958 and a key figure in establishing Progressive Judaism in Israel. A protégé of Martin Buber, Schalom Ben-Chorin, an ardent ecumenist, is perhaps best remembered as a pioneer in promoting interreligious dialogue between Jews and Christians and improved relations between Israel and Germany. In recognition of his work and scholarship, Ben-Chorin received many honors, among them: professor, *honoris causa*, at the University of Stuttgart; and doctorate, *honoris causa,* from the University of Munich. In 1975, he was invited to the University of Tübingen as a visiting professor. With the publication of *Bruder Jesus: Der Nazarener in jüdischer Sicht*[31] in Munich in 1967, Ben-Chorin joined a diverse group of twentieth century Jewish scholars in their quest to better understand and appreciate Jesus from a Jewish perspective. *Bruder Jesus* was translated into English in 2001 and published as *Brother Jesus: The Nazarene through Jewish Eyes* in the United States.

Schalom Ben-Chorin is perhaps unique among modern Jewish authors writing on Jesus in that he has encountered Jesus, not merely through the Christian Gospels. In his foreword to *Brother Jesus*, he explains:

> Over and over again I have met him, as it were, in the streets of the Old City, but also on the hills of Galilee and especially on the banks of Kinnereth, the Sea of Gennesaret. Over and over again I have heard his brotherly voice, which calls to us and teaches us how the law is to be fulfilled through love. This is the way I see Jesus of Nazareth. This is the way I hear him. Not as exalted Lord but as the picture of my "eternal brother." . . . This picture has engraved itself in my soul, and only from this perspective can I bear witness—Jewish witness—to the Rabbi from Nazareth, not to the Christ of the Church.[32]

The book is addressed primarily to Christians. Throughout *Brother Jesus*, the prose of which is more akin to a conversation than a scholarly treatise—though scholarship informs the narrative—Ben-Chorin presents Jesus from a Jewish perspective. Clearly embracing a Jewish *Heimholung Jesu* (bringing home Jesus), Ben-Chorin's interests lie in recovering from the Gospel the Jewish Jesus of history, not the Hellenic Christ of faith. To do this, "to recover Jesus' picture from the Christian overpainting,"[33] Ben-Chorin seeks to discern beneath the Greek text of the Christian Gospels the oral Hebraic-Aramaic Jesus tradition that underlies it.[34] His hermeneutic? Intuition.

Ben-Chorin distinguishes between intuition, which he uses; and fantasy, which he rejects as irresponsible reinterpretation: "Intuition, as I understand it, grows out of a lifelong familiarity with the text and allows it to be interpreted subjectively. Subjectively, to be sure, but not in an unbridled fashion."[35] He describes this approach as "intuitive interpretation," which "proceeds from a deep kindred empathy with Jesus within the Jewish world in which he lived, taught, and suffered."[36]

In a journal article, Ben-Chorin clarifies his approach: "Although the principle of intuition is here expressly admitted, anything imaginary is vigorously avoided, and only what seems exegetically possible is presented."[37] Intuitive interpretation strides the middle ground between "an unverifiable historical position, on the one hand, and theological-literary fantasy, on the other."[38]

Admittedly influenced by Martin Buber,[39] Ben-Chorin defines his position: "Jesus is for me an eternal brother—not only my human brother but [also] my *Jewish brother.* I sense his brotherly hand clasping mine and asking me to follow him. It is *not* the hand of the Messiah, this hand marked by a wound; it is certainly *no divine hand.* It is rather a *human hand,* in whose lines the deepest sorrow is inscribed."[40]

Ben-Chorin, describing Jesus as "a great and faithful witness in Israel,"[41] captures the crux of the matter poignantly: "The belief of Jesus unifies us, but the belief in Jesus divides us."[42] The belief *of* Jesus—meaning Judaism, which Ben-Chorin believes is the unifying factor between Jews and Christians—and Jewish ethos provide Ben-Chorin with a privileged, essential perspective to discern the Jewish face of Jesus beneath the Christian overlay. He writes: "I have always found so much in this land of Israel, in this city of Jerusalem, and so much in Judaism, even in our own day, that lent to the reports of the Gospels a burning actuality that is always with me."[43]

As to the divisive elements within Christianity, such as the belief *in* Jesus, Ben-Chorin sees these doctrines—Jesus as the Messiah, the apotheosis of Jesus, and so forth—as "entirely foreign to the *Jewish insight* into Jesus that we wish to describe here."[44] Thus, these matters are not entertained in the discussion.

Jesus, Jewish Brother, Tragic Figure

This is the kind of man Jesus understood himself to be: a man who lives, as a man, a typically human life, without possessions and subject to pain. In designating himself "Son of Man," Jesus does not stand before us as a prophet or the Messiah but as our brother. And since he is the Son of Man, the human question erupts within him, "Who am I?"

Schalom Ben-Chorin, *Brother Jesus,* 107

Ben-Chorin, grappling with the various possible interpretations of the phrase "Son of Man" found in Matthew 16:13, chooses as the most likely identification the vulgar form *barnash*, from the Aramaic phrase *bar-'ĕnoš* found in Daniel 7:13–14. *Barnash* means "everyman." But where does one situate this everyman within the milieu of Judaism in the first century? To whom could Jesus be compared or likened? With the Gospels before him, the recent scholarship emerging from the studies of the Dead Sea Scrolls at hand, and his knowledge of Jesus research and of Jewish literature,[45] Ben-Chorin ably, intuitively, sketches a portrait of Jesus the Jew.

Ben-Chorin discounts Jesus as a *navi'* (*nābî'*), an Old Testament prophet, and yet allows a comparison to Elijah and Elisha.[46] Jesus then is not a *navi'*, but rather, one who appears more akin to contemporary teachers of the law, such as Hillel and Shammai, and yet unique.[47] Ben-Chorin describes Jesus as a third authority in relationship to the law; and yet he admits that Jesus' interpretation of the law is not easy to define. Still, he believes "that we can recognize in Jesus' interpretation a clear tendency toward the *internalization of the law*, whereby *love* constitutes the decisive and motivating factor."[48] He admits to knowing nothing about the teaching and education of Jesus.[49] So who influenced Jesus?

Surveying the various Jewish groups—especially Pharisees, Sadducees, Essenes, and Zealots—and sects, such as the Hasidim, that were Jesus' contemporaries, Ben-Chorin posits: "We may conclude that Jesus cannot be reckoned entirely to have belonged to any single group known to us, although it is to the Pharisees—as peculiar as that may sound—that he has the closest links."[50]

Jesus appears as a rabbi, and yet he is not so easily cast. Ben-Chorin, utilizing the lens of intuitive interpretation, sees Jesus as married, yet estranged somewhat from mother and family. In view of Jesus' healing miracles, Ben-Chorin casts him as a Jewish wonder-worker, one of the Hasidim; and somewhat akin to Honi the Circle-Drawer. No Messiah, this *moshel* (*môšēl*), this master of parables, approaching Jerusalem; but nonetheless influential and controversial, given both his constituency and his opposition. Through this prism of intuition, light refracts upon a Jesus who is a man of prayer, echoing "the brotherly voice of a praying Jew";[51] but he is no Zealot. The prism's light displaces shadows, revealing a nonviolent Jesus; and yet we catch glimpses of outrage, as in the commotion Jesus provoked in the temple. With provocation comes condemnation and Jesus' subsequent martyrdom. Ben-Chorin describes Jesus' path to Jerusalem as "a pilgrimage, a victory procession, and a path of martyrdom, all in one."[52]

Like Schweitzer, Ben-Chorin recognizes an internal development in Jesus' personality between the ages of thirty and thirty-three. He describes this as "three stages of development or tragic disappointment, in the life of Jesus: eschatology, introversion, and passion."[53] Though acknowledging that Jesus, in the Jewish historical view, is a "tragic failure," given the events surrounding his death, Ben-Chorin asserts that this

"does not, however, belittle his greatness, not even in terms of Jewish historical understanding," inasmuch as others, such as Rabbi Akiba and Bar-Kokhba the Messiah,
have experienced similar failure and no diminishment of honor among Jews.[54]

Ben-Chorin succinctly states that "the Jesus revealed to us in both exegesis and
intuition (these do not exclude but condition each other) is a historical figure, even if
not all details of his life can be historically validated."[55] As to Jesus' essential Jewishness, Ben-Chorin enlists the voice of another. Adopting the words of Rabbi Leo Baeck
as his own, he echoes poignantly:

> Jesus is a genuine Jewish personality, all his struggles and works, his bearing and feeling,
> his speech and silence, bear the stamp of a Jewish style, the mark of Jewish idealism, of
> the best that was and is in Judaism, but which then existed only in Judaism. He was a
> Jew among Jews; from no other people could a man like him have come forth, and in no
> other people could a man like him work; in no other people could he have found the
> apostles who believed in him.[56]

Ben-Chorin affirms confidently: "Jesus of Nazareth lived. He continues to live, not
only in the church that rests on him, . . . but also in his Jewish people, whose martyrdom
he embodies."[57]

David Flusser, 1917–2000

David Flusser was Professor of Early Christianity and Judaism of the Second Temple
Period at the Hebrew University of Jerusalem. He was born in Vienna in 1917 but raised
in Prague. In 1939 he left Eastern Europe for Palestine and later studied at the Hebrew
University of Jerusalem, where in 1957 he received his doctorate. Flusser, an Orthodox
Jew, was appointed Professor of Comparative Religions at the Hebrew University in
1962. As a Jewish New Testament scholar skilled in philology and historical research,
Flusser concentrated his studies on the origins of Christianity from the Judaism of the
late Second Temple period to the compilation of the New Testament. He became in-
ternationally known for his work on the Dead Sea Scrolls and his critical research on
Jesus and Christianity's Jewish origins. He is credited with establishing the modern
study of Christianity in Israel. Flusser was a member of the Israel Academy of Sciences
and Humanities. In 1989 the Catholic Faculty of Theology of Lucerne, Switzerland
awarded him the degree of Doctor of Theology. Notable among his books are *Jesus,*
first published in 1968, a biography of Jesus of Nazareth (which he updated in 1997,
in collaboration with R. Steven Notley) and *Judaism and the Origins of Christianity*,
a collection of previously published articles, in 1988.

In several ways David Flusser is unique among the authors considered in this text.
First, Flusser's Jesus scholarship is not focused primarily on the Jewishness of Jesus,
but rather upon the scholarly quest for the Jesus of history. Flusser challenges the
prevalent "despairing trend" in Jesus scholarship by demonstrating with his book *Jesus*

in Selbstzeugnissen und Bilddokumenten "that it is possible to write the story of Jesus' life."[58]

Second, concurring with Robert L. Lindsey's resolution of the Synoptic Problem, Flusser accepts that the Gospel of Luke and not the Gospel of Mark preserves the original Jesus tradition and therefore is primary among the Synoptics.[59] Accepting the primacy of Luke necessarily influences Flusser's hermeneutic.

Third, as noted by R. Steven Notley:

> Flusser's philological-historical approach calls for a reconsideration of how we read the literary sources. He brings to bear the wealth of new information concerning the first-century setting in light of the Dead Sea Scrolls, historical inquiry, and recent archaeological discoveries. What results is a portrait of Jesus which gains additional depth because it is viewed within the context of Jewish thought and life of the first century.[60]

And finally, Flusser, a pioneer of a new understanding of the Jewish background of early Christianity, argues that undergirding Jesus' teachings, especially those considered most radical, are Jewish preconditions that have facilitated a new Jewish sensitivity, making Jesus' message possible and more palatable.

An original thinker who questions previous assumptions, Flusser writes a biography of Jesus based primarily upon his interpretation of the New Testament, specifically the Synoptic Gospels, to which he concedes historical reliability, though not uncritically. Flusser employs archaeology, history, and philology creatively, optimistically, to render his schema of Jesus. However, Flusser does so not simply as a Jew writing about the Jewish Jesus, but rather as a scholar who personally identifies himself with "Jesus' Jewish *Weltanschauung,* both moral and political,"[61] one not limited by his Jewish faith, nor confined by the Christian doctrine. Flusser explains: "I believe the content of his [Jesus'] teachings and the approach he embraced have always had the potential to change our world and prevent the greatest part of evil and suffering."[62]

In the aftermath of the Holocaust, Flusser reaches back into the Jewish tradition and brings forth Jesus as the paradigmatic voice capable of initiating and sustaining this sought-after change. He does not do this primarily because Jesus is a Jew, but rather because Jesus, as an effective, innovative moral teacher, is from Flusser's perspective the optimum catalyst of change. Herein lies a tension in Flusser's approach. His interest in Jesus stems primarily from his study of him as a historical person and not primarily as a Jewish person.

That Jesus is a Jew is, from Flusser's point of view, a matter of historical record, a position not widely disputed. As mentioned above, it is Jesus' teaching and his pedagogical approach that stimulate Flusser's interest. Jesus' Jewishness, though formative, is ancillary. Notley captures succinctly Flusser's distinct passion for the historical Jesus:

> As Israel's foremost scholar on Jesus and nascent Christianity, he is often asked to give comment on "the Jewishness of Jesus" or to provide the "Jewish perspective." Few requests irritate him more. Flusser's close attention to philology and textual analysis cuts against the grain of New Testament scholarship's penchant for "trendiness," in which Jesus is re-created in the mold of whichever psychological or political trend is in vogue.

He reminds his students that his is not the study of "the Jewish Jesus" but the Jesus of history. . . . His optimism that careful philological-historical research can produce fruitful results will surprise some skeptics.[63]

Flusser does not, however, ignore the question of Jesus' Jewishness. He writes:

> I am personally interested in this question because the exegesis of the Gospels is far more determined by prejudices than I once thought. Some exegetical distortions are already reflected in the extant text of the Gospels themselves. Thus, they are quite old. Moreover, I think that many of the false interpretations that have persisted through history have become second nature to most modern scholars, whether they are willing to acknowledge it or not.[64]

Flusser's early encounter with Jesus and his teachings were mediated to him by Josef Perl and the Unity of Bohemian Brethren and later reaffirmed in his subsequent encounter with the Mennonites of North America.[65] This early experience led him to dedicate himself to Jesus scholarship. Many years later, responding to a question as to whether the book *Jesus,* published in German in 1968, was a Christian book or Jewish book, Flusser replied that "if the Christians would be Mennonites, then my work would be a Christian book."[66] Flusser, referring to his efforts in his book, *Jesus,* asserts: "What I have set out to do here is to illumine and interpret, at least in part, Jesus' person and opinions within the framework of his time and people. My ambition is simply to serve as the mouthpiece for Jesus' message today."[67]

In the preface of the 1997 updated text, written in collaboration with R. Steven Notley, Flusser describes his thrust: "This present volume not only reflects the truism that Jesus was a Jew and wanted to remain within the Jewish faith but [also] argues that, without the long preparatory work of contemporaneous Jewish faith, the teaching of Jesus would be unthinkable."[68]

Jesus the Son, Faithful, Law-Observant Jew

> To Christians it may appear paradoxical that a Jew can learn from Jesus how he should pray, the true meaning of the Sabbath, how to fast, how to love one's neighbour and the meaning of the kingdom of heaven and the last judgment. An unprejudiced Jew will always be deeply impressed by Jesus' point of view. He understands he is a Jew speaking to Jews.
>
> David Flusser, "To What Extent Is Jesus a Question for the Jews?" in *Christians and Jews*, 71–72

Quoting Martin Buber, Flusser concurs "that if a man has the gift of listening, he can hear the voice of Jesus himself speaking in the later accounts of the Gospels."[69] Even so, while generally acknowledging the historical reliability of the Synoptics, Flusser also recognizes, for example, that "Jesus' attitude toward the Law has sometimes become unrecognizable as the result of 'clarification' by the evangelists and touching up by later revisers."[70] Such ambiguity does not shake Flusser's confidence. The above withstanding, he argues that "the Synoptic gospels, if read through the eyes of their own time, still portray a picture of Jesus as a faithful, law-observant Jew."[71]

Flusser begins his narrative by following the Gospel of Luke. With Jesus' baptism as his point of departure, he discerns an emerging Jesus bedewed and marked with a nascent sense of intimate sonship with the Father. Flusser sketches a Jesus who, though influenced by, is both similar to and yet markedly different from both the Essenes and the Pharisees, both contemporary groups within first-century Judaism. Nonetheless, Jesus is a Jew, a nonsectarian Jew, who, as pointedly asserted by Flusser, remains within Jewish faith.

Flusser persuasively argues that Jesus builds upon the Jewish teaching of both predecessors and contemporaries. He questions Jesus' originality, as in his teaching on ritual purity; marvels at his creative innovation, as in the rationale for healing the man with the withered hand on Sabbath; endorses Jesus' ethical preaching, as in the radical interpretation of the commandment of mutual love;[72] and applauds Jesus' skill in employing the Jewish hermeneutic: "Jesus did not accept all that was thought and taught in the Judaism of his time. Although not really a Pharisee himself, he was closest to the Pharisees of the school of Hillel who preached love, and he led the way further to unconditional love—even of one's enemies and of sinners."[73]

The Lukan Jesus, after his ordeal in the desert, returns to Galilee a controversial teacher and miracle-worker. Motivating this enigmatic young man is what Flusser describes as Jesus' "high self-awareness." Undergirding Jesus' self-awareness is the knowledge that within the Judaism of his day, a miracle-worker was believed to be closer to God than other men. It is this intimacy with God, this self-awareness, an awareness of his unique sonship, confirmed in the aftermath of his baptism, which motivates and sustains Jesus. Flusser posits:

> Jesus' consciousness of his exalted value—though, as in Hillel's case, connected with personal meekness, and though he was opposed to any "cult of personality"—was connected with the knowledge that his person was not interchangeable with any other man. As the Son, he considered himself to have a central task in the divine economy: "He who is not with me is against me, and he who does not gather with me, scatters."[74]

Jesus' central task is embodied in his proclamation and demonstration of the presence of the kingdom of heaven within the midst of the current age. Jesus posits an eschatological tension when speaking of the inbreaking of the kingdom of heaven. Flusser, commenting on the uniqueness of Jesus' proclamation and its effect, asserts:

> A movement had begun in Israel, the realization of the kingdom of heaven on earth (Matt. 6:10). The movement necessarily centered around the person of Jesus; separate initiatives, independent of Jesus, would not gather, but scatter. One can recognize again how important the concept of the kingdom of heaven was for Jesus. His main task was to be the center of the movement which realized the kingdom of God among mankind—with the aid of co-laborers. . . . With John the Baptist the biblical period came to an end and a new era—that of the kingdom of God—began.[75]

Flusser suggests that Jesus, when constructing his messianic timetable, deliberately named this intermediary period "the kingdom of heaven," so as to draw a contrast between the more widely accepted title "the Days of the Messiah." Flusser posits that "the fact that Jesus spoke about this period of the kingdom of heaven, instead of the Days of the Messiah, hints at his own messianic self-awareness."[76]

The Jewish face of Flusser's Jesus mosaic is wrought in stones that give one a glimpse of a confident, beloved Son, a Galilean miracle-worker, a Pharisaic-like teacher-preacher, an eschatological prophet, one who recognizes his role as pivotal in the inbreaking of God's reign. Flusser concludes: "Jesus' acute self-awareness cannot be denied, and I am convinced that he eventually embraced the conviction that he would be revealed as the Messiah of Israel. The inscription placed over Jesus on the cross, 'This is the King of the Jews,' suggests that others had reached the same conclusion about how he perceived himself."[77]

Pinchas E. Lapide, 1922–1997

Pinchas Lapide was born on November 28, 1922, in Vienna. Though he was detained in a concentration camp in 1938, Lapide escaped Nazi-occupied Austria, eventually arriving in England. Traveling from England in 1940 by ship, he reached the English-mandated territory of Palestine. During World War II, Lapide, an Orthodox Jew, served as a British Army liaison officer between Allied and Russian Armies. After the war, he returned to Palestine and began studies at Hebrew University in Jerusalem. During this period he was influenced by the writings of Martin Buber. His interest in Judaism and early Christianity culminated in an MA degree from the Hebrew University of Jerusalem in 1967. In Israel, he served as an officer in the Israeli Defence Forces in three wars, 194–49, 1956, and 1967. Lapide also served in the Israeli Foreign Service as a diplomat. From 1956 to 1958 he was the Israeli consul in Milan, Italy. He was acquainted with Pius XII, John XXIII, and Paul VI, whom he first met when the latter was archbishop of Milan. In 1969, Lapide settled in Frankfurt, Germany. He attained a doctorate at the University of Cologne in 1971. A Jewish New Testament scholar and an avid promoter of dialogue between Jews and Christians, he lectured widely and participated frequently in ecumenical conversations with prominent Christian theologians, such as Luz, Moltmann, Küng, and Rahner. These exchanges, often first radio broadcasts, were eventually published as books. As author of numerous books on Jewish-Christian relations—such as *Jesus in Two Perspectives: A Jewish-Christian Dialog / Pinchas Lapide and Ulrich Luz*; *Encountering Jesus—Encountering Judaism: A Dialogue / Karl Rahner and Pinchas Lapide*; and *The Resurrection of Jesus*—Lapide stands alone among his Jewish colleagues in his belief that the resurrection of Jesus was not only an historical event, but also undeniably a "Jewish faith experience." Though, like David Flusser, devoted to Jesus the Jew, he is singular in his articulation of a positive Jewish theology of the Christian church.

Pinchas Lapide occupies an unusual place among the post-Holocaust Jewish scholars who have contributed to the Jewish mosaic of the Galilean rabbi of Nazareth. Perhaps "enigmatic" would be a more apt characterization, since Lapide, an Orthodox Jew, posits rather unorthodox positions regarding Jesus, his resurrection, and the church that emerged after his parting.

Pinchas Lapide explains his interest in Jesus of Nazareth:

> In my view, I can neither speak for all Jews—no one can—nor am I an outsider. The love of Jesus and the academic interest in him and his impact were implanted in me by Jewish teachers like Joseph Klausner, for whom Jesus was "the most Jewish of all Jews," Martin Buber, who perceived him as "his great brother," and Leo Baeck, . . . who in the year 1938 at the time of the Nazi *Kristallnacht* managed to write of him: "We see before us a man who according to all the signs of his personality discloses the Jewish character, in whom the purity and worth of Judaism is so specially and so clearly revealed."[78]

Thus captivated, Lapide, an unorthodox Jewish ecumenist, argues for renewed relations among Christians and Jews, especially in the aftermath of the Shoah. While not denying the centuries of historic hostilities between Jew and Christian, Lapide does not allow these hostilities to remain or become obstacles anew. Reiterating this in his introduction to *Jesus in Two Perspectives,* Lapide writes: "The following pages are not so much concerned with accusation and denunciation as they are with overcoming a traumatic past that continues to poison the present and overshadow every dialog with its horrifying memories."[79]

To assuage the consequences of centuries of hatred and suspicion, Lapide vies for renewed efforts at dialogue that would engender better appreciation and understanding among Jews and Christian communities. He asserts:

> First, all of us, whether we gather in houses of worship that bear the star of David or the cross, [we] know next to nothing about the first and the last things. We *believe* with the firmest convictions of our hearts, but none of us [neither Christian nor Jew] can logically demonstrate the foundations of his or her religion. This should instill in all of us that essential humility which ought to characterize every proper frank conversation. True dialog must be based on complete frankness which leads to no giddy deception of artificial fellowship such as Martin Buber warned against, but rather which clarifies and discusses everything that lies on our hearts. So let us be honest, even if it is not without pain.[80]

Anticipating a Christian's question as to his interest, as a Jew, in the New Testament, Lapide responds candidly:

> Inasmuch as Christian Old Testament scholars have for hundreds of years engaged in exploring the Hebrew Bible, it is only right that Jewish New Testament scholars be involved in today's quest for the earthly Jesus and his message—all the more since, as we have learned from experience, the influence of Christian theologies will surely have a direct effect on the future generations of Jews.[81]

Citing that which is both his opportunity and challenge, Lapide ventures: "As the first step on this long journey we must correct three errors that have served as the roots of that ancient 'Christian' animosity for the Jews: Jesus was the Messiah of Israel; Jesus was rejected by the Jews; Jesus has in turn repudiated them."[82]

With the above framing his inquiry and debate, Lapide affirms his intent: "In the following pages we are not interested in syncretism, or in developing a Jewish antithesis to the church's teaching, and certainly not with the reputation of Christian truths. To eliminate antiscriptural hostility and to undergird biblical love of one's neighbor is the sole intention of the author."[83]

To apprehend Lapide's portrait of Jesus, one must eavesdrop, as it were, on various conversations or dialogues that Lapide had with both Protestant and Catholic theologians. One must contend with Lapide's distinctive view of the resurrection event and his positive Jewish theology of the Christian church. Moreover, given that "it is the author's chief purpose to provide theological building blocks for the construction of a biblical bridge"[84] between Judaism and Christianity, one must also take into account Lapide's perspective on the Gospels. He affirms that "all the New Testament passages quoted . . . are treated primarily according to *the history of their effect* rather than from a historical-critical perspective."[85] Lapide agrees that "whoever reads the Gospels carefully and with a critical eye knows that they are not objective reports but rather statements of faith, inevitably conditioned by the spirit of the times in which they were written."[86]

An irenical Lapide, seeking to correct the above-cited errors, proposes a reconsideration of the church's position and expands upon the aforementioned theological building blocks:

> If the following should be proved, on the basis of the New Testament accounts:
>
> - that Jesus never revealed himself to his people as their Messiah;
> - that Israel therefore could not accept him as their redeemer;
> - that the majority of the Jews whom Jesus addressed gave him an enthusiastic reception;
> - that it is impossible to speak of "Jewish guilt" in connection with crucifixion;
> - that even as Jesus never rejected his people, Israel never rejected Jesus; and
> - that Jesus' undivided love for his people continues to be valid even beyond his death;
>
> then Christian theology could not silently skirt these facts. It would have to examine them seriously, in order to ascertain the extent to which they would necessitate a new interpretation of the Jewish rejection of Christology after Jesus, as well as a reevaluation of its own theological position regarding Judaism.[87]

Lapide provides such evidence from a Jewish perspective, and in doing so he offers the church both opportunity and challenge.

From the various bits of stone and glass culled from texts and conversations, Lapide's mosaic emerges. Jesus—a Galilean, Pharisaic-like teacher, an eschatological instigator of a unique interpretation of Judaism, though not the Messiah, neither rejected by nor a rejecter of Judaism, destined to become "the Savior of the Gentiles"[88]—ushers in the *"praeparatio messianica,"*[89] for which Lapide is deeply grateful.

Jesus, a Pious, God-Fearing Jew and Savior of the Gentiles

> Still Jesus, if I understand him rightly, was neither an illusionist regarding fulfillment
> nor a triumphalist regarding salvation, but rather, like many Jews, an incorrigible optimist
> and hero of faith, whose entire striving was directed toward the future. Like all his fellow
> believers it was precisely the miserable, unredeemed condition of this world, that kindled
> his vibrant hope—a hope in the day of the Lord which was still to come.
>
> Pinchas Lapide, *Jesus in Two Perspectives*, 54

Lapide embarks upon a reclamation of Jesus, whom he regards as *the fifth Jesus*—in
contradistinction to the Evangelists' Jesus—who is "no lofty, fleshless figure of light
but a Jew with deep roots in the faith of his people."[90] Invoking a Pharisaic principle
that disallows negative testimony, Lapide argues for a positive assessment of Jesus:

> In Israel no one can state before a court what an accused person has *not* said, or done, or
> been involved in. There is just as little ground for anyone today to testify who Jesus was
> not. Using the sources at our disposal we can attempt to determine who Jesus was, what
> he accomplished, and which sayings were mostly his. But what he became after Easter
> Sunday for believing Jewish Christians and later for the Gentile church in addition to
> and beyond this remains an untouchable prerogative of faith that belongs to the mystery
> of the church.[91]

Of that which transpired after Easter Sunday, Lapide states simply, "'I do not know'—
this is the only honest reply a Jew can give to the Christology of the church."[92] And
yet, he equally asserts: "The outer shell of the church's Christology may be thick and
gnarled, but the inner kernel that determines its nature and lends it radiance is Jesus,
the Jew from Nazareth."[93]

Lapide, concentrating his scholarship upon the Jesus of history rather than becoming embroiled with the "God-man of Greek alloy,"[94] affirms: "Any Jewish scholar who
examines the New Testament will find that Jesus was undoubtedly a Jew—not just a
marginal Jew, nor a lukewarm, *pro forma* Jew, but a true Jew, whose spiritual roots
rose out of the prophetic core of Israel's faith, that he was closely related to the Pharisees, that he was a Galilean, and that, on top of everything else, he was a master in the
art of telling parables."[95]

To a direct question as to the identity of Jesus of Nazareth, Lapide responds: "For
me, Jesus is less the founder of Christianity than the instigator of a Christian way of
life that has as its great manifesto in the Sermon on the Mount: a Christian way of life
that at bottom amounts to a Jewish way of life and, like it, unfortunately, finds far too
few imitators in either community of faith."[96]

In answer to the question as to Jesus' place within Judaism, Lapide expands his
description of this instigator:

> If you want it simplified, in a very brief form, I would say that Jesus presented to the
> Judaism of his time a harmony of contrasts, and both parts of this term make him for me
> primitively Jewish—I would almost say, only Jewish. You may ask why. It is certain
> that he was Jewish in spirit in at least six respects: in his hope, in his eschatology, in his

Jewish ethos, in his blind trust in God, in his very Jewish messianic impatience and—last but not least—in his Jewish suffering; this we can gather without difficulty from all four Gospels. The fact that he often presented a contrast with his milieu also makes him Jewish, for I know no luminary of Judaism from Moses onwards who did not provoke lively opposition among the Jewish people.[97]

Arguing, moreover, that Jesus was not the Messiah of Israel, given the unredeemed state of the world, but acknowledging that he did become the Savior of the Gentiles, Lapide asserts:

It is true: as a Jew among Jews, Jesus was not unique. As teachers of Torah and interpreters of Scripture, other rabbis also contributed their special insights and ideas to the overall wisdom of Israel. Thousands of his fellow Jews died as religious heroes and martyrs on Roman crosses like the one on which he lost his life. As messianic prophets, others called for repentance in the face of the new age which was expected to dawn any day. And more than a dozen messianic contenders were crucified.[98]

And yet, Lapide admits:

It is equally true that only in the case of the Nazarene did his disciples experience him as the resurrected One; and as a result, that he would return as Messiah became the certainty of their existence. It is no less true, moreover, that this certainty soon crossed the borders of Israel to become the certainty of salvation which called innumerable Gentiles away from their idols to the living God of Abraham, Isaac, and Jacob.[99]

He concludes: "Last but not least, it is an indisputable fact that Jesus of Nazareth—and he alone—became a person of vital significance for millions of believing Christians whom he has helped, and continues to help, to a better life, an undying hope, and a peaceful death."[100]

Pointedly, Lapide asks: "How did the believing Nazarene become the Savior in whom others believed, the proclaimer become the proclaimed, the earthly Son of Man become the heavenly Son of God, the preacher of the Sermon on the Mount, the bringer of salvation? In short, how did the Jesus of history become the Christ of faith?"[101]

The answer is embodied in the resurrection of Jesus.

Géza Vermès, 1924–

Géza Vermès was born in Mako, Hungary, on June 22, 1924.[102] He studied in Budapest and in Louvain, where he read Oriental history and languages. In 1953, Vermès earned a doctorate in theology with a dissertation on the historical framework of the Dead Sea Scrolls. From 1957 to 1991 he taught in England at the universities of Newcastle-upon-Tyne (1957–65) and Oxford (1965–91). He is now Professor Emeritus of Jewish Studies and Emeritus Fellow of Wolfson College. Vermès has edited the *Journal of Jewish Studies* since 1971, and since 1991 he has been the director of the Oxford Forum for Qumran Research at the Oxford Centre for Hebrew and Jewish Studies. Vermès is a Fellow of the British Academy, the holder of an Oxford DLitt degree and honorary doctorates from the Universities of Edinburgh, Durham and Sheffield.

Though or perhaps because Vermès is a Qumran scholar, he was drawn into the historical Jesus search when he was invited to expand upon an article that he wrote at Christmas 1967 concerning issues related to the topic. The result in 1973 was his widely received book *Jesus the Jew: A Historian's Reading of the Gospels*, wherein he described Jesus as a Hasid (*ḥāsîd*), a Galilean, charismatic wonder-worker. What has emerged since is a trilogy: *Jesus the Jew* (1973); *Jesus and the World of Judaism* (1983); and *The Religion of Jesus the Jew* (1993). In a fourth book, *The Changing Faces of Jesus* (2001), Vermès discerns four diverse faces of Jesus in the Gospel of John, the Letters of Paul, the Acts of the Apostles, and the Synoptic Gospels, respectively. He then suggests that underlying these first-century Christian texts is a "fifth face": the elusive face of the "real" Jesus. His recent work *The Authentic Gospel of Jesus* (2003) finds Vermès wrestling, critically, with the Gospels themselves in the hope of recovering the "genuine religious message preached and practiced" by Jesus.

Géza Vermès is a prolific Jewish author. His writings on Jesus the Jew span three decades, beginning in 1973 with the publication of *Jesus the Jew: A Historian's Reading of the Gospels*—which developed into an unexpected trilogy—and continuing to *The Passion* in 2005.[103] Describing "Jesus the Jew" as "an emotionally charged synonym for the Jesus of history,"[104] he recalls for his readers the obvious: Jesus was a Jew, and therefore the portrait of the historical Jesus remained incomplete without a Jewish perspective (which today is equally obvious but in 1973 was not persistently argued or well received). Equally apparent to Vermès was the labyrinth into which one entered as one embraced historical Jesus scholarship.

Distancing himself from the overtly negative Jesus tradition of medieval Jewish polemics and the *modernen Heimholung Jesu in das jüdische Volk* (the modern repatriation of Jesus into the Jewish people), Vermès, emboldened by contemporary resources—including recent archaeological finds, such as the Dead Sea Scrolls, and modern hermeneutics—chooses a self-described quest for truth:

> My intention has been to reach for the historical truth, for the sake, at the most, of putting the record straight; but definitely not in order to demonstrate some theological preconception. . . .
>
> My purpose, both in the written and the verbal examination of "Jesus the Jew," has been to look into the past for some trace of the features of the first-century Galilean, before he had been proclaimed either the apostate and bogeyman of Jewish popular thought or the second person of the Christian Holy Trinity.[105]

Géza Vermès, positioning himself between conservative Christian fundamentalists and liberal Protestant theologians—the former arguing that no quest for the historical Jesus should be attempted; and the latter, influenced by Rudolf Bultmann, arguing the futility of any quest because of the lack of pertinent data—poses a different perspective, a historian's reading:

> Against both these viewpoints, and against Christian and Jewish denominational bias, I seek to reassert in my whole approach to this problem the inalienable right of the historian to pursue a course independent of beliefs. Yet I will at the same time try to indicate that, despite widespread academic skepticism, our considerably increased knowledge of the

Palestinian-Jewish realities of the time of Jesus enables us to extract historically reliable information even from nonhistorical sources such as the Gospels.[106]

As to how much history can be extracted from the sources, which are not primarily historical, is Vermès's to demonstrate. As he embarks on his "plan of reintegration and the corresponding work of detection,"[107] Vermès offers this caveat:

> Since it is always an arduous, and an often hopeless, task to try to establish the historical value of the Synoptic story, the plan here is not to attempt to reconstruct the authentic portrait of Jesus but, more modestly, to find out how the writers of the Gospels, echoing primitive tradition, wished him to be known. What did they think was important about him, and what secondary? On what did they expatiate fully, and what did they gloss over? Who, in brief, was the Jesus of the evangelists?[108]

Thirty years later, with the publication of *The Changing Faces of Jesus*, Vermès reaffirms the approach—more finely honed—that he pioneered in *Jesus the Jew*:

> Our three-pronged approach—from stories, titles, and teachings—to the Jesus of Mark, Matthew, and Luke has yielded a coherent picture, the portrait of Jesus intended by the Synoptics. It mirrors in some way, but is not identical with, the Jesus of history. Alas, owing to the nature of the Gospel material, strict historical accuracy is bound to elude us, but a strenuous effort can be made—and will be attempted presently—to authenticate this image as far as possible by integrating it into the cultural and religious setting of contemporaneous Palestinian Judaism.[109]

Jesus the Galilean Jew, Charismatic Healer, Teacher, and Eschatological Enthusiast

> Jesus was a Galilean Hasid: there, as I see it, lies his greatness and also the germ of his tragedy. . . . But Jesus was also, and above all, an exemplary representative of the fresh and simple religiousness for which the Palestinian North was noted.
> Géza Vermés, "Jesus the Jew," in *Jesus' Jewishness*, 118

In *Jesus the Jew*, Vermès first affirms the essential Jewishness of the Synoptic Jesus and, from his hermeneutical palette, enhances his canvas of first-century Galilee. Then in chapter 3 he expounds upon what for him is the uniqueness of Jesus' Jewish character, not that of an Essene or Pharisee, but rather of a charismatic Hasid.

Comparing the Synoptic accounts of Jesus' healings and exorcisms to the Jewish Hasidim—with its the charismatic tradition of healings and exorcisms, the portraits thereof derived primarily from comparative rabbinic traditions—Vermès ventures: "The representation of Jesus in the Gospels as a man whose supernatural abilities derived, not from secret powers, but from immediate contact with God, proves him to be a genuine charismatic, the true heir of an age-old prophetic religious line."[110]

Asking if Jesus' contemporaries may be similarly defined, thus confirming a paradigm, he asserts: "The answer is yes. Furthermore, far from digressing from the main theme of the present enquiry, it is very pertinent to a search for the real Jesus to study these other men of God and the part they played in Palestinian religious life during the final period of the Second Temple era."[111]

Vermès's descriptions of Honi the Circle-Drawer and Hanina ben Dosa, both Jewish pietists, demonstrate his hypothesis:

> One of the prime characteristics of the ancient Hasidim or Devout is that their prayer was believed to be all-powerful, capable of performing miracles. . . .
>
> To understand the figure of Honi it is necessary to remember that from the time of the prophet Elijah, Jews believed that holy men were able to exert their will on natural phenomena. Thus, in addition to offering formal, liturgical prayers for rain, in times of drought people urged persons reputed to be miracle-workers to exercise their infallible intervention on behalf of the community. Such a request for relief from their misery is reported to have been addressed to Honi sometime before the fall of Jerusalem to Pompey in 63 BC.[112]

Of Jesus' contemporary, Hanina ben Dosa, who was "one of the most important figures for the understanding of the charismatic stream in the first century AD,"[113] as well as one who "offers remarkable similarities with Jesus,"[114] Vermès writes:

> Hanina's intervention was principally sought in cases of sickness. His fame was such that the outstanding personalities of his own time are portrayed as requesting his help. Nevertheless, though later hailed as the saviour and benefactor of his generation, there are signs that he was in part resented by the leaders of contemporary Pharisaism and by representatives of the later rabbinic establishment.[115]

Vermès cites several parallels between Jesus and Hanina ben Dosa. Despite "all the precautions imperative to a thesis which, owing to the nature of the sources, must remain hypothetical,"[116] he disallows coincidence as the explanation for the similarities between Jesus and Hanina ben Dosa. Instead, he surmises:

> It would appear, rather, that the logical inference must be that the person of Jesus is to be seen as part of first-century charismatic Judaism and as the paramount example of the early Hasidim or Devout.
>
> It may have been their charity and loving-kindness that inspired the affection felt for these men, but it was through their "miracles" that they made their strongest impact. When rabbinic tradition attempts to define Hanina, it refers to him as a "man of deed."[117]

In support of his hypothesis, Vermès posits:

> That a distinctive trend of charismatic Judaism existed during the last couple of centuries of the Second Temple is undeniable. These holy men were treated as the willing or unsuspecting heirs to an ancient prophetic tradition. Their supernatural powers were attributed to their immediate relationship with God. They were venerated as a link between heaven and earth independent of any institutional mediation.
>
> Moreover, although it would be forcing the evidence to argue that charismatic Judaism was exclusively a Northern phenomenon because Jesus, Hanina ben Dosa, and possibly Abba Hilkiah were Galileans, this religious trend is likely to have had Galilean roots. It is, in any case, safe and justifiable to conclude that the unsophisticated religious ambiance of Galilee was apt to produce holy men of the Hasidic type, and that their

success in that province was attributable to the simple spiritual demands of the Galilean nature, and perhaps also to a lively local folk memory concerning the miraculous deep of the great prophet Elijah.[118]

After careful study and analysis, Vermès concludes that Jesus is best situated in first-century Judaism as a Galilean charismatic Hasid (*ḥāsîd*): a "man of deed."[119]

After completing his first task, he turns to the second: "It remains now to be seen whether the fundamental definition thus established is sufficient in itself, or is to be completed, or even replaced, by applying to Jesus the specific roles and functions ascribed by the Bible or post-biblical Jewish tradition to eschatological figures awaited with intensity by first-century AD Palestine."[120]

In both the latter half of *Jesus the Jew* and, more recently, *The Changing Faces of Jesus*, Vermès demonstrates how, without their christological overlay, various New Testament titles attached to Jesus—such as teacher, exorcist, preacher, prophet, Son of God—are thoroughly Jewish.

Jacob Neusner, 1932–

Jacob Neusner was born on July 28, 1932 in Hartford, Connecticut. He earned an AB degree at Harvard University in 1953 and then did graduate work at Lincoln College, Oxford, in 1953–54; at Hebrew University, Jerusalem; and at Union Theological Seminary. Neusner completed his doctorate at Columbia University, receiving his PhD degree in 1960. Throughout the 1960s he held posts at various universities before settling as a Professor of Religious Studies at Brown University in 1968. He was named vice-president and program chair of the American Academy of Religion in 1967–68 and president in 1968. Neusner was a founding member of the Association for Jewish Studies, the Council on the Study of Religion, and the Max Richter Foundation. In 1972, he was named a fellow of the American Academy for Jewish Research and became a member of its executive committee four years later (1976–81). In 1975, Neusner was honored as the Ungerleider Distinguished Scholar of Judaic Studies. In 1990, he moved to Tampa, Florida, as the Distinguished Research Professor of Religious Studies at the University of South Florida. In 1994, he also joined the Faculty at Bard College, Annandale-on-Hudson, New York, as Professor of Religion. Currently he is Research Professor of Religion and Theology at Bard College and Senior Fellow, Institute of Advanced Theology.

Neusner, a renowned scholar of Judaism in the first century of the Christian era, is a prolific writer. He is an acknowledged world expert in rabbinic literature. His latest effort, *The Babylonian Talmud: A Translation and Commentary* (22 vols.), bears a copyright year of 2005 and was released with a CD-ROM in March 2006. Neusner has published over five hundred books on Judaism, for Jewish and non-Jewish audiences. Notable among these are *The Rabbinic Traditions about the Pharisees before 70* (first ed., 1971); *Between Time and Eternity: The Essentials of Judaism* (1976); *Judaism in the Beginning of Christianity* (1984); *Judaism and Story* (1992); *The Talmud of Babylonia: An American Translation* (1984–95); and *The Rabbinic Traditions about the Pharisees before 70* (augmented ed., 1999). In 1993, in anticipation of the third millennium, Neusner, imagining himself in conversation with the Matthean Jesus, with whom he respectfully disagrees, published *A Rabbi Talks with Jesus: An Intermillennial, Interfaith Exchange*. In 2001 this was followed by a revised and expanded version simply titled *A Rabbi Talks with Jesus*. Two other books pertinent to Jesus scholarship followed. The first was released in 2001: *Jews and Christian: The Myth of a Common Tradition* is a reprint and expanded version of the 1997 edition. The second book, *The Missing Jesus: Rabbinic Judaism and the New Testament*, published in 2002, is a collaboration between Bruce Chilton, Craig Evans, and Jacob Neusner.

Jacob Neusner, unlike his contemporaries, issues a respectful but critical "no" both to the tendency among Jewish scholars to laud Jesus' facility with and reverence for the Torah and the equally erroneous tendency, as Neusner views it, of those involved in the Jewish-Christian dialogues to presuppose some level of success. He claims that the preconditions for dialogue have not been met largely due to a misperception about a common tradition. In *Jews and Christians: The Myth of a Common Tradition*, Neusner, explains:

> Judaisms and Christianities never meet anywhere. That is because at no point do Judaism, defined by the Torah, and Christianity, defined by the Bible, intersect. The Torah [Hebrew Scriptures] and the Bible [OT and NT] form two utterly distinct statements of the knowledge of God. The Torah defines Judaism— all Judaisms—and the Bible, Christianity, all Christianities. The differences between the Torah and the Bible cannot be negotiated, and those shaped by the one can never know God as do those educated by the other. That is why the faithful of Judaism can never concede the truth of Christianity: at its foundations it rests on a basis other than the Torah of Sinai. Once God has made himself known in the Torah, the Torah must stand in judgment on all other claims to know God. And that judgment, for Christianity and for Islam, takes the form of the persistence of Israel, the holy community of the Torah. That is why, when a Jew adopts Christianity or Islam, he can no longer claim a portion in the God of Jacob. That implacable judgment, broadly shared among Jews, will never change and is beyond negotiation.[121]

To grasp Neusner's perspective, not only on the Jewish-Christian dialogue but importantly also on Jesus, it is appropriate to allow Neusner full voice regarding his premise that modern Jews and Christians have gotten it wrong:

> Recognizing the diversity of Judaic and Christian religious systems in the formative age, we may still speak of Judaism and Christianity as distinct religious traditions, incompatible from the beginning. That is because all Judaic religious systems of antiquity privilege the Pentateuch, within the larger canon of ancient Israelite Scripture, and affirm that through the Torah Israel knows God. All Christian religious systems of antiquity concur that through Jesus Christ, Christianity knows God. So far as the two large families of kindred religions intersect, it is at Scripture. Judaisms read forward from Scripture, Christianities read backward from Christ to Scripture. The reason that Judaism can never formulate a Judaic theology of Christianity that [the] Christian faithful can comprehend then is simple. Judaism—all Judaisms—begin in the Torah and find there the criterion of theological truth. *And Christianity, for its part, from the important teachings of Jesus*

forward, violates the teachings of the Torah. By that criterion Judaisms and Christianities can never meet. The faithful of Judaism and the faithful of Christianity pray to the same God, the God who made himself known to Abraham and at Sinai. But they cannot say the same prayers, because, from the perspective of Judaism, we know God through the Torah, and judge all truth by the criterion of the Torah. *Much that Jesus taught, and still more that his disciples taught, do not meet that criterion but violate the teaching of Moses our rabbi.*[122]

His is the unapologetic voice of Jewish dissent, through which he hopes to stimulate religious dialogue. Neusner explains: "It [Jewish dissent] is a gesture of respect for Christians and honor for their faith. For we can argue only if we take one another seriously. But we can enter into dialogue only if we honor both ourselves and the other. In these pages I treat Jesus with respect, but I also mean to argue with him about things he says."[123]

Jesus, Galilean Sage, a Teacher of torah

The Jesus with whom I compose my argument is not the historical Jesus of a scholar's studious imagination, and that is for a simple reason: those fabricated historical figures are too many and diverse for an argument. . . . I write for believing Christians and faithful Jews; for them, Jesus is known through the Gospels. I address one of those Gospels.[124]

Jacob Neusner, *A Rabbi Talks with Jesus*, 7

Neusner enters into the discussion of Jesus not simply from a different angle but decidedly unlike his twentieth-century Jewish contemporaries. He disallows the possibility of rescuing the Jesus of history held bound within the overlays and accretions of Gospel redaction. He resists the temptation, the fabrications of other scholars both Jew and Christian, to reconstruct Jesus from the confines of the Gospels by utilizing historical-critical scholarship and creative intuition or other hermeneutics. Nonetheless, Neusner does engage Jesus.

Creatively, Neusner, "taking a different path,"[125] proposes to listen and respond to Jesus. Specifically and importantly, Neusner as a twentieth-century rabbi converses with the first-century itinerant Jesus. Of the four canonical Gospels, he selects Matthew's Gospel since by common consensus it is acclaimed as the most Jewish. Neusner proceeds to construct an imaginative conversation, an argument—as Neusner describes it—with the Matthean Jesus. Of his proposed creative encounter, Neusner writes: "I can see myself meeting this man and, with courtesy, arguing with him. It is my form of respect, the only compliment I crave from others, the only serious tribute I pay to people I take seriously—and therefore respect and even love."[126]

As to the impact of such a meeting, he speculates: "We would meet, we would argue, we would part friends—but we would part. He would have gone his way, to Jerusalem and the place he believed God had prepared for him; I would have gone my way, home to my wife and children, my dog and my garden. He would have gone his way to glory, I my way to my duties and my responsibilities."[127]

Eugene B. Borowitz, 1924–

Eugene B. Borowitz was born on February 20, 1924, in New York. He received his BA degree from Ohio State University in 1943; and an MHL from Hebrew Union College in 1948. Borowitz was ordained a rabbi by the college that same year. He earned a DHL at Hebrew Union in 1952 and a EdD from Columbia University in 1958. From 1953–57 he served as a rabbi in Port Washington, New York. In 1957–62 he was the director of education for the Union of American Hebrew Congregations, New York City. Borowitz is currently the Sigmund L. Falk Distinguished Professor of Education and Jewish Religious Thought at Hebrew Union College—Jewish Institute of Religion, New York City, where he has taught since 1962. He is the editor of *Sh'ma: A Journal of Jewish Responsibility,* a magazine of social ethics. Borowitz has received honorary degrees from Lafayette College, Colgate University, and Gratz College. In 1982–83 he was the first occupant of the Albert T. List Professorship of Jewish Studies at Harvard University Divinity School. Borowitz is the dean of American Jewish philosophers and specializes in contemporary Jewish thought and ethics.[128] Among his Jewish peers he has argued for a distinct Jewish theology, a position that has met with critical response. Borowitz has delivered papers and talks throughout the world. He is the author of numerous articles and twelve books, including *Exploring Jewish Ethics: Choices in Modern Jewish Thought; Liberal Judaism;* and *Contemporary Christologies: A Jewish Response.*

Eugene Borowitz is deeply committed to the Jewish-Christian dialogue and yet, among the seven authors considered here, has perhaps the least to say about the Jesus of history. His reason is simple enough: Jesus is an elusive figure.

This became abundantly clear to Borowitz as he prepared two lectures at the invitation of The Center for Jewish-Christian Learning at The College of St. Thomas, St. Paul, Minneapolis, in 1987. The first was titled "Jesus the Jew in Light of the Jewish-Christian Dialogue." The second explored "The Challenge of Jesus the Jew for the Church." While composing the first lecture, what he presumed would be a "relatively accessible theme, one which it would be easy to get one's hand on,"[129] turned out to be more difficult as Jesus the Jew proved to be "a quite illusive [elusive] figure."[130]

His exploration of the sources, both historical and contemporary, yielded similar results: ambiguous sources, diverse methodologies, enigmatic images, "less a picture of Jesus the man in that historical period than an account of how a modern theory of structuring history produces its historical Jesus."[131] His decision, given the elusiveness of Jesus, was to take the subject of the session literally:

> That is to say I understand my invitation to speak to you about "Jesus the Jew in the Light of Jewish-Christian Dialogue," to mean "Who is the Jesus mediated to me, a Jewish theologian, by a dialogue partner?" I now seek to encounter not the Jesus of history or of any popular theology, but the Jesus of the person who comes to meet and speak with me out of his or her Christian faith; the one who, standing beside me in all openness, yet

believing in his or her own faith. . . . Who is the Jesus mediated to me and communicated to me by this dialogue partner? I can hope to recognize the Jewishness of this because, in fact, I am being asked to recognize something about myself which the other has seen in me and the faith I bear and [has] identified with the Jesus of his or her Christian faith.[132]

Borowitz, thus, provides us with a unique, if somewhat unconventional, Jewish perspective, one mediated to him by his encounter with a Christian believer.

Jesus, Light and Shadow

This Jesus is a Jewish type that I can easily place. He's Galilean pietist, an itinerant preacher and teacher who wants Jews to be more Jewish, who wants them to take their religion more seriously, to express its inner belief in their lives, to add sanctity to their day-by-day affairs as part of the people dedicated to God and pledged to see that God's rule ultimately triumphs in history. When I meet this Jesus, the Jesus I find in the eyes of someone who meets me in honest dialogue, I recognize [that] I have come across something particularly precious.

Eugene B. Borowitz, "Jesus the Jew in the Light of the Jewish-Christian Dialogue," 17

Borowitz describes this Jesus, communicated to him vis-à-vis Christian disciples, fundamentally as a lover of God, a God whom Borowitz recognizes as "the God of Abraham and Sarah, of Isaac and Rebecca, of Jacob and Leah and Rachel."[133] Jesus' love for God is expressed in service. Borowitz observes that Jesus serves God in a familiar fashion: "loving people and reaching out to them."[134] He does this primarily as a teacher, one with "a quite familiar pedagogic style."[135] Calling Jesus an unusual teacher, both in his use of parables and choice of diverse audiences, Borowitz comments:

What I find particularly attractive about this Jewish teacher—particularly compared to some religious leaders today—is his activism. He seeks to serve God by doing things with people amid general society. . . . He is in the world. Indeed he is willing, despite the risks, to go up to Jerusalem, the center of his society and its power. I like that kind of religion; it reminds me of Nathan's and Amos' faith, the reality of human life and social existence, one that confronts and seeks to change real people facing real situations.[136]

Encountering this Jesus is "particularly precious." Yet Borowitz is not naive. He knows well that standing beyond the light of the Jewish-Christian dialogue is the Jesus of the shadow. As do all Jews, Borowitz fears this Jesus whom he encounters "when dialogue is not fully present," lest "the old Jewish-Christian animosities somehow reassert themselves."[137] Borowitz poignantly describes the shadow's darkness: "This Jesus is the one who validated the hatred and oppression of his own people. He is the Jesus who stands for crusades, inquisitions, ritual murder charges and forced conversions. He is the Jesus who did not protest the Holocaust. That Jesus may not hate his kinfolk in his heart, but he has stood idly by while his kinfolk bleed."[138]

Borowitz affirms: "We remain fearful of that Jesus, the one who is the only way to the Father, the son who comes to supersede all prior covenants, the Lord whom everyone should and one day will come to serve. If you do not see the shadow, you won't appreciate the light."[139]

Wary of the shadow Jesus, Borowitz engages Jesus of the Light. This Jesus, Jesus the Jew, admired by Borowitz, is poised as a challenge for the church.

Summary

Whether it is Sandmel's serious effort to distill and distribute pertinent scholarly New Testament knowledge concerning Jesus to thoughtful Jews; Lapide's dialogue with Catholic and Protestant theologians in hopes of redressing errors that bedevil the deepening of mutual respect and understanding between Jews and Christians; Vermès's thoughtful assessment of Jesus as a Galilean Hasid; or Neusner's respectful dissent, these diverse Jewish voices are raised to urge both Jews and Christians to take a fresh look at Jesus from a different angle.

2

Of Glass and Stone

Sources and Inquiry

Whatever the problems in reconstructing the life and career of Jesus (and they are immense), it is more plausible than otherwise that the general outline of his career as presented in the Gospel biographies is correct, simply because the hypothesis that these accounts were entirely composed, rather than partially altered, to make a theological point is more implausible than the belief that the outlines of Jesus' career are correctly described. Among other objections to the former (and commonly held) view are the survival within each Gospel of contradictory views of Jesus and the oddness of biography as a vehicle for theological didacticism.

Martin Goodman, *The Ruling Class of Judea*, 22

Géza Vermès, quoting Goodman, in his book *The Religion of Jesus the Jew,* succinctly captures the issue at hand: a reasoned rebuttal to Rudolf Bultmann's dissent and the subsequent historical skepticism it has engendered regarding the quest for the Jesus of history.[140] In the light of *Formgeschichte,* Bultmannian skeptics, arguing against the credible recovery of the life and personality of Jesus from the Gospel narratives, since these lay beyond the range of the Gospels' voice, turned their considerable attention to the Gospels' kerygmatic tenor. Having done so, first in Germany and then in North America, Jesus scholarship, vibrant before the 1920s, entered a virtually dormant period.

Though historical skepticism held sway over New Testament scholarship, a nascent quest reemerged in Germany in the 1950s, spurred on paradoxically by some of Bultmann's former students, especially Ernst Käsemann and Günther Bornkamm. In the latter half of the twentieth century, there was an explosion of scholarly efforts demonstrating the viability of this renewed quest for the historical Jesus. The 1980s saw a resurgence of Christian and, notably, Jewish New Testament scholarship that grappled with the above-described sources to discern within them a more decidedly Jewish hue to the features of Jesus.

Vermès provides an apt description of this third quest: "Unlike Bultmann and his followers, the authors of this latest historical quest, while investigating the subject from within the (Synoptic) Gospels, pay not mere lip service to the essential contribution of post-biblical Jewish literature to a genuine perception of Jesus, but in their various ways make substantial use of it."[141]

Vermès has specifically in mind A. E. Harvey and E. P. Sanders.[142] John P. Meier, N. T. Wright, James D. G. Dunn, and James H. Charlesworth could also be added as further representing Christian scholarship. As to Jewish representation in this third venture, given the time period, one would include Géza Vermès, David Flusser, and Jacob Neusner—though Neusner's dissent could arguably disallow his inclusion.

Serious scholarship, delving critically and favorably into postbiblical Jewish literature, coupled with a significant advancement in Jesus studies, the influx of new pre-70 CE Palestinian data, gave rise to a distinction between a quest for the historical Jesus[143] and research. Charlesworth explains:

> The singular most important difference between the quest and Jesus research, which began about 1980, is that during the former periods, both the old and the new quest, scholars were searching for Jesus. Now, scholars find themselves *bumping into* pre-70 Palestinian phenomena: some Old Testament Pseudepigrapha, all the Dead Sea Scrolls, houses in Capernaum (one that may well have belonged to Peter and in which Jesus would have spoken), streets and the remains of massive houses, stairways, gates, and thousands of artifacts—especially stone jars—from pre-70 Jerusalem. . . .
>
> In doing research on historical (but not historic) documents and stones, we are deeply involved in history and are attempting to reinterpret the life of pre-70 Jews. We find ourselves eventually engaged in Jesus research, which may be defined simply as the attempt to understand the man of history in light of all the evidence that is now pouring our way. The New Testament traditions about the pre-Easter Jesus are subsequently read in appreciably different ways.[144]

The renewed optimism undergirding the Jesus scholarship of the latter half of the twentieth century, the advent of significant, new pre-70 phenomena paralleling the life and culture of Jesus, and the unique perspectives of Jewish New Testament scholars upon this data and New Testament parallels—among whom Flusser and Vermès may qualify as Jesus researchers—form the vehicle for a distinctively Jewish contribution to our understanding of the man Jesus. Weighing in on this debate, on either side, one finds the diverse, sometimes discordant, voices of our post-Holocaust, Jewish authors.

This chapter and the one following present the authors' choice of sources, methodologies, and perspectives culled from their respective investigations. To better facilitate this presentation, the authors are gathered into two groups. In this present chapter, Sandmel, Flusser, and Vermès are representative of the aforementioned critical approach since they scrutinize the sources through the prism of acceptable critical scholarship: historical scrutiny, historical-critical hermeneutics, philological exegesis, and archaeological investigation. In the works cited, Ben-Chorin, Lapide, Neusner, and Borowitz have chosen to ignore, creatively interpret, or subjectively nuance the pertinent data—as in Ben-Chorin's hermeneutic of intuition or Neusner's granting of the historicity of Matthew's portrait of Jesus—and they thereby constitute a creative approach.[145] Their subsequent consideration comprises chapter 3.

Before exploring the groups' use of sources and methodologies, it is appropriate to provide a brief explanation concerning the sources and the coherent criteria of authenticity widely employed to discern the historical reliability of the sources and their content.

Sources

The primary sources for a historical investigation of the figure of Jesus are the canonical Gospels of the New Testament, especially the Synoptic Gospels: Mark, Matthew, and Luke. John's Gospel poses obvious difficulties, as Vermès explains:

> Research has to be restricted to Mark, Matthew and Luke and to exclude John because, despite the occasional historical detail it contains, its Jesus portrait is so evolved theologically as to be wholly unsuitable for historical investigation. By contrast, a reading, devoid of doctrinal preconceptions, of the Synoptic Gospels has disclosed a figure of Jesus as a popular teacher, healer known directly from Josephus, and indirectly from rabbinic literature.[146]

Though the Gospels, together with other pertinent New Testament Scriptures, are obvious internal texts within the Christian tradition, sources from outside the tradition also contribute to the body of evidence accumulated in the pursuit of Jesus, such as the writings of Josephus, a Jewish historian, who in a limited, though "monumental" way[147] affirms the historical existence of Jesus; the Qumran texts, indirectly; and the corpus of rabbinic literature, including the Mishnah and the midrashim.[148] To these external sources one could add the Old Testament Pseudepigrapha, which includes Jewish apocalyptic literature; the writings of the Hellenistic Jewish philosopher, Philo of Alexandria; the Roman commentators Tacitus and Pliny the Younger, both of whom document, in a limited way, the historicity of the man Jesus and his subsequent followers; the Nag Hammadi Codices, fourth-century AD Coptic texts, which include the *Gospel of Thomas*; and significantly, recent archaeological evidence that corroborates and enhances our understanding of first-century Palestinian life and culture.

Notably, it is the influx of new information, such as comparative Jewish literature and archaeological evidence, that provides our Jewish authors an opportunity to discern and explore, from a Jewish perspective, first-century Jewish parallels vis-à-vis the Gospel texts. However, an obstacle to the viability of such comparisons may dampen enthusiasm, given the possibility of anachronistic interpolation.[149] This dual nature of the Jewish contribution to the historical Jesus study is both the opportunity and the obstacle, which raises both the praise and the critique of their contemporary colleagues, Jew and Christian.[150]

These sources, especially the Jewish literature and archaeology, together with the Christian Gospels and pertinent New Testament writings, such as the Pauline corpus, are either critically appraised by our authors to illuminate the figure of Jesus from within the texts or creatively interpreted to craft a Jewish portrait of Jesus.[151]

Criteria of Authenticity

Oral traditions, Jesus traditions, circulating among his disciples during his life and especially after the death of Jesus, are relatively quickly, comparatively speaking, gathered and eventually redacted into written texts that preserve and facilitate access to the Jesus kerygma. Such transmission and subsequent redaction invite questions as to authenticity and historical reliability. The literary form—such as narrative, poetry, or prose—of the documents, as well as the archaeological evidence, invites critique and interpretation.

To address this question of historical reliability, scholars have reached wide consensus upon a body of criteria—such as the criterion of embarrassment, the criterion of discontinuity or dissimilarity, and the criterion of multiple attestations—to ascertain or argue, not for certitude but rather for degrees of probability when confronting internal and external sources.[152]

Samuel Sandmel's Critical Approach

In his book *We Jews and Jesus*, Sandmel explores the Jewish attitude toward Jesus and writes primarily for a Jewish audience. His goal is to assist the thoughtful, twentieth-century Jewish reader as to where one may stand with respect to Jesus. The specific audience that Sandmel has in mind, though, is much more focused. Sandmel addresses himself primarily to Jewish parents and their college-bound children, who are encountering and contending with, perhaps for the first time, Christianity and Christian perspectives on Judaism vis-à-vis Jesus. Though Sandmel's purpose is pastoral and his perspective Jewish, this does not preclude others from benefiting from his noteworthy accomplishment.

Though a serious Jewish New Testament scholar, adept with contemporary historical-critical hermeneutics, Sandmel with his target audience necessarily chooses to translate scholarly acumen in a nontechnical manner. This is no small task since Sandmel does not seek simply to frame the question, but also to enflesh his timely presentation "with what I hope is a little more profundity."[153] Sandmel, commenting upon previous Jewish attempts to address the question of Jesus, describes the scope of his task:

> It is not, as some think, a new problem for our time; for almost two hundred years a host of Jews have addressed themselves to it. I do not try to reflect all of the Jewish opinions, for many are repetitious of each other, but I do try to cite some of the major motifs of Jewish writing on the subject so that the reader can see, or at least glimpse, the earnestness with which Jews have approached the question.[154]

Along with these major motifs of Jewish writing, Sandmel wrestles also with the data culled from recent biblical scholarship and the challenge of representing that body of evidence to the novice. He explains:

Second, on the conviction that an informed opinion can be superior to an uninformed one, I have devoted the major part of this book to reproducing some of the concerns and the conclusions of technical scholars, both Christians and Jews. . . . To reflect for the general reader what scholars have written in technical books poses for the interpreter the acute problem of conveying clarity while at the same time dealing responsibly with the scholarship he is citing. I have earnestly tried to accomplish this.[155]

Sandmel provides the reader with an overview of Jewish attitudes toward Jesus; a useful survey of the historical Jesus study; and a critical assessment of the Gospels as both primary sources for historical Jesus research and Christian literature.

As to methodology, given the nontechnical parameters of Sandmel's task, it is not surprising that, though clearly informing his presentation, there is no overt exploration of the coherent criteria or the diverse sources that the various authors, highlighted by Sandmel, utilize to construct their respective portraits of the historical Jesus. Unlike some of the authors whom we will later consider, Sandmel, though conversant with the sources, does not expound upon them in *We Jews and Jesus*.[156]

Since his intention is to offer a nontechnical work, Sandmel does not elaborate upon the criteria that undergird his assertions. This intent, coupled with his reluctance to reconstruct a portrait of the historical Jesus from the primary sources because of both his consternation at the apparent impotence of the historical-critical method to get behind the Gospel texts and the multiplicity of images already mined from these texts by other scholars—which, in Sandmel's estimation, also points to the futility of the methods employed—leaves us little to explore critically in *We Jews and Jesus*. It would be wrong, however, to assume that he lacks the necessary facility to engage the sources critically. One need only survey his later works—*The First Christian Century in Judaism and Christianity* (1969), *A Jewish Understanding of the New Testament* (augmented edition, 1977), and *Judaism and Christian Beginnings* (1978)—to dispel such an assumption. Though here, too, one realizes how dated Sandmel's material is compared to today; thus when speaking of biblical scholarship, Sandmel repeatedly refers to lower criticism and higher criticism rather than, for example, to diverse methodologies, redaction criticism, and criteria of authenticity.

It is the bits of glass and stone, meaning Sandmel's choice of evidence sifted from the sources, to which we must turn our attention if we are to glimpse Jesus from Sandmel's perspective.

The prism through which his perspective is refracted is Jewish New Testament scholarship. It therefore is appropriate, by way of preface, to add Sandmel's description of himself as both a Jew and a scholar since this self-understanding undergirds and informs his perception of Jesus. Speaking of himself and his scholarly task, Sandmel, in *Judaism and Christian Beginnings*, states succinctly:

If I were to set forth a claim of some tolerable mastery, it would be in Bible (Old Testament), in Hellenistic Judaism, and in New Testament. I am experienced in Rabbinic literature, but am by no means an unqualified expert; I have studied and taught the Apocrypha and the Dead Sea Scrolls, but make no claim of special eminence. . . . I have dared to hope that where expertise has eluded me, responsible competency has not.[157]

Speaking specifically about Jewish New Testament scholarship, he states in *A Jewish Understanding of the New Testament*:

> I am writing on the significant religious content of the book [the New Testament], as a scholar of it, not as one religiously committed to it. In the sense that I am a Reform Jew it is undeniable that the modernism and rationalism of Reform Judaism shape my approach, as such factors shape the approach of anyone to a traditional literature. A Reform Jew is selective in what he accepts as valid in the ancient Jewish traditions; it is to be expected, then, that he will exercise similar selectivity in his approach to Christianity, and that an earnestly sympathetic understanding, therefore, of one facet or another of that tradition is not to be equated with a doctrinal acceptance of it.[158]

Sympathetic understanding should not be misunderstood or misconstrued as doctrinal acceptance. Here Sandmel frames the scope of his inquiry. While his interest is scholarly, his intent is both educational and ecumenical. He is not attempting, however, to legitimize nor proselytize. He offers to his readers a positive assessment of the New Testament literature. In doing so, he assesses the biblical evidence, striving to justify a positive, contemporary Jewish portrait of Jesus as discerned by a Jew analyzing predominantly Christian sources from a Jewish perspective.

After offering this explanation, Sandmel further describes his scholarly bias:

> My own bias will be evident in that I find myself operating within the suppositions of the liberals. The liberal Protestant scholarship is free, objective, and rigidly honest. In it, predisposition and prejudgment are reduced to the vanishing point, and reverence for the New Testament has seemed to evoke as full and open-minded a study and investigation as fallible man can undertake. The fair-mindedness of most liberal Christian scholars has been one of the delightful discoveries of my study of the New Testament.[159]

Sandmel, however, is not content to leave his self-portrait abstract. In *We Jews and Jesus*, Sandmel asserts: "In addition to my being Jewish, I am a product of the intellectual stream of modern times. My spiritual legacy from the past, like that of other American Jews, includes, in addition to Judaism, Greece and Rome, the Protestant Reformation, Humanism, the French Revolution, Darwin and Freud, and for that matter, Shakespeare and Beethoven and Puccini."[160]

Pointedly, though, it is as a Jew that Sandmel enters into the discussion. He concludes: "All these factors are involved in how I think, and what I think. Yet they are involved also in how I feel. Since to all these things I react in some measure with the heart, obviously in this matter of Jesus and us Jews I do so too. So do most Jews."[161]

Sandmel, an American rabbi, admits that his experience of Judaism is vastly different from that of a European Jewish peer. "The challenge is comparable, but the environments are totally different, for we American Jews have never had to struggle for political rights, having been born into a relatively high measure of religious toleration, and we have enjoyed an unprecedented high peace and harmony with our Christian neighbors."[162]

Nonetheless, Sandmel plainly asserts that the historic animosities that exist between Jews and Christians have distorted not only their appreciation of one another's religions but also the image and appreciation of Jesus.[163] It thus should come as no surprise that his own appreciation for Christianity is not shared by some of his Jewish contemporaries. In fact, Sandmel knowingly runs the risk of their disdain by entering into the debate. In the introductory pages of *We Jews and Jesus*, he feels compelled to acknowledge his fidelity to Judaism.[164] Convinced of the necessity—and the opportunity, given modernity's expectation of religious toleration—to answer the probing questions of "thoughtful Jewish people," Sandmel persists.

Sandmel Grappling with the Sources

Rabbinic Literature and Extrabiblical Texts

> Jesus is mentioned in the rabbinic literature, but passages are rather late retorts to post-New Testament Christian claims. They are of no value for the history of Jesus.
>
> Samuel Sandmel, *A Jewish Understanding of the New Testament*, 194

In *We Jews and Jesus*, Sandmel assesses the contribution of the Jewish historian Josephus. Sandmel argues that of the three passages in question, the one that specifically mentions Jesus, *Jewish Antiquities* 18.3.3 (63–64), wherein Josephus describes Jesus as the Christ,[165] is widely regarded as a Christian interpolation. The second and third passages are from the Slavonic Josephus and as such pose their own difficulties.[166] Because of this presence of a Christian interpolation and the inherent difficulties with the Slavonic texts, Sandmel disallows Josephus as a viable source for Jesus study.

In *Judaism and Christian Beginnings*, Sandmel provides the following general description of rabbinic literature, which may prove helpful:

> The Rabbinic literature is known among Jews as the Oral Torah, in contradistinction to the Written, which is Scripture. Paradoxically, the Oral Torah came to be set down in writing; for example the Mishna was recorded around A.D. 175–200. This literature can, however, justly be known as Oral in that its recalls the opinions of Sages and the events of the time long before its written form, these transmitted orally. As a repository of quite old oral traditions, some as early as about 200 B.C., and of events in the first and second centuries of the present era, the Rabbinic literature is a source of some knowledge of the historical events of the period with which we deal. This testimony to history is quite indirect and in manner coincidental, and far from full; one could not from the Rabbinic literature assemble materials that would enable one to write a sequential account of events. The chief utility of the Rabbinic literature, as we shall see, is in the realm of religious ideas and practices, of worship, and of pious observance, but not in that of history.[167]

Given the above statement, it is not surprising that, while analyzing the few mentions of Jesus in the Talmud, Sandmel asserts:

In sum, the contribution of Rabbinic literature to knowledge about the figure of Jesus, is scant, and even that material is of no value for Jesus himself, as independent testimony to him, but is derived from hearsay about what is in the Gospels. . . .

Accordingly, though Jesus was a Jew, there are no Jewish sources of any value about him.[168]

Commenting on *The Dead Sea Scrolls,* Sandmel dismisses their usefulness in the quest for the historical Jesus. He writes in *We Jews and Jesus*: "I would personally emphasize that the scrolls have contributed in quantity little to what we already had, and that in quality this little is worthy but of much less significance than it was sometimes initially deemed. . . . For the scrolls turn out not to have added one jot to the previous knowledge about Jesus."[169]

As to other sources, such as the Talmud, Sandmel observes: "What knowledge we have about Jesus comes only from the New Testament. He went unmentioned in the surviving Jewish and pagan literature of his time."[170]

Sandmel concurs with mid-twentieth-century scholarly assertions that credible sources apart from the New Testament texts mentioning Jesus are limited, lacking, or anachronistic.

The New Testament

A Jew will find some particular answers of the New Testament unsatisfying, but he can find that the questions asked are universal among men.

Samuel Sandmel, *A Jewish Understanding of the New Testament,* 11

The New Testament corpus, specifically the Pauline letters, the Gospels, and the Acts of the Apostles, provides pertinent data about Jesus and the emerging Christian communities. In his book *A Jewish Understanding of the New Testament,* Sandmel provides his American Jewish audience, those who possess "a thoughtful curiosity and an earnest desire for information,"[171] with an introduction to New Testament material based upon contemporary New Testament scholarship, albeit a palatable distillation thereof. Sandmel, with an eye toward facilitating a better understanding of Christianity by Jews, provides a thorough and yet concise summary of the New Testament material.

In explaining the historical approach that he takes in examining the New Testament literature, Sandmel counsels his readers:

To understand the New Testament as it was understood in its own time, the historian must understand the circumstances and concerns of that time, as well as the languages which voiced its history. We have seen that the minimum equipment for the purpose of establishing the New Testament text is a knowledge of Greek, Aramaic, and Hebrew. In order to examine the text more deeply and analytically, even beneath the level of the words themselves, further specialized tools arc essential. Jewish history and religion, rabbinic literature, Greek philosophy and popular religion, and the social and political conditions of the Graeco-Roman world—all must be known to the scholar, to supply him with the content out of which the New Testament arose.[172]

Though Sandmel acknowledges the sacred character of the texts he studies, he does so as a Jew. Sandmel, reflecting upon his efforts in *A Jewish Understanding of the New Testament,* states: "I tried to write with fullest respect about beliefs which I have not shared. In a word, I tried to write about Christian sacred literature in the way I would have wanted Christians to write about what is precious to us Jews."[173]

In *The First Christian Century in Judaism and Christianity,* he asserts: "I do not think that it was ever my assumption that my Jewish eyes would see better than Christian eyes, but only that they would see from a different angle."[174] From the perspective of this different angle, Sandmel delves more deeply into the New Testament literature to extract from its testimony the historical Jesus.

Given the genesis of the New Testament corpus, Sandmel argues that "the historian must reconstruct a kind of jigsaw puzzle, many significant pieces of which are lost or were never made."[175] When considering what may be a gained from the New Testament material about Jesus, he admits to the following:

> Certain bare facts are historically not to be doubted. Jesus, who emerged into public notice in Galilee when Herod Antipas was its Tetrarch, was a real person, the leader of a movement. He had followers, called disciples. The claim was made, either by or for him, that he was the long-awaited Jewish Messiah. He journeyed from Galilee to Jerusalem, possibly in 29 or 30, and there he was executed, crucified by the Romans as a political rebel. After his death, his disciples believed that he was resurrected, and had gone to heaven, but would return to earth at the appointed time for the final divine judgment of mankind.[176]

To develop this historical figure more completely, more convincingly, is the challenge.

The Letters of Paul

> Strangely, Paul gave little data about Jesus. We know from him only that Jesus was crucified, that Paul believed he was resurrected, that Jesus had a brother named James, and that Jesus taught that divorce was prohibited.
>
> Samuel Sandmel, *We Jews and Jesus*, 26

In his analysis of the Pauline corpus, widely acknowledged as the earliest Christian writing to the fledging Christian communities cropping up around the Mediterranean basin, Sandmel admits both to the complexity of the man and his material for the average reader and the Jewish reader especially:

> The Epistles of Paul are not easy reading; the New Testament itself contains the view that they are difficult. The Jewish reader, in crossing over from the Old Testament directly to the Epistles, must make an abrupt transition from the familiar simplicity of Palestinian Judaism to a complex Graeco-Roman doctrine. He will encounter an exposition of an abstruse theological viewpoint and a metaphysical explanation of Jesus as the Christ rather than the attractive Gospel narratives, partly familiar to him, of Jesus as a personality.[177]

Counseling the Jewish reader, he adds: "We Jews should notice not so much the answers Paul gives—these are foreign to us—but his question, which is part of the matrix of Judaism."[178]

Our purpose is not an exposition of Sandmel's analysis of the Pauline corpus; rather, of interest to us and to Sandmel is Paul's information about Jesus the historical person. And this, in Paul, is sorely lacking. Sandmel comments: "Whatever may be the reason for the absence of information about Jesus, this much is clear, Paul was interested in the significance of Jesus, not in details about him. One might say that Paul tried to tell us *what* Jesus was, not *who* he was. To Paul, Jesus was a human being who represented an interval in the eternal career of a divine being."[179]

More specifically, Paul, influenced by a Greek philosophical worldview that differed from Palestinian Judaism, sees in the person of Jesus the means of salvation. Sandmel, in *A Jewish Understanding of the New Testament*, writes:

> For Philo, observance of the laws of Judaism was the soul's path to salvation. The essential difference between this point of view and that of Palestinian Judaism is that Palestinian Judaism never conceived of a man requiring such salvation. Traditional Judaism to this day has no such doctrine, since it never accepted the Greek premise that the material world is evil, but insisted that it was good. But for Philo and Paul, who were Jews inclined by the Greek atmosphere towards the goal of transcending physical nature, salvation from the material world was the very focus of religious aspiration. Philo paved his road to salvation with allegorical midrash on the meaning of Jewish Law. Paul found salvation in his interpretation of the meaning of the career of Jesus.[180]

Sandmel's assessment of Paul's soteriology follows:

> To Paul, Jesus was God's Logos. The Christ was that aspect of deity which could be apprehended by man. It miraculously had come to earth in human form and had graciously gone through the experience of crucifixion, death, and resurrection. Christ Jesus, in dying, had left his human form to ascend to heaven; and he had provided an example and a means for men to do the same. God had graciously provided man with salvation, Paul insisted, if man would believe and identify himself with the Logos.[181]

Clarifying Paul's use of the term 'Christ' and its unique Pauline interpretation, Sandmel asserts:

> The older Jewish term, Christ (Messiah), was used by Paul in a new sense as the designation for this ultimate Logos, in whom the earlier Jewish idea of the Shekinah [cf. the holy spirit], transmuted into the Greek concept of the divine mind, now lost its philosophical abstractness to become dramatically epitomized in one individual. The force of personalities—Jesus, the inspiration, and Paul, the inspired—thus brought to birth out of Greek-oriented Judaism and its search for salvation a new religion, a religion clearly the product of its ancestry and yet uniquely itself.[182]

Furthermore, Sandmel argues:

> It is not Jesus, the man, who might conceivably have been accepted as the Jewish Messiah, but the divine Christ whom Paul encountered in a revelation who fills Paul's concern and to whom Paul is dedicated. He is determined not to know Christ "from the human point of view" (II Cor. 5:16); his interest in the significance of Jesus' career

completely overshadows the details of the career, and his writings give few data about Jesus.[183]

Though Sandmel praises Paul's creative, persuasive literary skills, he concludes that, for Paul, "Jesus was a human being who represented an interval in the eternal career of a divine being."[184] Paul, therefore, provides little data that will assist in the recovery of the historical Jesus.

The Gospels

> The Gospels in telling about Jesus are dealing also with the human career of a being considered divine.
>
> Samuel Sandmel, *We Jews and Jesus*, 26

In his quest to recover the historical Jesus, the primary texts through which Sandmel must sift critically are the revered documents of the nascent Christian communities, whose interest in writing and preserving these Gospels was kerygmatic. Because the Gospels' purpose is kerygmatic and not historical, at least not in a modern sense,[185] scholars searching for remnants of the historic Jesus amid Gospel redaction are faced with the challenge of discerning historical fact from accretions and anachronisms. Sandmel states the obvious question with which he and others, before him and after, must grapple:

> If we assume that the Gospels contain both reliable materials and also accretions, additions from later times, then the next question can be this: is it possible through objective study, through pain-staking, fair-minded analysis, to separate these two from each other? Is it possible to separate the Jesus of reliable history from the Jesus of legend and the Jesus of theological belief? Is it possible to separate the man, purely the man, Jesus, from the view of him as divine?[186]

The attempts to recover the man Jesus from the Gospel overlay have given rise to three consecutive quests for the historical Jesus, not to mention the clamor of dissenting voices disparaging such efforts. Sandmel is situated within the second quest: a period characterized by a renewed optimism in critical research. At first, he embraced the critical scholarship, especially form criticism and source criticism, and shared in the optimistic enthusiasm. However, Sandmel began to doubt the objectivity of both the scholars and the critical methods of form criticism and source criticism that they employed to parse the Gospel texts. Recognizing that he had less of a stake in historicity of events within the texts than form criticism and its adherents, Sandmel, a competent historical-critical scholar, ultimately disparaged the effort to rescue the Jesus of history from the Gospels.

Sandmel recalls the dilemma that led to the eventual abandonment:

> What has constantly preoccupied and even troubled me is not the intertwining of questions of history and literature, for this intertwining is simply a fact. Rather my

difficulty is the equivalent of a paradox, that on one hand we possess only a bare minimum of data, and on the other hand the question of isolating precise history seems to me to continue to hold the center of the stage of the accumulated scholarship.[187]

Confident at first that form criticism would assist in the unraveling of the paradox, Sandmel embraces it, only later to despair of its objectivity. He writes:

Form Criticism had its supposedly objective method by which to differentiate between the historical and unhistorical. Yet, in my dilemma of wanting precise history and of finding it constantly elusive, I was discovering Form Criticism to have more of a stake in history than I had, and to be very subjective, rather than completely objective. I found myself concluding that all too often the method argued in a circle.[188]

Critical of form criticism's subjective tendencies, evidenced by frequent presupposition and inference that cast doubt rather than clarity upon the Gospel texts, Sandmel affirms:

I found myself tending to the conviction that in reality there has been, and there can be, no *objective* method whereby the historical can be separated from the unhistorical, in either the Pentateuch or in the Gospel materials or in Acts. My contention was not, and is not, that there are not historically reliable materials in them, but only that there does not exist in scholarship the tools whereby to make the differentiation. Predisposition, whether of religious conservatism or religious radicalism, necessarily enters in, and so do the other traits of the individual researcher, so that the assertion of history, or its denial, is a matter more of the personality of the scholar than the clarity of the documents.[189]

Sandmel, "rebelling against an overabundance of subtleties, acute distinctions, and eisegeses which seemed . . . to go beyond all reasonable prudence,"[190] begins to question the demands of modern scholarship for precise history and overprecise theology when confronting the pertinent sources. Underlying his question is Sandmel's appreciation of the distinction between ancient and modern concepts of history. It is this distinction that prompts his caution. Sandmel argues:

What all the writings, Old Testament, New Testament, and the quasi-biblical literature, have in common is that history is for them not the quasi-science it tried to become in the nineteenth century, but rather an interpretation of accepted but unproven events. No author in those days had a Ph.D. from a modern university, or worked in archives, or strove to present "the events as they really happened." For us to confront those authors on the plane of "pure" history is to expect what they neither intended nor were able to provide. It is a hopeless task to disentangle history from nonhistory in the narratives of the Tanak or of the extra-biblical literature, or of the New Testament.[191]

Decrying this tendency for precision or overprecision, Sandmel counters: "Precise history seemed to demand being set over and against a merely general history, and precise theology over and against a merely general theology. That is to say, I felt that I could accept, and even begin to formulate, some broad and general history and theology of Christianity, but I was debarred from precision."[192]

Aware and critical of the implications of scholarly practice, Sandmel writes:

Certain refinements of the scholarship have seemed to me so completely speculative as to merit on my part only acquaintance but not familiarity, and flirtation rather than courtship and marriage. I am no longer carried away by the ability of a scholar to tell us exactly where and when some New Testament or Old Testament document was written, and the sources it has been derived and adopted from, and the precise conditions under which the composition issued forth.[193]

He thus compares the hermeneutic of the ancients when offering a historical narrative vis-à-vis the moderns' quest for historical precision. This insight is coupled with or undergirds his growing appreciation for approximation rather than historical certitude. It all contributes further to Sandmel's growing disillusionment with the retrieval of a historical Jesus.

Sandmel describes his perspective, seeing through Jewish eyes, as seeing from a different angle. The different angle of which Sandmel speaks is not simply a Jewish angle. It is that, but it is also an angle influenced by his growing scholarly diffidence and critique of form criticism and its adherents. Embracing this perspective leads Sandmel to disavow both the critical method in vogue and the benefits thereof, at least as they pertain to advancing the historical Jesus quest.[194]

From his Jewish perspective, Sandmel sees an alternative to viewing the Gospels as documents from which to mine pure history. He theorizes that the Gospels are better understood as midrashim, as meditative piety, not unlike the midrashim that inform and interpret the Old Testament. Sandmel comments on this similarity: "I find myself regarding the Gospels as midrashic. The apocryphal Gospels I would take to be midrashim on the canonical Gospels, or on the Gospel tradition. But the Gospels themselves are the midrash on the career of Jesus; they are not the career, in somewhat the same way that the midrashic Abraham is not the same as the Abraham of Genesis."[195]

Though exploring the Gospels as comparative Jewish literature is a viable approach, Sandmel concedes that little is gained from a perspective that limits the Gospels to being midrash:

> But a written Gospel is more than a concatenation of midrashim, for none of the canonical Gospels lacks an inherent unity or an inherent integrity. They are portraits of Jesus. What is more natural than for modern historians to attempt, again and again, to use scholarship so as to paint a new "authentic" portrait of him? If, from the midrash on Abraham, we cannot re-create the Abraham of Genesis, can we from the midrash on Jesus re-create him and his age?[196]

Sandmel's exploration of the Gospels as midrash fails—not surprisingly, given its failure to retrieve from Old Testament midrash Abraham or Moses—to yield to him a greater clarity of insight into the Jesus behind the Gospels.

Dovetailing with his consideration of the Gospels as midrash, Sandmel explores a third alternative when approaching the Gospels from a Jewish perspective: the Gospels as literature. As a scholar, Sandmel approaches the Gospel texts critically; as a Jew, he finds them ordinary. In *We Jews and Jesus*, specifically in the chapter titled "The Jewish Reader and the Gospels," wherein Sandmel suggests that Jews approach the Gospels as literature, Sandmel slips off the mantle of New Testament scholarship and explains:

A Christian reading the Gospels has an empathy with Jesus, but I find that I have only a sporadic empathy with the Gospels in general, and I warm up only to scattered items . . . .

I simply do not see in the Gospels any special profundity and startling perceptiveness, or tremendously acute religious insight, surpassing other sacred literature. They are human, they are occasionally touching, they are here and there engaging. Since they are like anthologies of rabbinic anecdotes, I find myself quite often in full accord with some act of Jesus', or some word attributed to him. Indeed where I am not repelled, as I am by Matthew 23 with its cruel words, I find myself attracted and acquiescent, but not more so than by other edifying literature. I do not find in myself a feeling that the Gospels are superlative either as literature or as religious documents. They are for me antiquarian materials absorbing to study, but I cannot in any honesty evaluate them as superior to a simple book like Ruth, or IV Maccabees (an extraordinarily beautiful book), or Plato's *Symposium*, or Goethe's *Faust*, or Dostoyevsky's *Crime and Punishment*. If I felt that I knew more about Jesus than I do, I would be able to verify, or reject, a conjecture that the Gospels do not rise to the level of Jesus. I do not, then, find myself among the admirers of the Gospels as literature, and it would be false for me to pretend that I do.[197]

Sandmel, fearing misunderstanding, adds: "I am only commenting on the Gospels *as literature,* not on the Gospels as objects of study for a knowledge of early Christianity."[198] It is these "objects of study" that he assesses critically and objectively (to the degree that one may claim objectivity) to weigh the historical reliability of the evidence therein contained. Coupling this effort with his critique of the contribution of scholars of former historical Jesus quests, Sandmel concludes, not surprisingly, that the Jesus of history is irrecoverable; just as is the Abraham of Genesis. He writes in *We Jews and Jesus*:

There is, then, no unmistakable agreement on the Jesus of history to be found in the labors and written works of New Testament scholars. What Schweitzer said almost sixty years ago is just as true now, that the Jesus of history is beyond recovery, and that the Jesus of the Gospel scholars of the nineteenth century and of the twentieth, never existed, for that Jesus emerges more from the intuition and from the anachronisms of the scholars than from the pages of the Gospels.[199]

A decade later Sandmel puts it this way in *A Jewish Understanding of the New Testament*:

Though a voice here and there questions the validity of the liberal scholarship, the prevailing view is this: the evangelists disclose Jesus to us only after the church has meditated on his significance as the Christ. The form of the Gospel writings is such that it is not always possible to penetrate effectively beyond the Gospel portraits of Jesus to Jesus himself. We can know what the evangelists saw in Jesus the Christ. We can know what the evangelists report of his teaching; we can be sure that however the Gospels have shaped his words, some echo of them is discernible. But we cannot describe with exactness and precision the details of the life and career of Jesus.[200]

In his 1977 augmented edition of *A Jewish Understanding of the New Testament*, Sandmel contends at length with this dilemma involving historical reliability and scholarly objectivity. He acknowledges the controversies stirred by a historical-critical approach to biblical texts and observes that there is no unequivocal voice among

Christian scholars in this debate. Regardless of the controversies, the disharmony and the uncertainties occasioned by liberal scholarship, Sandmel declares that the significance of Jesus is not lost:

> Obviously, variety exists among such New Testament scholars, and no single description can fit all. But however negative the results from pure historical study, they have not been accompanied in liberal Christianity by negative approaches to the significance of Jesus. The usual liberal Christian has a positive conception of Jesus, difficult as it may be to contain it within definitions. It may be said, in general, that Jesus, as a man, serves the liberal as the model for those things which he considers the most cherished human ideals. Uncertain as he may be about the details of the career of Jesus, even to the point of rejecting this or that item of the traditional faith as unreasonable, or as untenable, he sees in that career the supreme idealism which he considers worthy of imitation. In this, at least, he concurs in the faith of the evangelists, who saw in Jesus the pinnacle of human achievement, love, and solicitude. To an outsider, it may appear that an idealized man, not a real man, has been accepted as the model to emulate; to the liberal Christian, Jesus seems to be not an idealized man, but the ideal man of history.[201]

Though appreciating the perspective of Christian scholars vis-à-vis the man, Jesus, he offers this Jewish rebuttal:

> In the Jewish tradition there have been many men who have inspired in modern Jews ideals such as self-effacement, nobility, and exaltation, yet neither the Old Testament nor rabbinic literature depicts the ancient worthies—Abraham, Moses, David—as perfect. Not perfection, but goodness, has been the Jewish demand from the individual, a goodness which we Jews have urged upon ourselves as a personal responsibility to be as nearly perfect as possible. But we Jews have not equated strict perfection and goodness as interchangeable. If the standard seems deceptively lower than Christian perfectionism, we Jews would reply that the standard is not less exacting, but only more humanly tolerable. In the Jewish view, there have been many great men, but not any perfect man to be exalted above all others.[202]

Scholars have and continue to construct their image of Jesus based upon diverse criteria employed by them to ascertain the degree of historical probability that such evidence arising from the Gospels warrants. Sandmel, however, does not do so. In *The First Christian Century in Judaism and Christianity*, he explains his dilemma:

> I am troubled by this personal inability to go beyond the Gospels back to Jesus himself. This is just as much the case respecting the teachings attributed to him in the Gospels as respecting the events of his career. I have tried to express this inability in a variety of ways. . . . The paradox, then, is that I can neither dismiss the Gospels, especially Mark, as totally unhistorical, nor yet accept all the specific details as reliable history. And I know no unchallengeable way of objectively distinguishing between the history and the non-history. If I know anything, it is the Gospels, not Jesus. Moreover, I think I have been fairly consistent in holding that the Gospels are not about the man Jesus, but about the human interval in the eternity of the divine Christ. Jesus the man is nineteenth and twentieth century, and not the first. The question "What manner of man?" is asked not so much to elicit an answer about a human, but so as to stress the supernatural character of Jesus. Only in the sense that I deny the Christ myth and its assertion that there never

was a man Jesus, am I willing to discuss Jesus. To affirm as I do that there was such a man is different from asserting that I possess precise information about him.[203]

To affirm Jesus' existence is different from positing precise details about him. In *Juda ism and Christian Beginnings*, in the chapter entitled "Jesus and Judaism," Sandmel echoes this conclusion: "Precisely what kind of person Jesus was—a teacher, a leader, a wonder-worker, a prophet, a social reformer, a political rebel—cannot be ascertained. But that Jesus was a Jew, a son of the Synagogue, is beyond doubt."[204]

Not surprisingly, Sandmel, when confronted with the question of historicity and the lack of the means to discern between fact and accretion, argues: "We cannot be precise about Jesus. We know what the Gospels say, but we cannot know Jesus. If our objective is an accurate history of Jesus, then we are more apt to find that the Gospels obscure than reveal him. The acute differences in the Gospels rise to impede a merely literary appreciation of them."[205]

The lack of tools whereby to differentiate between what is and is not historically reliable and the lack of an objective method with which to use the tools if they existed, combined with a preoccupation with precise history and the tendency toward subjectivity—these all lead Sandmel to abandon the effort.

What then does Sandmel offer to his reader about Jesus, the Jesus of whom we cannot be precise? He offers a viable, contemporary Jewish perspective and an appreciation for the limits that we may impose on the ancient text and author. Though Sandmel does broadly and intuitively affirm the Jewishness of Jesus, he shrinks from statements of certitude. In *The First Christian Century*, he argues, in two points, the value of uncertainty: "In the first instance, it is far better for scholarship to know where it stands than for it to fail to know. . . . Scholarship seems to me to be at its best when its claims are not extravagant and when they are substantial."[206]

As to the second point, wherein Sandmel grapples with the question of the supernatural, Sandmel writes:

> In the second instance, when we deal with the internal question of the supernatural, it is perhaps worth pointing out that it is at all times difficult to recapture the past, but it is especially so in the case of highly significant religious movements. There seems [to be] an inevitable mystery relating to elements that go into the fashioning of some particular personality, and relating also [to] the impact which he makes on his environment and which the environment makes on him, and the resultant movement which ensues and which goes through growth and development.[207]

The logical progression of Sandmel's reasoning leads him to affirm, not simply the value of uncertainty, but also the a priori status given the presence of mystery:

> It seems to me to be quite consistent with the mysterious nature of religion that the early phases of particular religions should be shrouded in some darkness. Rationalist that I am, I still feel that that which is essentially religious in religions loses much of its significance when it is all too easily and too readily explainable. All too often there is a tendency in man to explain too much and, indeed, to explain away.[208]

He concludes: "To know too much can destroy in man the intuitive creativity which is the element in our being that enables us to fashion or propagate our tremendous religious institutions."[209]

With the above as preface, we may now ask with Sandmel, where, then, may a thoughtful Jew stand with respect to Jesus? Seeking to deliver on his initial intent in writing *We Jews and Jesus*, "a reasoned and reasonable approach by a modern Jew" to Jesus, Sandmel opts paradoxically for a creative solution.

Familiarity with the Gospels and employing inference and even intuition in trying to present Jesus afresh may be appropriate, if not also necessary. In *We Jew and Jesus*, Sandmel does just this when he poses several hypothetical questions:

> Yet, suppose someone were to say to, "You keep stressing the scholars. Aren't you making too much of scholarship? Forget for a moment the problems of historical reliability. Here are the Gospels; they tell you about Jesus. Isn't it possible for you to have some view of him which is the essence of the Gospels but kept free from the piddling questions of whether or not that detail is historical?"[210]

He responds: "I have at various times tried to formulate some such thing, but I have not succeeded in satisfying myself. I once spoke, on the spur of the moment, of likening the portrait of Jesus to an oil painting rather than a photograph; if one stands too near to an oil painting, he sees the brush marks rather than the portrait."[211]

Sandmel describes his efforts in retrieving Jesus from the Gospels as a personal inability, a frustration, a confusion, a paradox, and an elusive task. Plainly, from Sandmel's scholarly perspective, Jesus the man is irretrievable. Yet Sandmel, equipped with Jewish religious sensibilities and scholarly acumen, attempts his mosaic of the historical Jesus even so, borrowing bits of stone and glass from a wide and diverse tray, and sketching the shape of this Jesus with a Jewish hand.

David Flusser's Critical Approach

Whereas Sandmel despairs of the effort to retrieve Jesus from the Gospel texts, Flusser embraces it—but with a different purpose. Flusser, uninhibited by Bultmannian pessimism, determines to demonstrate that "it is possible to write the story of Jesus' life."[212] Using the Gospels as his primary sources, Flusser provides us with a biography of Jesus. His aim, however, is not irenical, but rather an effort "merely to present Jesus directly to the reader."[213] He does so because he believes that such a study is timely. Flusser explains:

> The present age seems especially well disposed to understand him [Jesus] and his interests. A new sensitivity has been awakened in us by profound fear of the future and the present. Today we are receptive to Jesus' reappraisal of all our usual values. Many of us have become aware of his questioning of the moral norm, which was his starting point. . . . If we free ourselves from the chains of dead prejudices, we are able to appreciate Jesus' demand for an all-embracing love, not as philanthropic weakness, but as a realistic approach to our world.[214]

In the aftermath of the holocaust, Flusser seeks a model that will assuage the fear and embolden human society to greater moral rectitude. The paradigm for this rectitude, from Flusser's perspective, is Jesus of Nazareth, a Galilean Jew.

Straightaway, Flusser asserts that "the only important Christian sources concerning Jesus are the four Gospels: Matthew, Mark, Luke and John."[215] However, scholars debate the sequencing and interrelatedness of these texts. Flusser's approach to this Synoptic Problem, the question of literary independence of the Synoptic Gospels, as mentioned in chapter 1, is unique among the Jewish authors considered in this text. Flusser, following Robert Lindsey, posits that the Gospel of Luke, which Flusser perceives as best in preserving and transmitting the original Jesus tradition, is the primary Gospel, followed by Matthew, with Mark trailing as a thorough revision of the Lukan material. Hence, Flusser concludes that "Luke and Matthew together provide the most authentic portrayal of Jesus' life and teaching."[216]

To this minority approach, Flusser blends philology, first-century Jewish history and literature, and the nascent evidence emerging from the study of the Dead Sea Scrolls and biblical archaeology to arrive at his biographical mosaic of Jesus. Flusser, in *Jesus,* states succinctly both his aim and his methodology: "The present biography intends to apply the methods of literary criticism and Lindsey's solution to unlock these ancient sources. In order to understand the historical Jesus, it is not sufficient to follow the literary development of the Gospel material. We need also to possess intimate familiarity with Judaism in the time of Jesus."[217]

This last point he further develops, focusing specifically upon his quest for the Hebrew sayings that Flusser posits to underlie the Greek, which became the linguistic vehicle for transmitting the written text. Flusser explains his interest philologically: "The Jewish material is important not just because it permits us to place Jesus in his own time, but because it also permits a correct interpretation of his original Hebrew sayings. Thus, whenever we can be sure that there is a Hebrew phrase behind the Greek text of the Gospels, we translate that, and not the literal Greek."[218]

Though not ignoring the question of Jesus' Jewishness, Flusser is not essentially motivated by this thesis. Rather, he offers a scholarly study of the life of Jesus deduced from the Jewish milieu, to which the Synoptics attest, that gave rise to Jesus and his movement. And yet, Flusser is motivated to grapple with Jesus' Jewishness if only to challenge what he describes as persistent distortions on the part of previous redactors and exegetes. In the epilogue of his book, *Jesus,* he writes:

> I am personally interested in this question [Jesus' Jewishness] because the exegesis of the Gospels is far more determined by prejudices than I once thought. Some exegetical distortions are already reflected in the extant text of the Gospels themselves. Thus, they are quite old. Moreover, I think that many of the false interpretations that have persisted though history have become second nature to most modern scholars, whether they are willing to acknowledge it or not. What I set out to accomplish in this book was sound scholarship in the quest for the historical Jesus, and not simply in the points of his Jewishness.[219]

For our consideration, the pertinent sources from which Flusser sifts the essential evidence to construct his portrait of Jesus are the Synoptic Gospels, the Dead Sea Scrolls, Jewish history, literature, and archaeology.[220] Flusser's philological-historical critical approach is the primary hermeneutic through which he critically views these sources.

Flusser Grappling with the Sources

Jewish Literature

> One should view Jesus against his Jewish background, the world of the Sages, to recognize and appreciate his great influence on those around him. . . . Jesus was part and parcel of the world of the Jewish Sages. He was no ignorant peasant, and his acquaintance with the Written and the Oral Law was considerable.
>
> David Flusser, *Jewish Sources in Early Christianity*, 18–19

Not surprisingly David Flusser is conversant with the Jewish sources cited by Sandmel, especially Josephus and the talmudic and midrashic literature. Regarding talmudic literature, Flusser cites but one example, "the conversation between Rabbi Eliezer ben Hyrcanus and Jacob, the disciple of Jesus,"[221] as evidence of mention of Jesus within Jewish literature. Conceding that one should not look primarily among talmudic sources for confirmation of Jesus—just as one should not look within Christian sources for confirmation of illustrious Jewish personages, such as Rabbi ʿAkiva—Flusser nonetheless throughout the New Testament corpus recognizes significant Jewish motifs. Examples are atonement, martyrdom, messianic expectation, as well as Jewish midrashim. Many of these motifs, found both in the midrash *Tanḥuma* and in Christian midrashim, such as the Letter to the Hebrews, present the concept that the Messiah is greater than Moses and more sublime than the archangels.[222] This recognition, coupled with the lack of similar parallels for this Second Temple period among surviving talmudic and midrashic sources, fires Flusser's interest in the study of early Christianity, from which to glean further knowledge of Second Temple Judaism. From this initial inquiry, he deduces:

> Jewish sources alone cannot teach us enough about Second Temple Judaism. Our information on Rabbinic Judaism from these sources, for example, dates from a few generations after the rise of Christianity. The Sages began to chronicle their own history only after the destruction of the Second Temple (70 C.E.), and most of those who recorded the earlier oral tradition in the Midrashim (book of Biblical exegesis) and in the rabbinic legends lived at least a generation after the destruction of the Temple or later. Nevertheless, even the superficial reader of these sources will soon find that they reflect an oral tradition which is in many cases considerably earlier than the period of those in whose names it is reported.[223]

He posits: "Early Christian literature thus reflects the world of the Sages at an earlier stage than its reflection in the Jewish sources. It reflects Jewish life in the Hellenistic diaspora, details of which we otherwise know chiefly from the writings of Philo of Alexandria. We can learn from it about other Jewish diasporas and about Jewish customs which have not been recorded in early Jewish sources."[224]

In a reversal of expectation, Flusser mines first-century Christian literature, especially the Synoptic Gospels, to retrieve from it both new and corresponding information concerning Second Temple Judaism. Paradoxically, his hermeneutic, which provides the essential refraction, is talmudic literature. Flusser, in his article "The Dead Sea Sect and Pre-Pauline Christianity," asserts: "Talmudic literature remains our principal source for the interpretation of the Synoptic Gospels—which proves, to my mind, that Jesus and his followers were nearer to Pharisaic Judaism than to the Qumran sect."[225]

His method enhances both the understanding of Judaism and early Christianity. Thus enriched, Flusser handily shapes his narrative of Jesus, whose life and activities mirror and advance our perspective of the worldview of the sages of Israel and the diverse Judaisms prevalent during the late Second Temple period.

Unlike Sandmel, who dismisses rabbinic literature as contributing to the Jesus study, Flusser sees an opportunity to enrich Judaism itself through the study of the New Testament corpus since this body of Christian literature reflects the diverse motifs, beliefs, and practices of Second Temple Judaism, some of which are known to Judaism only through its encounter with the Christian Scripture. Flusser argues that these same Jewish sources that underlie and inform the New Testament literature provide evidence of a new sensitivity in the Judaism before and during Jesus' period that forms the *precondition* for the reception of Jesus' message. This is especially true of the pedagogical elements that are unique to Jesus.[226] This new sensitivity, of which Flusser speaks, constitutes the milieu in which Jesus is steeped, the evidence of which is perceived from within his teaching and preaching. Flusser posits that such a comparative study enhances and affirms the figure of Jesus in his Jewishness. Thus, he arrives at a better understanding and appreciation of Jesus as a Jewish teacher in the late Second Temple period.

Reprising Flusser's leitmotif, we may better apprehend, for example, his observations regarding Jesus and the question of messiahship. Flusser contends that by studying the origins of Christianity, one gains significant insights into a period, and oral traditions therein, less documented in Jewish sources for Second Temple Judaism. Flusser's Jesus scholarship bears testimony to this foundational premise. Thus, when considering the question of Jesus' messiahship, we find him consistent in writing: "Since Jesus was regarded as Messiah and Son of God and was literally identified with God, the New Testament has preserved expressions and views current in Judaism at the time of Jesus and ascribed to him. Thus we can reconstruct some chapters in the history of Jewish faith at the time, with its various sects and streams."[227]

Affirming that "this applies not only to Jesus and his conception of himself, but especially to the literature of the New Testament, the Epistles of Paul and other Epistles,"[228] Flusser demonstrates his premise:

Christianity brought about a combination of the sublime view of the Messiah as someone who was already present at the hour of creation, as we are told in the Book of Enoch, and the Jewish motif of atonement for the sins of Israel through the martyrdom of the saints. This conception, which is in no way central to Judaism, resembles the popular idea that "they died to bequeath us life." Marginal to this conception, we have the mythological idea that the death of those who have sacrificed themselves for our sake atone for our sins just as a proper sacrifice.[229]

Advancing his observation that a martyr's death is an atoning sacrifice for the sins of Israel, Flusser asserts:

> It appears that this mythological conception was current in those days [during the Roman period]. It was later connected to the Christian belief that Jesus was the Messiah in the sublime form of *Bar Enash*, and thus the sublime Jewish conceptions of the Messiah [the Messiah is greater than the patriarchs, and especially Abraham; that he is greater than Moses and more sublime than the archangels], which did not occupy a very central position in the world of the Sages, were amalgamated with the idea that there is no atonement except through Jesus. Christian do not believe—as Jews have always done—that their martyrs atone for their sins; the atonement for sins through the blood of Jesus is reserved only for the Son of God, for Jesus himself.[230]

He concludes:

> To sum up: the celestial biography found in the New Testament consists entirely of Jewish motifs: Jesus the Messiah had existed before the creation of the world; he entered the world, or even created it; he became flesh—this is an innovation—and then brought about redemption; he is the Messiah—the *Bar Enash*, the Last Adam; and he atones for sins just like those who had atoned for the sins of Israel and then comes back to life.[231]

One can demonstrate that the New Testament writers did perceive within the Hebrew Scriptures—the Old Testament—messianic typology that they incorporated into their Jesus narrative. Yet one would be less confident of their use of rabbinic sources—though Flusser argues thus. Whether or not his observations are based upon anachronistic assumptions is debatable.[232]

Given this reciprocal learning, Flusser both applauds the significance of the New Testament corpus for Jewish study and situates Jesus within the larger context of Second Temple Judaism, with its new sensitivity. Flusser contends that Jesus builds upon and advances the teachings of the sages of Israel, to which Jesus is heir, transmitter, and innovator. Given this, it is not surprising that Flusser includes among his sources the pertinent passages from the teachings of these sages, such as Antigonos of Socho, ben Sira, Hillel, and Shammai, and compares Jesus' contribution to theirs.

Both Jewish midrash and Christian midrash are put to service by Flusser in his quest to write his biography of Jesus.[233] As previously mentioned, Flusser argues that Christian midrash, as a hermeneutic, emerges from, provides evidence for, and advances the extant collection of Jewish midrashim, while at the same time becoming a distinctively Christian exegetical expression. In *Jewish Sources in Early Christianity*, he distinguishes between the two:

Jewish Midrash is one of the expressions of Jewish creative activity during the periods of the Second Temple and the early Rabbinic literature. It appears that all the books of the New Testament and all those persons who were active during the period of early Christianity also had an affinity to the world of Midrash. The New Testament contains whole Midrashim, and it also has, especially in the sayings of Jesus, allusions to Midrashim, whether these specific Midrashim have reached us or not. There are also typically Christian Midrashim, which set out to demonstrate the truths of Christianity from verses of the Bible. Jesus' death and the belief in his resurrection and in his divine origin are explained through Midrashim which were created by Christians of their own accord or which originated in Jewish Midrash.[234]

Flusser investigates the evidence within both, discerning similar and dissimilar patterns, pericopes, sayings, and teaching representative of the sages of Israel, among whom Flusser numbers Jesus.

With regard to Josephus, specifically *Jewish Antiquities* 18.63–64, wherein Josephus tells us that Jesus was more than merely human, Flusser favors a tenth-century Arabic text as opposed to the Greek manuscripts that are considered normative. The Greek text carries a Christian interpolation, that Jesus was the Messiah and was resurrected, but the Arabic text makes no such assertion. The manuscript does affirm, as does the Greek text, that Jesus was an historic personage: "At this time, there was a wise man called Jesus, and his conduct was good, and he was known to be virtuous."[235]

Given the lack of a Christian interpolation in the Arabic manuscript, Flusser asserts that the Arabic text is more faithful to Josephus. He further concludes that Josephus's attitude toward early Christians, as represented in both manuscripts, is favorable. Unlike Sandmel, Flusser sees Josephus as a viable, though limited, source for his Jesus study.

The Dead Sea Scrolls

> The people of Qumran had a dissenting theology, and it is precisely this element of dissent which was later a moving force in Christianity.
>
> David Flusser, *Jewish Sources*, 70

Flusser's study of the Dead Sea Scrolls yields the following concise assessment of the Dead Sea Scrolls' contribution to Jesus research: (1) The Essene doctrine contained within the Dead Sea Scrolls serves to indicate Essene influence upon the emerging Christian doctrines reflected primarily within the Johannine and Pauline communities. (2) Though the scrolls are not primarily a source for historical data concerning Jesus' person, personality, and personal history, they do, upon comparison with the canonical Gospels, firmly secure Jesus' place within the Judaism of his time.

Flusser agrees that Christianity developed upon two strata: "The first stratum of Christianity had special affinities with rabbinic Judaism, whereas the second stratum, from which Paul sprang, was influenced by the Essenes and their world-view."[236] From

Flusser's perspective, Jesus and his disciples, the information for whom he derives primarily from the Synoptic Gospels, form the first stratum; and the Johannine and Pauline writings, including the Letter to the Hebrews, form the second stratum. Within this second stratum Flusser perceives Essenian influence—dualism, predestination, election, and baptism—as a formative factor. The corroborating source for this determination of Essenian influence is the Dead Sea Scrolls.[237]

No such explicit influence is documented in the Synoptic Gospels, which are constitutive of the first stratum. Given that Essenian influence is discernible within Christianity's second stratum of theological development and not the first, Flusser doubts the Dead Sea Scrolls' benefit as a source for a biography of Jesus. Flusser contends that the Dead Sea Scrolls reveal little that would enhance the Gospel portrait of Jesus, specifically as this relates to his *personality* and *person*:

> A closer examination of the nature and occurrence of the parallels to the Scrolls in various NT writings yields, to my mind, the following results: (1) In contrast to the Gospel of John, the synoptic Gospels show few and comparatively unimportant parallels to the Sectarian writings. This seems to indicate that the Scrolls will not contribute much to the understanding of the personality of Jesus and of the religious world of his disciples.[238]

When, however, the Dead Sea Scrolls are juxtaposed with Jesus' *teaching* as preserved in the Synoptic texts, Flusser contends for Essenian influence, though in a mitigated form.[239]

The Dead Sea Scrolls provide much more than evidence of limited, mitigated Essenian influence upon Jesus. As the scrolls indicate and elaborate upon the diversity of Jewish belief and practice prevalent during the time of Jesus, they offer a contemporary Jewish perspective for the study of Jesus, Judaism, and early Christianity. Flusser agrees that the scholarly study of the scrolls situates Jesus squarely within the diversity of Second Temple Judaism, confirming Jesus as a faithful, yet creative Jewish teacher:

> Study of the recently discovered Dead Sea Scrolls enables us now to define more precisely the place of Jesus within the spectrum of contemporary Judaism. Jesus' message and self-awareness are firmly embedded in the Judaism of his time. Thus, if one studies thoroughly the pertinent Jewish sources, one is able to discern where Jesus accepts the teaching of others, where he modifies it, and where his sayings are really revolutionary.[240]

The New Testament

> From the New Testament we learn of great intellectual and literary achievements which had already been attained during the generations before Jesus. The New Testament reflects these achievements and is genuine evidence of this flowering of literature and culture.
>
> David Flusser, *Jewish Sources*, 66

Given the interplay discerned by Flusser between Jewish midrash and the subsequent Christian midrash described above, his appreciation for and facility with the New

Testament is apparent. However, this facility and appreciation will do little to advance his mosaic of the historical Jesus since the New Testament data, with the exception of the Gospels and the Acts of the Apostles, is extremely fragmentary. Flusser offers a concise analysis:

> Outside the Gospels, there are very few sayings of Jesus, and these are not theological or doctrinal, but "halakhic." There we learn that Jesus was a Jew from the family of David, that he was born under the Law (Gal. 4:4), and that he became the "servant" to the "circumcised" (Rom. 15:8). In the Epistle to the Hebrews we read about the temptation of Jesus (2:18; 4:15; cf. Luke 22:28) and about his agony and his receiving of the heavenly voice ([Heb] 5:5–7), which is also mentioned in II Peter 1:16–18 in connection with the transfiguration. This is essentially all that we can learn from the New Testament outside of the Gospels and Acts about Jesus' life prior to his passion and death. Naturally the latter is often mentioned, but we do not learn much about the attending circumstances. From Rev. 11:8 we can deduce that it occurred in Jerusalem and in Hebrews 13:12 we read that Jesus "suffered outside the gate." In I Tim. 6:13 we find the name Pontius Pilate mentioned, but outside the Gospels and Acts the Romans are never mentioned in connection with the crucifixion of Jesus. Instead of this, in one passage Jewish guilt appears: the Jews killed Jesus Christ (I Thess. 2:15). According to the famous passage in I Cor. 15: 3–8, Christ died, was buried, and was raised to life on the third day. The fact of the resurrection is often mentioned: it is both an historical experience and a cornerstone of Christ's metahistorical biography.[241]

Flusser necessarily restricts himself primarily to an investigation of the Synoptic Gospels and comparative Jewish and rabbinic literature in his effort to construct his mosaic of Jesus.

The Letters of Paul

> Paul, one of the most important of the founders of Christianity, is probably the most famous early Christian besides Jesus. Many regard him as a second founder of Christianity. Paul did not know Jesus.
>
> David Flusser, *Jewish Sources*, 67

The same scholarly parameters that exclude much of the New Testament as a primary source for Jesus research also eliminate the Pauline corpus as a significant source for Flusser's historical Jesus construct. Given this and Flusser's above assessment of the New Testament data, in which Pauline material figures prominently, there can be little surprise at this exclusion. The Pauline corpus, situated as it is within the second stratum of Christian theological development, reflects kerygmatic doctrines pertaining to the risen Christ and the fledging communities from which such doctrine emerges, and thus it contributes little to advance Flusser's efforts.

The Synoptic Gospels

> We shall say nothing new if we maintain that Jesus was a Jew in every way. The Gospels
> have preserved his maxims and sayings, and thus it is not only the views and opinions
> of Jesus himself that have been preserved for us, but also details concerning the various
> streams in Judaism during the period of Jesus' life and activities.
>
> Flusser, *Jewish Sources*, 7

Flusser, like Sandmel, regards the canonical Gospels as midrashim pertaining to the
person and public life of Jesus of Nazareth. This midrash, redacted and woven into
literary tapestries, emerges as portraits of Jesus. New Testament scholars examine these
portraits critically in an effort to retrieve from the texts a more accurate image of Jesus.
Where Sandmel despairs of the historical-critical effort, Flusser embraces it. Flusser
brings two elements into unique focus: (1) the historical value of the Synoptic Gospels
and (2) the Hebrew origins of the Gospels.

Flusser agrees that of the four canonical Gospels, John's Gospel, given its kerygmatic, post-Easter Christology, is the least reliable from a historical perspective.
Therefore, he focuses his attention upon the Synoptic Gospels, which he deems more
historically reliable, more so than some of his contemporaries would allow:

> The early Christian accounts about Jesus are not as untrustworthy as people today often
> think. The first three Gospels not only present a reasonably faithful picture of Jesus as a
> Jew of his own time, but they even consistently retain his way of speaking about the
> Savior in the third person. An impartial reading of the Synoptic Gospels results in a
> picture not so much of a redeemer of mankind, but of a Jewish miracle-worker and
> preacher. . . . The Jesus portrayed in the Synoptic Gospels is, therefore, the historical
> Jesus, not the "kerygmatic Christ."[242]

Flusser argues that for Jewish Christianity this emphasis upon Jesus' role "as
miracle-worker, teacher, prophet and Messiah was more important than the risen Lord
of the kerygma."[243] This latter focus upon the risen Lord marks a shift of emphasis from
the historical Jesus of Jewish Christianity to the kerygmatic Christ of early "Hellenistic
Christian congregations founded by Greek Jews, and composed predominantly of non-
Jews."[244] The heart of their kerygma was "redemption through the crucified and risen
Christ."[245]

Given this focus, Flusser suggests:

> It is perhaps a stroke of luck, as far as our knowledge of Jesus is concerned, that the
> Synoptic Gospels were written fairly late—apparently around 70 A.D.—when the dy-
> namic creativity within the Pauline congregations had diminished. For the most part, this
> later stratum of the Synoptic tradition found its expression in the redaction of the separate
> evangelists and was styled in Greek. If we examine this material with an unprejudiced
> mind, we learn from its content and its manner of expression that it is concerned not with
> kerygmatic statements, but with Christian platitudes.[246]

Flusser questions if it is "indeed credible to suggest that when the Synoptic Gospels
are studied scientifically they present a reliable portrayal of the historical Jesus, in spite

of the kerygmatic preaching of faith by the Church."[247] He responds in the affirmative, arguing:

> My research has led me to the conclusion that the Synoptic Gospels are based upon one or more non-extant early documents composed by Jesus' disciples and the early church in Jerusalem. These texts were originally written in Hebrew. Subsequently, they were translated into Greek and passed through various stages of redaction. It is the Greek translation of these early Hebrew sources that were employed by our three evangelists. Thus, when studied in the light of their Jewish background, the Synoptic Gospels do preserve a picture of Jesus which is more reliable than is generally acknowledged.[248]

He further asserts:

> In order to understand the historical Jesus, it is not sufficient to follow the literary development of the Gospel material. We also need to possess intimate familiarity with Judaism in the time of Jesus. The Jewish material is important not just because it allows us to place Jesus in his own time, but because it also permits a correct interpretation of his original Hebrew sayings. Thus, whenever we can be sure that there is a Hebrew phrase behind the Greek text of the Gospels, we translate that, and not the literal Greek.[249]

From this Christian matrix, wherein Jewish voices echo, Flusser conceives a biography of Jesus: a biography that identifies and perpetuates a new sensitivity that undergirded and facilitated the message and ministry of Jesus. Flusser, aware of what he deems as yet another new, yet markedly different, sensitivity prevalent in the latter part of the twentieth century—a sensitivity "awakened in us by profound fear of the future and the present"[250]—seeks through a biographical mosaic to offer to his contemporary, post-Holocaust world a balm to assuage fear and eliminate prejudice. Ironically, to this diverse world village poised at the dawn of the third millennium, he offers Jesus: a first-century Galilean Jew, a sage of Israel, a faithful and yet creative teacher, and his innovative and yet eminently Jewish teachings, seen darkly, perhaps, through a Christian mirror as exemplar and moral compass.

Géza Vermès's Critical Approach

Vermès's task is seemingly not markedly different from that of those who have preceded him in their quest for the historical Jesus since the portrait that emerges is one largely deduced from the Synoptic tradition. This would be true of Vermès except for one important distinction: his "particular slant." Vermès, describing this slant in the prologue of *The Changing Faces of* Jesus, explains: "A particular slant characterizes my approach to the study of Jesus. I envisage the New Testament not as an independent and autonomous literary composition standing apart from the Jewish world, but look at it through the prism of contemporaneous Jewish civilization, the matrix of the primitive Christian Church."[251]

To gain further insight into Christianity through the perusal of contemporary Jewish sources is not distinctive in and of itself, since critical New Testament scholarship has often used Jewish intertestamental literature—such as the Septuagint, the Apocrypha, the Pseudepigrapha, the Dead Sea Scrolls, the philosophical writing of Philo of Alexandria, and the historian Flavius Josephus—as a hermeneutical tool. Yet the use of this tool, according to Vermès, was hardly evenhanded because scholars, mostly Christian churchmen, had "explicitly or implicitly introduced a qualitative distinction between the New Testament and the nonbiblical Jewish writings."[252] This distinction, this presumed superiority, according to Vermès, prejudiced their consideration of pertinent Jewish material and thus limited their view.

As a corrective, Vermès suggests that, rather than merely viewing Jewish intertestamental literature as a background upon which a superior Christian literature rises, scholarship would benefit more if all the pertinent materials, Christian and Jewish, were viewed more equitably, albeit, critically. Vermès proposes a different approach:

> The procedure which I advocate is much more democratic. Both parties are granted a voice, an equal voice. Put differently, as a historian I consider Jesus, the primitive Church, and the New Testament as part and parcel of first-century Judaism and seek to read them as such rather than through the eyes of a theologian who may often be conditioned, and subconsciously influenced, by two millennia of Christian belief and church directives.[253]

In his first book of the trilogy, Vermès, grapples with the seeming dichotomy presented by the Jesus of history and the Christ of faith and explains the difference between his task and that of a theologian: "By contrast to these imperatives of faith, the issues which writer and reader will explore together are concerned with the primitive, genuine, *historical* significance of words and events recorded in the Gospels. What they are *believed* to signify is the business of the theologian; the historian's task is to discover the original meaning of their message."[254]

Such a historical reading is facilitated by recent archaeological discoveries, including not only but significantly also manuscript discoveries and their subsequent study, as Vermès affirms:

> In fact, with the discovery and study of the Dead Sea Scrolls and other archaeological treasures (see Illus. 1, 11, 19, and 21), and the corresponding improvement in our understanding of ideas, doctrines, methods of teaching, languages, and culture of the Jews of New Testament times, it is now possible not simply to place Jesus in relief, against this setting (as students of the Jewish background of Christianity pride themselves on doing) but to insert him foursquare within first-century Jewish life itself.[255]

Given this, he suggests: "The questions then to be asked are where he [Jesus] fits into it, and whether the added substance and clarity gained from immersing him in historical reality confer credibility on the patchy gospel picture."[256]

Vermès hopes that his historical approach will yield "the significance of words and ideas in their original language, as the original speakers meant the original listeners to understand them."[257] He agrees with majority scholarship—and therefore disagrees with Flusser's position—that "the language of Jesus and his Galilean disciples was Aramaic, a Semitic language akin to Hebrew, then spoken by most Palestinian Jews."[258] Vermès posits, given the lack of an extant Aramaic Gospel—if one ever existed—and the predominance of a Greek New Testament, albeit one which is both "a 'translation' of the genuine thoughts and ideas of Aramaic-thinking and -speaking Jesus and of his immediate disciples"[259] and "a 'transplantation' of the ideology of the Gospels into the completely alien cultural and religious environment of the pagan Graeco-Roman world,"[260] that his task is twofold:

> Therefore my task as a historian and exegete is first to find the way back to the Jewish Jesus speaking to his Jewish followers in his Jewish mode of communication and in his familiar Semitic tongue. The next step is to examine the words attributed to Jesus, and teachings about Jesus, in the Greek New Testament in order to discover changes or developments in meaning, and even potential deformation, arising from the transmission of ideas through the channel of Hellenistic civilization.[261]

Yet, in his quest for "the Jewish Jesus speaking," Vermès concedes that the search for *ipsissima verba* is elusive and therefore unwise, futile. Rather than search the texts for the actual words of Jesus, he argues that one would benefit more profitably and convincingly from a search for the ideas, the *ipsissimus sensus*. Vermès affirms this position, which guided his earlier works, in his more recent book:

> Since Jesus did not record his message in writing, it has to be handed down by his disciples orally, first in Aramaic and later in Greek when the evangelization moved outside Palestine among Jews and Gentiles who spoke Greek. The written word soon became the medium of transmission in the various geographically distinct regions in the Graeco-Roman world and as a result the gospel [the message of Jesus] was bound to acquire a considerable degree of variation. In such circumstances the possible recovery of a literally authentic saying is most of the time beyond reasonable expectation. Therefore it is wiser to lower one's aim and try to reconstruct, not the *ipsissima verba*, the original word-for-word version of a saying of Jesus, but the general gist [*ipsissimus sensus*] of his message.[262]

As to finding "the way back to the Jewish Jesus," one may broadly describe Vermès's methodology as historical since his aim is historical. More specifically, one may discern a philological, historical-critical methodology, though he himself at the outset of his Jesus research decried describing his approach and the principles therein as a "methodology." In his trilogy of early works, he ascribes, admittedly, to certain guidelines, yet he resists being bridled by unwieldy strictures. In *The Religion of Jesus the Jew*, Vermès asserts: "It would be quite inappropriate, however, to attach to these guide-lines the grandiloquent, but highly fashionable, label of *methodology*. In my opinion, research aiming to be innovative should not be bound by strict, predetermined rules."[263] Though criticized for his candor, Vermès does, in fact, utilize a methodology, but not one that finds a warm reception among his nemeses, "the transatlantic dogmatists."[264]

In the preface of the latest edition of *Jesus the Jew*, Vermès calls his a "pragmatic approach," attune to "patterns," such as the *ipsissimus sensus*, rather than grappling with the actual sayings—though he will grapple with these, in due course, in later works. Nonetheless, his thrust throughout is the same: innovative, unconventional, observing patterns, typologies, adducing evidence from what some deem "spurious" data.[265] When considering Jesus the teacher, Vermès asserts in *Jesus the Jew*: "This enquiry will be concerned not so much with the contents as with the mode of his preaching, and the impression it left on sympathetic listeners."[266] Though methodology, by which we understand him to mean the paths *sanctioned* by the transatlantic dogmatists' sacrosanct rule book, makes him see red,[267] Vermès does in fact explain his approach. In *Jesus and the World of Judaism*, chapters 5 and 6, "Jewish Studies and New Testament Interpretation" and "Jewish Literature and New Testament Exegesis: Reflections on Methodology," respectively testify to this.

Moreover, as Vermès's Jesus exploration continues and expands throughout a thirty-year period, so too does Vermès's approach. Moreover, perhaps in keeping with this innovative spirit, Vermès in *The Authentic Gospel of Jesus* recently critiques the manner in which the standard criteria, utilized to suggest parameters for determining authenticity, were formulated. After pointing out this flaw, he tries to formulate more adequate principles that would allow for the proper determination of the parameters of authenticity.[268]

To answer the questions that he poses, Vermès sifts the New Testament corpus, specifically the Synoptic Gospels, through a Jewish sieve, a comparative Jewish matrix, the composition of which reflects both Jewish intertestamental literature (ca. 200 BCE–200 CE) and, though seemingly incongruent, subsequent rabbinic literature (200–500 CE): the Mishnah, midrash, Talmud, and Targum. In doing so, he confirms the validity of the second portion of his double conviction upon which his contribution to Jesus research is based, "that it is possible to extract, thanks to our considerable increased knowledge of Palestinian-Jewish realities of the time of Jesus, historically reliable information from non-historical sources, such as the Gospels."[269]

In contrast to Sandmel, Vermès argues for the inclusion of Jewish intertestamental and rabbinic literature as viable sources for Jesus research. Vermès's optimism in this regard exceeds that of Flusser's—though Flusser cautiously concedes benefit.[270] After endorsing rabbinic literature as a viable source, though not carte blanche, Vermès cautions that "their use for interpreting the New Testament requires familiarity and critical skill, but if handled competently they can shed an invaluable light both on Jesus and primitive Christianity."[271]

Vermès's description of his task anticipates the work of a growing number of scholars, such as James H. Charlesworth, who in the 1990s have regarded their scholarly activity as it relates to Jesus as "Jesus research." As mentioned earlier in this chapter, Jesus researchers such as Vermès and Flusser distinguish themselves from the "questers" who precede (and accompany) them since they, the Jesus researchers, seek "to understand the man of history [Jesus] in the light of all the evidence that is now pouring our way,"[272] avoiding a less-expansive hermeneutic.

Before delving into the pertinent and diverse sources, Vermès offers a proviso:

> I intend to leave to one side the speculations of the early Christians concerning the various divinely contrived roles of Messiah, Lord, Son of God, etc., that their Master was believed to have fulfilled before or after his death. Instead, I will rely on the accounts of the first three gospels, which suggest that Jesus impressed his countrymen, and acquired fame among them, chiefly as a charismatic teacher, healer, and exorcist.[273]

From an informed, literary-historical study of pertinent, correlative first-century Jewish texts and the de rigueur Synoptic Gospel texts, Vermès gathers glass and stone, evidence from which first-century Judaism and primitive Christianity emerge anew. From this matrix, Vermès ventures a description not simply of the Jesus of the evangelists, but rather a narrative of the person and the personality cloaked within an overlay of traditions and teachings—Christian and Jewish—of Jesus, a Galilean Hasid (*ḥāsîd*).[274]

Vermès Grappling with the Sources

Jewish Intertestamental and Rabbinic Literature

> These sources will not be treated merely as a backcloth, however, but as witnesses. They will not be employed simply as aids in answering queries arising from the New Testament, but as independent spokesmen capable, from time to time at least, of guiding the enquiry, either by suggesting the right angle of approach, or even the right questions to ask.
>
> Géza Vermès, *Jesus the Jew*, 16–17

Vermès views the inclusion of the Jewish intertestamental material and the subsequent collection of rabbinic literature as both an integral hermeneutic for interpreting the New Testament corpus and as *primary* sources.[275] This is possible since he allows no qualitative distinction between the Jewish writings and Christian texts in his effort to discern the *ipsissimus sensus* of Jesus' gospel. The inclusion of these sources shapes his image of Jesus. He maintains and affirms this contention in his most recent book:

> To understand the Gospel evidence within its historical framework, the accounts of the evangelists must be compared with the many parallels preserved in Jewish writings of the intertestamental age (*c.* 200 BCE–200 CE) and in rabbinic literature. Although the latter was recorded in script roughly between AD 200 and 500, it none the less comprises many religious traditions which stem from, or even antedate, the age of the Gospels. These writings have survived in Hebrew and Aramaic and thus bring us near to the ideas of Jesus, and to their expression in words and images. Without their study, it is often impossible to catch the nuances or even the basic meaning of the sayings, parables, and Bible interpretation handed down by the evangelists in the name of Jesus.[276]

He recognizes that "the New Testament is in some way connected, not only with Hebrew Scriptures (which it often cites), but also with post-biblical Judaism,"[277] and that its message makes a transition from an initial Jewish setting to a Greek milieu. Hence, Vermès seeks "a linguistic and religious-cultural 'retranslation' from Greek into Aramaic/Hebrew concept and thought-forms."[278] Such a retranslation may facilitate "a valid approximation of his [Jesus'] genuine message"[279] and therefore, with a better sense of the *ipsissimus sensus*, give greater credibility to a Jewish portrait of Jesus.

Though in customary, if sporadic, use since the seventeenth century,[280] Vermès's confidence in the potential of these Jewish documents to assist in this retranslation as well as his familiarity with and critical skill thereto, which aid him in realizing this potential, exceeds that of some his colleagues.[281] Of this potential benefit, he writes:

> The sectors likely to benefit most from comparison with Jewish sources are those of religious concepts and motifs such as Messiah, Lord, son of God, holy man/miracle-worker, exorcist/healer, etc. With the proviso that an acceptable method of evaluation is agreed on, the juxtaposition of the New Testament and Jewish parallels is sure to lead to the discovery of how the original audience or readership understood the words, phrases or themes in question.[282]

The Writings of Josephus

Is it nevertheless possible to add a little flesh to bones?
Géza Vermès, *Jesus the Jew*, 42

Recognizing the limited value of the Gospel material as historical documentation per se, Vermès suggests that one might better enflesh, meaning enhance historically, these bones through a comparative reading of the Synoptic texts, "devoid of doctrinal preconceptions," and the writings of the Jewish historian, Flavius Josephus:

> Research has to be restricted to Mark, Matthew and Luke and to exclude John because, despite the occasional historical detail it contains, its Jesus portrait is so evolved theologically as to be wholly unsuitable for historical investigation. By contrast, a reading, devoid of doctrinal preconceptions, of the Synoptic Gospels has disclosed a figure of Jesus as a popular teacher, healer and exorcist, who fits perfectly into the first-century Galilee known directly from Josephus, and indirectly from rabbinic literature.[283]

Vermès concludes: "He [Jesus] represents the charismatic Judaism of wonder-working holy men such as the first-century BC Honi and Jesus' younger contemporary, Hanina ben Dosa, modeled on the biblical prophets such as Elijah and Elisha. They feed the hungry, cure disease, physical and mental, both often attributed to demonic possession."[284]

Although his Jewish contemporaries focus narrowly upon Josephus's mention of Jesus, as in *Jewish Antiquities* 18.63–64—wherein Sandmel dismissively sees a Christian interpolation; and Flusser, reading from a tenth-century Arabic text void of Christian interpolation, pragmatically embraces a historical note—Vermès values Josephus, not exclusively but significantly, for his observations of first-century Galilean culture and history. Viewing this Jewish parallel literature as a means "to fit Jesus and his movement into the greater context of first-century Palestine,"[285] Vermès puts flesh to bone. He enhances the scant historical portrait of Jesus, his disciples, and his Palestinian environs with the historical data provided by Josephus, positing:

> A much more reliable picture of the Galilee of Jesus is reflected in the writing of Flavius Josephus who, as rebel commander-in-chief of the Northern region during the first Jewish

War (AD 66–70), possessed a first-hand knowledge of it. Clearly, it was a territory *sui generis*. Not only did it have its own peculiar past, but its political, social and economic organization also contributed to distinguish it from the rest of Palestine. The conflict between Jesus and the religious and secular authority outside Galilee was at least in part due to the fact that he was, and was known to have been, a Galilean.[286]

The Dead Sea Scrolls

The most revolutionary change in the position of the New Testament exegete concerned with Jewish comparative data occurred in 1947 with the discovery of the Dead Sea Scrolls. Not only did he find himself equipped with non-biblical Qumran documents written mostly in Hebrew and Aramaic, and in a broad sense contemporaneous with Christian beginnings, but they [also] derive in addition from a sectarian setting more or less similar to the early church. Also, practically all of the literature is religious, including a fair amount of Bible interpretation.

Géza Vermès, *Jesus in His Jewish Context*, 70

Although the Dead Sea Scrolls[287] certainly fall within category of Jewish inter-testamental literature, the magnitude of the discovery and the subsequent correlative evidence marks it as *the* watershed in twentieth-century biblical archaeology and literary-biblical study and therefore worthy of separate consideration.

Vermès, an eminent scholar of the Dead Sea Scrolls,[288] commenting upon the significance of the Qumran Scrolls—Vermès's preferred appellation—writes:

Looking at the Qumran discoveries from an overall perspective, it is—I believe—the student of the history of Palestinian Judaism in the inter-Testamental era (150 BCE–70 CE) who is their principal beneficiary. For such an expert, the formerly quite unknown sectarian writings of the Dead Sea literature have opened new avenues of exploration in the shadowy era of the life of Jesus, the rise of Christianity and the emergence of rabbinic Judaism.[289]

Another windfall for both historian and exegete, given the age of the texts and their 2000-year concealment, is that they did not undergo redaction by either early Christianity or later rabbinic Judaism. Vermès explains:

The rabbis of the first and second centuries CE had not permitted religious writings of that epoch to go down to posterity unless they conformed fully to their ideas, and although some of these texts were preserved by Christians (viz. the Apocrypha and many of the Pseudepigrapha), the fact that they had served as a vehicle for Church apologetics caused their textual reliability to be suspect. But the Scrolls are unaffected by either Christian or rabbinic censorship, and now that the evidence is complete, historians will be thoroughly acquainted, not with just another aspect of Jewish beliefs or customs, but with the whole organization, teaching and aspirations of a religious community flourishing during the last centuries of the Second Temple.[290]

Since their discovery beginning in 1947, the Qumran texts have continued to "add substance and depth to the historical period in which Jewish Christianity and rabbinic Judaism originated."[291] As Vermès points out:

> By dwelling in such detail on the intimate organization of their society, on the role attributed to their Teacher and on their ultimate hopes and expectations, the sect of the Scrolls has exposed its own resulting synthesis. This in turn has thrown into relief and added a new dimension to its dissenting contemporaries. Thus, compared with the ultraconservative rigidity of the Essene Rule, rabbinic Judaism reveals itself as progressive and flexible, while the religion preached and practised by Jesus of Nazareth stands out invested with religious individuality and actuality. Also, by comparison to all three, the ideology of the Gentile Church sounds a definitely alien note. Yet at the same time, the common ground from which they all sprang, and their affinities and borrowings, show themselves more clearly than ever before. It is no exaggeration to state that none of these religious movements can properly be understood independently of the others.[292]

Vermès gathers his observations on the relationship between the scrolls and the New Testament under a threefold heading: (1) the fundamental similarities of language, ideology, and attitude to the Bible; (2) the similarities in administration (e.g., monarchic) and social organization (e.g., religious communism), suggesting an Essenian paradigm for the emerging Church; and (3) similarities in the charismatic-eschatological elements in both traditions, Essene and Jesus. This last observation bears most directly upon the study of the historical Jesus since the Gospels bear witness to Jesus as healer, exorcist, and eschatological prophet.[293]

Vermès and Flusser sound a similar note of agreement regarding the scrolls' import for Jesus research, though Flusser is less ambitious in his estimation of Essenian influence upon Jesus and Jewish Christianity. Both scholars recognize and incorporate the fruit of comparing the Qumran Scrolls with Jewish Christianity and rabbinic Judaism as they image the face of Jesus. Whereas, Vermès and Flusser view the Dead Sea Scrolls as corroborating evidence that secures for Jesus his place within Judaism vis-à-vis the Synoptic Gospels, Sandmel disavows any measurable benefit to be gained from the sectarian scrolls.

Finally, as important as Vermès views the contribution of the comparative study of the Dead Sea Scrolls to New Testament scholarship and Jesus research, he does not restrict comparison exclusively to them at the detriment of other parallel Jewish literature.[294]

Rabbinic Literature

> The hypothesis I prefer would envisage a common source, written or oral—it may be called Jewish (doctrinal, legal, exegetical) tradition—firm in substance but variable in shape, on which both the evangelists and the later rabbis depended.
> Géza Vermès, *The Religion of Jesus the Jew*, 9

In a historical investigation that has spanned thirty years, Vermès has maintained two primary goals. Throughout his works, he seeks to situate Jesus securely within first-century Jewish life and, having done so, ask whether this immersion confers credibility on the "patchy gospel picture." To accomplish his goals, Vermès, fired by the double conviction that informs his methodology,[295] relies upon a comparative scrutiny of Synoptic Gospels and parallel Jewish literature and archaeological evidence, such as Josephus's writings, the Dead Sea Scrolls, and select rabbinic literature.

In his first book, *Jesus the Jew*, Vermès identifies the character of the historical Jesus as a charismatic, Galilean Hasid: a Jewish holy man, typified by Honi the circle drawer and Hanina ben Dosa, whose attributes are recorded, preserved, and transmitted by Josephus and the subsequent rabbinic tradition. In his third book, *The Religion of Jesus the Jew*, Vermès presumes this portrayal of Jesus as his starting point and turns his attention to the teaching of Jesus to further "add flesh to bone." In this pursuit of the authentic teaching of Jesus, which Vermès deems "even more hazardous than an attempt to discover his historic contours,"[296] he defends the inclusion of rabbinic literature as a viable source—not one relegated to an ancillary role vis-à-vis the New Testament—and hermeneutic for Jesus research.

Vermès recognizes the "serious chronological snag"[297] that one encounters when contemplating a comparison of the earlier New Testament corpus with the later rabbinic traditions and the "new circumstances"[298] presented by the more-recent scholarship derived from the Dead Sea Scrolls, which provide "a considerable body of comparative material contemporaneous with the first Christian writings or only slightly predating it, whereas prior to 1947 no such documentation was extant."[299] Hence, he grapples with the emerging question as to the benefit gained from *any* use of rabbinic literature—the Mishnah, Tosefta, Talmud, midrash, or Targum—as a New Testament hermeneutic and critical source. Positing both the unfamiliarity with and lack of enthusiasm for rabbinic sources as well as partisanship among "pan-Qumranists,"[300] Vermès disallows a negative response to the question at hand.

Vermès concedes the elimination of rabbinic material that "definitely postdates by a century or more the New Testament in substance and not only in formulation or redaction, or if the similarity between them is due to the rabbis' dependence on the evangelists."[301] He discounts this latter suggestion, however, since it is "most unlikely, indeed unthinkable, that the Jewish sages would directly borrow from the Gospels."[302] Vermès further asserts that "equally improbable is the theory that all the contents recorded in the rabbinic compilations were created in the Talmudic age."[303] This last assertion is derived from "both the evidence included in the writings themselves, and critical scholarship,"[304] which "tend to show that these documents largely consist of teachings dating from earlier centuries and handed down, often re-shaped and re-edited, by the redactors of the Talmud, etc."[305] Affirming that "it is impossible to assert with any degree of confidence that Jewish works similar [to] or identical in form and content to rabbinic Targum and Midrash existed in writing in the first century AD or before,"[306] Vermès agues that it would be "wholly unsound to postulate that the evangelists used such purely conjectural literature, and further assume that they were substantially the same as the much more recent texts known to us."[307]

Having offered his readers a précis of this historical-critical dilemma, Vermès reasserts an earlier hypothesis: his theory of a common source, a Jewish tradition upon which both evangelists and rabbis relied. Vermès explains this hypothesis in his book *Jesus and the World of Judaism* (1983), more recently reissued as *Jesus in His Jewish Context* (2003), and concedes that such a proposition is problematic but not insurmountable.[308]

Arguing from a historical perspective for a common Jewish tradition from whence both the New Testament and rabbinic doctrine emerge, Vermès suggests:

> Divested, however, of its denominational garb, the matter takes on another colour. The New Testament then ceases to be insignificant for Jews or autonomous and in every sense primary for Christians. Jesus and the movement that arose in his wake are recognized as belonging to first-century Jewish history. Furthermore, a good deal of the New Testament appears as reflecting a brief moment in the age-long religious development of Israel that starts with the Bible and continues via Apocrypha, Pseudepigrapha, Qumran, Philo, the New Testament, Josephus, Pseudo-Philo, the Mishnah, Tosefta, Targum, Midrash, Talmud—and so on and so forth.[309]

Viewed from this perspective, the New Testament, as a brief moment, fills a void from which Jewish and Christian scholarship benefit: "For Jews, the study of rabbinic literature benefits greatly inasmuch as the New Testament is able to fulfil the exceedingly important function of providing a chronologically well-defined segment of tradition applicable as a yardstick in dealing with undated material."[310]

Flusser agrees with Vermès's estimation of viewing the New Testament as part of a larger environment of Jewish religious and cultural history and the benefit thereto. Moreover, both Vermès and Flusser assert that not only may the *ipsissimus sensus* be ascertained from a close comparative scrutiny of New Testament and rabbinic texts, but also, and significantly for Jesus research, Vermès declares:

> The sectors likely to benefit most from comparison with Jewish sources are those of religious concepts and motifs such as Messiah, Lord, son of God, holy man/miracle-worker, exorcist/healer, etc. With the proviso that an acceptable method of evaluation is agreed on, the juxtaposition of the New Testament and Jewish parallels is sure to lead to the discovery of how the original audience or readership understood the words, phrases or themes in question.[311]

The New Testament

> By the end of the first century Christianity had lost sight of the real Jesus and the original meaning of his message. Paul, John, and their churches replaced him by the otherworldly Christ of faith, and his insistence on personal effort, concentration, and trust in God by a reliance on the saving merits of an eternal, divine Redeemer. . . . Within decades of his death, the message of the real Jesus was transferred from its Semitic (Aramaic/Hebrew) linguistic context, its Galilean/Palestinian geographical setting, and its Jewish religious framework, to alien surroundings.
>
> Géza Vermès, *The Changing Faces of Jesus*, 282

Though the New Testament as a whole does not contribute significantly to Vermès's emerging Jewish portrait of Jesus, he is, nonetheless, familiar with its corpus and the pertinent texts, the Synoptic Gospels, which do confirm and enhance the Jewishness of Jesus. As we have seen, Vermès seeks to clarify the historical significance of the New Testament's nonhistorical documents, the Gospels, through a comparative scrutiny with other parallel sources, especially Jewish intertestamental and rabbinic sources. In *The Changing Faces of Jesus*, Vermès ventures further. He sketches four diverse portraits of Jesus that he discerns from within the Johannine and Pauline literature, the Acts of the Apostles, and the Synoptic Gospels. He concludes:

> The most prominent features of the Synoptic portrait of Jesus, those of a charismatic healer and exorcist, teacher and champion of the Kingdom of God, are essentially dependent on the historical figure which other authors of the New Testament progressively disguised. The fact that Jesus was admired, or suspected, as a potential Messiah started a complex process of theological speculation which in the course of three centuries culminated in the elevation of the carpenter from Nazareth to the rank of the second person of the triune Godhead, the Holy Trinity[312]

Probing this disguise, while lamenting the lack of the real gospel (message) of Jesus by Jesus, Vermès asserts that "the only chance to transform Jesus into a lifelike character beckons from the realities of the Jewish world of his day."[313] Such an effort might yield a glimpse of Jesus:

> By re-creating the milieu of his time, we may be able to catch a glimpse of what he really was. So we must try to retrieve the atmosphere he breathed, together with the ideas and ideals which animated his small world of people living in first-century Palestine, and especially the backwaters of Galilee: their religious dreams and petty jealousies, and— particularly in Galilee—their love of (relative) independence springing from a freedom from immediate Roman rule and the direct influence of the distant Judaean priestly authority, and from the doctrinal domination of the urban intellectual classes represented by the Pharisees.[314]

To the extent that a study of the New Testament may contribute to this canvas, it will be of significance to Jesus research.

The Gospels

> Unlike the theological pictures of Christ revealed in John and Paul and of the recently glorified and no longer physically present Master disclosed in the Acts of the Apostles, the portrait of Jesus in the Synoptic Gospels takes the form of a biographical sketch. Admittedly Mark, Matthew, and Luke were not professional historians in search of critical objectivity; nevertheless they acted as narrators of the life, ideas, activities, teachings, and death of a holy man of flesh and blood who lived a few decades before they sat down to record traditions forming around him.
>
> Géza Vermès, *The Changing Faces of Jesus*, 157

Vermès, writing in 1983 of his search for "Jesus' authentic religious thought,"[315] concedes that both his confidence in and use of a historical-critical approach among the pertinent parallel first-century Jewish literature, in which may be numbered, in some measure, the Synoptic Gospels—indeed the New Testament as a whole (see n. 158)—runs apparently counter to the prevailing thrust of a historical skepticism inaugurated by Bultmann, though inadequately defused by subsequent New Testament scholars, such as Käsemann. This inadequacy, according to Vermès, stems primarily "in the absence among its developers and practitioners of any *real* familiarity with the literature, culture, religion and above all spirit, of the post-biblical Judaism from which Jesus and his first disciples sprang."[316] We recognize this as a consistent critique coming from Vermès. And yet, for all his hesitation, Vermès, unlike Sandmel, does not despair of the benefits gained from employing literary-critical techniques and the criteria of authenticity.

Vermès concedes that "none of the evangelists were professional historians, not even the Synoptists."[317] He grants that "each had his own theological vantage-point and told his story with a specific end in view."[318] Concurring with dominant scholarship, he asserts: "The four Gospels are conceived as accounts conveying the life story and message of Jesus. In their final version, that is to say in the form in which they have reached us, the aim of these Gospels was to transmit, not the report of a chronicler, but the doctrinal message of the early church. Their purpose was primarily didactic, not historical."[319]

Of this he writes, justifying his historical scrutiny:

> But a theological interest is no more incompatible with a concern for history than is a political or philosophical conviction. As long as this interest is recognized, and as long as the interpreter realizes that it is likely to affect the whole work under scrutiny, he ought with a minimum of critical skill to be able to make allowances for it. In this connection, the fact that we have *three* theologically motivated accounts, and not just *one*, is in a sense fortunate and helpful because those elements which are common to them all are thus easily detectable and the historian is enabled to exercise his judgement on these basic data.[320]

As such, then, the Gospels were composed in Greek, and "like all ancient sources, they must be subjected to a critical analysis if we are to grasp the reality and authentic significance of the events and the teaching contained in them."[321]

Though he agrees that the Synoptic authors were not primarily historians, Vermès puzzles over their "choice of *biography* as their medium"[322] and asks how we are to explain this given "that they cannot have been influenced by tradition; no Jewish convention exists that the sayings of sages should be transmitted in this way."[323] Citing discrepancies and incongruities within the Synoptic text, he points to other difficulties:

> For if there is one certain conclusion which no serious reader endowed with insight and logic the size of a mustard seed can escape, it is that these hundreds of sayings have not been produced by one and the same teacher. They patently represent irreconcilable variations; indeed again and again they display flat contradictions. Jesus could not declare the proclamation of the good news to be restricted to the Jews alone, yet simultaneously

wish it to be addressed to all the nations of the earth. He could not have expected the Kingdom of God to burst into the world in his own lifetime, yet maintain that it would be postponed until the infinitely distant consummation of the ages, thus making room for a long-lasting church, etc., etc. If one of these alternatives is true, the other must inescapably be false.[324]

To this he adds the fact that other first-century Christian teachers, such as Paul, James, and the author of the *Didache*, "saw no advantage in a life-story as the vehicle of theological doctrine, moral exhortation, and disciplinary of liturgical rules,"[325] All of which leads Vermès to conclude:

> It is consequently difficult to avoid concluding that if the evangelists chose to tell the story of Jesus' life, it was because, whatever else they may have intended, they wished also to recount history, however unprofessionally. And if they included circumstances which were doctrinally embarrassing, it was because they were genuinely believed to be part of the narrative. In that case, Bultmann's dictum about the impossibility of knowing anything about Jesus or his personality, "because the early Christian sources show no interest in either," becomes a plain misjudgment.[326]

Vermès affirms the germ of historicity within the Synoptic seed. But how does one identify and quantify what is historically significance from what is theologically motivated? As we have seen, Vermès employs a historical approach that views the New Testament as part of the larger Jewish literary corpus in whose critical light historical significance and circumstance may be properly discerned. It is this methodology, coupled with the criteria of authenticity—as qualified by Vermès—that facilitates his necessary discernment of the authentic sayings of Jesus, from which he casts his Jewish mosaic of Jesus. Noting the "gospel's" evolutionary transmission, he writes:

> These various stages in the formulation and revision of the "gospel" or message of Jesus are all merged in the traditions which finally resulted in the written Synoptic Gospels. If we can link these evolutionary stages to the successive phases of the early history of the Christian movement, we will be in a position to distinguish, on some solid basis, between the treasures left by Jesus and the later growth which affected them.[327]

Reasserting the measure by which he will determine authenticity, Vermès concludes: "No saying of Jesus can be reckoned authentic unless it was intelligible to first-century Jews in a Palestinian/Galilean setting."[328]

Summary

Sandmel, Flusser, and Vermès, though grappling with similar sources, weigh the evidence differently and deduce from this evidence often similar and yet markedly distinct perspectives vis-à-vis the person of Jesus. They strive for objectivity, yet scholarly critique, varying hypotheses, subjective conjecture, and differing ideologies, as well as their respective audiences and motivation, influence their perspectives.

In this effort Flusser and Vermès are more closely allied. Though all are critical scholars conversant with the sources and the prevalent methodological hermeneutics,

Flusser and Vermès share an optimism in the historical-critical analysis that eludes Sandmel. Moreover, their work, in contrast to Sandmel's, situates Jesus securely within first-century Judaism and brings greater depth to his person and interaction.

Sandmel is more modest in his assessment of both the scholar's objectivity and the hermeneutic's effectiveness in sifting through the evidence to ascertain historical probability vis-à-vis the question of authenticity. It is this skepticism that leads him to affirm little critically about Jesus. As we have indicated previously, this does not preclude him from providing a portrait of Jesus. The emerging mosaic, however, is not deduced from his scholarly inquiry but rather from his musings. In this, one may ask why Sandmel is grouped within this chapter and not the next.

Sandmel is one of the first, certainly the first American, Jewish New Testament scholar to grapple critically with the question of Jesus' Jewishness. His facility with the sources and the hermeneutics secure for Sandmel this consideration. Moreover, it is his scholarship that leads him to confirm little. Sandmel's critical faculty informs his skepticism, a skepticism that prompts him to abandon the effort. His is no haphazard dismissal of the evidence or simple innovation. Though muted, his effort is critical. Moreover, it is the scholarship that permits Sandmel to cautiously advance a portrait of Jesus that has been of some benefit. It is the initial rendering of a positive image of Jesus that will be more securely advanced, by others, within the first-century Jewish matrix.

Among "those others" who view Jesus with greater appreciation within the context of Jewish thought and life, we number the Jesus researchers, Flusser and Vermès.

3

Creative Variations

Intuition and Imagination

The Jesus that has been missing is the figure within the culture of Galilean Judaism, recoverable only by inference, who gave rise to the movement or movements that our sources attest in all their diversity.

Bruce Chilton, *The Missing Jesus*, 44

Schalom Ben-Chorin, Pinchas Lapide, Jacob Neusner, and Eugene Borowitz, largely due to the manner in which they choose to engage the Jesus debate and assess the evidence—which may be described as idiosyncratic, enigmatic, or ambiguous—have been designated for our purposes as *creative*. The dilemma with which these scholars confront us is twofold. First, though they are conversant with the pertinent sources and normative methods of literary and historical critique, their presupposition, superficiality, or optimism seemingly prejudice or preclude a critical analysis.[329] This would be more true of Ben-Chorin and Lapide and less true of Neusner and Borowitz, though these latter two are less engaged in the Jesus debate—which in itself poses a difficulty for comparison and critique. Second, their motivation for engaging in the quest for the historical Jesus and their appreciation of Jesus from a Jewish perspective vary—which in turn facilitates or obscures objectivity.

Ben-Chorin and Lapide are ardent ecumenists who see Jesus as an elder brother: a Jewish brother capable of bridging the enmity that has for centuries divided kindred communities: Jewish and Christian. Neusner and Borowitz, though irenic, are more modest in their assessments. Their motivation and appreciation in this regard stem largely from invitations extended by group or occasion. The occasion for Neusner's conversation with Jesus, a reasoned encounter with the Matthean Jesus, is the conclusion of the second millennium, a period ripe with historical Jesus controversy. Borowitz, invited to address a Jewish-Christian dialogue, avoids the complex nuances of Jesus scholarship and offers instead a subjective encounter with Jesus, that is to say, an encounter mediated through a Christian dialogue partner.

Though each of these Jewish scholars offers variations on the theme, if you will, all four of them, logically and confidently, from their perspectives, situate Jesus in the milieu of first-century Palestine. To the degree that they do so, they may be identified as participants in the third quest for the historical Jesus: the quest for the Jewish Jesus.

70

Schalom Ben-Chorin

Schalom Ben-Chorin, like David Flusser, is a Jewish scholar who is passionate about Jesus. As an ecumenist, Ben-Chorin calls into service disciplines—etymology, psychology, and theology—that may facilitate his irenic quest. Fundamental to this quest, and his portrait of Jesus, is his astute observation that "the belief of Jesus unifies us, but the belief in Jesus divides us."[330] Jesus, Ben-Chorin asserts, is the pivotal figure that may bridge the chasm between Jew and Christian; his belief is the catalyst transforming enmity into friendship.

In his encounters with Jesus, Ben-Chorin finds not an alien figure nor the Christ, but rather a human brother, a Jewish brother. These encounters with Jesus are not restricted to an encounter with the Jesus of the Gospels. Rather, Ben-Chorin encounters Jesus in the hills of Galilee and the streets of the Old City. This Jesus, whose presence and voice seemingly permeate the city of Jerusalem and the land of Israel, captures both the heart and the imagination of Ben-Chorin. It is this Jewish Jesus whom he perceives deftly beneath a Christian overlay, and whom he seeks to reclaim and present to both Jews and Christians. Ben-Chorin explains:

> After centuries of a Christology that has sacrificed the human side of Jesus more and more to his divine nature, attempts are being made today to see the person Jesus, the *human being Jesus*. Nevertheless, the prevailing tendency is still to view Jesus as the mediator, divested of his bodily nature. . . . But this is not a realistic view of the Jew Jesus—not merely *a* Jew but *the* quintessential Jew, to whom representational faith was entirely alien.[331]

How he frees Jesus from such a disguise remains to be explained.

Ben-Chorin's Creative Variation: Exegesis and Intuition

> I have always found so much in this land of Israel, in this city of Jerusalem, and so much in Judaism, even in our own day, that lent to the reports of the Gospel a burning actuality that is always with me.
>
> Schalom Ben-Chorin, *Brother Jesus*, 7

Unlike Flusser, Ben-Chorin, though conversant with various pertinent sources—such as Jewish intertestamental literature, rabbinic writings, and the Christian Scripture, notably the Gospels—does not grapple critically with the sources. Rather, he acknowledges the dilemma posed by Bultmannian skepticism vis-à-vis historicity on one hand; and on the other hand, theological-literary fantasy, among which Robert Aron's *Jesus of Nazareth: The Hidden Years* is representative. Though he rejects the tendency to embrace theological-literary fantasy as a viable means to create a Jesus narrative, he does not embrace historical skepticism. He suggests that the solution to the dilemma is a discernible middle ground that lies between the two extremes of skepticism and capriciousness. This middle ground, from Ben-Chorin's vantage point, is *intuition*.

Though introduced in chapter 1, this principle bears repeating. Ben-Chorin is adamant that the intuition of which he speaks must not be confused with fantasy or mere imagination, but rather "grows out of a lifelong familiarity with the text and allows it to be interpreted subjectively."³³² Seeking to clarify this principle, while bridling its subjectivity, Ben-Chorin asserts that "anything imaginary is vigorously avoided, and only what seems exegetically possible is presented."³³³ Furthermore, from Ben-Chorin's experience, this "intuitive interpretation proceeds from a deep kindred empathy with Jesus within the Jewish world in which he lived, taught, and suffered."³³⁴ Kindred empathy, familiarity, indeed an intimacy and pathos, garnered from years of accompaniment, dialogue, and study, provide Ben-Chorin with the confidence to craft his mosaic from intuition and exegesis.

Aware of the inherent struggle among scholars to ascertain the probability of historical certitude vis-à-vis the Gospels and correlative texts in the quest for the historical Jesus, Ben-Chorin acknowledges both the limited historicity conveyed therein and the equally limited ability to ascertain the same with measured probability. He is also wary of what he deems *arbitrary* reinterpretations of the sacred tradition, such as Robert Graves's *King Jesus*, wherein Jesus is depicted as the son of Herod. It is this arbitrariness, this capriciousness, which he holds as untenable.

Ben-Chorin's intolerance vis-à-vis theological-literary fantasy and his idiosyncratic hermeneutic of intuition are seemingly contradictory inasmuch as he admits to a subjective hermeneutic. Yet he maintains that this principle is informed—and its subjectivity corralled—by an acquired knowledge, an intimacy, a kindred empathy that permits him the freedom to enter more confidently into the endeavor as opposed to one who abandons all constraint when constructing a narrative of Jesus or one ensnared by the intricacies of historical critique.

Ben-Chorin, like several of his Jewish contemporaries—of which Sandmel would be the exception—with little critique accepts the historicity of obvious Jewish elements preserved and transmitted in the Gospels while at the same time stripping away or ignoring other elements involving the theological overlay within the same text. Their interest is in history, not theology. They try to reclaim the decidedly Jewish Jesus of history and free him from Christian theology.

Given this, it is best to allow Ben-Chorin to voice his estimate of some of the pertinent sources. In so doing, one may demonstrate his reasoning and perhaps lessen a suspicion of poetic license, a license that Ben-Chorin disdains.

Considering the New Testament, Ben-Chorin writes:

> For me, the New Testament is certainly not Holy Scripture in the canonical sense. Nevertheless, I agree with Rabbi Leo Baeck ("Gospel") that it is a document that belongs to the history of the Jewish faith and preserves much of the relevance to the salvation of Israel. Accordingly I find it unjustifiable to alter the figure of Jesus in any arbitrary fashion, just as it seems wrong to me to make an Egyptian of Moses, as Sigmund Freud did in his late work *Moses and Monotheism* (1939).³³⁵

Of the Gospels and the question of historical reliability, he succinctly reports:

> For Bultmann and his followers the *Sitz im Leben,* the cultural and historical context, is precisely the preaching not the actual event; events are no longer considered to be reconstructible. These scholars base their premises on the undeniable fact that the Gospels do not represent a historical report but attest only to the missionary purpose of the risen Lord, the savior of Israel and the world. In academic circles it is commonly held today that missionary documents of this type cannot yield a valid historical picture. The elements of the picture are of course lacking, since it was not the intention of the New Testament authors to provide a historical report.[336]

From this point of view, neither the New Testament in general, nor the Gospels specifically, attest primarily to the historicity of the events therein contained. Rather these events woven into compelling narratives serve as a vehicle for the transmission of kerygma for the fledging Christian communities. If this is true, then the historical figure of Jesus is beyond retrieval. This is a position reminiscent of Sandmel. Yet Ben-Chorin, given his Jesus narrative, is obviously less restrained.

This, in part, may be due to his confidence that, though often contradictory and therefore subject to historical skepticism, the Gospels nonetheless affirm the historical existence of the man Jesus. Ben-Chorin writes: "There are so many contradictory features, traits, and details in the reports of the Gospels that we must conclude, on this fact alone, that we are dealing not with a didactic abstraction or invented messianic myth but with the living reminiscence of a son of man—a son of *a* man—notwithstanding the aura of apotheosis surrounding him."[337]

Ben-Chorin affirms that "the few sources we do have beyond the New Testament are, if anything, even less useful for historical evaluation."[338] He adds:

> The apocryphal gospels, for example, certainly have no historical value, even where they preserve a statement of Jesus here and there that has an authentic ring to it. The few passages in the Talmud and the Midrash that may refer to Jesus (these have been compiled by Joseph Klausner in his *Jesus of Nazareth*) are likewise of little historical value, since they grew out of the polemic with the early Christian community.[339]

What then, one may ask, constitutes the matrix from which Ben-Chorin confidently constructs his portrait of Jesus? *Alles wiederholt sich nur im Leben,* the first line of Friedrich Schiller's poem "An die Freunde," may provide the clue. "Everything returns only in life." It is a sentiment that Ben-Chorin interprets and renders applicable to Jesus: "Prefigured in the life of Jesus was much that has been repeated in the lives of his followers. Fantasy and belief have extracted much from his life, transporting it from the sphere of secular history into the higher sphere of salvation history. But the *Sitz im Leben,* the real context of these episodes in the historical report of Jesus, is unmistakable to Jewish eyes."[340]

The matrix from which Jesus emerges, the *Sitz im Leben,* for Ben-Chorin, unlike Bultmann, is the context, not the kerygma. The context is historical and, from Ben-Chorin's perspective, unmistakably Jewish and therefore familiar and not fantasy. From his scrutiny of Jesus and his familiarity with the matrix—past and present—in which Jesus moved and taught, Ben-Chorin discerns both Jesus' historicity and heritage.

After glimpsing a familiar face obscured beneath a Christian overlay, Ben-Chorin asserts: "Layer after layer must be removed in order to penetrate to the original countenance of Jesus. But this countenance and this form do not stand in an empty space; they must be examined within the context of the Palestinian Judaism contemporary to him. Any other viewpoint fails to see the true nature of Jesus."[341]

Ben-Chorin, like Flusser and Vermès, perceives and presents Jesus best from within his Jewish context. His tools are intuition and exegesis. Of his effort, he writes: "In this book the results of New Testament scholarship are consciously assimilated; nevertheless the Judaism contemporaneous to Jesus is constantly referred to, so that speeches, parables, prayers, and deeds of Jesus are fitted together smoothly. Jesus is seen here neither as Messias nor as prophet, but as a revolutionary of the heart."[342]

Pinchas Lapide

Pinchas Lapide is a *Wegbereiter*, a forerunner among the post-World War II Jewish scholars who seek to assuage the centuries-old enmity between the Jewish and Christian communities by urging a better understanding between and appreciation of both Jewish and Christian traditions. As a survivor of the Shoah, who later trained as a diplomat and a scholar, Lapide in the aftermath of the war employs the wisdom garnered from these experiences to build a biblical bridge between the Jewish and Christian communities.

In the introduction to his book *Jesus in Two Perspectives,* Lapide pointedly assesses the situation and articulates his strategy:

> It is the author's chief purpose to provide theological building blocks for the construction of a biblical bridge. But whether or not the bridge can be built remains an open question. Nineteen hundred years without dialog have generated colossal mounds of mutual mistrust and polemical debris that block almost every theological access. This book must be understood as an attempt to clear away the debris that has for so long hampered and inhibited communication. It aims to uncover that which has been buried and encrusted, especially the mutual recognition of Jews and Christians as closely related faith communities, who despite their admitted differences, live as brothers and sisters under the same Father-God, build upon his gracious love, pray for his succor, and earnestly hope for his salvation.[343]

In his zeal to promote ecumenism while insisting upon honest dialogue in which differences are appreciated and not ignored, Lapide seizes paradoxically upon the person of Jesus as *the* primary bridge that could span such a grievous chasm. His task is made all the more difficult in that the figure for whom he reaches, this Jesus, this Jew, who might unite and bring clarity, has in fact historically been the stumbling block, the obstacle, to peace and civility among Christians and Jews. Lapide explains: "For almost two millennia, a pious, devoted Jew has stood between us, a Jew who wanted to bring the kingdom of heaven in harmony, concord, and peace—certainly not hatred, schism, let alone bloodshed."[344]

Standing between Jew and Christian is the pious, Galilean Jew, Jesus, whom the Christians divested of his heritage and whom the Jews, given the hostility heaped upon them in his name by his followers, denied kinship. Lapide's task, given that "the Gentile church tried to de-Judaize Jesus, to Hellenize him, and to render the name of Jesus loathsome to all Jews,"[345] is to re-Judaize Jesus, to reclaim Jesus as a Jew and bring him home.

Lapide's Creative Variation: Irenic and Unorthodox

> Certainly the glad tidings are not without textual incongruencies. . . . However, legends *can* also be bearers of truths, which by no means deprive the kernel of the narrative of its historicity, as any scholar of religion will bear out.
>
>   Pinchas Lapide, *The Resurrection of Jesus*, 93

Lapide, conversant with the pertinent sources, especially the Gospels and Jewish intertestamental literature, is convinced of a Hebraic primary source underlying the Gospel narratives. This Hebraic subscript, once retrieved, would confirm and clarify the blurred features of Jesus the Jew.

As to motivation and appreciation, Carl E. Braaten, in his introduction to Lapide's book *The Resurrection of Jesus*, succinctly describes Lapide's approach:

> Dr. Lapide himself characterizes his approach as a process of rediscovering the authentically Jewish aspects of early Christianity, one that includes the rediscovery of Jesus and the witness of the first believers, who were all Jews. . . . Lapide calls this process *"Heimholung"*—"bringing home" to Judaism today what is originally rooted in Jewish experience, thus overcoming the alienation that Jews have felt toward those elements of their own tradition which served as the foundation stones of Christianity. . . . Pinchas Lapide does not let his readers forget the painful history of Jewish agony, and yet he hopes to transcend the negatives of the past on the way to a rapprochement at a deep level of faith and theology.[346]

A *Heimholung*. A rapprochement. A quest for true, previously unimaginable, dialogue, "the first impartial conversation about faith between the actual living brothers of Jesus and his spiritual disciples—since church and synagogue parted ways."[347] These aspects of Lapide's efforts form the "theological building blocks for the construction of the biblical bridge"[348] that he hopes will span the chasm that separates kindred communities.

With *Heimholung* as his goal, Lapide, unimpeded by Bultmannian skepticism, asserts that the time for historical Jesus study could not be more suitable, especially for a Jewish scholar equipped with the tools of modern sciences and unencumbered by Christian kerygma—and one might add, exempted from the rigors of historical criticism. Lapida argues that "Israel's threefold return—to the land of its fathers, to existence as a nation, and to the mother tongue of the Bible—favors a vivid appreciation of Jesus and the context of his life such as scarcely possible till now."[349] He therefore embarks upon a reclamation of Jesus, whom he regards as *the fifth Jesus*—in contradistinction to the Evangelists' Jesus—who is "no lofty, fleshless figure of light but a Jew with deep roots in the faith of his people."[350]

It is a task to which, from Lapide's perspective, a Jew is aptly called. Lapide, in a radio broadcast with Hans Küng, later published as *Brother or Lord?* gives an expansive rationale for this assertion, describing "five bonds with Jesus which—if I may say so—perhaps bring him closer to me than to many a Christian theologian in Europe today."[351]

Lapide, like Ben-Chorin, argues that he, as an Israeli Jew, shares certain affinities with Jesus that facilitate empathy and intimacy that elude a non-Jew. Of the five bonds that undergird this intimacy between Jesus and himself, Lapide sees their shared bond with *the land of Israel* as primary. Next, Lapide asserts that his familiarity and facility with both *Hebrew and Aramaic*, both secular language and sacred, serve to bring Jesus closer to him. Third, as further evidence of their commonality, he advances their shared understanding and appreciation of *the Hebrew Bible*, which both he and Jesus revere as Sacred Scripture and which both interpret according to rabbinical rules. Fourth, Lapide posits that he and Jesus share *an oriental imagination*: a way of thinking that finds expression in metaphors and parables and is averse to Western literalness. Such metaphorical prose is not easily translated nor comprehended once it is removed from its Jewish context; rather, that which is familiar to the Jew sounds, to the Jew, as strange and distorted in any other tongue. Finally, in his efforts to demonstrate his solidarity with Jesus, Lapide suggests that he and Jesus share *a concern for the land of Israel*. Citing similarities between both external and internal dangers, hostilities and unbelief respectively, then and now, Lapide insists: "This anxious love for Israel with its thirst for redemption—I hope and believe—gives Jesus and myself *a certain psychological solidarity*."[352]

Carl Braaten concurs:

> Lapide is convinced that perhaps only a Jew with an ear to the real ground underlying the sources will discover strong affinities with the Nazarene. And with well-pointed irony he claims to feel closer to Jesus than do many Christian theologians in Europe today, some of whom still grudgingly concede the Jewishness of Jesus, perhaps still reading the Gospels through Hellenistic, if not Aryan anti-Semitic, spectacles.[353]

One could easily imagine that Schalom Ben-Chorin and David Flusser would also concur with Lapide's assessment of this solidarity with Jesus.

After providing a rationale for his *Heimholung* approach and asserting his distinctive solidarity with Jesus given their common heritage, Lapide enlists the evidence culled from the pertinent sources to support his overall effort: *Heimholung*. His primary source is the Hebraic tradition underlying the Greek Synoptic tradition.

Lapide, writing in *Israelis, Jews, and Jesus*, accepts as self-evident the existence of a Hebrew stratum underlying the four Greek Gospels. He asserts what others disclaim:

The earliest writing about Jesus was composed in Hebrew and appeared, most probably, in Jerusalem. It was a collection of sayings which perhaps one of his disciples wished to record to guard them from the possible distortions of oral tradition. Or it may have been a protogospel designed to make the glad tidings of the rabbi of Nazareth accessible to all his fellow believers. We do not know for sure.[354]

He continues that "it is certain, however, that all four Greek Gospels display distinct traces of an original Hebrew text in their vocabulary, grammar, syntax, and semantic pattern."[355]

His secondary sources, deemed primary by the majority of New Testament scholars, are the Gospels, specifically the Synoptic Gospels. Lapide, like Flusser and Ben-Chorin, employs etymology, philology, and exegesis as well as archaeological evidence in his assessment of the sources. Given his arguments and the evidence presented, it is clear that Lapide is conversant with the Synoptic tradition, pertinent Christian doctrine, the Talmud, and significant rabbinic literature. He employs the evidence therein to demonstrate his claim of a Hebrew stratum underlying the Gospel traditions.[356]

Lapide, an Orthodox Jew, does not employ historical criticism in the customary fashion. Rather, he seeks to study the history of the effect rather than ascertain the historicity of the event. In the introduction to *Jesus in Two Perspectives*, he explains that the New Testament passages quoted therein "are treated primarily according to the history of their effect rather than from a historical-critical perspective."[357] *The history of their effect.* His unorthodox and unexpected assertion that the resurrection of Jesus was indeed a historical event is paradigmatic of this approach. His argument for historicity in this regard stems not from a historical-critical analysis of the texts and the criteria inherent therein, but rather from *the effect* that the resurrection of Jesus had on the apostles and disciples: the transformation of previously cowering men into fervent witnesses. For Lapide, what makes such a metamorphosis explicable is the cause: the resurrection of Jesus. From Lapide's perspective, this in turn validates the historicity of the causal event: Jesus' resurrection.

Though Lapide expresses an enthusiastic confidence in the fruit harvested from the study of the Qumran texts, he offers no critical assessment. Yet he is more guarded as to his assessment of the New Testament evidence. The history of their effect is a history marred by enmity, mutual hostilities, and pogroms, creating the Jewish ghettos and culminating in the Shoah. It is this enmity that Lapide seeks to overcome by gaining a better appreciation of commonality that exists between the two separate communities through a retrospective approach to the person of Jesus. To this end he employs the process of *Heimholung*; his overall purpose is irenic.

In several books and in numerous radio interviews—some of which were transcribed and published—with notable Christian theologians, such as Ulrich Luz and Karl Rahner and Hans Küng, Lapide wrestles with the complexities of both traditions in his effort to demonstrate *Heimholung*, an aspect of which is Jesus' continuity with Judaism—a continuity that though obscured, is more clearly discernible to Jewish eyes, and to facilitate, in light of *Heimholung*, Judaism's rapprochement with Christianity.

Jacob Neusner

Jacob Neusner, an advocate of the modern historical-critical method and literary analysis, is an ardent critic of those who employ both methodologies improperly or
inappropriately. He brings to our discussion a voice of dissent and critique, of affirmation and challenge. Among the authors considered in this study, Neusner's voice is
a distinctive voice critical of Jesus and his teaching. His dissent and critique are not
confined to Jesus and his message but extend, significantly, to Jewish and Christian
scholars in pursuit of the historical Jesus as well as to ecumenists engaged in the Jewish-
Christian dialogue. His affirmation and challenge are given to both Jew and Christian,
orthodox or secular.

Briefly, his critique of Jesus, which informs his dissent, is emboldened by
Jesus' claims to reform or improve Torah. From Neusner's perspective such a presumption contradicts Torah insofar as it introduces distortion and error. This forms his
dissent to some of the teachings of Jesus that Neusner deems wrong. It is this, Jesus'
torah, with which he takes issue when confronting Jesus.[358]

As to the questers and ecumenists, he charges the questers with issuing theology
masquerading as history, and he diagnoses the ecumenists as producing shallow po-
liteness or naiveté, devoid of substantial debate, posing as dialogue. Neusner's dissent
and critique will be explored more appropriately in chapter 5. Here, since our focus is
upon sources and method, we may but introduce them.

Regarding his dissent, Neusner writes broadly:

> My dissent is entered not against "Christianity" in all its forms and versions, nor is it
> against the apostle, Paul, nor even against that complex and enormous "body of Christ"
> that the Church was and would become. I mean to offer no apology for a "Judaism" that
> focuses upon that negative "Why not Christ?" Judaism does not have always to explain
> "why not," when the message of the Torah is always: Why . . . , because . . . Judaism in
> all its complex forms constitutes something other than merely Christianity without Christ
> (the Old Testament without the New, in terms of revealed writings). Judaism is simply
> another religion, not merely not-Christianity; and at issue here is not Judaism as against
> Christianity or Jesus as against Christ (in that formulation in narrowly biographical-
> historical terms, which I find irrelevant to argument).[359]

The issue, of which he speaks, is his, Neusner's, own response to Jesus: "In these pages,
I take a different path altogether. I am not interested in what happened later on; I want
to know, how, *if I were there*, standing at the foot of the mountain where Jesus said the
words that came to be called "the Sermon on the Mount," I would have responded."[360]

Neusner refuses to follow the path of Jewish apologists who advance a "rather tired
claim, yes to the historical Jesus, no to the Christ of Christianity."[361] Instead, he suggests
a different approach, one in which he directly engages Jesus in conversation and debate.
The Jesus whom Neusner engages in conversation is not "the historical Jesus of a
scholar's studious imagination,"[362] but the Jesus of the Gospels.

Neusner advances a simple reason for his departure from the customary approach
to Jesus study: "Those fabricated historical figures," discerned by a scholar's studious

imagination, "are too many and diverse for argument."[363] Instead, he focuses upon a Jesus familiar to both Jew and Christian:

> When Jews open the New Testament, they assume they are hearing from the same Jesus Christ of Christianity, and when Christians open the same book, they surely take the same view. That is not to say the historical Jesus is not present within and behind the Gospels; it is only to affirm that the Gospels as we read them portray Jesus to most of us who propose to know him. I write for believing Christians and faithful Jews; for them, Jesus is known through the Gospels. I address one of those Gospels.[364]

Candidly, Neusner in *A Rabbi Talks with Jesus* cautions his readers: "This is a not a book about scholarship. I address only one picture of what Jesus said, that of the Gospel according to Matthew."[365] In addressing Matthew's Jesus, Neusner not only provides a studied response, but also advances a paradigm for true religious dialogue—the subtext, if you will, of Neusner's argument.

Neusner's Creative Variation: A Different Path

> What made at all possible a Judaic reading of Jesus was, of course, the separation of "the historical Jesus" from "the Christ of faith." Judaism could then consider the former and ignore the latter.
>
> Jacob Neusner, *Telling Tales*, 87

Since Jacob Neusner chooses to converse with the Matthean Jesus, his primary source for this construct is obviously the Gospel of Matthew. It would be erroneous, however, to presume that Neusner is confined simply to Matthew. It should not be forgotten, or missed, that Neusner is *the rabbi* talking with Jesus: a rabbi formed in Torah and skilled in Jewish hermeneutic and argumentation. Rabbi Neusner talks, converses, and argues with Rabbi Jesus. A twentieth-century American university professor engages a first-century itinerant Galilean teacher of torah in debate.

Explaining the Jewish concept of argument—the method of his approach—Neusner anticipates an accusation of disrespect and instructs:

> In my religion, argument forms a mode of divine service, as much as prayer: reasoned debate on substantive issues, debate founded on respect for the other and made possible by shared premises. That kind of contention is not only a gesture of honor and respect for the other, but in the context of the Torah, it forms a gift of intellect on the altar of the Torah. I do not think a non-Christian can pay to him whom Christians know as Christ a more sincere tribute than a good, solid argument.[366]

Neusner, asserting that "Matthew's Jesus comes closest to an account of Jesus that a believing and practicing Jew can grasp in terms of Judaism,"[367] explains the plausibility of his choice and his proposal:

> An argument with Matthew's Jesus is plausible because there is a shared Torah between us, so we can agree sufficiently on the main thing to disagree on other things. By contrast, there is a very good reason that I cannot argue with John's Jesus or Luke's Jesus or Mark's

Jesus. John and therefore his Jesus simply loathes "the Jews"—and enough said. Mark's and Luke's Jesus, sharing much to be sure with Matthew, do not represent figures for whom the Judaic connection nourishes.[368]

The goal is not winning, but rather providing reaffirmation and example, as Neusner emphasizes:

> This is not an argument I want to win. It is an argument to make plausible to both Jews and Christians that other position, the one of the Torah, that Jews have affirmed in the nearly two thousand years since they went their own way and chose not to follow Jesus at all. This I say without apology, without deceit or guile. What I do is simply reaffirm the Torah of Sinai over against Matthew's Jesus Christ: Moses would want no less of any of us, or Matthew's Jesus, I think, [would want] no more. So when I say, if I heard those words that day, I would have offered an argument, it is with the living mortal man, walking among us and talking with us, that I set forth my argument.[369]

Matthew presents Jesus as a Jew among Jews. It is this Jew, Jesus, whom Neusner engages. Neusner views Matthew's "representation of Jesus as a teacher, with an important message forming part of the evidence that here is the Christ, in whom Israel should believe,"[370] as most compelling: one that invites a Jewish response—a response focused upon both the teacher and his teaching.

Of this, Neusner writes: "In response to the message of Matthew's Jesus, a practicing Jew such as myself, speaking for myself alone of course, but well within the faith of eternal Israel, can frame an argument."[371] Honing his argument, Neusner observes:

> There is much in Matthew's story of Jesus that simply reviews well-known teachings of the Torah of Moses, for example, Jesus' well-known paraphrase of Leviticus 19:18: "Love your neighbor as yourself." With that and much else that is good Torah-teaching, no faithful Jew would want to argue. But much set forth in fulfillment of the Torah in fact either violates the clear teaching and intent of Torah, or offers a religious message inferior to that of the Torah as Israel reads Torah. And an argument on that set of teachings to which judgments such as these pertain is what I offer in these pages.

Describing Jesus, then, as "a Torah-teacher teaching his torah to his disciples,"[372] Neusner engages Jesus on a single subject: "what God wants of me." As to his criterion, given that both he and Jesus are explicit in their fidelity to the integrity of the Torah, Neusner claims that "the Torah is a legitimate criterion of truth, since both parties to the argument share the same conviction."[373] It is Jesus' torah with which Neusner will take issue. The Torah of Moses will be his criterion of truth.

Beginning with Matthew's Gospel, while making "no claim whatsoever about the historical veracity of what Matthew says Jesus said and did,"[374] Neusner states:

> I insist then that we meet Matthew's Jesus on his own ground, taking as a fact that he said the things that Matthew said he said: I take this Gospel seriously. To appreciate this effort of mine at religious dialogue, in a religious spirit, on religious issues, scholarly or theological readers, with their own conceptions of what Jesus really said or did, will have to suspend doubt. Everyone else, I hope will go forward with me.[375]

Eugene Borowitz

In 1975 Eugene Borowitz, a Reform Jew, was invited by the American Theological Society to address the question of contemporary Christologies from a Jewish perspective. The specific Christologies—represented by Knox, Barth, Rahner, Moltmann, and others—to which he was to offer a Jewish response were provided by the society, at Borowitz's request.[376] Because Borowitz is responding to what contemporary Christian theologians are saying about *Jesus as the Christ*, his efforts, published as a book in 1980, bear no direct interest to our discussion of the historical Jesus. Nonetheless, Borowitz's book *Contemporaries Christologies: A Jewish Response* is a significant and praiseworthy accomplishment.[377] More to our purpose are the papers that Borowitz delivered at a 1987 lecture series at the College of St. Thomas, St. Paul, Minnesota. Though limited in scope, the lectures let us glimpse Borowitz's creativity and sensitivity vis-à-vis the rigors of religious dialogue.

Borowitz's Creative Variation: Acquaintance and Observation

> Accepting the Jewishness of Jesus means accepting the fact that the piety from which he arose continues in living faithfulness to this day.
>
> Eugene Borowitz, "The Challenge of Jesus the Jew for the Church," 26

Eugene Borowitz poses a difficult dilemma for us who seek to fathom sources and method, given the brevity of his response to the question of Jesus from a Jewish perspective and the lack of documentation. This dilemma is compounded in that Borowitz is also wary of the pertinent sources, the prevalent methodologies, and trends in popular culture that tend to obscure, exaggerate, or contradict what may be gleaned from the data vis-à-vis the historical Jesus. The habit of reading back into history elements from a later period—such as Jewish elements from rabbinic literature read back into the Gospels, which predate them—to enhance or verify the Jewishness of Jesus is but one such example that legitimizes, from his perspective, his apprehensions.

Though the New Testament accounts, the Gospels, "are the best documents available to us for the practice of Judaism in Jesus' lifetime,"[378] Borowitz is aware that they are not purely objective or significantly biographical. Questioning their historical accuracy, he states, "These records come to us from people who are speaking out of Christian faith, not out of a desire to record data as impartially or sympathetically as possible."[379] Candidly admitting to the stumbling blocks posed by these incongruencies or deficiencies, Borowitz chooses not to engage in a critical analysis of the sources.

As to his methodology, there seems to be none, at least not in the usual sense. Rather Borowitz, a nonhalakic Jew,[380] adopts an unconventional strategy: acquaintance and observation. He advances a description of Jesus acquired from—or mediated by—his acquaintance with and observation of his Christian dialogue partner. As noted previously, this Jesus is described sympathetically, yet candidly, in lectures later published as articles in an ecumenical journal. Given this subjective, unconventional approach—which warrants Borowitz's inclusion in this chapter—the brevity of his address and the lack of book or monograph, there is little to assess critically. His unconventional approach does not diminish, however, his contribution to our presentation of Jesus from Jewish perspectives.

Summary

These, then, constitute the variations on sources and techniques advanced by our four authors as they creatively assess "glass and stone" before casting them in distinctive mosaic patterns. Ben-Chorin and Lapide, the Reform Jew and the Orthodox Jew, weigh the evidence differently but cast similar portraits, given their common hope of *Heimholung Jesu*. Neusner and Borowitz, both American Reform rabbis, advance more cautious renderings, given their reservations about Jesus scholarship and methodologies.

We now have reviewed both the critical and creative efforts employed by our seven authors to advance their comprehension of Jesus as a Jew. Thereby we may better appreciate and comment upon the various positions that give shape to the emerging Jewish mosaic of Jesus.

4

Jesus within Judaism

A Triptych

In the closing decades of the twentieth century the most hopeful advance in life of Jesus research was the recognition that the quest must primarily have in view Jesus the Jew and a clearer and firmer grasp of the consequences. What distinguishes this "third quest of the historical Jesus" is the conviction that any attempt to build up a historical picture of Jesus of Nazareth should and must begin from the fact that he was a first-century Jew operating in a first-century milieu. After all, when so much is historically uncertain, we can surely assume with confidence that Jesus was brought up as a religious Jew.

James D. G. Dunn, *Jesus Remembered*, 85–86

In *Jesus Remembered*, James Dunn distinguishes the third quest for the historical Jesus from the second quest, which was preoccupied with the criterion of dissimilarity and thus focused upon what set Jesus *apart from* Judaism. This third quest does just the opposite. Rather than separate Jesus from Judaism—a separation that reflects the continued denigration of Judaism vis-à-vis Christianity and Christian scholarship—this third quest, reacting against both this denigration and its subsequent separation of Jesus from Judaism, places Jesus squarely within his Jewish milieu: first-century Palestinian Judaism.

The third quest, imbued with this *Jewish* perspective, emerged in the 1980s. Nevertheless, it did not arise out of a vacuum. Rather, as Dunn acknowledges, the third quest is indebted to the previous efforts of Jewish scholars whose work, though "curiously ineffective in regards to the mainstreams of Jesus research,"[381] nonetheless has prepared the groundwork for the assertions that would follow and that came to typify this third quest for the historical Jesus. The Jewish authors included in this study are numbered among those who preceded and, in some measure, influenced the efforts of E. P. Sanders and N. T. Wright, whom Dunn heralds as most significant among the third questers.[382]

Of these Jewish authors, Dunn credits Vermès with having "a subtle and significant influence"[383] upon the third quest, so much so that he dubs Vermès "the *John the Baptist* of the third quest."[384] Hence, we turn to Vermès especially and to those others considered here, who preceded and prepared the way for that which has become the commonplace, though not uncontroversial, portrayal of Jesus within first-century

Palestinian Judaism. Specifically, we return to their portraits of Jesus, cast from a Jewish perspective, and more thoroughly examine them.

This chapter explores the portraits of Jesus as discerned in the works of Sandmel, Flusser and Vermès, respectively. Chapter 5 will explore the figure of Jesus as discerned in the work of Ben-Chorin, Lapide, Neusner, and Borowitz. Both chapters give each author's composite of Jesus. Concomitantly, where appropriate, I will offer a juxtaposition of these portraits: their points of convergence and divergence. This latter analysis will take into consideration, where applicable, Jesus' identity, as a Galilean Jew, prophet, rabbi, messiah, and so forth; his relationship to the law of Moses; his teaching, such as his themes of forgiveness and the advent of the kingdom of God; his healing miracles, as in the tradition of Honi the Circle-Drawer and Hanina ben Dosa; and his arrest, trial, and death. Also, where warranted, Jesus' resurrection will be considered. This juxtaposition will give shape and form to the Jesus mosaic that emerges from the efforts of these diverse authors. Chapter 6 will indicate, where applicable, their contribution to Jewish theology and Christian theology. To better assess our authors' contributions, this final chapter will survey various critical voices, both positive and negative critiques, raised in response to our authors' perspectives on Jesus.

Jesus, Jewish *Nazir,* Icon of Western Culture

> It is not part of our Jewish disposition to regard any man as supreme over all others. We say this without animus towards the figure of Jesus. A good and worthy man, yes. A man whose impact on others, directly or indirectly, and on subsequent human history was greater than any other man in history, yes. But we persist in seeing him as only one of the many whose lives dot Jewish history.
>
> Samuel Sandmel, "Jesus: A Jewish Perspective," 141

In *We Jews and Jesus*, Samuel Sandmel lists four factors that the modern-day Jew should take into consideration when trying to grapple reasonably with Jesus. Four questions constitute his approach and his recommendation: "First, what has traditional Christianity thought of him? Second, what does modern scientific scholarship tell about him? Third, what have modern Jewish scholars told us of him as far as their historical studies disclose? Fourth, what are the characteristics of Judaism, and how does Jesus fit into both our inherited Judaism and into the Judaism of today?"[385]

These four factors form the outline of his book *We Jews and Jesus*, which was written primarily for a Jewish readership. Of these factors, the fourth is more pertinent to our current discussion inasmuch as this factor when juxtaposed with the canonical Gospels forms the milieu from which Sandmel's Jesus portrait—though timorously rendered, given his reservations about historical certainty—emerges.[386]

Sandmel begins by telling us what we do *not* know about Jesus, given the "insufficient material [gleaned from the Gospels] for a biography, especially in the modern sense."[387] From Sandmel's perspective, we do not know for sure or only vaguely know the following:

- The year Jesus was born.
- The year of his death, though we do know that Pontius Pilate served as Roman governor in 26–36 CE.
- The environment and the times, which we know only sketchily. Judaea became a Roman province in 63 BCE, which later included Palestine. Given its previous history, Grecian culture and civilization were well represented in Palestine.
- Adversity under foreign occupiers, which intensified Jewish yearning for a *māšîaḥ*, messiah, who would destroy the foreign occupiers and gather the dispersed Jews into one kingdom, Israel.
- The Sadducees, from whom we have inherited no literature.
- The Pharisees, whose literature is abundant but in its written forms dates chiefly from a period much later, so that we have little secure data about Pharisaism in the period of Jesus.
- The Essenes, for whom we have uncertain, unreliable data.
- The connection in religious atmosphere and influence between Galilee in the north and the Essenes, who presumably were in the south, remains dark for us.
- The Fourth Philosophy (one of Josephus's categories for the Jewish groups in first-century Palestine), apparently to be understood as patriotic guerillas rather than thinkers: a sporadic, unorganized, recurrent impulse of activists.
- The overly praised Dead Sea Scrolls, especially the "sectarian" documents; at best, a small portion of the scrolls throw light on the Judaisms of the time, but not specifically on Jesus.
- The title "rabbi": we are uncertain whether it was already in common use in Jesus' day or if it became common two or more decades later.
- That unique development, the synagogue: it is unclear whether in Jesus' day it was the act of meeting, or as later, the place of meeting and hence an edifice.
- The temple: yet in some clarity (given the information provided by Josephus, the Hebrew Bible, and rabbinic literature), we see that the temple was priestly and the synagogue laical, and that animal sacrifice was central in the temple, while Scripture was central in the synagogue.
- Scribes, whom we can conjecture were the scriptural experts and teachers, whose role eventually passed to the rabbis.
- The Sanhedrin, which had certain prerogatives relating to governing of Jews, but the exact rights which it had under either a Jewish ruler or under a Roman governor are uncertain.
- Priests, about whom we find some surprising and dubious materials: "chief priests" is a New Testament term unknown and quite unlikely in other Jewish literature.
- Other compositions written in that age: we do not know to what extent they circulated and to what extent they were influential.
- Apocalyptic writings (purportedly end-time revelations), which failed to gain a full and acknowledged status, Jewish or Christian.
- Messianism: though the precise connection is far from clear to us, there is some relationship between apocalyptic writing and messianism, to the extent that messianic thought in part dealt with the end of time.[388]

The above is what we do not know about Jesus or only vaguely know about him.

What we *do know* about Jesus comes to us also primarily from the Christian Gospels. Not only is the data insufficient to secure biographical information, the narratives therein, in Sandmel's estimation, "are not about the man Jesus, but about the human interval in the eternity of the divine Christ."[389] To learn of this divine Christ, qua Jesus, Sandmel provides his Jewish readers with a survey of select New Testament titles, many of which reflect Greek influence.

Christ, qua Jesus

In the third chapter of his book *We Jews and Jesus*, Sandmel tries to better inform his readers as to *who* or more precisely *what* Jesus was. He titles the chapter "The Divine Christ." Sandmel explains that, in the aftermath of the parting of the ways between Judaism and Christianity over the question of *what* Jesus was, distinctive Jewish concepts—*messiah, lord, son of man,* and *son of God*, none of which conveyed divine status on the bearer—take on, in the Hellenistic milieu where Christianity first flourished, decidedly Greek overtones that do convey divine status upon Jesus.[390]

As previously indicated, Sandmel, unlike our other authors, does not engage the New Testament evidence critically. He therefore does not try to provide a historical-philological analysis. Rather, he simply conveys to his readers the meaning of the New Testament titles of Jesus in their Christian, meaning Greek, context. All of which affirms for the reader, in Sandmel's estimation, what is conveyed by the New Testament: Jesus, rather than merely human, is the divine Christ. Sandmel's reticence to engage the texts critically prevents us from commenting further.

Sandmel's summary comments, however, may be instructive: "When we Jews have understood Christian explanations, and when we have not, we have consistently rejected the Christian claims about Jesus. We have not believed that Jesus was the Messiah; we have not been willing to call him Lord; we have not believed that the Logos became incarnate as Jesus; we have not believed that Jesus was, or is, the very Godness of God."[391]

Uncertainties and Nuances

Sandmel affirms that "for all we do know, there is more that we do not know."[392] Moreover, he asserts that "the uncertainties about the Jewish scene in the age of Jesus are kindred to the central problem of Jesus himself."[393]

The problem to which Sandmel refers is the question of historical reliability vis-à-vis the Gospels. From Sandmel's perspective, this complex question (treated in chapter 2 above) yields no satisfactory conclusions. This, as we have seen, prompts Sandmel to abandon the effort of retrieving the Jesus of history from the Gospels. And yet, he does not entirely despair of the effort, even though he dismisses such efforts based on the Gospels as dubious.

It is this very uncertainty, and his understanding of the value thereof, that permits Sandmel to offer a conjecture, albeit, one unsubstantiated by his own scholarship, as to *who* was Jesus. Sandmel explains: "It is far better for scholarship to know where it stands than for it to fail to know. It is far better for us to present guesses as guesses than to pass them off as reflections of accurate and unmistakable knowledge. Scholarship seems to me to be at its best when its claims are not extravagant and when they are substantial rather than hazardous."[394]

Sandmel further comments that "to know too much can destroy in man the intuitive creativity which is the element in our being that enables us to fashion or propagate our tremendous religious institutions."[395]

Before presenting his conjecture vis-à-vis the question of *who* Jesus was, we must allow Sandmel two more nuances.

First, in *We Jews and Jesus*, Sandmel provides us with a survey of previous research on the life of Jesus. While commenting upon early nineteenth-century efforts, he introduces us to what he describes as the emergence of "the Jesus of Western society." Speaking about the subtle connection between the Jewish reclamation of the Jesus of history and the emergence of the Jesus of Western society, Sandmel explains:

> This Jesus [of Western society] is not quite the same as the Jesus of historical scholars, but rather an intuitive assumption on the part of Western man that there are certain high points in human intellectual and spiritual attainment which characterized Jesus, and hence that Jesus the man represents a kind of benevolent humanitarianism to mankind at large and he serves as exemplar, a model for the aspirations of the individual. This Jesus of Western culture is held to have been a man of keen insight into the psychology of men, a kindly and benevolent person who unbrokenly manifested goodwill, and whose mission in life was to bring about universal peace and to provide guidance for men in either solving the acute social, economic, and political problems of the age, or at least of setting forth the standard by which the problems might be solved. This Jesus of Western culture is only remotely connected with the Christ of Christian faith, and even less directly connected with the historical Jesus. When the ghetto walls fell, this Jesus of Western man came more and more into the ken of Jews in the West.[396]

Second, Sandmel explains that Jews fail to grasp the significance of Jesus for two important reasons. Briefly, we may reduce his explanation to two tendencies found in Christian scholarship and Christianity respectively. In Christian scholarship, Sandmel, using Abraham Geiger's critique of Ernst Renan's *Life of Jesus* (1863) as paradigmatic, discerns "an antecedent conditioning" that allows liberal Christian scholars to deny or severely question the historicity of the Gospels vis-à-vis the quest for the historical Jesus, while at the same time heralding Jesus as an ideal man, affirming such from the very evidence that they have previously eschewed.[397] This first tendency, coupled with the second—that Sandmel describes as "iconoclastic scholarship," a scholarship wherein "Jesus himself remains free from equation with other humans"[398] and is heralded intuitively as the ideal man—perplexes the Jewish scholar.

From Sandmel's Jewish perspective, given "that there is often [in the various books called *The Life of Jesus*] very little correlation between the denials of the scholars of this or that detail in the Gospel and the *intuitive determination* to see in Jesus the 'ideal man,'"[399] one would expect a less-favorable assessment of Jesus. However, this is not the case. Jesus is inevitably affirmed as the ideal man. What Geiger views as an inconsistency, given "this anomaly of abiding reverence in the midst of ruthless negative scholarship,"[400] Sandmel posits as the preeminence of Jesus in the mind of the Christian. He asserts that "in the minds of Christians the person of Jesus is so central as to be immune to the logic and even the data of scholarship."[401] Geiger failed to appreciate this factor due to "a certain naïveté."[402] In Sandmel's estimate, "Geiger was quite unprepared to discover that *intuitive imagination* was even stronger in Renan than pure scholarship."[403]

Bridling his own New Testament scholarship, Sandmel posits his own "intuitive assumption" and renders a portrait of Jesus, a portrait that, despite his reservations, reflects the influences described above.

Jesus, Jewish Nazir

Sandmel, stepping outside his scholarly perimeter, renders his mosaic of Jesus in response to a hypothetical question that challenges him to give an assessment of Jesus, "some view of him which is the essence of the Gospels"[404] unencumbered by scholarly debate. He muses:

> It seems to me not to violate the documents or that scholarship which I have imbibed to think of Jesus as someone who had gifts of leadership and who was something of a teacher. I believe too that I discern in him a Jewish loyalty at variance with the views both of Christian and Jewish partisans who, through opposing motives that cancel each other out, detach him from Judaism. I believe that Jesus firmly believed that the end of the world was coming soon. I believe that he believed himself to be the Messiah, and that those scholars who deny this are incorrect.[405]

A tentative portrait emerges of Jesus as a leader, a teacher, a loyal Jew, the Messiah— from Jesus' perspective, not Sandmel's—and one convinced of the imminent end time.

Sandmel, reflecting on the teaching qualities of Jesus teacher, continues:

> I own to seeing no originality in the teachings of Jesus, for I hold that those passages which deal with his supernatural role reflect not his authentic words but the piety of the developing Church. As to those teachings which are conceivably his, they seem to me to be of a piece with Jewish teaching, and that they range from the commonplaces of that Jewish teaching through a sporadic flash of insight that other Jewish teachers also achieved.[406]

Having said this, Sandmel states that, from his point of view, "the question of originality is a misguided one."[407] Sandmel dismisses the question of who said what first, such as Hillel or Jesus, and asserts the supremacy of value over priority:

> To my mind the issue is that of value, not of priority; I find that there is more in the teachings of Jesus that I admire than that I do not; purely by chance I would deny that the hateful and hating chapter Matthew 23 goes back authentically to Jesus. There is, then, a general sense in which I see abiding values in many of the teachings of Jesus,

and I also see that Christians have found affirmative values in passages which do not stir me; for example, I believe that Christians have been motivated to noble act and deed by the injunction not to resist evil, but I cannot in good conscience agree with this sentiment.[408]

Explaining that Jesus' uniqueness lies not in the particulars but rather "in the totality of what we may perhaps glimpse of him,"[409] Sandmel concedes: "Thus he was in part a teacher, a Jewish loyalist, a leader of men, with a personality unquestionably striking enough to be a leader, and his career must have been exceedingly singular for his followers to say that he had been resurrected."[410]

In commenting upon Jesus' suffering and death, Sandmel affirms somewhat ironically: "He was a martyr to his Jewish patriotism. So many Jews became martyrs at the hands of later Christians that his martyrdom seems to us perhaps too unexceptionable for special notice. We Jews have so suffered, because Christians in ages past made us suffer, that it is difficult for us to acknowledge that Jesus suffered unusually. I believe that he did."[411]

Sandmel does not, however, embrace the recurrent theme of triumphalism vis-à-vis Jesus' career and subsequent martyrdom as found in Paul and the Gospels. Rather, he admits to the opposite: "I can certainly acknowledge that martyrdom partakes of the overtone of triumph. Yet the dominant note to me of his career is overwhelmingly one of pathos, of sympathy, that a man, with the normal frailties of men, aspired and labored and worked, and yet experienced defeat."[412]

Though Sandmel does acknowledge these tragic circumstances, he does not find Jesus' tragic demise unique. Moreover, he finds that the warm sympathy that he feels toward this Jewish *nazir* (*nāzîr*, Nazarite), this person dedicated to God, is "obstructed by a feeling that he [Jesus] remains always in some measure alien to me."[413] Sandmel expands upon his dilemma, explaining:

> When I ask myself why this is so, I do not ascribe it to any conscious bias—this may be the case, but I do not think so—but rather because I am inherently unable to see in Jesus that extra attribute which Christians and quasi-Christians see in him. Perhaps the impediment is not so much what my mind and heart may tell me about Jesus, but simply my resistance to what admirable and noble Christians tell me about him. I can agree that he was a great and good man, but not that he exceeded other great and good men in the excellency of human virtues.[414]

Not surprisingly, Sandmel, who "cannot share in the sentiments of Montefiore . . . nor in Klausner's distant dream of a reclaimed Jesus,"[415] disavows any religious assessment of Jesus, exclaiming:

> I must say most plainly that Jesus has no bearing on me in a religious way. . . . I am not sensible of any such incompleteness. A religion is, after all, a complex of more than just theological viewpoints, for a religion has its own tone and texture which arises from its history, its group experience, its mores and norms, and even its folkways. I confess that there arises in me from time to time, in moods of self-criticism, some occasional feeling about certain inadequacies in Judaism. . . . But I do not discern any religious

incompleteness which the figure of Jesus would fill in, just as I see no incompleteness
which a Mohammed or a Confucius would fill in.[416]

Culturally the situation is quite different. Encounters with the Jesus of Western culture,
given his presence in art, music, and theatre, are unavoidable—and perhaps enriching
from a cultural perspective—for Sandmel and other Western Jews. Even so, Sandmel
accords no preeminence to this Jesus, stating: "I cannot value him above the martyr
Socrates, but I cannot conceive of myself as unaware of him, or isolated from him."[417]
Nor could other Jews.

As to other Western Jews and their position vis-à-vis this icon of Western culture,
Sandmel writes "I see no valid reason for Jews to insulate themselves from the Jesus
of Western culture, any more than they should, or would, from Plato."[418] As to the fear
of undue influence, corruption, or conversion of the Jew vis-à-vis- these encounters
with this Jesus, Sandmel offers a candid assessment:

> Here and there some Jews will cross over to Christianity. . . . I venture to suppose that
> these crossings arise much more from Western freedom, and freedom to court and woo,
> than from theological concessions. To my mind there is a greater likelihood of the per-
> petuation of Jewish loyalties through the understanding by Jews of where they stand
> religiously in respect to Jesus than to their retaining this as a somewhat forbidden area,
> even though it enters into our ken and into our lives.[419]

He concludes his assessment on a confident note:

> Jews need not shy away from such cultural encounter. They will not, and they should
> not, compromise their convictions about the Christ Jesus of the Christian religion. They
> should know and understand the Jewish religion, certainly as a higher priority to their
> understanding Christianity. But Jews can be trusted to discern the difference between the
> Jesus of religion and the Jesus of Western culture.[420]

Sandmel's Jesus is unquestionably striking, exceedingly singular, a man with normal
frailties, who experienced defeat. His Jesus is a great and good man, but not extraordinarily so. Though Sandmel can apprehend the above characteristics of Jesus, from a
certain disinterested perspective, Jesus has no impact upon him in a religious way. In
the end, Sandmel presents us with a Jesus who is a *nazir*,[421] a person dedicated to God,
not unlike Samson or Hillel. From Sandmel's perspective, Jesus is a Jewish teacher, a
rabbi,[422] with messianic overtones, who, like those before and after him, met with a
martyr's end. Jesus is an unavoidable icon in Western culture, whom Jews may relate
to much as they would Bach or Plato or Michelangelo; he may be considered unique
within Jewish history, but not extraordinary.

Jesus the Son, Faithful, Law-Observant Jew

> What I have set out to do here is to illumine and interpret, at least in part, Jesus' person
> and opinions within the framework of his time and people. My ambition is simply to
> serve as the mouthpiece for Jesus' message today.
>
> David Flusser, *Jesus*, 16

David Flusser's narrative on Jesus—written from a predominantly Lukan bias—
wherein Jesus emerges as a moral exemplar for both ancient and modern worlds, begins
with a concise assessment of Jesus' ancestry. After Flusser ponders the difficulties
inherent in reconciling the genealogical lists recorded in the infancy narratives found
in Luke and Matthew, lists that link Jesus to the house of David and the messianic
expectation, he posits:

> It would have been quite natural that any expected Messiah be retrospectively legitimized
> by his followers as the Son of David. On the other hand, it has become clear that in Jesus'
> time there were indeed many real descendants from the family of the famous king David
> (as there are today many descendants of Charlemagne). . . . So, knowledge that one was
> from the family of David would not necessarily legitimize a person for messianic claims.
> It is important to reiterate, moreover, that even though there were those in the first century
> who could trace their lineage to David, we cannot be certain that Jesus himself belonged
> to David's line.[423]

Whether or not Jesus was of the house of David and whether or not he was born in
Bethlehem, Flusser cannot ascertain. He does concede that, from a Christian perspective, these two conditions actually do undergird the messianic claims attributed to Jesus
by the fledging Christian community. Flusser's study of Jesus is not contingent upon,
nor diminished by, ascertaining either. This aside, Flusser asserts broadly: "Historically, Jesus was a Galilean Jew who was probably born in Nazareth. Certainly that
was where he lived for about thirty years until the time of his baptism by John (Luke
3:23). He was baptized either in 27/28 A.D. or 28/29 A.D. It is more difficult to determine the duration of his public ministry, namely, the period between his baptism and
crucifixion."[424]

To resolve this question, he follows the Synoptic tradition, which chronicles one
year of public ministry before Jesus' crucifixion. Continuing his overview, Flusser
explains his choice:

> There is material evidence to suggest that on these chronological and geographical points
> the synoptists are to be trusted [rather than John]. Jesus may have ministered in Judea
> and in Jerusalem before his final journey to death, but his real sphere of operation was
> in Galilee on the northwest shore of Lake Gennesaret. It will also become evident that
> the events of Jesus' life are best understood on the presumption that the baptism and the
> crucifixion were separated by only a short space of time. There are scholars who suggest
> that Jesus died at Easter in the year 30 or 33. Most likely, Jesus was baptized in 28/29
> and died in the year 30.[425]

As to Jesus' family, Flusser, following the Gospel narrative, affirms that Jesus had
brothers and sisters. This does not preclude him from allowing for the possibility of a
virginal conception, though Flusser would not ascribe to it. He writes: "If one accepts
the virgin birth as historical and also concedes that the brethren of Jesus were his true
brothers and sisters, one must conclude that Jesus was Mary's first-born child. Even
those who regard the birth narratives of Matthew and Luke as unhistorical must admit
that Jesus may well have been the eldest of the family."[426]

Flusser speculates that Jesus' father died before he was baptized, most probably while Jesus was a child. No mention is made of the father during Jesus' public ministry. Luke last mentions Joseph visiting Jerusalem with Mary and Jesus, when Jesus was twelve. Flusser finds this pericope significant not because of its mention of Joseph, but because it gives us a first glimpse of Jesus' debate with Jewish teachers in the temple precinct. In this exchange between Jesus and the teachers, Flusser sees "a story of a precocious scholar, one might almost say of a young talmudist."[427]

Flusser believes that "Luke's story [of finding Jesus in the temple, Luke 2:41–51] may well be true."[428] This, coupled with other evidence, leads him to dismiss the suggestion that Jesus was uneducated or that he never studied. Juxtaposing Jesus' teaching with that of contemporaneous Jewish teaching, Flusser concludes that "he [Jesus] was perfectly at home both in Holy Scripture and in oral tradition, and he knew how to apply this scholarly heritage."[429]

Moreover, following Josephus in *Jewish Antiquities* (18.63–64), though distancing himself from the Christian interpolation therein, Flusser accepts that Jesus was a wise man. Expanding upon this, he allows that "evidently by these words Josephus identifies Jesus with the Jewish Sages."[430] Whether Jesus would have preferred to be seen as a Jewish rabbinic scholar is unimportant in Flusser's judgment. What was significant, from Flusser's perspective, was Josephus's reference to Jesus as a wise man. It challenges "the recent tendency to view Jesus as merely a simple peasant."[431]

Debunking a current trend suggesting that Jesus was a simple peasant, Flusser discerns a more realistic assessment. From Flusser's scrutiny of the sources and comparative texts, Jesus emerges as a precocious scholar: a young Talmudist, learned, clever, respected. Not simple, not uneducated, but a wise man, a Jewish sage. Moreover, "although he was not an approved scribe, some were accustomed to address him as 'Rabbi,' 'my teacher/master.'"[432] Lest there be confusion, Flusser stresses:

> Nevertheless, it should be noted that according to the oldest sources, as reflected by Luke, Jesus was addressed as "Rabbi" only by outsiders. Those numbered among the inner circle of his followers and those who came to him in need addressed him as "[the] Lord" (*ha-'adon* [*hā-'ādon*]). Apparently this is the title that he preferred. . . . This title should not be confused as a sign of his deity (i.e., *Adonai*), but an indication of his high self-awareness.[433]

Jesus, then, is *rabbi* to the outsider and *lord* to the inner circle, but also *carpenter*. Flusser, expanding upon this last assertion, explains a metaphorical sense familiar to the cognoscenti:

> Arrogance may have been prevalent among the scribes, but they were not effete academicians. They demanded that everyone teach his son a trade, and many of them were themselves artisans. Carpenters were regarded as particularly learned. If a difficult problem was under discussion, they would ask, "Is there a carpenter among us, or the son of a carpenter, who can solve the problem for us?" Jesus was a carpenter and/or the son of a carpenter. This in itself is no proof that either he or his father was learned, but it counts against the common, sweetly idyllic notion of Jesus as a naive and amiable, simple, manual workman.[434]

Our discussion of the education and academic skill of Jesus leads us full circle: from the family of the child Jesus in Nazareth to the family of the adult Jesus in Galilee. In both times and places, the family is rendered astonished at the presence and teaching of their brother and son, Jesus. It is this astonishment that provokes familial tension, to which Flusser turns in his attempt to better capture the person of Jesus.

Like Ben-Chorin, Flusser sees heightened familial tension between Mary his mother and his brothers and sisters (e.g., John 2:4; Luke 8:21; 11:27–28; Mark 3:34–35). He observes that "notwithstanding the evidence of the evangelists' editorial creativity, Jesus clearly understood that uncompromising religious commitment sometimes results in breaking family ties."[435] As to the probable cause of this tension, Flusser, again like Ben-Chorin, can only surmise. He ventures:

> An emotion-laden tension seems to have arisen between Jesus and his family in Nazareth, and it would appear to have been this psychological fact—the background to which we do not know—that contributed powerfully to his personal decision that was so decisive for mankind. The impetus for his departure from Nazareth probably lies in the fact that his family regarded the mission that led Jesus to his death as a dangerous illusion (John 7:5). Jesus correctly suspected that his own kith and kin would not favor his mission, and for this reason he did not return home after his baptism, but went to Capernaum. Later, when he returned to visit his native town, he proved that *no one is a prophet in his own country* (Matt. 13:57; Mark 6:4; Luke 4:24; John 4:44).[436]

The baptism proved a watershed for Jesus. John's baptism was unlike traditional Jewish baptismal baths since the latter "merely washed ritual uncleanliness from the body."[437] Flusser, comparing the Synoptic texts that describe both John and his ritual baptism with the writings of Josephus, observes parallels between the baptism that John preached and the Essene baptism. This was to be expected. Flusser believes, given the similarities between John and the Essenes, that John may have been an Essene. He posits that "he left later because he disapproved of the sectarian separatism of the Essenes and wanted to offer the opportunity of repentance and forgiveness of sins to the whole of Israel."[438]

The prerequisite for John's baptism was repentance, as it was for the Essene baptism. The water immersion followed, for "water can cleanse the body only if the soul has first been purified through righteousness."[439] Flusser observes that the "Essene baptism linked repentance with the forgiveness of sins, and the latter with the Holy Spirit."[440] So, too, it is in John's baptism. Both elements are crucial: the repentance of sins and the reception of the Holy Spirit in baptism.

John baptized Jesus in the waters of the Jordan. It was a defining moment in the life of Jesus inasmuch as he emerges from the waters graced with the Holy Spirit and possessing a heightened sense of identity. On moving from the water's edge, he is convinced both of his call and his unique sonship with the Father. Flusser views both of these aspects as keys to understanding the drama that was to unfold.

As Luke records the event, the freshly baptized Jesus, deep in prayer at the water's edge, receives the gift of the Holy Spirit. A voice, accompanying the descent of the Holy Spirit, proclaims Jesus a beloved son with whom the Father is well pleased (Luke 3:21–22). According to Flusser, these pneumatic-ecstatic experiences were not uncommon among the Jews who went out to John.[441] Yet Jesus' baptism held a significance that the others lacked. This significance is directly related to the acclamation of the heavenly voice.

Flusser does not doubt the historicity of the event. He believes that Jesus had a special pneumatic-ecstatic experience of the Holy Spirit, during which he heard a heavenly voice acclaiming his special favor. Flusser posits that this voice did not simply affirm Jesus' sonship, but rather, and importantly, the voice also conveyed to Jesus his special character in quoting to him Isaiah 42:1: "Here is my servant whom I uphold, my chosen with whom I am pleased, upon whom I have put my spirit; he shall bring forth justice to the nations."

Stating that this quotation from Isaiah is "probably the original, for the reason that the prophetic word fits the situation,"[442] Flusser muses:

> If we accept the traditional form of the heavenly message, Jesus is described as "My Son." If, however, the heavenly voice intoned the words of Isaiah, Jesus must have understood that he was being set apart as the Servant of God, the Chosen One. For him the gift of the Holy Spirit, which was part of John's baptism, held another special significance that was to become decisive for his future. None of the designations, Son, Servant or Chosen One were exclusively messianic titles—the last two could also denote the special status of the prophetic office. By these titles, Jesus learned that he was now chosen, called, set apart.[443]

Of the relationship between John and Jesus, postbaptism, and their respective missions, Flusser writes:

> At his baptism, Jesus was illuminated by the heavenly voice concerning the beginning of the messianic kingdom. John was the precursor, "the breaker," for the advent of that kingdom, but he himself did not belong to the kingdom. He was, so to speak, a member of the previous generation. This paradoxical insight on the part of Jesus highlights both the distinction between John and the messianic kingdom, as well as the historic link between Jesus and the Baptist. Nevertheless, Jesus' experience at his baptism invested him with a new and separate function. Jesus could not become a disciple of John. He would have to move on to the villages around the Sea of Galilee and proclaim the kingdom of heaven.[444]

Flusser, recalling Jesus' enigmatic verse (Luke 7:31–35; Matt 11:16–19) wherein he compares himself and John, finds in it the hallmark of their respective messages: "From this saying of Jesus we learn indirectly that the content of each man's preaching was closely linked with his character. The good news of love related to Jesus' Socratic nature; penitential preaching was related to John's somber inclination toward asceticism."[445]

A New Sensitivity

A necessary digression on our part follows. Flusser has previously argued that the Jewish people of Jesus' day had imbibed a new sensitivity—one representative of the diverse trends and movements of the intertestamental Jewish period—within Judaism that predated and accompanied Jesus' emergence into Jewish history. Flusser concisely captures this unfolding theocentric philanthropism:

> The rigid moral code of the old covenant was clearly inadequate for the new sensitivity of the Jews in the Greek and Roman period. Having recognized that people are not sharply divided into the categories of the righteous and sinners, one is compelled to admit the impossibility of loving those who are good and hating the wicked. Because of the difficulty of knowing how far God's love and mercy extended, many concluded that one ought to show love and mercy toward all, both righteous and wicked. In this they would be imitating God himself. Luke puts this saying into the mouth of Jesus: "Be merciful, even as your Father is merciful" (Luke 6:36).[446]

The new sensitivity emphasized love, the unconditional love of God—and not compensatory doctrine or awe—as the motivation for just moral action.[447] Positing this new sensitivity, the fruit of Pharisaic discrimination and differentiation between love of God and awe of God, as a precondition for Jesus' reception by the Jewish crowds, Flusser asserts:

> This superior rating of love over awe prevailed and took hold upon all Jewish groups. The date of the oppositional fraction was approximately contemporary with the first controversies within the school of Hillel more than a century after Antiginos. This novel discrimination and differentiation between love and awe, with preference for the former, finds its reflection in the early prayer texts, which contain a plea for divine assistance in serving him in awe, to which now "love" was specifically added and even put first.[448]

After providing this précis, Flusser confirms the presence of the new sensitivity, the precondition of Jesus' fruitful advent:

> In our investigation of the new religious sensitivity with the Judaism of the Second Commonwealth, the conflict between the oppositional fraction among the Pharisees, the love-Pharisees, and the veteran Pharisees who allegedly confined themselves to the compensatory idea, is of relevant importance. The new emphasis on love for love's own sake, irrespective of any compensation, would indicate a relaxation of the compensatory doctrine and perhaps render circumstantial evidence for a growing discontent and uneasiness over the black-and-white presentation of good and evil in the doctrines of the Old Testament. This was the new Jewish sensitivity concerning divine justice manifested in the world.[449]

He concludes by suggesting:

> In summing up this discussion, we arrive at the conclusion that the last era of the Second Commonwealth saw a complex dialectic about righteousness and justice, about the pitfalls of sin and the actual, real human aspect of religious conduct which excludes practically the perfectly good person and the completely abandoned sinner; failure and straying from the godly way of life can be corrected by returning to God and the straight path. Virtue and vice are relative terms in light of this humanism.[450]

This "new sensitivity" that Flusser describes is essentially one of the diverse phenomena of Jewish religiosity in the intertestamental period; it advanced the joint concept of divine and altruistic love beyond just moral action. This divine and altruistic love finds its zenith of expression in the dual commandment: the Great Commandment, to love God and one's neighbor as oneself (Deut 6:5; Lev 19:18; Mark 12:28–34; Luke 10:25–28). The idea of compensation is introverted in that "expected compensation now is not inductive to awe of God, but to love of fellow men."[451] Moreover, "in those circles where the new Jewish sensitivity was then especially well developed, love of one's neighbor was regarded as a precondition to reconciliation with God."[452]

Flusser observes "that there is no controversy between Jesus and the rabbis concerning the dual commandment of love, divine and altruistic."[453] After perusing the pertinent Jewish traditions, Flusser affirms: "In any event, the dialectic reflected in these and similar statements demonstrates the intricate struggle within Jewish circles that provides the matrix for discussions in the days of Jesus."[454] This matrix, imbued with a new sensitivity, a theocentric philanthropism, served as the seedbed and garden for Jesus' moral teaching. In the hands of this master vinedresser, the vineyard would yield distinctive fruit.

After demonstrating the *"praeparatio evangelica"*[455] that preceded Jesus, Flusser asserts that "the theocentric philanthropism [the fruit of the dialectic] of certain scribal circles, mainly the disciples of Hillel (Beth Hillel), served Jesus as one of the two pillars of his doctrine of love."[456] The second pillar reflects semi-Essenian influence.[457]

This second influence embodies a semi-Essenian pietistic approach to neighbor, which permits moral improvement even among the Sons of Darkness. This concept of "all-embracing love toward all, righteous and sinners,"[458] gravitates against the Essenian doctrine of double predestination and its subsequent theology of hatred. Flusser agrees that this emerging, semi-Essenian theology of undivided love is amenable to the parallel Pharisaic new sensitivity.

It would be erroneous, however, to suggest that Jesus was untouched by Essene influence, as Flusser cautions:

> Jesus, belongs, if it is permitted to say, to rabbinic Judaism, but he accepted also some Essene achievements, especially through John the Baptist, who was a dissident Essene. Jesus opposed Essene sectarian theology even more strongly than John, but he accepted from Essenism the positive evaluation of poverty as a religious value and the opinion that wealth is dangerous for the faith. He also did not like the intelligentsia. All these three points were common to Jesus, to the Essenes, and in some degree to the charismatic holy men, and there is a possibility, as we have already said, that the latter were indirectly influenced by the Essene movement.[459]

Flusser, speculating upon this perceived dual influence upon Jesus' moral teaching, nonetheless affirms the uniqueness of Jesus. He writes:

> But even if it seems probable that the moral doctrine of Jesus is influenced by the semi-Essene "pietism" and the "rabbinic" sensitivity, it is clear that Jesus' moral approach to God and man, even in points which are possibly influenced by others, is unique and incomparable. Let me mention one aspect of Jesus' sublime teaching. . . . According to the teaching of Jesus you have to love the sinners, while according to Judaism you have not to hate the wicked. It is important to note that the positive love even toward enemies

is Jesus' personal message. We do not find this doctrine in the New Testament outside the words of Jesus himself. But later in Christianity Jesus' doctrine of love became important and cannot be forgotten even by those who do not live according to it. The consequence of the doctrine is today that a Christian knows that you must not make a difference in treating your neighbor according to his moral qualities or his good or bad attitude toward you. In Judaism hatred is practically forbidden but love to the enemy is not prescribed.[460]

This, then, was the moral climate in which Jesus was steeped and of which he was both reformer and innovator. From this matrix emerges what Flusser describes as Jesus' Jewish *Weltanschauung*. It is this philosophy of life, "the germ of revolution in Jesus' preaching,"[461] that captivates Flusser. From his perspective, Jesus' worldview has the potential to beneficially change a post-Holocaust world—if we would but heed Jesus' voice.

Juxtaposing Jesus' philosophy of life, as conveyed primarily by the Synoptic Gospels, with other Jewish literature, Flusser divides his consideration into three foci: Jesus and the law of Moses; his extraordinary emphasis on love; and Jesus' ethics.

Jesus and the Law

In his book *Jesus*, Flusser begins with an obvious assertion—obvious, that is, to a Jew—that Jesus' peculiar problem with the law and its precepts was not unique, for "this arises for every believing Jew who takes his Judaism seriously."[462] Elsewhere, Flusser asserts: "Even though he [Jesus] gave his own personal bent on Jewish ideas, selected from among them, purged and reinterpreted them, I cannot find a single word of Jesus that could seriously exasperate a well-intentioned Jew."[463]

Flusser discerns a greater difficulty. He contends that the Gospel redactors eschew Jesus' relationship to Jewish law and its precepts. Flusser, perusing these Christian texts through a Jewish prism, observes:

> In the gospels, we see how Jesus' attitude to the law has sometimes become unrecognizable as the result of "clarification" by the evangelists and touching up by later revisers. Nevertheless, the synoptic gospels, if read through the eyes of their own time, still portray a picture of Jesus as a faithful, law-observant Jew. Few people seem to realize that in the synoptic gospels, Jesus is never shown in conflict with the current practice of the law—with the single exception of the plucking of heads of grains on the Sabbath.[464]

Exploring the Jewish practice of washing one's hands before a meal, Flusser makes both of his opening assertions clear: (1) Given the degree and extent to which this obligation, founded a generation before Jesus, varied, it is apparent that people grappled with the law and its interpreters. (2) Jesus, distinguishing himself as a faithful teacher, enlarges the debate on washing of hands to his advantage.[465] He affirms his position: "What Jesus said, thus, has nothing to do with a supposed abrogation of Judaic law, but is part of a criticism directed at the Pharisees. The general truth that strict observation of ritual purity can encourage moral laxity, was applicable even in Jesus' day."[466]

Moreover, this orthodox Jesus, the Pharisaic-like preacher, advances his perspective not only with debate but also with deeds. Flusser observes:

> Jesus knew how to capitalize on a suitable occasion for a pedagogic offensive against the bigots. He did this, for example, when he performed a miracle of healing on the Sabbath. To understand the situation properly, we must keep in mind that if there was even a slight suspicion of danger to life, any form of healing was permitted. Moreover, even when the illness was not dangerous, while mechanical means were not allowed, healing by word was always permitted on the Sabbath. According to the synoptic gospels, Jesus adhered to these restrictions in all of his healings.[467]

Jesus, Flusser concludes, had "no desire to oppose the law of Moses."[468] Rather, "he only wanted to expose the rigidity of the bigots, using this case as an example."[469]

Emphasizing his thesis that Jesus was a faithful, law-observant Jew, Flusser asserts:

> We assume that in reality Jesus' relation to the Jewish sages was not different from that of the pious charismatics. As to the understanding of the law, he surely followed the teaching of the sages (see Matt 23:2–3 and 5:17–20). It is true that when one reads the reports in the gospels uncritically, one can gain the impression that Jesus' behavior was often in conflict with the actual law, but the facts which are behind the reports contradict this impression. In reality, one cannot discover any factual transgression of religious practice as it was observed by his rabbinic contemporaries. This evidently shows that those later redactors of the gospel narratives who needed to create a gap between Jesus and the Jewish religious practices were not experts in Jewish law, and therefore, they were not able to handle the historical facts themselves. Jesus lived according to the law of Moses, both in its written and in its oral form, i.e., the teaching of the Jewish sages.[470]

Asserting Jesus' orthodoxy vis-à-vis his relationship with the law, Flusser continues: "The fact that Jesus was an 'orthodox' Jew does not mean that he did not have his personal opinion about the way Jewish legal practice should be performed. Variety of opinion and decisions in this field were (and are) the rule in Judaism, especially in Jesus' time, some decades before the main points of *halakhah*, the Jewish legal way, were fixed in Jamnia and became normative."[471]

Flusser, citing the Gospels reports as "precious sources of a situation of transition of the *halakhah* towards its more normative stage,"[472] describes Jesus' emphasis:

> The leading principle of Jesus' teaching about the law was evidently that a legal attitude which can cause evil or suffering cannot be in accord with God's will and is, therefore, not valid. "Is it lawful on the Sabbath to do good or to harm, to save life or to destroy it?" (Luke 6:9; see also Matt 15:3–6 and Mark 7:9–13). Jesus, then, emphasized the moral side of the law in preference to the purely formal side of legal observance. But the germ of revolution—if I may speak thus—in Jesus' preaching does not emerge from his attitude to the law, but from other premises altogether. In reality, one cannot speak about a real revolution of Jesus in the sphere of ethics; Jesus' "revolution of love" is but a further, consequent step in the evolution of Jewish humane approach to God and to human beings.[473]

Jesus' Message of Love

Focusing upon the new sensitivity in Judaism, of which Jesus is beneficiary and contributor, Flusser continues:

> We have already said that the highest ideal of the Pharisees was in Jesus' days the "Pharisee of love" (of God). The doctrine of God's love for Israel and the imperative necessity of Israel's love of God are rarely found in the first four books of the Bible, but they constitute the basic principle of the Deuteronomic teaching. We have already mentioned that the love of God became a device in the inner-Pharisaic controversy. The decisive biblical verse in this connection is Deut 6:5: "You shall love the LORD your God." It was easy for the Jewish revolution of love to combine this verse with Lev 19:18: "You shall love your neighbor as yourself," as both verses began with the words ("you shall love"). In this way, so to speak, a mountain with two summits emerged, the famous twofold command, an expression of the essence of the biblical message regarding God and neighbor. Jesus *repeated* this teaching (Matt 22:34–40; Mark 12:28–34; and Luke 10:25–28) *and added* that from these two rules "depend all the law and the prophets." Thus, Jesus accepted as his own this sublime homily.[474]

Thus, Flusser observes that "Jesus, with his commandment of unrestricted love, belonged to the left wing of rabbinism, and he surely rejected the Essene doctrine of dualistic hatred."[475] This assertion Flusser more fully demonstrates in his juxtaposition of Jesus and other contemporary Jewish wonder-workers, the Hasidim, with both the Essenes and the Pharisees. I shall consider the juxtaposition later in this segment.

Though Flusser situates Jesus within rabbinism, meaning Pharisaic Judaism, his effort is not without nuance. Flusser posits: "It would not be wrong to describe Jesus as a Pharisee in the *broad* sense. Yet, even if his criticism of the Pharisees was not as hostile as that of the Essenes, nor as contradictory as that of the contemporaneous writings that we have cited, (i.e., *The Assumption of Moses*, chap. 7), he did view the Pharisees as outsiders, and did not identify himself with them."[476]

Nonetheless, tension did exist between Jesus and some of the Pharisees.[477] I shall examine this tension more appropriately in the juxtaposition to follow. Nevertheless, we may speak of it briefly.

Jesus' Ethics

Given Jesus' affiliation with the charismatic wonder-workers, the revolutionary element of his preaching as in his love ethic, and his Galilean origins, tension with institutional Judaism was inevitable. This tension was not peculiar to Jesus or a negation of him as a faithful Jew. Flusser, concurring with this inevitability, ventures: "It will become evident also that the authentic teaching of Jesus questioned the very foundations of the social structure. Nonetheless, we should bear in mind that this tension never implied negation, nor were the views of Jesus and the Pharisees contrary or did they ever degenerate into enmity."[478]

As previously explained, Flusser presents Jesus as heir, beneficiary, and innovator of the new sensitivity, the moral revolution in intertestamental Judaism that served as a precondition for his preaching. This revolution embodied "the radical interpretation of the commandment of mutual love, the call for a new morality, and the idea of the kingdom of heaven."[479] In Jesus, this new sensitivity is radicalized further. The dual commandment becomes the sublime paradigm. God's love is expansive, inclusive, indiscriminate, and unconditional; so too should be one's love of neighbor. This mutual love is the hallmark of the kingdom of heaven present and unfolding in and through the person of Jesus.

Jesus and the Kingdom of God

A new age was unfolding. Flusser explains:

> For Jesus and the rabbis, the kingdom of God is both present and future, but their perspectives are different. When Jesus was asked when the kingdom was to come, he said, "The kingdom of God is not coming with signs to be observed; nor will they say, 'Lo, it is here!' or 'There!' For behold, the kingdom of God is in the midst of you" (Luke 17:20–21). . . . There are, therefore, according to Jesus, individuals who are already in the kingdom of heaven. This is not exactly the same sense in which the rabbis understood the kingdom. For them the kingdom had been always an unchanging reality, but for Jesus there was a specific point in time when the kingdom began breaking out upon the earth.[480]

Of Jesus' unique perspective and proclamation, Flusser exclaims:

> This, then is the "realized eschatology" of Jesus. He is the only Jew of ancient times known to us who preached not only that people were on the threshold of the end of time, but that the new age of salvation had already begun. This new age had begun with John the Baptist who made the great break-through, but was not himself a member of the kingdom. The eruption of the kingdom of God also meant its expansion among the people.[481]

He continues: "Thus, for Jesus, the kingdom of heaven is not only the eschatological rule of God that has dawned already, but a divinely willed movement that spreads among people throughout the earth. The kingdom of heaven is not simply a matter of God's kingship, but also the domain of his rule, an expanding realm embracing ever more and more people, a realm where there are both great and small."[482]

Flusser, having probed the significance of Jesus' kingdom image, concludes:

> That which Jesus recognized and desired is fulfilled in the message of the kingdom. There God's unconditional love for all becomes visible, and the barriers between sinner and righteous are shattered. Human dignity becomes null and void, the last become the first, and the first become the last. The poor, the hungry, the meek, the mourners, and the persecuted inherit the kingdom of heaven.[483]

The hallmark of Jesus' revolution of love is "the transvaluation of all the usual moral values,"[484] as Flusser perceives it:

Jesus' concept of the righteousness of God, therefore, is incommensurable with reason. Man cannot measure it, but he can grasp it. It leads to the preaching of the kingdom in which the last will be first, and the first last. It leads also from the Sermon on the Mount to Golgotha, where the just man dies a criminal's death. It is at once profoundly moral, and yet beyond good and evil. In this paradoxical scheme, all the "important," customary virtues, and the well-knit personality, worldly dignity, and the proud insistence upon the formal fulfillment of the law, are fragmentary and empty. Socrates questioned the intellectual side of man. Jesus questioned the moral. Both were executed. Can this be mere chance?[485]

What enlightens such vision, fires such enthusiasm, encourages such risk? Conviction. Divine election. A heightened self-awareness as favored son. An innovative prowess as teacher, revolutionary, but not in the expected sense. One, bedewed with John's baptism, imbued with the Holy Spirit, and convinced of his unique sonship and mission.

Jesus, Sonship, and Mission

Flusser, contradicting a liberal trend that downplays Jesus' high self-awareness and his self-esteem, is convinced that Jesus possessed a high self-awareness similar to and yet distinctive from that of Hillel, for example.[486] Flusser focuses upon this sense of identity, exploring its possibilities, and extrapolating its significance. This high self-awareness bespeaks an understanding or an appreciation of oneself and one's unique role in the "meta-historical economy of the universe."[487]

Advancing this perspective, Flusser affirms, in contradistinction to opposite views, that both Hillel and Jesus demonstrate this confidence, though in Hillel's case this confidence becomes paradigmatic for others. Flusser observes:

> As we have seen, Hillel's paradigmatic sayings are either put in the second person so as to demand from others to act, or in the first person. In the latter sayings his own person is exemplary for all other people. In this way he shares the characteristic mistake of great men who are at the same time humble, in thinking that any human being is able to perform what he as a gifted genius can. The strong existential meaning of all these sayings is rooted not only in Hillel's strong and goodly personality but also in the special contemporaneous situation of religious crisis. History had put the right man in the right time. And thus he could successfully fulfil his own demand: "In a place where there are no men, there be a man!"[488]

After citing evidence that supports a description of the exalted self-awareness of Hillel—who predates Jesus but of whom Jesus is aware—Flusser ventures:

> It may be assumed that Hillel's high consciousness about himself had some influence on Jesus' personal experience. But there is a great difference between the two. Hillel's high self-awareness is not limited to his person, but is paradigmatic for everyone. Jesus' consciousness of his exalted value—though, as in Hillel's case, connected with personal meekness, and though he was opposed to any "cult of personality"—was connected with the knowledge that his person was not interchangeable with any other man. As Son, he

considered himself to have a central task in the divine economy: "He who is not with me is against me, and who does not gather with me, scatters" [Luke 11:23].[489]

Of Jesus' task, Flusser writes:

> A movement had begun in Israel, the realization of the kingdom of heaven on earth (Matt. 6:10). The movement necessarily centered around the person of Jesus; separate initiatives, independent of Jesus, would not gather, but scatter. One can recognize again how important the concept of the kingdom of heaven was for Jesus. His main task was to be the center of the movement which realized the kingdom of God among mankind—with the aid of co-laborers.[490]

Significantly, Flusser concludes his juxtaposition of Hillel and Jesus by asserting somewhat enigmatically:

> The fact that some of Hillel's saying in which he expresses sublime views about himself were followed by biblical quotations in which God himself speaks caused the erroneous understanding, as early as in ancient rabbinic sources, that the "I" of Hillel in these sayings was the divine "I." In this connection it is interesting to note that already in the New Testament some biblical verses about God were quoted as referring to Jesus of Nazareth (e.g., Phil. 2:10; cf. Isa. 45:23). An exalted self-awareness thus caused in both cases a somewhat similar development, though Hillel, who wanted to express the sublime dignity of man, was never deified.[491]

Before we delve further into Jesus' identity as advocated by Flusser, and the ramifications of such a self-awareness, we must ascertain first where, within the spectrum of Second Temple Judaism, Flusser locates Jesus.

Jesus and Charismatic Judaism

Flusser argues that, to some degree, given the dualistic aspect of angelology and demonology prevalent in Second Temple Judaism, Jesus is influenced by Jewish apocalypticism. The degree to which he may be influenced is difficult to ascertain. However, that Jesus experienced the existence of the wicked forces in the world is not to be denied.[492] Flusser himself is convinced that "the description of Jesus' temptation by the devil is based upon a real encounter."[493] Thus, "Jesus believed that his fight with the realm of evil forces was part of his mission,"[494] Flusser affirms and then ventures: "On one hand, he fought with success against the demons as an exorcist and charismatic healer. On the other hand, his success in this field was, according to his view, simply a part of the realization of the kingdom of Heaven, a process in which he thought he had been appointed to play the central role."[495]

Flusser' Jesus is cast both as a charismatic holy man and eschatological prophet. Flusser explains:

> One aspect of the person of Jesus is that, from the point of view of social typology, he belonged—not least because of his miracles and supernatural healings—to the category of Jewish charismatic wonder-workers. One of the activities of such persons was, as in the case of Jesus, to use their charismatic powers in order to heal. As the charismatic

wonder-workers were rightly considered highly pious men, their powers were able to overwhelm the sins of others.[496]

In Jesus' actions, these supernatural deeds of healing, Flusser sees greater purpose. He affirms:

> There is no doubt that Jesus the wonder-worker was a great helper of the afflicted. Nevertheless, these supernatural deeds which Jesus performed in order to help the suffering were not done for their own sake. It is evident that the healing of the paralytic was a didactic act. His healing of the man with a withered hand was destined to exemplify Jesus' view about healing on the Sabbath. And all his mighty acts had the higher purpose of bringing the people to repentance. They were also understood by Jesus as eschatological acts: "If it is by the finger of God that I cast out demons, then the kingdom of God has come upon you" [Luke 11:20].[497]

Jesus' relationship to the charismatic wonder-workers, the ancient Hasidim, will be explored more fully and appropriately in this presentation when we consider Géza Vermès's significant contribution to the development of this perspective in his Jesus trilogy. Though Flusser is conversant with Vermès's scholarship, citing it in his own work, his interest in this Hasidic juxtaposition serves primarily to advance his perspective of Jesus as beloved Son.

Flusser introduces us to four Hasidic contemporaries of Jesus and offers a précis on each: Honi the Circle-Drawer (65 BCE) and Hanan the Hidden, his grandson; Abba Hilkia, also a grandson of Honi; and Rabbi Hanina ben Dosa, who lived a generation after Jesus.[498] Flusser's comparison of Jesus to Jewish charismatic wonder-workers is not confined to supernatural deeds. Citing two other points of similarity, he continues: "Two other important similarities must be stressed: on the one hand, sociological ties between the behavior of these pious Jewish charismatics and between Jesus' divine sonship and, on the other hand, tension with the Pharisaic establishment."[499]

Sociologically, the five Hasidim share things broadly in common: divine election, a unique sonship with the Father, poverty, miraculous healing, a favored status as intercessor before God, a hidden life in a humility that avoids a cult of personality, and martyrdom. In their shared hiddenness, their self-deprecation vis-à-vis their status among the people, Flusser sees a vindication of his position regarding Jesus' high self-awareness: an awareness that undergirds Jesus' image of himself as son.

However, Jesus' sonship is significantly unlike the other Hasidim, as Flusser explains:

> Jesus' relationship with the Jewish holy wonder-workers also has something to do with his divine sonship. We have seen how the connection to God of three of the Jewish wonder-workers belonging to the period of the Second Temple was described as that of a son to his father. The earliest, Honi, prayed to God as a member of his household, and was likened to a son who was accustomed to ingratiate himself with his father. Hanina stood before God as his personal servant, and was addressed by a heavenly voice as "my son." Hanan the Hidden took up the children's word "Father" and in prayer described God as "the Father who can give rain." Could it have been otherwise than that such men who were like sons to God should have addressed God as "Father"? That Jesus also spoke

in the way is certain, but one should not forget that Jesus' tie to God as his Father, even if it fits his task as a charismatic wonder-worker, is only a point of departure for a deeper and broader concept of his divine sonship. . . . Here it must suffice to remember that Jesus spoke about "your Father" on one hand and "my Father" on the other hand, but never about "our Father," with one characteristic exception, namely the Lord's Prayer (Matt 6: 9–13; Luke 11: 2–4). This exception proves the rule, because the Lord's Prayer is not his own prayer, but the prayer recommended by him to his hearers. Thus the different use of the term "Father" for God shows that, in the eyes of Jesus, his sonship was of a different kind than that of others.[500]

Following a digression wherein Flusser juxtaposes the Matthean version of the Lord's Prayer with that of an older version of the Kaddish, Flusser asserts: "I have shown the Jewishness of the Lord's Prayer because I wanted to claim that in Jesus' mind there was a difference between God as the common Father and his own specific sonship. In this he is not identical with the other Jewish charismatic wonder-workers who were believed to have a direct contact with God as sons to their heavenly Father."[501]

Flusser, contending that "charismatic pious men believed their ties to God were stronger than those of other men,"[502] asserts that in Jesus this awareness was more firmly felt.

Yet while stressing the importance of the similarities between these wonder-workers and Jesus, Flusser still affirms:

All these points of contact between them are also in a certain manner common to Jesus: he healed in a supernatural way, and used to hide himself and sometimes to conceal his healings; he knew that he was near to God as a son to his father and liked little children, evidently because they were simpleminded. It is important to notice that both Abba Hilkia and Rabbi Hanina ben Dosa were very poor; . . . Moreover, Jesus suspected wealth and praised poverty: "Foxes have holes and birds of the air have nests, but the son of man (i.e., Jesus himself) has nowhere to lay his head" (Matt 8:20; Luke 9:58). Finally, what is especially meaningful for understanding Jesus is that there existed a tension between most of these wonder-workers and the Pharisaic establishment. This tension was ambivalent, because at the same time these pious charismatics formed a part of rabbinic Judaism.[503]

The term "charismatic" describes one who possesses a divinely conferred power or talent, a charisma. It is a form of authority distinct from those of tradition or law.[504] Flusser observes that "this type of piety—not only among the Jews—tends to develop a tension against institutionalism of the religious establishment."[505] Paupers possessing divinely conferred power, men who held the intelligentsia in disdain, valued deeds rather than worldly wisdom. Flusser writes:

Now one can understand that these Jewish charismatics who performed wondrous deeds were called "the pious one [Hasidim] and men of *deed*." Their deeds, and not worldly, intellectual wisdom, were for them decisive. These deeds comprised not only acts of fulfilling God's commandments, but also voluntary good works, and all this led them to the supernatural gift of theurgy, the gift of performing supernatural deeds.[506]

Of this tension between the Hasidim and some of the Pharisees, Flusser observes that "the element of pauperism, the appreciation of simplemindedness, and the opposition to intellectual pride are common both to Jewish charismatic wonder-workers and the Essenes."[507] Even though Flusser deems Essenian influence upon Jesus, in this regard, "quite palatable,"[508] he disallows, however, a strong affiliation. In the above-cited essay he recognizes decisive differences between the charismatic wonder-workers and the rigorous Essene sect from Qumran, and Flusser situates these charismatic men of deeds within Pharisaic, rabbinic Judaism:

> It is probable that the Jewish charismatic wonder-workers formed a distinct group within the Judaism of their time, and even possessed not only common ethics and common religious concepts but also their own halakhic rules. Yet, in contrast to the Essenes, they apparently did not want to become a separate sect with their own rule. They would have certainly opposed the Essene dualistic theology of double predestination. They belonged to Pharisaic, rabbinic Judaism, and even if there existed a certain tension between them and the Pharisaic establishment, their attitude towards the members of that establishment was ambivalent and there existed cordial contacts between them and important Pharisaic sages, from the time of Honi the Circle-Drawer and Simeon ben Shatah on.[509]

Affirming Jesus' fidelity "to the Torah in its entirety,"[510] Flusser proposes Jesus as a bridge within divergent Jewish currents. He observes: "In his attitude to people, . . . he was closer to the School of Hillel, and the love of man was central to his teaching. His acceptance of the more astringent rulings of the School of Shammai had its origins in his fear of sin and his desire that man should live in an atmosphere of perfect holiness. Thus Jesus formed a bridge between the two positions of the School of Hillel and the School of Shammai."[511]

Flusser, stressing that "all this fits Jesus as well,"[512] suggests that "the character of Jesus' piety and his association with the charismatic holy men explains, at least partially, Jesus' critique of the Pharisees."[513] Interpreting Jesus' polemics against the Pharisees through this charismatic paradigm, Flusser speculates:

> We see again that, on the one hand, Jesus accepts rabbinic Judaism as his own but, on the other hand, he shows a tension with it. We have already recognized ambivalent ties between similar Jewish holy wonder-workers and the rabbinic establishment. It is true that our knowledge about these holy men is far smaller than what we have about Jesus. It is especially a pity that we are in complete ignorance of their sayings about rabbinic authorities, but it is certain that they lived among the Jewish sages, that their religiosity was a part of rabbinic thought, and that their religious practice was rabbinic. But one cannot know if, e.g., Honi the Circle-Drawer would answer affirmatively and without hesitation the question of whether he was a Pharisee. And how great would be the difference in the answer between Jesus and the other charismatics?[514]

Elsewhere, though, he ventures an answer. In *Jesus*, Flusser suggests:

> Those who listened to Jesus' preaching of love might well have been moved by it. Many in those days thought in a similar way. Nonetheless, in the clear purity of his love they must have detected something very special. Jesus did not accept all that was thought and taught in the Judaism of his time. Although not really a Pharisee himself, he was closest to the Pharisees of the school of Hillel who preached love, and he led the way further to unconditional love—even of one's enemies and of sinners.[515]

In the above-cited essay, Flusser argues, as he did previously in his book *Jesus*, that Jesus' high self-awareness is demonstrated in the distinctive manner in which he addresses God the Father as compared to the manner in which he instructs his disciples to pray to the Father. Moreover, Flusser stresses that Jesus was aware of a relationship with the Father that was distinctive and different from that of other charismatic holy men. This, he argues, is evident in the Synoptics—but less so in John, though John 20:17 does seem to preserve this sense of high self-awareness.[516] Flusser emphasizes this in reaction to the liberal trend in twentieth-century theology that denied or restricted such high self-awareness. He also defends his assertion because it is key to his depiction of Jesus as Son.

Flusser believes that Jesus understood himself to be the son, the chosen servant, of the Father. Advancing this perspective, he argues: "According to the Gospels, Jesus was addressed by the heavenly voice as 'Son' as early as his baptism. The assumption is justified, however, that at the time he was simply being addressed as the chosen servant. Not until the voice at the Transfiguration was he truly named 'Son.'"[517] The transfiguration experience is pivotal.

Jesus, Messianic Prophet

Flusser, with an ear attentive to the Lukan version of the transfiguration with its mention of Jesus' imminent death, contends that "Jesus linked his sense of sonship, his predestination as prophetic preacher, and his knowledge of his tragic end, in the parable of the tenants of the vineyard (cf. Luke 20:9–19)."[518] Flusser is aware of a similar Jewish parable of a proprietor and his wicked, thieving tenants, but in that version the son sent by the proprietor does not die.[519] In Jesus' prophetic rendition, the son dies at the hands of the wicked tenants, whom Flusser identifies as the Sadducees. Having heard the parable with its new ending and understanding correctly Jesus' harsh critique, the Sadducees were incensed. The consequences proved tragic for Jesus.

Flusser stresses that "here we are at the epicenter of Jesus' clash with Sadducees, the Temple aristocracy—the clash that was to lead to his death."[520] Assessing Jesus' sense of sonship in this light, he writes: "Jesus' sonship therefore leads, not to life, but to the death that other prophets before him had suffered. After the Transfiguration (Luke 9:28–36), his awareness of the sonship of God was linked with the premonition that he had to die."[521]

Yet Flusser does not equate Jesus' knowledge of divine sonship with that of his consciousness as Messiah.[522] Nor does he allow that Jesus saw himself as the suffering, atoning servant of God, given his careful philological analysis of relevant texts.[523] Rather, Flusser concludes: "Jesus had neither subtly nor mythically worked out the idea of his own death from the ancient writings, let alone did he carry it out. He was no 'Christ of the festival,' of a medieval sacred drama, for he wrestled with death to the very end."[524]

As to the question of whether or not Jesus saw himself as a prophet, Flusser answers in the affirmative:

> Indeed, Jesus saw himself as a prophet. His remark, "for it cannot be that a prophet should perish away from Jerusalem" (Luke 13:33), confirms this. His words reflect the notion that Jerusalem "kills the prophets and stones those who are sent to it" (Luke 13:34 and Matt. 23:37). Furthermore, Jesus speaks in the parable of the wicked husbandmen (Luke 20:9–19) about himself as a prophet—and at the same time as the Son of God—who would be killed, just like the prophets before him.[525]

While doubting that Jesus identified himself as the eschatological prophet,[526] Flusser is aware that others did recognize him as such, and more, as Flusser adds: "We have heard that many recognized him only as the eschatological prophet, but there were obviously others who thought that he was (or aspired to be) the Messiah. This we learn indirectly from the inscription on the cross ('the King of the Jews')."[527]

Exploring the question of Jesus' messiahship, Flusser examines Jesus' use of the phrase "Son of Man" in reference to himself. The Aramaic phrase *bar-'anosh* (*bar-'ĕnoš*), son of man, and its meaning have been presented in chapter 1 (above). Flusser and Ben-Chorin agree on the standard threefold understanding of the use of the phrase *bar-'anosh*: an eschatological figure; a circumlocution to refer to Jesus himself; or simply a term for "man." However, Flusser, unlike Ben-Chorin, senses that the eschatological designation of *bar-'anosh*, the Danielic Son of Man (Dan 7:9–14), may have been used enigmatically by Jesus. Admitting to the difficulty in ascertaining such, Flusser speculates: "If I am right, then the threefold meaning of the designation of 'son of man' in the mouth of Jesus betrays his manner of sometimes creating a kind of fourth dimension behind his utterances. He is in solidarity with other human beings and is subject to the same humanity, but he personally has to suffer a cruel death, and he will also be revealed as an eschatological figure."[528]

Flusser argues that Jesus, who he believes taught in Hebrew, would use the Hebrew phrase *ben-'ādām* (cf. Ezek 2:1) when referring to the "son of man."[529] In any case, Flusser advances his analysis, exploring the relevance of this concept to Jesus' doctrine of the Savior.

Describing the Danielic Son of Man as "the manlike eschatological judge,"[530] who is frequently identified with the Messiah or Enoch, Flusser adds:

> According to the *Testament of Abraham,* the Son of Man is literally the son of Adam—*ben Adam*—Abel, who was killed by the wicked Cain. God appointed Abel to be the eschatological judge, because he desired that every man would be judged by his peer. At the second judgment the twelve tribes of Israel will judge the whole of creation. Not until the third judgment will God Himself judge. This apocalyptic tradition explains why Jesus said to the twelve, "You, who have persevered with me in my tribulations, when the Son of Man sits upon his glorious throne will also sit upon thrones, judging the twelve tribes of Israel" (cf. Matt. 19:28; Luke 22:28–30).[531]

Continuing this perspective in an essay, Flusser contends that—given a comparison of Sirach 44:16 (mention of Enoch as example), the book of *Jubilees* 4:9–12; 10:17 (mention of Enoch as sign), and Luke 11:29–32 (the sign of Jonah pericope)—Jesus juxtaposes Jonah and the Son of Man concomitantly with the Ninevites and Jesus' generation (Luke 11:29–32). Thus, he "spoke in a way that, though all his hearers understood generally what he wanted to say, only a few of them could catch the hidden and profound allusion embedded in his words."[532] Flusser discerns, especially through the hermeneutic of *Jubilees*, that this hidden allusion to Enoch was in fact an allusion to himself, Jesus, as the eschatological Son of Man.

Moreover, Flusser argues, given the results of his investigation, "that Jesus' saying in Luke 11:29–32 is his profound *ipsissima verba*, because it is practically impossible to imagine that such a profound saying with hidden hints to Enochic motifs could have been invented later by others."[533] He, therefore, concludes: "And if the gospel preserved this original saying of Jesus, it has a further, far-reaching consequence for the self-awareness of Jesus. One cannot escape the conclusion that in our saying Jesus identified himself with the eschatological Son of Man, the supreme judge who will witness against his wicked generation."[534]

Again, in *Jesus*, Flusser, juxtaposes an Essene fragment, wherein "Melchizedek, the Old Testament priest-king of Jerusalem in the time of Abraham, figures as the eschatological heavenly priest at the end of times,"[535] with Psalm 110, which speaks of Melchizedek as the executor of the last judgment: "The LORD says to my lord, 'Sit at My right hand. . . .You are a priest forever after the order of Melchizedek." Flusser asserts that Jesus understood this distinction, to sit at the right hand of God, to be reserved for "one who is the same kind of person as Melchizedek."[536]

Jesus: Son of Man, *ben Adam* like Abel, the manlike eschatological judge. Jesus: an Enochic sign of Jonah. Jesus: priest-king, one like Melchizedek, but not Melchizedek. Jesus: Messiah? Flusser asserts that during his Passion, when questioned by the high priest as to whether or not he was the Messiah, Jesus answers by alluding to the words of Psalm 110: "If I tell you, you will not believe me, and if I question you, you would not answer. This much only will I say: 'From now on, the Son of Man will have his seat at the right hand of the Power of God'" (Luke 22:67–69). Flusser contends that "those present correctly understood this as Jesus' indirect admission of his messianic dignity."[537] Yet, he is reluctant to assert that Jesus himself intended this meaning.

Puzzling over this, Flusser admits:

> It is quite certain that in his own lifetime Jesus became accepted by many—not just by Peter—as the Messiah. Had it not been so, Pilate would not have written above the cross of Jesus, "King of the Jews." On the other hand, one cannot rule out the possibility that Jesus sometimes referred to the coming Son of Man in the third person simply because he wanted to preserve his incognito. At first he was possibly awaiting another. In the end, however, the conviction prevailed that he himself was the coming Son of Man. Otherwise Jesus' answer to the high priest makes no sense.[538]

Flusser, questioning whether or not, given the sublime status of the Redeemer-judge, Jesus of Nazareth understood himself thus, muses: "Let us not forget that he felt he was God's chosen one, His servant, the only Son to whom the secrets of the heavenly Father were open. This very sense of sublime dignity could have led him finally to dare that he would be revealed as the Son of Man; and in Judaism the Son of Man was frequently understood as the Messiah."[539]

To his musing, we may add his observation, which is suggestive if not certain: a "hint" discerned by Flusser from Jesus' messianic timetable. He writes:

> It was (and is) a common Jewish opinion that the kingship of God is both present and future, and that it has existed from the creation of the world, or at least from Abraham's time. This was not the position of Jesus. According to him the concept of the kingdom of heaven was not static but dynamic. It was a movement which began with John the Baptist. There are a number of reasons why Jesus differs on this point. One is that Jesus understood the kingdom of heaven as not only God's kingship but as we have noted, a kind of intermediary epoch between the historical period and the end of history. In his messianic timetable it occupied the same place that is represented in other Jewish tri-partite systems as "the Days of the Messiah." The fact that Jesus spoke about the period of the kingdom of heaven, instead of the Days of the Messiah, hints at his own messianic self-awareness.[540]

Flusser acclaims Jesus' identification of the messianic age with the rabbinic kingdom of heaven as "the most important innovation of Jesus."[541] Moreover, Flusser sees in this innovation proof of Jesus' messianic self-awareness given that he, Jesus, would occupy the central task. He writes:

> The identification by Jesus of the Messianic age and the kingdom of heaven in which Jesus would have the central task is, by the way, an additional proof that Jesus was sure that he was the Messiah. In his answer to John the Baptist he claimed (Matt. 11:4–6; Luke 7:22–23) that his own blessed activities show that the time of salvation is here. There were at that time many who believed that John was Elijah. Jesus described John as the man who opened the way for the realization of the kingdom (Matt. 11:12–15). He finished his words saying that "if you want to accept it, he [John] is Elijah who is to come." According to popular belief, Elijah will announce the coming of the Messiah. "He who has ears to hear, let him hear!"[542]

Clearly, Flusser believes that Jesus believed that he was the Messiah and that he would be revealed eventually as the divine Son of Man.[543] Convinced of his own assessment, Flusser concludes:

> Our study indicates that for Jesus the messianic period no longer lay as a hope in the future. It had already begun with John the Baptist, and Jesus was now the Messiah. It is also possible to understand how Jesus modified the structure of the concept of the king-dom of heaven. In the understanding of Jesus, the kingdom of heaven became more dynamic than in rabbinic thinking. Since according to Jesus the kingdom was identical with the messianic period, it was no longer, as in rabbinic thought, an eternal suprahis-torical entity. It became a dynamic force which broke through into the world at an identifiable point in history. The kingdom of heaven began to break through with John, and Jesus—the Messiah—was in the center of the movement. "He who is not *with me* is against me, and he who does not gather *with me* scatters" (Matt.12:30).[544]

Yet Flusser does not believe the Jesus connected the tragedy of the cross with Messi-ahship. Rather, Flusser suggests: "The New Testament links Jesus' death with his Messiahship, but it seems that Jesus himself connected his tragedy on the cross with his divine sonship. Moreover, both ideas of his sonship and his death were in his mind connected with his prophetic task."[545]

Of these links, Flusser speculates:

> These links were evidently expressed by the heavenly voice at the Transfiguration. "This is my only (or beloved) son, listen to him!" (Matt. 17:5; Mark 9:7; Luke 9:35 with variants). The first part alludes to the sacrifice of Isaac, the only beloved son of Abraham (Gen. 22:2), and in the second half the heavenly voice hints at the eschatological prophet (Deut. 18:15). Also, in the parable of the wicked husbandmen (Luke 20:9–19 and par.), Jesus speaks about the prophet, the son of the proprietor (i.e., God) who will be killed.[546]

Flusser concludes: "I believe that this connection between Jesus' prophetic task, his sonship, and the final tragedy originated in Jesus' own intuition. He who had commanded us not to resist evildoers, went to his death without a fight. At the end, did he realize that his execution was the crown of his transvaluation of all the usual values? By it the highest was indeed made the lowest and the lowest, highest."[547]

Throughout his study of Jesus of Nazareth, a presentation not confined to his book *Jesus*, Flusser has enlisted a comparative study of contemporary Jewish literature, notably, the Synoptic texts, Jewish Pseudepigrapha, rabbinic literature, and various Dead Sea Scroll texts, such as Essenian texts. His methodology is not without controversy or criticism. Nevertheless, with confident ease and facile argumentation, Flusser navigates deftly around or through exegetical hazards deemed insurmountable to others, such as Sandmel. Where Sandmel hesitates, Flusser ventures. He has no qualms in accepting certain Gospel events as historical and select literature as contemporary, pertinent, and therefore comparative. All of this leads Flusser in his Jesus study to affirm what others evaluate as ambiguous or tentative: Jesus' messianic self-awareness and his unique and yet Jewish *Weltanschauung*.

Jesus the Galilean Jew, Charismatic Healer, Teacher, Eschatological Enthusiast

> During his short charismatic ministry in Galilee, although he encountered some jealousy and hostility among small-minded local scribes and synagogue elders, he was on the whole a highly popular and much-sought-after healer, exorcist, and teacher. For the local people of the region of Lake Gennesaret, Jesus was a man of God, and even in Jerusalem he was hailed as "the prophet from Nazareth in Galilee" (Matt. 21:11).
>
> Géza Vermès, *The Authentic Gospel of Jesus*, 404

If Pinchas Lapide is *ein Wegbereiter*, a pioneer or forerunner, of the Jewish ecumenists strategizing to reconcile Jew and Christian in the aftermath of the Shoah, then Géza Vermès may be viewed as *ein Wegbereiter* of those deemed third questers, scholars who study Jesus historically through the prism of his Jewish milieu: first-century Palestine, as refracted by recent archaeological discoveries, such as the Nag Hammadi codex cache, the Qumran Scrolls, and subsequent philological investigation.[548] Though this may be one of a limited number of points of convergence between these two Jewish authors, Lapide and Vermès, the characterization is nonetheless accurate.

Vermès, uniquely equipped as historian and distinguished Dead Sea Scroll scholar—though not a New Testament scholar per se—navigates a distinctive course. What began as a distraction from his Qumran studies evolved into a major study and the impetus for a renewed effort to retrieve the historical Jesus from the christological overlay.

Though Vermès's Jesus, the Galilean Hasid, has remained a constant type throughout a thirty-year period of research and writing, the matrix in which he dwelled and from which this Hasid emerged continues to be enhanced by further archaeological finds and exegetical inquiry. This emerging first-century matrix is integral to grasping Vermès's Jesus. Given this, the reader should not be surprised that the following reconstruction moves discriminately among Vermès's varied texts so as to present more clearly Jesus as he emerges from Vermès's perspective.

We begin with *Jesus the Jew.* Vermès succinctly recaps his efforts:

> The purpose of *Jesus the Jew* was to rebuild the picture of the historical Jesus, a task considered to be beyond the scholar's means during the preceding half century because, according to the then-current views, hardly anything could be known "concerning the life and personality of Jesus, since the early Christian sources show no interest in either." To achieve this aim, I endeavored to explore the figure of Jesus as preserved in the Synoptic Gospels, in the framework of the political and social history of first-century BC–first-century AD Galilee, and especially in that of contemporaneous popular, charismatic Judaism of prophetic derivation. The hero of this type of Palestinian religion was not the king, the rabbi or the priest, but the man of God, believed to be capable of working miracles and mastering forces of evil and darkness, namely the devil and sickness. In the first century BC, Honi the Rainmaker was such a holy man, and so also was Jesus' younger Galilean contemporary, Hanina ben Dosa, renowned for curing the sick, even from a distance, and helping the needy. His many wondrous interventions earned him the title of protector, saviour and benefactor of humankind. The Galilean Jesus of the Synoptic Gospels is perfectly at home in such a company.
>
> Having thus sketched the background and setting of Jesus' existence, I needed a checking mechanism, which I found in a historical and linguistic analysis of the titles borne by Jesus in the Gospels. Of these, three—"prophet," "lord" and "son of God"— when examined in their Semitic (Aramaic/Hebrew) context are found in biblical and post-biblical Jewish literature applied to charismatic holy men. Hence, I concluded that the historical Jesus could best be situated "in the venerable company of the Devout, the ancient Hasidim" (*Jesus the Jew*, p. 223). I hastened to add, however, that compared to the portrait of minor charismatic figures preserved in post-biblical Jewish sources, Jesus stood out as incomparably superior.[549]

It remains for us to follow Vermès as he confirms what he above asserts.

Vermès, begins his exploration of the figure of Jesus, admitting to a limitation. The Jesus that he constructs is not an authentic portrait of Jesus, but rather a portrait gleaned from the Synoptic Gospels, which he considers to be nonhistorical.[550] Given this, Vermès hopes to discern more clearly how the evangelists, "echoing primitive tradition, wished him [Jesus] to be known."[551] Vermès, in *Jesus the Jew*, asks simply: "Who, in brief, was the Jesus of the evangelists?"[552]

The Synoptic Jesus

Following the Gospel of Mark, unlike Flusser, who yields primacy to Luke's Gospel, Vermès sketches a preliminary response to his question. In brief, Vermès affirms Jesus' name; his father's name, Joseph; his mother's name, Mary; and their domicile, Nazareth in Galilee. He observes that Jesus' place of birth, birth date, and marital status are not mentioned. Since his father, Joseph, was reportedly a carpenter, so too Jesus may have been. Vermès allows this and adds itinerant exorcist and preacher to his profession. As to a death certificate, based on Mark, Vermès affirms Jesus' place of death, Jerusalem; date of death, under Pontius Pilate, between 26 and 36 CE; cause of death, crucifixion by order of the Roman prefect; place of burial, Jerusalem.[553]

As to Jesus' family background and personal life, Vermès, widening his lens to encompass the Synoptic corpus, points out the following:

- Apart from the infancy stories of Matthew and Luke that "inject an element of doubt into the issue of paternity," Luke names the father as Joseph, whereas Matthew speaks of the carpenter.
- Unless belief in Mary's perpetual virginity dissuades one, then Jesus had four brothers, Jacob, Joseph, Judah, and Simon and several sisters.
- Though Matthew and Luke speak of Bethlehem as Jesus' place of birth, Mark does not mention his birthplace. Rather, his implied birthplace is Nazareth, "the unimportant little Galilean locality where he and his parents lived."
- Reportedly Jesus was approximately thirty years of age when John baptized him "in the fifteenth year of the reign of Tiberius, probably in AD 28/29."
- No wife is mentioned, though several women accompanied him and his group.
- Jesus is not depicted as a widower, "so one is to assume that he was unmarried, a custom unusual but not unheard of among Jews in his time."
- His secular profession, though uncertain, may have been a carpenter. Traditionally this is affirmed. Vermès, however, notes the metaphorical use of carpenter, craftsman, in ancient Jewish writing wherein "the Aramaic noun, carpenter or craftsman (*naggar*) stands for a 'scholar' or 'learned man.'" Thus, Jesus may not have been a carpenter per se.
- However he earned his living before his public ministry, "the Synoptics are unanimous in presenting him as an exorcist, healer and teacher."[554]

Vermès focuses his gaze upon this unanimous representation of Jesus as exorcist, healer and teacher.

Jesus, Exorcist and Healer

Though agreeing that even a cursory reading of the Synoptic text affirms Jesus as an exorcist and healer, Vermès prefaces his remarks with an instruction:

> To access correctly Jesus' healing and exorcistic activities, it is necessary to know that in bygone ages the Jews understood that a relationship existed between sickness, the devil and sin. As a logical counterpart to such a concept of ill-health, it was in consequence believed until as late as the third century BCE that recourse to the services of a physician demonstrated a lack of faith since healing was a monopoly of God. The only intermediaries thought licit between God and the sick were men of God, such as the prophets Elijah and Elisha.[555]

Viewing Jesus in this perspective, as one "believed to be acting as God's agent in the work of liberation, healing and pardon,"[556] Vermès observes: "Jesus' healing gifts are never attributed to the study of physical or mental disease, or to any acquired knowledge of cures, but to some mysterious power that emanated from him and was transmitted to the sick by contact with his person, or even his clothes."[557]

Given this, Vermès confirms: "Jesus was an exorcist, but not a professional one: he did not use incantations such as those apparently composed by King Solomon, or foul-smelling substances intolerable even to the most firmly ensconced of demons. . . . Instead, Jesus confronted with great authority and dignity the demoniacs (lunatics, epileptics, and the like) and commanded the devil to depart."[558]

And he concludes: "Jesus, curing the sick and overpowering the forces of evil with the immediacy of the Galilean holy man, was seen as a dispenser of health, one of the greatest blessings expected at the end of time, when 'the blind man's eyes shall be opened and the ears of the deaf unstopped'; when 'the lame man shall leap like a deer, and the tongue of the dumb shout aloud' (Isa. 35:5–6)."[559]

Another task of the Galilean holy man, related to healing and exorcism, is the task of forgiveness of sin. Vermès cites as an example of Jesus' forgiving prowess Mark 2:3–12, the healing of the paralytic lowered through the roof into Jesus' presence. On this account he comments and then instructs:

> "My son, your sins are forgiven you" is of course not the language of experts in the law; but neither is it blasphemy. On the contrary, absolution from the guilt of wrong-doing appears to have been part and parcel of the charismatic style: this is well illustrated in an important Dead Sea Scrolls fragment, the Prayer of Nabonidus, which depicts a Jewish exorcist as having pardoned the Babylonian king's sins, thus curing him of his seven years' illness. In the somewhat elastic, but extraordinary perceptive religious terminology of Jesus and the spiritual men of his age, "to heal," "to expel demons," and to "forgive sins" were interchangeable synonyms. Indeed, the language and behaviour of Jesus is reminiscent of holy men of ages even earlier than his own, and it need cause little surprise to read in Matthew that he was known as "the prophet Jesus from Nazareth in Galilee" (Matt. 21:11), and that his Galilean admirers believed that he might be one of the biblical prophets, or Jeremiah, or Elijah redivivus (Matt. 16:14).[560]

In this latter regard, Vermès ventures that "in fact, it could be advanced that, if he modeled himself on anyone at all, it was precisely on Elijah and Elisha."[561]

Jesus, Preacher and Teacher

Turning his focus upon the Synoptic memory of Jesus as teacher, Vermès observes the following:

- The Gospels from the outset portray Jesus as a popular preacher and preserve various types of sayings ascribed to him.
- Contrary to the Essene practice of reserving instruction to initiates only, but imitating John the Baptist, Jesus addressed his preaching in Galilee to all who had ears to hear—or rather, to all Jews with ears to hear, for he never envisaged a systematic mission to the Gentiles.
- His ethical message was also aimed at all and sundry, as were also his parables, a form of homiletic teaching commonly used by rabbinic preachers.
- He did not employ parabolic instruction as a means to conceal his message. Non-Jews, unaccustomed to Palestinian teaching methods, would have needed explanations, not Jesus' direct disciples.
- The equally traditional Jewish method of preaching in the form of Bible interpretation is less frequently attested in the Gospels. If Jesus was primarily a teacher of morals, he might be expected to have shown a liking for short, pithy, colorful utterances, the kind of rabbinic *logia* with which the pages of the *Sayings of the Fathers* in the Mishnah are filled.
- He several times taught in the synagogues and once delivered the liturgical sermon after reading the prophetic lesson of the day in Nazareth.
- Unlike the doctors of the law, Jesus spoke with authority. New Testament commentators usually see in this a contrast between Jesus' method of teaching and the rabbis' habit of handing down a legally binding doctrine in the name of the master from which they had learned it.
- Jesus was no expert in Jewish law, and therefore it is misleading to compare his style of instruction to that of later rabbinic academies. It is more probable that people saw his exorcisms and cures as confirmation of Jesus' teaching.
- His personal style of teaching does not evidence doctrine purporting novelty or rejection of the law or Judaism.[562]

Vermès, in *The Religion of Jesus the Jew*, expands his exploration of Jesus as preacher and teacher, writing:

> Whatever else he may have been, Jesus was unquestionably an influential teacher. He was popular rather than a professional figure, an itinerant master who did not deliver his message in a fixed location such as a "school" (*bet midrash* [*bêt-midraš*]) or a particular synagogue. Instead, surrounded by a group of disciples, the nucleus of which was established, he traveled up and down the Lower Galilean countryside, proclaiming his

gospel and healing. Later rabbinic writings mention "wandering Galilean" Bible interpreters (*b. Sanh.* 70a; *b. Ḥul* 27b), but the evidence is too meager to permit us to speak
of representatives of an institution and wonder whether Jesus was one of them.[563]

Vermès recognizes that, though Jesus was an influential teacher and itinerant preacher,
he does not fit conveniently into established Jewish patterns. Such lack of continuity
does not bode well for Jesus vis-à-vis the established religious authorities, as Vermès
notes: "As he was not a member of any recognized teaching group such as the
scribes' (*soferim* [*sopērîm*]) or even the less clearly defined 'preachers' (*darshanim*
[*daršanîm*]), who pronounced homilies on Bible readings in the synagogues, the nature
of his mission was bound to be questioned in his own day and throughout the ages."[564]

Given the lack of continuity, Vermès focuses his inquiry upon the nature of Jesus'
mission in an effort to situate Jesus within the broader corpus of Judaism. To investigate
such, Vermès delves into "the character of his teaching."[565]

After providing his readers with a synopsis of the development of doctrinal authority
in Judaism and its various criteria of validity, Vermès reasserts his question: "To revert
to our original question, it must be asked where and how Jesus' manner of teaching fits
into this canvas [of first-century Judaism] and what his personal attitude is to the an-
cestral Holy Scriptures?"[566] Vermès believes that resolving this question with "a literary
analysis of the Gospel passages which include Bible citations will, it is hoped, assist
in the search for the genuine message of the Galilean master."[567]

Exploring the use of the Bible in the teaching of Jesus, Vermès masterfully delivers
a précis of the exegetical styles representative of first-century Jewish scriptural
hermeneutics and discerns: "All in all, the main impression emerging from this survey
of five classes of didactic form employing scriptural proof-texts is that in general they
figure only on a small scale in Jesus' teaching as presented by the evangelists and that
most of the examples lack the force necessary for a strong hypothesis, let alone a
demonstration, of authenticity."[568]

On this he comments:

> This not withstanding, it would be unreasonable to doubt that Jesus ever had recourse to
> biblical arguments, and of these, as has been suggested, the adoption of biblical idiom,
> the use of scriptural precedents and the emphatic or hyberbolical interpretation of com-
> mandments with which all his contemporaries were familiar, enjoy the strongest claims
> for genuineness. But they seem to be few and far between and in no way form a suffi-
> ciently solid corpus to endow the preaching of Jesus with exceptional power. Yet from
> the outset, from the very first reference to his teaching in the synagogue of Capernaum,
> all three synoptists portray him as a man speaking with *exousia*, i.e., authority. This
> remarkable claim necessitates some further investigation.[569]

Vermès underscores that "the principal evidence regarding Jesus' personal power and
particular doctrinal authority appears at the very beginning of the Gospel, in the account
of his first public pronouncement in Galilee [Mark 1:21–28; Luke 4:31–37]."[570] He
concludes:

> Compared to the preaching to which the members of the Capernaum synagogue were
> accustomed, that of Jesus is defined as "new" (*didachē kainē* [Mark 1:27]), and its novelty

is assigned to its being delivered "with authority." Since this *"exousia"* is parallel to the "authority and power" (*en exousia kai dynamei*) with which Jesus is depicted in Luke 4.36 as an exorcist, it logical to conclude that both as teacher and as miracle-worker, he was primarily perceived as a charismatic, that is a person whose paramount authority was spiritual in nature. Also, acts of healing and exorcism were seem as tangible confirmation of the validity and compelling character of his teaching. Hence both provoked astonishment (Mark 1.22/Luke 4.32) and amazement (Mark 1.27/Luke 4.36), the natural reaction to unexpected, unusual, enigmatic phenomena.[571]

Such characterization, from Vermès's perspective, points to "an early standard Galilean portrayal" of Jesus: charismatic Galilean Hasid.

Commenting upon this charisma of Jesus, he writes:

In Palestinian Jewish parlance—*charisma* being a Greek concept, absent from the Gospels and used only by Paul in the New Testament—a person wielding such authority is known as a prophet, a term appearing a little further in the same passage (Mark 6.4/ Matt. 13.57) relating to Jesus. Such a divine messenger had no need to verify his utterances by suitable biblical proof-texts. His personality, his presence, the power of his voice, his awe-inspiring reputation as a wonder-worker, ensured that his words were accepted.[572]

Concluding his investigation into the character of Jesus' teaching and the source of his authority, Vermès asserts:

In short, it was the people's belief in the heavenly origin of Jesus' and John [the Baptist]'s teaching, reinforced in the case of the former by his apparent mastery over the corporal and mental sickness, that dispensed them both from the need to demonstrate the truth of their doctrine. Their words were endowed with authority not because they were confirmed by Scripture, but because both men were revered as *prophets*, inspired by the spirit of God. To use again the language of Rudolf Otto, it was the constant experience by Jesus' disciples of the holy and the numinous, springing from his words and deeds, that rendered superfluous any traditional form of biblical argument or proof.[573]

Jesus as prophet will be explored (below) in our presentation of Vermès's assessment of the Synoptics titles associated with Jesus. To perceive more clearly the portrait of Jesus emanating from his teaching, we may inquire—but concisely, following Vermès in *The Changing Faces of Jesus*—into three elements of his teaching: "his attitude to the Jewish religion of his day, to God the Father, and to the idea of the Kingdom of heaven."[574]

The Jewish Jesus

Given Jesus' teaching function, as evidenced by the titles "lord," "prophet," and "messiah," Vermès explores "the question of the exact position of Jesus toward Judaism as it was understood and practiced in his time"[575] in his effort to enhance his portrait of Jesus. He observes:

The evangelists implicitly portray Jesus as a Jew profoundly attached to the laws and customs of his people, and some of his most obviously authentic sayings confirm this picture. The Gospels attest his presence in Galilean synagogues and in the Temple in Jerusalem. We are told that he had eaten the Passover just before he was arrested. His garment was like that of the Pharisees (Matt. 23.5), with the traditional tassels hanging from its edges (Matt. 9.20; Luke 8.44; Mark 6.56; Matt. 14.36; cf. Num. 15.38–40; Deut. 22.12). Following an anecdote, which is to be taken with a pinch of salt, he arranged for a miracle to find the right amount of money to pay the Temple tax. His respect for the ritual legislation is revealed in the story of the leper already cured by him whom he ordered to submit himself to the judgment of the priests and offer the prescribed sacrifice in the Temple (Mark 1.44; Matt. 8.4; Luke 5.14; cf. Lev. 14.1–57).[576]

Pointedly, at issue here is Jesus' relationship to the law of Moses, the torah, given the various Gospels accounts that suggest that he is opposed, in some measure, to the law or is abrogating it. From Vermès's perspective, this assertion of Jesus' opposition to the law stands in direct contradiction to the Jesus saying found in Matthew 5:18 wherein Jesus asserts the permanent validity of torah. Luke 16:17 provides a parallel saying.[577] Vermès is conversant with Christianity's position vis-à-vis this question concerning the permanence of the torah, wherein the church argues that Jesus "disregarded two of the most fundamental obligations imposed by the law, the observance of the Sabbath and the dietary regulations of the Bible,"[578] thus demonstrating his [Jesus'] superiority—and therefore Christianity's vis-à-vis Judaism.

Vermès, asserting the inability of these allegations to withstand objective scrutiny, especially when compared "against the testimony of the maxims, proverbs, and parables of Jesus, and against the broader canvas of first-century Jewish religious ideas and aspirations,"[579] offers the following arguments.

As to the criticism that by curing the sick on the Sabbath, Jesus broke the law, Vermès counters:

> The question of healing on the day of rest is explicitly raised in the Gospels themselves (Mark 3.4; Matt. 12.10; Luke 6.9), as well as in the debate of rabbis outside the New Testament. The evangelists make Jesus answer it affirmatively through his actions, and this is in conformity with the view of the rabbis for whom the saving of life superseded the Sabbath precepts. In any case, the form of healing by word of mouth or touch which Jesus adopted did not really count as "work" prohibited on the Sabbath. . . . Enlightened rabbis of the Mishnah advocated leniency and held that if any doubt existed about the potentially life-threatening character of a sickness, that was enough to overrule the Sabbath precepts (*m. Yoma* 8.6).[580]

As to the claim that Jesus abolished the distinction between clean and unclean foods, as reported in the Synoptic memory (Mark 7:15, 18–19; Matt 15:11, 17–18), Vermès responds: "The patent meaning of the words is that defilement is caused not by the foodstuff as such but by the heart's disregard for a divine prohibition, a customary ethical interpretation of a legal precept."[581] He pointedly adds:

> To return to the dietary laws, the comment by the editor of the Gospel to Mark 7:18—"Thus he [Jesus] declared all foods clean" [7:19]—is a secondary gloss which had nothing to do with Jesus and was meaningful and beneficial only in the Gentile-Christian

church for which this Gospel was ultimately destined. Jewish Christianity's difficulty with prospective Gentile converts in the Acts of the Apostles and Paul's row with Peter in Antioch demonstrate that in the first Christian generation no one was aware of Jesus having declared all foods clean![582]

Last, after dealing with the two preceding allegations, Vermès focuses upon the third proof of Jesus' claim of superiority over the law: the sayings in the Sermon on the Mount known as the "antitheses" (Matt 5:21–48). Of these supposed antitheses, he writes:

> However, when objectively analyzed, his [Jesus'] declarations strengthen and clarify, rather than contradict, the Torah. By forbidding anger Jesus does not permit murder but ensures that its root is pulled up. To mistake the antitheses for a "shattering of the letter of the Law," as Ernst Käsemann, a German New Testament scholar, put it, reveals an extraordinary blindness to which theologians of a certain type are often prone.[583]

Deeming these three allegations spurious, Vermès vindicates Jesus, endorsing his fidelity to torah while admitting to a certain "elasticity" or originality in Jesus' approach: an elasticity that is in concert with Vermès's Hasidic hypothesis. Clarifying this observation, Vermès comments: "Again, . . . the *elasticity* of Jesus in regard to a strict interpretation of the sabbatical rest must be envisaged from the point of view of a *charismatic* for whom the healing of the sick overrides all other constraints, however legitimate they may be in themselves."[584]

In the conclusion to the second chapter of *The Religion of Jesus the Jew*, "Jesus and the Law: The Judaism of Jesus," Vermès's rebuttal vis-à-vis the question of Jesus' superiority over the law situates Jesus and his charismatic tendencies vis-à-vis the torah securely within Judaism. Vermès affirms:

> Whereas the rabbinic sages are mostly portrayed as practical experts in the finer details of what is forbidden or permitted, that is to say, the correct way to implement the Torah, and only less frequently as moralists or theologians, the most outstanding feature in Jesus' attitude is an all-pervading concern with the ultimate purpose of the law which he perceived, primarily and essentially and positively, not as juridical, but as a religious-ethical reality, revealing what he thought to be right and divinely ordained behaviour towards men and towards God.[585]

Jesus, the Worshipper of God the Father

Exploring Jesus' relationship with God the Father as discerned from the Synoptics, Vermès observes:

> If the Torah is presented by the Synoptists as the focal point of the devotion of the "Jewish" Jesus, careful examination of the Gospels indicates that the wellspring of his religion lay in his perception of God as Father, his Father, the Father of the Jewish people and of the whole of mankind. The God of Jesus is less remote, transcendent and awesome than the God who could show Moses not his face, but only his back (Exod. 33:21–23).[586]

This difference was not due to Jesus' innovation but is more representative of the "new sensitivity" of which Flusser wrote, which formed the precondition for the reception of Jesus' message. Vermès, though not using Flusser's language, concurs:

> By the time of Jesus, the God contemplated by Jews appeared less awe-inspiring. Already the postexilic Third Isaiah (sixth century B.C.) repeatedly addressed the deity as "our Father" (Isa. 63:16; 64:8), and the paternal imagery is regularly employed from the second century B.C. onward in Jewish literature, including the Dead Sea Scrolls.... Indeed, by the earliest stages of the era of the rabbis the phrase "the Father who is in heaven" was a standard formula.[587]

Discerning that "the loving and caring heavenly Father is the model for Jesus' religious action,"[588] Vermès observes the following:

- Jesus was the imitator of the forgiving and merciful Father.
- His imitation of God is epitomized in the commands, "You must be perfect, as your heavenly Father is perfect" (Matt. 5:48), or "Be merciful, even as your Father is merciful" (Luke 6:36).
- The imitation of God was direct, without intermediaries, and his disciples were encouraged to follow the same direct path.
- This imitation of the forgiving and merciful Father was a central topic of his teaching, occurring throughout the Synoptics.
- In addition to the quality of forgiveness, the divine virtue extolled by the Jesus of the Synoptics as supreme and essential to emulate is the Father's solicitude toward the weak, the poor, and the helpless, a solicitude inspiring limitless trust (see the Sermon on the Mount).
- With eastern Mediterranean Semitic exaggeration, Jesus opted for an extreme example to bring home his admiration for the paternal generosity of God. He chose what goes most against the grain, the love for an enemy.[589]

To gain greater insight into Jesus' relationship with God the Father, Vermès examines the Synoptic memory of Jesus' prayer since "prayer is the most direct source [for] disclosing a person's attitude and feelings towards God."[590] He records the following observations:

- Although the Gospels frequently locate Jesus in synagogues, and during his Passover pilgrimage in the temple in Jerusalem, they never mention that he prayed there, let alone participated in sacrificial worship.
- With the exception of the Lord's Prayer, which is meant for a group, he is always depicted as a practitioner of individual prayer either in solitude or at least some distance from other people.
- His advice on prayer insists on privacy (Matt 6:6).
- Whether the words reported as his in the Gospels are authentic or not, there is no doubt about the conviction of the evangelists, who make him address all his supplications to God the Father.

- As an example of the validity of the above observation, Vermès cites Mark's Gospel, wherein a single prayer is recorded: a petition address to *Abba* ("Father" or possibly "my Father") in Jesus' own Aramaic.
- Mark 14:36 contains this single invocation, conveying reverence and intimacy. However, *Abba* is not "daddy" nor does it represent "baby language."
- All the other prayer formulas preserved in Matthew and Luke begin in Greek with "Father" or "Our Father," and they convey the ideas of blessing, supplication, and thanksgiving.
- All three characteristics of the formula comprise the most famous of Jesus' prayers, the Lord's Prayer par excellence, a paradigm of a plea to God taught by Jesus to his disciples.
- Of the two versions that have been handed down to us in Matthew and Luke, the shorter version (Luke 11:2–4) is nearer the original—contrary to the common view.
- As far as substance is concerned, both versions seem to reflect the religious cast of the mind of Jesus.
- The Lord's Prayer is admirably concise (cf. Matt 6:7). The chief topics concern the sanctification of God's name; a plea for *today's* bread—tomorrow's or [for] the day after; and a plea for divine remission of our debts, presupposing repentance and mutual forgiveness among the members of the community.
- The petition "Thy Kingdom come" is the best warranty for tracing the Lord's Prayer to Jesus himself, for the primitive Christian community would have expressed its eschatological hope in a prayer for the return of Christ, *Marana tha* [cf. 1 Cor 16:22; Rev 22:20], rather than for the advent of the Kingdom.[591]

Jesus and the Kingdom of God

Vermès prefaces his remarks concerning Jesus and the kingdom of God by observing: (1) This powerful concept—modeled on the biblical idea of God's sovereignty as king over the Jewish people and by extension, as Creator of the world—which figures more than a hundred times in the Synoptics, was not Jesus' creation. (2) This eschatological concept permeated the whole of Palestinian thinking of the epoch. (3) Though the development of primitive thinking about the kingdom of God is traceable in the Acts of the Apostles and in Paul, the idea is virtually extinct in John's Gospel (cf. John 3:3, 5; 18:36).[592]

Confirming that this "same notion continued to flourish in the postexilic age to the end of the period of the Second Temple (538 B.C. to A.D. 70),"[593] Vermès further observes:

- The literature of this intertestamental era, including the Dead Sea Scrolls, further enriched the kingdom imagery with the apocalyptic features of a cosmic battle between good and evil on the eve of the final manifestation and triumph of the divine King.

- Apocalyptic fervor often transformed itself into political action, as the history of Palestinian Jews shows.
- In the subsequent centuries [after 66–70 CE], despite two calamitous defeats, the political concept lingered on, contrasting the kingdom of heaven with the wicked Roman Empire.
- Nevertheless Jewish thinkers increasingly imagined entry into the kingdom in a nonviolent form, through taking the "yoke of the kingdom" by means of a whole-hearted obedience to the Torah. A typical example is furnished by the famous Aramaic prayer called Kaddish, the origins of which are thought to belong to the earliest phases of the rabbinic era, if not before.
- Jesus' kingdom perfectly fits between the apocalyptic and the rabbinic pictures, and due to its unwarlike character it rather foreshadows the latter than develops the former.
- The idea of a bellicose march toward the new Jerusalem in the footsteps of a combative Messiah is exclusive to the book of Revelation in the New Testament.[594]

Asserting that "nothing indicates more clearly the importance ascribed by the writers of the Gospels to the idea of the kingdom of God than the fact that it opens and closes the story of Jesus,"[595] Vermès affirms:

> The evangelists give us correctly to understand that preoccupation with the kingdom of God and devotion to doing what he had to do about it constitute the essence of the vocation of Jesus. Not being an abstract thinker, he never set out to determine the exact meaning of the concept; he sought to describe the kingdom in similitudes rather than [to] define it, and strove to make known how he and his followers were to act when the moment was ripe for action.[596]

Observing that "Jesus nowhere distinctly spells out his concept of 'kingdom,' even in the metaphorical language of the parables, his approach is oblique and his outline hazy,"[597] Vermès discerns:

> The kingdom of God is a mystery attainable only with human co-operation. The climax is expected, suddenly and soon, in an unheralded yet triumphal manifestation of divine power. In the mind of Jesus the *nature* of the kingdom comes second to the *role* to be played by the actors of the drama, himself and his adepts, in ushering it in. The "what" of the philosopher gives way to the "when" and "how" of the prophet and wisdom teacher. It is therefore not surprising that the bulk of the surviving material relates to the moral and religious qualities required of those who seek the kingdom, and the exigency of the mission facing them.[598]

Of the God of Jesus, Vermès writes:

> Perhaps the most paradoxical aspect of the teaching on the kingdom of heaven which can safely be attributed to Jesus is that unlike the God of the Bible and of intertestamental and rabbinic literature, the God of Jesus is not a regal figure, but is modeled on a smaller, hence more accessible, scale. He is conceived in the form of the man of influence familiar to Jesus and his listeners, the well-to-do landowner and paterfamilias of rural Galilee. As I have argued elsewhere, the chief characteristic of Jesus' doctrine

is that it "transforms into reality the 'unreal' ingredients of the inherited imagery of the kingdom" (*JWJ*, 36) [*Jesus and the World of Judaism*].[599]

As to the date of the kingdom's arrival, though Scripture speculates (see Dan 9–12; Mark 13:5–20; Matt 24:4–22; Luke 21:8–24; 2 Thess 2:1–9), the Synoptic Jesus' response is innovative and distinct. Vermès states:

> Yet with the exception of the dissonant eschatological discourse, the Synoptics depict Jesus as someone whose mind was totally alien to such an outlook. He was opposed to giving clues because he did not believe in premonitions: "The kingdom of God is not coming with signs to be observed" (Luke 17:20; cf. Mark 8:11–13; Matt. 12:38–39; 16:1–4; Luke 11:16, 29). Even more positively—and flatly contradicting all the warnings he is supposed to have issued in the eschatological discourse—Jesus firmly denied any knowledge of the date of the coming of the kingdom; it was the exclusive privilege of God: "But of that day and that hour no one knows, not even the angels of heaven, nor the son, but only the Father" (Mark 13:32; Matt. 24:36).[600]

Confirming that "imbued with eschatological enthusiasm, Jesus saw himself and his generation as already belonging to the initial stages of the kingdom and called to expedite its final manifestation,"[601] Vermès asserts:

> He and his disciples entered wholeheartedly into the eschatological age and recognized a fundamental difference between their own time with no future, and the centuries that preceded it. From the moment when Jesus obeyed the Baptist's call to repentance, time for him became the end time, demanding a decisive and irrevocable *teshuvah* [*těšûbāh*, "return, repentance"], which necessitated for himself and his followers a new way of life.[602]

Of the kingdom and Jesus' metaphorical language, Vermès writes:

> In many of the relevant parables and in all the preserved sayings the kingdom is an existing but as a rule concealed reality, which nevertheless at times allows its presence to be felt. According to Jesus, the kingdom is symbolized by the concerted action of the field, the farmer sowing and the seed (Mark 4:26–29), or by the tiny mustard seed which invisibly and astonishingly grows and is transformed into a tall plant (Mark 4:30–32; Matt. 13:31–32; Luke 13:18–19), or by the leaven which mysteriously turns flour into bread (Matt. 13:33; Luke 13:20–21). The coexistence of good and evil shows that the scene is in the here and now, antedating the final settlement and the new age. Seeds of corn and weeds, fish fit and unfit to eat, remain together in the parable[s] of the sower and [of] the net (Matt. 13:24–30, 47–50). As for the similitudes of the wedding feast, wise and foolish virgins and worthy and unworthy guests await together the bridal procession or try to enter the banquet hall (Matt. 25:1–13; 22:1–14; Luke 14:16– 24). In the words of Jesus of the Synoptics, "the kingdom of God is in the midst of you" (Luke 17:20).
>
> However, another aspect of the teaching of Jesus which the evangelists emphatically underscore is that the still-hidden kingdom now and then reveals its presence in charismatic manifestations. Jesus declares that victory over evil in the form of exorcism by the spirit or the finger of God signals that the kingdom "has come upon you" (Matt. 12:28; Luke 11:20).[603]

Trying to summarize Jesus' message, Vermès writes:

Motivated by a central vision of God as King and Father, the main purpose of his short existence was to give reality to his own filial relation by living as a son of God, and to show to the repentant and the receptive how to live similarly. His understanding of his own obligations, and those of his followers, combined with the pressures of the escha-tologico-apocalyptic world-view which they had all inherited, conferred a quality of urgency and uncompromising self-surrender on his entire religious action. It is this sin-gle-minded, unreserved, enthusiastic piety, this unceasing struggle to reproduce in himself, in his dealings with the world, the attributes of his heavenly Father, that strikes the historian as *Jesus' unique contribution* to the history of religion, one which as a source of inspiration and model of holiness possesses a real, timeless, and universal significance and appeal. They are the qualities that so overwhelmed the apostles and disciples that even the collapse of Jesus' ministry was unable to extinguish the faith which he had kindled in them.[604]

As to how Jesus conceived entry into the kingdom, Vermès, observing the absolute clarity in the Synoptic Gospels in this regard, reports:

- The conduct prescribed by Jesus is set out in the Synoptic Gospels.
- The gate opens only to those who have the simplicity, trust, and intensity of desire of a child (Matt. 18:3; Mark 10:15; Luke 18:17).
- No one could become a citizen of the kingdom without total devotion to the cause (Matt. 13:44–46). The ideal devotee is the destitute widow who gave "everything she had, her whole life" (Mark 12:44; Luke 21:3–4).
- It is preferable to rid oneself of an eye or a limb and to sacrifice sex if that is the price of entry into the kingdom of God (Mark 9:45–47; Matt. 18:9; 19:12).
- This willingness to surrender oneself for the sake of the kingdom is an empty pre-tense in Jesus' eyes unless it is turned into immediate action.
- In harmony with his stress on the primacy of today over tomorrow, he obliged his disciples to throw themselves at once into the work for the kingdom.
- No delay or procrastination was tolerated, not even on the pretext of filial piety (Luke 9:60; Matt. 8:22).
- Once recruited by Jesus, a laborer for the cause of heaven was no longer allowed to hesitate or wonder. He had to press ahead (Luke 9:62).[605]

Given this, Vermès asserts:

If we bear in mind the constant emphasis laid on the immediacy, single-mindedness and unrestrained giving of self vis-à-vis the kingdom of God, the inescapable conclusion will be that the eyes of Jesus were resolutely focused on the present, on the duty of the mo-ment, and closed to anything pertaining to the more distant future. Indeed, if we take his words in their most obvious sense, we are compelled to accept that Jesus refused to contemplate or prepare for eventualities that lay far ahead. For if the kingdom of God was already there and its glorious manifestation was due any moment, it would have been nonsensical to be concerned with matters of this age whose time would soon run out.[606]

In his last Riddell Memorial Lecture, Vermès pondered aloud the galvanizing principle that energized and sustained Jesus and his followers. In the closing pages of *The Reli-gion of Jesus the Jew*, Vermès echoes his earlier response:

The answer given then still strikes me as valid. Initiated by *teshuvah* [conversion] and nourished by *emunah* [*'ĕmûnāh*, "trusting faith"], the religion of Jesus can ultimately be summed up as an untiring effort to follow God as a model, a constant *imitatio Dei*. The doctrine is an essential part of one of the streams of biblical, inter-testamental and rabbinic Judaism, and as such constitutes the apogee of our description of the religion of Jesus the Jew.[607]

Vermès affirms this *imitatio Dei* in his more recent work *The Changing Faces of Jesus*:

Unshakable faith and trust in God, the biblical *emunah*, was the hallmark, the ideal of Jesus which he preached and practiced. It was the spiritual engine of his whole life's work and we may reasonably believe that it continued to his last day, during his trial before the high priest and Pilate, and even on the way to the cross. But there came the moment of realization that his Father would not intervene, which provoked the cry of anguish, "*Eloi, eloi, lama sabachtani?* . . . My God, my God, why hast thou forsaken me?" (Mark 15:34).[608]

Concluding this section on Jesus and the kingdom of God, Vermès renders a descriptive response to his query:

Far from being a "doom and gloom" merchant, Jesus was an eschatological enthusiast. It is a single-minded dedication to what he believed to be his special mission, the leading to a safe haven those entrusted to his charge, that defines the role of Jesus in the last act of the final drama. He is depicted in the Synoptics as the compassionate, caring and loving pilot and shepherd who, imitating the merciful, caring, and loving God, guides those most in need, the little ones (Matt. 18:10), the sinners, the whores, and the publicans, toward the gate of the kingdom of the Father.[609]

Exploring the Synoptic descriptions of Jesus as exorcist, healer, and teacher, Vermès discerns an emanating typology—the parallel of which he finds in comparative Jewish literature: a Galilean Hasid. Vermès affirms: "Jesus was a Galilean Hasid: there, as I see it, lies his greatness, and also the germ of his tragedy. That he had his share of the notorious Galilean chauvinism would seem clear from the xenophobic statements attributed to him. . . . But Jesus was also, and above all, an exemplary representative of the fresh and simple religiousness for which the Palestinian North was noted."[610]

This "fresh and simple religiousness of the Palestinian North" will prove to be a flashpoint between Jesus and his critics, especially the Pharisees.

Jesus, a Galilean Jew

In Vermès's view, Jesus' Jewish milieu is not merely coincidental, but also integral. Failing to comprehend this matrix would compromise one's ability to reconstruct the figure of Jesus with significant probability. Specifically, the Galilean setting, as described by Vermès, which both formed Jesus and served as his palette during his public ministry, is to be appreciated in order better to grasp Jesus and his personality.

In *Jesus in His Jewish Context*, Vermès deftly sketches Jesus' Galilean milieu:

In distant Rome, Tiberius reigned supreme. Valerius Gratus and then Pontius Pilate were governing Judea. Joseph Caiaphas was high priest of the Jews, the president of the Jerusalem Sanhedrin, and the head of the Sadducees. Hillel and Shammai, the leaders of the most influential Pharisaic schools, were possibly still alive, and during Jesus' lifetime, Gamaliel the Elder became Hillel's successor. Not far from Jerusalem, a few miles south of Jericho, on the western shore of the Dead Sea, the ascetic Essenes were worshipping God in holy withdrawal and planning the conversion of the rest of Jewry to the true Judaism known only to them, the followers of the Teacher of Righteousness. And in neighboring Egypt, in Alexandria, the philosopher Philo was busy harmonizing the Jewish life-style with the wisdom of Greece, a dream cherished by the civilized Jews of the Disaspora.

In Galilee, the tetrarch Herod Antipas remained lord of life and death and continued to hope (in vain) that one day the emperor might end his humiliation by granting him the title king. At the same time, following the upheaval that accompanied the tax registration or census ordered in 6 C.E. by the legate of Syria, Publius Sulpicius Quirinius, Judas the Galilean and his sons were stimulating the revolutionary tendencies of the uncouth Northerners, tendencies that resulted in the foundation of the Zealot movement.[611]

Though conversant with the general Galilean ambience of Jesus' day, Vermès notes: "We know nothing concrete, however, about his education and training, his contacts, or the influences to which he may have been subjected; for, quite apart from the un-historical nature of the stories relating to his infancy and childhood, the interval between his twelfth year and the start of his public ministry is wrapped in total silence by the four evangelists."[612]

Given this, Vermès turns his attention to the Synoptic record of Jesus' public ministry. Observing that the Synoptic Gospels confine Jesus and his public ministry primarily to Galilee, with notable exceptions, Vermès reasserts his conviction that "if we are to understand him [Jesus], it is into the Galilean world that we must look."[613]

As to the region and its inhabitants, Vermès reports:

The Galilee of Jesus, especially his own part of it, Lower Galilee around the Lake of Gennesaret, was a rich and mostly agricultural country. The inhabitants were proud of their independence and jealous of their Jewishness, in which regard, despite doubts often expressed by Judaeans, they considered themselves second to none. They were also brave and tough. Josephus, the commander-in-chief of the region during the first Jewish War, praises their courage and describes them as people "from infancy inured to War" (*War* 3.41).

In effect, in the mountains of Upper Galilee, rebellion against the government—any government, whether Hasmonean, Herodian, or Roman—was endemic between the middle of the first century BCE and 70 CE. . . . In short, the Galileans were admired as staunch fighters by those who sympathized with their rebellious aims; those who did not, thought of them as dangerous hot-heads.[614]

As to how the Galilean Jews were viewed in Jerusalem, Vermès writes:

In Jerusalem, and in Judean circles, Galileans also had the reputation of being an unso-phisticated people. In rabbinic parlance, a Galilean is usually referred to as *Gelili shoteh*, "stupid Galilean." He is presented as a typical "peasant," a "boor," an '*am ha-'arez* ('*am hā-'āreṣ*), a religiously uneducated person. Cut off from the Temple and the study centers of Jerusalem, Galilean popular religion appears to have depended—until the arrival at Usha, in the late 130s C.E., of the rabbinic academy expelled from Yavneh—not so much on the authority of the priests or on the scholarship of scribes as on the personal magnetism of their local saints like Jesus' younger contemporary, Hanina ben Dosa, the celebrated miracle-worker.[615]

Vermès has now examined the Synoptic record regarding its portrayal of Jesus as exorcist, healer, and preacher—juxtaposing it with other pertinent comparative Jewish literature—and the ambience of Galilee upon the person and personality of Jesus. Next he reaffirms his thesis and asserts:

> The chief finding of *Jesus the Jew* is the recognition of Jesus within the earliest Gospel tradition, prior to Christian theological speculation, as a charismatic prophetic preacher and miracle-worker, the outstanding "Galilean Hasid" who, thanks to the "sublimity, distinctiveness and originality" of his ethical teaching (Joseph Klausner), stood head and shoulders above the known representatives of this class of spiritual personality. Powerful positive and negative support for such a perception comes from the first-century Jewish historian, Flavius Josephus' characterization of Jesus as a "wise man" and a "performer of astonishing deeds" (*Ant.* 18.63), a description which expressed in neutral terms the positive Gospel portrait, and in its negative mirror image, the latter hostile Talmudic picture of Jesus, [as] "seducer" and "sorcerer".[616]

This Galilean "wise man" and "performer of deeds" was not so without controversy and reaction. Vermès writes: "Exorcist, healer and itinerant preacher, Jesus is portrayed by the Synoptists as a person toward whom his contemporaries rarely if ever, remained indifferent. Their reactions were by no means always favorable, but on the other hand they were not generally hostile either."[617]

Of Jesus' proponents and followers, Vermès observes:

- A small group of devotees, simple Galilean folk, joined him from the beginning—"after John had been arrested"—and became his traveling companions.
- The Twelve, an even smaller group, were later chosen to be his disciples par excellence.
- So impressed were they by his powerful personality that they left everything to follow him—work, possessions, and family.
- Heroic though they may have become after Jesus' death, concentrating themselves wholeheartedly to the continuation of his lifework, they are not depicted in the Gospels as particularly quick at understanding the mind and the preaching of their master while he was alive, or brave at the time of his ordeal, when they all deserted him.[618]

As to his reception in Galilee and its environs, Vermès adds:

- Among the Galilean crowds Jesus was a great success.
- Large groups formed and accompanied him when the rumor went round that he was on his way to heal the sick, or simply when he traveled.

- He preached to multitudes in Capernaum and by the lakeside, and soon acquired such a renown that he "could no longer show himself in any town, but stayed outside in the open country."
- Although his fame apparently also aroused curiosity outside of Galilee, he is not described as a welcome visitor in non-Jewish areas. The inhabitants of Gerasa requested him to leave their country, and as a Jew traveling to Jerusalem he is represented as a persona non grata in Samaria.
- The popularity of Jesus in Judea and Jerusalem did not match that which he enjoyed in his own country.[619]

Observing that "the true relationship between Jesus and his associates, and the company led by John the Baptist, is more difficult to determine," Vermès ventures to assert: "The aim of the Gospel writers was, no doubt, to give the impression of friendship and mutual esteem, but their attempts smack of superficiality, and closer scrutiny of the admittedly fragmentary evidence suggests that, at least on the level of their respective disciples, sentiments of rivalry between the two groups were not absent."[620]

As to the relationship between Jesus and John, given the diversity of the Synoptic record, Vermès discerns the following:

- That Jesus went to be baptized by John is enough to prove the Baptist's initial impact on him.
- Some saw Jesus, after John's death, a John redivivus, [as] the tetrarch Herod.
- At their first encounter, according to Matthew and Luke, John recognizes Jesus' superiority.
- Jesus, for his part, proclaims John as the greatest in the long series of Israelite prophets, the one in whom the words of Malachi have come true, . . . the returning Elijah, the precursor of the Messiah.
- Jesus is also reported to have said that though John may have been the greatest of men, "the least in the kingdom of heaven is greater than he."
- In Aramaic and Hebrew the phrase, "the least one," "the smallest one," can be used in the chronological sense to designate the youngest or last person in a series, allowing one to suggest that Jesus is implying that he is the greater of the two.[621]

Vermès concludes that while a rivalry between the two groups of disciples is indicated, it is "resolved [in Matthew and Luke] in the compromise that John, recognized as the precursor , acknowledges the superiority of Jesus at the time of his baptism or better still, when they are both in their mothers' wombs."[622]

Of Jesus' critics and opponents, those who find Jesus' teaching disconcerting or problematic, Vermès asserts: "As an exceptional and controversial religious teacher, it was inevitable that Jesus should encounter criticism and hostility as well as respect and love, but strangely enough, the first opposition came from those closest to him, his family and fellow-citizens in Nazareth."[623]

Of this first opposition, coming from Jesus' family and neighbors, Vermès puzzles over the opposition, as do both Flusser and Ben-Chorin, and argues, given "the scandalous incongruity"[624] of their reaction to Jesus—"He is out of his mind" (Mark 3:21)—that "this statement is the best guarantee of its historicity."[625] Like Flusser and Ben-Chorin, Vermès see the initial opposition of Jesus' family and his refusal to acquiesce to his family's influence as historical.[626] This would be true too of the reaction of Jesus' friends and neighbors.[627]

Vermès's preliminary remarks, before his assessment of Jesus' religious and secular opponents—those who find his "fresh and simple religiousness" an affront—warrant attention:

> Firstly, the identity of the opponents is often unclear because the sources are contradictory regarding them. For instance, the protagonists in what appears to be the same event are described by Mark as Pharisees and Herodians, by Matthew as Pharisees only, and by Luke as lawyers and Pharisees [Mark 3:6; Matt 12:14; Luke 6:7]. Secondly, interpretative tradition, both scholarly and popular, is too easily inclined to equate Pharisees, scribes and lawyers, but since Mark and Luke expressly refer to the lawyers of the Pharisees, it would follow that those not so described were not necessarily members of that party. Thirdly, in the various accounts of the plot which lead to the arrest of Jesus and his surrender to Pilate for trial and execution, the Pharisees as a class play no part. Lastly, the struggle with the chief priests and elders, and probably with the Sadducees too, is confined to Jerusalem.[628]

Observing that "the only serious clash reported in the Gospels between Jesus and the established authority finds him opposing the Sadducees in their denial of the resurrection of the dead,"[629] Vermès turns his attention to Jesus and the Pharisees. He writes: "Here [in Jesus opposition to the Sadducees regarding the resurrection of the dead], as well as in the identification of the greatest commandment—love of God and one's fellow-men—Jesus is represented as sharing the outlook and winning the approval of the Pharisees."[630]

Though they may share similarities, Vermès points out—as does Flusser—that Jesus and the Pharisees may not be equated. He asserts: "Yet it would be a gross overstatement to portray him as a Pharisee himself. Indeed, in regard to those customs which they invested with a quasi-absolute value, but which to him were secondary to biblical commandments, a head-on collision was unavoidable. Jesus ate with sinners and did not condemn those who sat down to table with unwashed hands or pulled corn on the Sabbath."[631]

As to the Pharisees' reception of Jesus and subsequent interaction, Vermès affirms:

> There is little doubt that the Pharisees disliked his non-conformity and would have preferred him to have abstained from healing on the Sabbath where life was not in danger. They obviously enjoyed embarrassing him with testing questions, such as whether tax should be paid to Rome. . . . But Jesus himself was not above employing the same methods: indeed, they were an integral part of polemical argument at that time. There is no evidence, however, of an active and organized participation on the part of the Pharisees in the planning and achievement of Jesus' downfall.[632]

In *Jesus in His Jewish Context*, Vermès is explicit, highlighting the tension that existed between Jesus and the Pharisees:

And yet it was in this respect [Jesus' fresh and simple religiousness] that he cannot have been greatly loved by the Pharisees: in his lack of expertise, and perhaps even interest in halakhic matters, common to Galileans in general; in his tolerance of deliberate neglect in regard to certain traditional—though not, it should be emphasized, biblical—customs by his followers; in his table-fellowship with publicans and whores; and last but not least, in the spiritual authority explicitly or implicitly presumed to underpin his charismatic activities, an authority impossible to check, as can be done when teachings are handed down from master to disciple.[633]

Vermès does not observe in Jesus a catalyst of schism. Regarding basic issues, he writes:

Not that there appears to have been any fundamental disagreement between Jesus and the Pharisees on any basic issue, but whereas Jesus, the preacher of *teshuvah,* of repentance, felt free rhetorically to overemphasize the ethical as compared with the ritual— like certain of the prophets before him—he perhaps could be criticized for not paying enough attention to those needs of society which are met by organized religion.[634]

There is no schism or fundamental disagreement, but rather a conflict upon which Vermès comments: "Nevertheless, the conflict between Jesus of Galilee and the Pharisees of his time would, in normal circumstances, merely have resembled the in-fighting of factions belonging to the same religious body, like that between Karaities and Rabbanites in the Middle Ages, or between the orthodox and progressive branches of Judaism in modern times."[635]

In normal circumstances. Yet, as Vermès and others have suggested, circumstances in Galilee were not normal. "An eschatological and politico-religious fever was always close to the point of eruption, if it had not already exploded, and Galilee was a hotbed of nationalist ferment."[636] This is not to suggest that Jesus was a Zealot. From Vermès's perspective, the Gospel records concur. Even so, he surmises that "it is likely that some of his followers may have been committed to them [the Zealots] and have longed to proclaim him as King Messiah destined to liberate his oppressed nation."[637]

In the midst of this eschatological and politico-religious fervor, Rome, the foreign occupier, ruled oppressively. Rome's representatives—Herod Antipas in Galilee and the chief priests and Sanhedrin of Jerusalem—did not look kindly upon anyone who provoked Rome or threatened the status quo. Vermès notes:

In their eyes, revolutionary propaganda was not only against the law of the Roman provincial administration, but also murderously foolish, contrary to the national interest, and liable to expose to the vengeance of the invincible emperor not only those actively implicated, but [also] countless thousands of their innocent compatriots. They had to be silenced one way or another, by persuasion or by force, before it was too late. . . . Such indeed must have been the mind of the establishment. Not only actual, but even potential leadership of a revolutionary movement called for alertness and vigilance.[638]

Making an obvious connection between the fate of John the Baptist and the death of Jesus, Vermès observes a similar preemptive intervention: "Jesus, I believe, was a victim of a similar preventive measure devised by the Sadducean rulers in the 'general interest' [of the common good]."[639]

As to the culpability of others, Vermès writes:

> The Synoptic Gospels know of two main plots to put an end to Jesus' activities: one in
> Galilee, which failed, and one in Jerusalem, which resulted in the cross. Probably, some
> individual Pharisees bore a measure of responsibility for this, but in both cases the prin-
> cipal, and certainly the ultimate, guilt lay with the representatives of the political
> establishment—Herod Antipas and his supporters in Galilee, and the chief priests and
> Pilate in the capital.[640]

Vermès, finding the assertion of a trial before the Sanhedrin dubious, concurs with Paul
Winter's thesis, writing:

> If such a trial did take place, and if it were possible to reconstruct its proceedings from
> the discrepant, and often contradictory reports of the Gospels, the only justifiable con-
> clusion would be that in a single session the Sanhedrin managed to break every rule in
> the book: it would, in other words, have been an illegal trial. Yet even those who are able
> to believe that a real trial occurred are compelled to admit that when the chief priests
> transferred the case from their court to Pontius Pilate's tribunal, they did not ask for their
> findings to be confirmed, but laid a fresh charge before the prefect of Judea, namely, that
> Jesus was a political agitator with pretensions to being the king of the Jews. It was not
> on a Jewish religious indictment, but on a secular accusation that he was condemned by
> the emperor's delegate to die shamefully on the Roman cross.[641]

With the echo of Jesus' dying lament resonating in his ears, Vermès exclaims:

> Nothing to my mind, epitomizes more sharply the tragedy of Jesus the Jew, misunder-
> stood by friend and foe alike, than this perplexed cry from the cross [*Elōi, elōi, lema
> sabachthani?*]. Nor was this the end of it. For throughout the centuries, as age followed
> age, Christians and Jews allowed it to continue and worsen. His adherents transformed
> this lover and worshipper of his Father in heaven into an object of worship himself, a
> god; and his own people, under the pressures of persecution at the hands of those
> adherents, mistakenly attributed to Jesus [the] Christian beliefs and dogmas, many of
> which—I feel quite sure—would have filled this Galilean Hasid with stupefaction, anger
> and deepest grief.[642]

There remains for us but to consider more clearly Vermès's juxtaposition of Jesus
with the contemporary, Galilean Hasidim and glean from his presentation of the New
Testament titles associated with Jesus those most applicable and appropriate, given his
Jewish milieu. Yet, before this endeavor, it is appropriate—though technically not
within the parameters of his historical inquiry—to allow Vermès to close his overview
of the Synoptic Jesus with some comments pertaining to the resurrection of Jesus.

On the resurrection narratives and its doctrine, Vermès observes:

> Although founded on evidence which can only be described as confused and fragile,
> belief in the resurrection of Jesus became an increasingly important, and finally central,
> issue in the post-Synoptic and especially post-Marcan stage of doctrinal evolution. This
> development is all the more astonishing since the idea of bodily resurrection played no
> part of any significance in the preaching of Jesus. Moreover, his disciples did not expect
> him to arise from the dead any more than their contemporaries expected the Messiah to
> do so.[643]

To this he adds: "A further point to take into consideration is that despite Luke and Paul, and the Creed, the resurrection of Jesus 'according to the Scriptures' cannot be seen as a logical necessity within the framework of Israel's prophetic heritage because, as has been indicated, neither the suffering of the Messiah, nor his death and resurrection, appear to have been part of the faith of first-century Judaism."[644]

Yet Vermès the historian is not prepared to dismiss the Synoptic memory of Jesus risen as mere fabrication or enigmatic myth. Rather, given that "John the Baptist and Jesus are both described as Elijah redivivus,"[645] he advances a conjecture: "It is conceivable that a belief of this sort prevailing among those who continued Jesus' ministry, including healing and exorcism, had a retroactive effect on the formation of the resurrection preaching, and liberal historians have long since seen the 'real Easter miracle,' not in a changed Jesus, but in metamorphosed disciples."[646]

In the end, though, "when every argument has been considered and weighed,"[647] Vermès concedes: "[These] are simply interpretations of the one disconcerting fact: namely, that the women who set out to pay their respects to Jesus found to their consternation, not a body, but an empty tomb."[648]

The Titles of Jesus in the Synoptics

In the first part of *Jesus the Jew*, Vermès argued persuasively that the figure of Jesus emanating from the Synoptic text was that of a Galilean Hasid. Though he believed this assessment eminently credible, he applied to his hypothesis a "checking mechanism," a historical and linguistic analysis of the titles borne by Jesus in the Gospels, to confirm it. This analysis comprised the second half of *Jesus the Jew*. Of the five titles—prophet, lord, messiah, son of man, and son of God—that met Vermès's gaze, "three—prophet, lord, and son of God—when examined in their Semitic (Aramaic/Hebrew) context, are found in biblical and post-biblical Jewish literature applied to charismatic holy men."[649] It remains for Vermès to demonstrate this latter assertion. We will follow Vermès's analysis of these titles, relying as he did on the disciples' response to Jesus' query: "Who do men say the son of man is?" (Matt 16:13–23). Our presentation, though representative of the analysis found in *Jesus the Jew*, will also move discriminately among pertinent pages of Vermès's more recent book *The Changing Faces of Jesus* and highlight salient features of his initial analysis.

Before applying his checking mechanism to the Synoptic titles, Vermès provides a necessary and insightful distinction regarding the task at hand:

> The historian's approach to the evolution of the Gospel titles is bound to differ from that of a theologian. The latter may admit that there was doctrinal development, but will claim that it was *intended*, that the modification he can detect in the New Testament, in Patristic thought, in the Councils and in the Church is "genuine," inspired, governed, protected and brought to maturity by the spirit of God. By contrast, the historian's task being to enquire into the metamorphosis of Jesus of Galilee into the Christ of Christianity, he must necessarily attach greater weight to the doctrinally least advanced tradition relating to Jesus and endeavour to trace from that point onward the successive stages of

theological change. In doing so, he needs to treat extraneous contemporary parallels with particular care, bearing in mind that the meaning of a religious title depends more on culture and traditional usage than on etymology. Epithets such as "lord" or "son of God" uttered in Greek by Gentile Christians in Antioch, Alexandria or Athens, evoke ideas other than those attached to their Hebrew or Aramaic originals by Palestinian Jews. The primary aim must therefore be to determine the importance of a title in a first-century AD Galilean milieu. If this can be done, there is a good chance of approaching closer to the thought of Jesus and his first disciples. But even a better acquaintance with the wider Palestinian usage will furnish an insight into the minds of those of his contemporaries who employed or witnessed the employment of the title in question.[650]

The "Son of Man" in the Synoptics

As a point of departure for our inquiry, the following summary attends to the pertinent data that confronts one's initial analysis of the phrase "Son of Man":

- In the Synoptic Gospels the "Son of Man" title appears some sixty-five times. As a key feature of John's Gospel, it appears eleven times. In the rest of the New Testament, it hardly figures: never in Paul, once in the Acts of the Apostles, and twice in Revelation in direct quotations from the Old Testament.
- From a philological point of view it is generally accepted that the Greek formula *ho huios tou anthrōpou* (the son of man) translates an Aramaic idiom *bar 'enasha* or *bar nasha* (or *bar-'ĕnoš*, as in Dan 7:13). In the Synoptic Gospels the phrase "Son of Man" is found exclusively on the lips of Jesus, who speaks of himself.
- His use of the phrase appears to be intelligible since no one asks what he means. It is perfectly acceptable to the listeners, upsetting no religious sensibilities.
- Outside the New Testament, "son of man" is most commonly employed in the Aramaic language spoken by the Jews either as a noun ("a man/the man") or as the indefinite pronoun ("one/someone") but neither of these usages is applicable to the Synoptic Gospels. Furthermore, in the Galilean dialect of Aramaic spoken by Jesus, "son of man" sometimes appears in a monologue or dialogue as a circumlocutional reference to the speaker himself. The purpose of such a periphrastic style was to camouflage something fatal dreaded by the speaker or something that would sound boastful if directly asserted.
- There is also a nonliteral, interpretative understanding of "son of man," displayed both within and outside the New Testament. It is based on the biblical book of Daniel (7:13). In the book of Daniel "one like a son of man" represents "the saints of the Most High," that is to say, the Jewish people (Dan 7:18, 22, 27), and this collective interpretation seems to have recently been confirmed by the first-century BCE Aramaic Daniel Apocryphon from Qumran.
- From the completion of the book of Daniel in the 160s BCE to the time of the destruction of Jerusalem in 70 CE, there is no attestation in extant Jewish literature of the use of "son of man" as describing a religious function. However, in the decades following the first Jewish war against Rome, which ended in 70 CE, during

the period of the composition of the Gospels, we possess independent literary evidence in which such a manlike figure is portrayed as a heavenly Messiah (*4 Ezra* 13 [= 2 Esd 13]), or a superterrestrial final Judge (Parables of Enoch, or *1 Enoch* 37–71). The Gospel of John reflects this titular function, this richer messianic significance of "Son of Man" as messianic judge.[651]

The second datum alone, Jesus' colloquial self-identification and solitary use, provides the raison d'être for an inquiry into the phrase.

Vermès, emphasizing the nontitular sense of the phrase "son of Man," asserts:

> In contrast [to the Johannine titular function of the phrase "Son of Man"], the bulk of the "son of Man" instances in the Synoptics can best be interpreted in a nontitular sense. They may be categorized as Aramaic circumlocutions in which the speaker, always Jesus in the Synoptics, wishing to avoid a direct reference to himself, replaces "I" by the equivocal and more modest "son of Man." Occasionally the context and/or the Synoptic parallels make absolutely plain that by "son of Man" the speaker is meant [e.g., Mark 2:10; Matt 16:13 and Mark 8:27].[652]

He does recognize, however, the allusion to the titular sense of "Son of Man" in the Synoptics, though he sees this as an exegetical construct:

> In the Synoptics, there are only two instances of "son of Man" which explicitly allude to Daniel 7:13. The first, "They will see the son of Man coming in the clouds with great power and glory" (Mark 13:26; Matt. 24:30; Luke 21:27), is introductory to the scene of eschatological judgment, and the second, "You will see the son of Man seated at the right hand of Power, and coming with the clouds of heaven" (Mark 14:62; Matt. 26:64; Luke 22:69), represents Jesus' answer to the high priest's question whether he was the Messiah. In short, the Synoptic "son of Man" combined with Daniel 7:13 coalesces into an exegetical construct, often called early church *midrash*, and qua title it has a definite messianic and eschatological significance.[653]

From Vermès's perspective, a nontitular usage of the phrase "son of Man" is normative in the Synoptics. The above is but a scant précis of the philological assessment provided in his seminal work *Jesus the Jew*. Summing up his lengthy treatment of this complex issue, Vermès, in *Jesus the Jew*, advances a provocative conclusion:

> To sum up, there is no evidence whatever, either inside or outside the Gospels, to imply, let alone demonstrate, that "the *son of man*" was used as a title. There is, in addition, no valid argument to prove that any of the Gospels passages directly or indirectly referring to Daniel 7:13 may be traced back to Jesus. The only possible, indeed probable, genuine utterances are sayings independent of Daniel 7 in which, in accordance with Aramaic usage, the speaker refers to himself as the *son of man* out of awe, reserve or humility. It is this neutral speech-form that the apocalyptically-minded Galilean disciples of Jesus appear to have "eschatologized" by means of a midrash based on Daniel 7:13.[654]

Vermès next focuses his gaze upon "the genuine titles capable of shedding light on how Jesus was perceived by his Galilean and Judaean country men. The foremost of these are Messiah or Christ, son of God, Lord and Prophet."[655] Vermès prefaces his remarks with a warning to his reader: "Their [the forthcoming titles'] significance has developed during two millennia of Christianity. Our task is to determine, not how they are understood today, but what they meant to Jews in the first century A.D."[656]

The Messiah or Christ

Vermès, beginning with an examination of Messianism in Jewish sources outside the Old Testament, explains:

- In its basic meaning, the Hebrew/Aramaic *Mashiah* [*māšîaḥ*]/*Meshiha* and the Greek *Christos* indicate someone anointed with oil. In the Hebrew Bible the rite of anointing occurs in ceremonies appointing an Israelite king like Saul (1 Sam. 10:1), a prophet like Elisha (1 Kings 19:16), or priests, for example, Aaron and his sons (Exod. 28:41). "The Anointed of the LORD," generally a royal title, is regularly given to David and his descendant.
- In traditional parlance and expectation the phrase "the Anointed King" acquired, after the dethronement of the Davidic rulers by the Babylonian emperor Nebuchadnezzar in 586 B.C., the specific sense of *the* Messiah, the final Jewish monarch who would defeat all the foreign nations, subject them to Israel and his God, and thus inaugurate the Kingdom of heaven.
- Such a savior figure was anxiously awaited in the intertestamental age, especially during periods of political agitation against the dominating foreign power, the Greeks in the Maccabaean period, and the Romans after the conquest of Palestine by Pompey in 63 B.C., and even more so in the course of the years leading up to the two wars of the Jews against Rome in the first and second centuries A.D.
- As to what kind of deliverer they hoped [for], consult their prayers, e.g., *Psalms of Solomon* (17 and 18), as well as most of the messianic texts among the Dead Sea Scrolls of a similar date, and the Eighteen Benedictions attributed to first century A.D. All convey a colorful picture of the hoped-for royal Messiah.
- Behind the central character of the eschatological anointed king, future conqueror of earthly empires and guardian of truth and justice in the Kingdom of God, stand in a less-prominent position other figures produced by theological speculation in the priestly and mystical circles of intertestamental Judaism. With the rise of the Maccabaean-Hasmonean priestly family to the leadership of the Jewish nation in 152 B.C., moves toward the institution of priestly Messianism began.
- The notion of the priestly anointed is firmly testified to in the Dead Sea community, which was awaiting a Messiah of Aaron and a kingly Messiah of Israel, a Priest and the Prince of the Congregation, or a priestly Interpreter of the Law and the Branch of David.[657]

Vermès concludes his summary presentation by observing the presence of further messianic concepts in Jewish literature that are of little value to a study of Synoptics.

Turning his attention to the Synoptics and the title "Messiah," he writes: "Of the two main usages of the title 'Messiah,' the eschatological high priestly function is plainly not applicable to the Jesus of the Synoptics: he was not a hereditary Jewish priest. Not even the heavenly Pontiff of the Epistle to the Hebrews has any proper messianic connotation. This leaves us with the image of the royal figure, the traditional anointed king of Israel."[658]

Exploring this latter, dominant image, Vermès observes:

- Clearly at some later stage clumsy attempts were made, especially by Matthew in his "infancy" story, to create a Davidic pedigree for Jesus, but main Synoptic tradition includes no support for it apart from the shout "Hosanna to the son of David" at Jesus' entry to Jerusalem (Matt. 21:9; Mark 11:9–10; Luke 19:38), and the occasional call of "Son of David," addressed to him by strangers.
- However, none of the latter appears in a context which has "political" connotations; they are all linked to stories of healing by the "son of David," that is to say, the miracle-worker of the messianic age (Matt. 9:27; 12:23; 15:22; 20:30–31; Mark 10:47–48; Luke 18:38–39).
- Peter's response, "You are the Christ" (Mark 8:29; Matt. 16:16; Luke 9:20) to Jesus' question, "Who do you [my disciples] say that I am?" is far from a political manifesto.
- Matthew's more detailed parallel, "You are the Christ, *the son of the living God*," seems to confirm [that] the Synoptic Gospels have not royal Messianism in mind; neither is such a suggestion implicit in the Acts of the Apostles, when Jesus is simultaneously proclaimed "Lord and Christ" (Acts 2:36).[659]

Vermès advances a frank conclusion: "Contrary to the claim of some contemporary New Testament interpreters, the general context of the portrait of Jesus in the Synoptics and in the rest of the New Testament shows that he was not a pretender to the throne of David, or a would-be leader of a revolt against Rome."

What then is one to make of the epithet "king of the Jews," attached to Jesus and his cross? Vermès responds:

> The accusation that Jesus sought to become king of the Jews or royal Messiah first surfaces in the Gospels on the day of his crucifixion, or more precisely at the moment of the transfer of the case from Jewish to Roman jurisdiction. Thereafter Pilate is always cited as referring to Jesus as the king of the Jews. The Roman charge or *titulus*, written on the cross, also read "The King of the Jews" (Mark 15:26; Matt. 27:37). The explicit indictment of disloyalty to the emperor is probably Luke's creation: "We found this man perverting our nation, and forbidding us to give tribute to Caesar, and saying that he himself is Christ the king" (Luke 23:2). . . . In fact, when under pressure from Pilate to substantiate their accusation, even in Luke's version the chief priests become rather vague: "He stirs up the people, teaching throughout all Judaea, from Galilee even to this place" (Luke 23:5). All in all, the whole political charge sounds hollow.[660]

Vermès next inquires as to how Jesus viewed himself in this regard "or, to formulate the question more accurately, how do the Synoptic Gospels describe his reaction when he is called Messiah or is questioned about his messianic status?"[661] He reports:

- Jesus' response to being publicly proclaimed the Messiah oscillated between the unenthusiastic and the negative.
- Demon-possessed people, we are given to believe, and Satan himself in the legend of the Temptation (Matt. 4:3; Luke 4:3), were regularly silenced by Jesus when they called him the Messiah or Son of God (Luke 4:41; Mark 1:34).
- More significantly, Peter's confession at Caesarea Philippi that Jesus was the Christ was also met, in what seems to be the original version of the story, with a strict order to keep silent (Mark 8:30; Matt. 16:20; Luke 9:21).
- Though this prohibition is not tantamount to a denial of messiahship, its ensuing reference to the future suffering and death of Jesus was a tacit rejection of his role as the triumphant Christ, the only kind of Messiah ordinary Jews were expecting, provoking a reprimand from Jesus, "Get behind me, Satan!" (Mark 8:33; Matt. 16:23).
- This latter exclamation juxtaposed with Jesus' previous praise of Peter, "Blessed are you, Simon Bar-Jona! . . ." (Matt. 16:17–18), yields irreconcilable statements. However, it would seem, given the circumstances, [that] it is more likely that the praise of Peter in Matthew represents a later attempt to alleviate the shocking impact of Jesus' unwillingness to confirm that he was the Messiah.
- As to the inquiries of the Jewish high priest and the Roman prefect regarding Jesus' messiahship, with one exception the answer quoted is at best equivocal and more often seems to be negative (Matt. 26:64; 27:11; Luke 22:70–23:3; Mark 15:2).
- The weight of probability found in the above citations favors an oblique denial: "So you have said so" followed by a tacit "not I."
- As to the one exception to Jesus' evasiveness, according to Mark in response to the high priest's inquiry about his messianic status, Jesus replies simply, "I am" (Mark 14:62). This is an unparalleled case, which may be explained as a deliberate editorial attempt to eliminate equivocation.[662]

Coupled with the above observations lending credence to the first datum, Vermès emphasizes:

> The fate of Jesus before the Roman authorities . . . demonstrates the risk that anyone rumored to be a political Christ incurred in the powder keg of Palestine in the first century A.D. If Jesus had had political ambitions, if he had as it were run for the office of Messiah and had encouraged his partisans to proclaim it to all and sundry, it is most unlikely that the Romans would have allowed his public career to last even the one year envisaged by the Synoptic Gospels.[663]

The above constitutes the essential points of Vermès's analysis. All of it coincides with Vermès's initial conclusion in *Jesus the Jew*:

> In fact, since the figure of the Messiah appears not to have been central to the teaching of Jesus, and since no record has survived of any hostile challenge concerning his Messianic status before his days in Jerusalem; since, moreover, he deliberately withheld his approval of Peter's confession and, in general, failed to declare himself to be the Christ, there is every reason to wonder if he really though of himself as such.[664]

There is yet another possibility, to which Vermès gives voice:

> Apart from such radicals as Bultmann, who denies that the Synoptic Gospels
> saw in Jesus the "promised Messiah," the large majority of New Testament scholars,
> including a number of non-Christians—this is not a denominational issue—champion
> the view that Jesus had a "messianic consciousness," but since his notion of "the Christ"
> differed from the popular one, he chose not to touch on the question.[665]

The Title "Son of God"

In *Jesus the Jew*, Vermès succinctly captures the dilemma confronting the scholar or curious vis-à-vis the title "son of God": "Within Christianity and without, accepted as an article of faith or rejected, the assumption is that when the evangelists apply this term to Jesus, they are acknowledging him as equal to God."[666] Unraveling this exegetical, historical, and chronological construct to discern its original meaning, what it meant to Jews in first century CE, is Vermès's challenge. We will follow his cogent assessment in *Jesus the Jew*.

Scrutinizing pertinent intertestamental literature to decipher the meaning of the notion "son of God," Vermès confirms:

> All in all, it would appear that a first-century AD Palestinian Jew, hearing the phrase *son of God*, would have thought first of all of an angelic or celestial being; and secondly, when the human connection is clear, of a just and saintly man. The divine sonship of the Messiah was expected to be within a royal context. In a Hellenistic milieu—and there alone—the epithet would allegedly have called to mind a miracle-worker.[667]

Of this last assertion, he writes: "Although the passages employing *son of God* in the sense of miracle-worker form the numerically largest group in the Synoptic material, and must consequently have played a significant part in the development of the Christian tradition, they—or at least the confessions by Satan and the Roman centurion—are considered to be of recent, i.e., Jewish-or Gentile-Hellenistic, origin."[668]

Admittedly, this would seem to argue against the possibility of enlisting the support of this epithet by Vermès in his quest to affirm his Hasidic typology vis-à-vis Jesus. As Vermès notes: "In short, average academic opinion of today would hold that the Messianic application of the son of God title was the original one in Judeo-Christianity; its association with a miracle-worker is secondary, and was possibly due to the impact of a parallel but wholly separate linguistic usage current in Hellenistic circles."[669]

However, he counters: "The only trouble with this well-articulated argument is that it is put together without the benefit of the evidence of a group of Jewish texts, not merely pertinent, but essential, to the correct approach to the issue, texts in which are incorporated demonic confessions, exorcism, the heavenly Voice and the designation 'my son.'"[670]

Focusing his gaze upon this supplementary evidence, especially rabbinic literature, Vermès affirms: "As had been said in regard to Jewish charismatics, it was a firmly held rabbinic conviction that saints and teachers were commended in public by a heavenly Voice. Furthermore, when such a commendation is directly accredited to God, the person in whose favour it is made is alluded to as 'my son.'"[671]

Offering several examples of this acclamation in the stories pertaining to Hanina ben Dosa, Vermès substantiates his thesis. He recalls the story of Agrat (Agrath) the demonic queen meeting Hanina (*b. Pesaḥim* 112b)[672] and the heavenly Voice parallel therein, Vermès affirms: "Taken together, the various elements of the Hanina tale coalesce to form a picture closely resembling that included in the Gospels. Like Jesus, he is commended by the heavenly Voice and proclaimed *son of God*. And as in the case of Jesus, this commendation is heard by the demons who, in consequence, know, fear and obey him."[673]

Affirming the viability of the phrase, *son of God*, vis-à-vis the charismatic Hasidic typology, Vermès concludes:

> Thus, if the Hanina parallel is given the attention it deserves, it may be argued that the greatest, and no doubt earliest, part of the Synoptic evidence concerning the divine sonship of Jesus corresponds exactly to the image of the Galilean miracle-working Hasid. The Hellenistic *son of God*/"divine man" then appears not as an original element in the Gospel tradition, but as one superimposed on a solidly established Palestinian Jewish belief and terminology. There is, in other words, no reason to contest the possibility, and even the great probability, that already during his life Jesus was spoken of and addressed by admiring believers as *son of God*.[674]

Given the above, asking if Jesus considered himself to be a *son of God*, Vermès answers in the affirmative:

> Jesus' recognition of himself as son of God, and his encouragement to others to develop the same self-awareness in their position vis-à-vis God, entailed putting into effect Judaism's foremost principle: the *imitatio Dei*. As Targum and Midrash insist, those who strive for holiness must "walk in God's ways." "As he is merciful and gracious, you must also be merciful and gracious" (*Mekilta on Exod.* 15.2). "As the Holy One is called righteous, . . . so you also must be righteous; as the Holy One is called *Hasid*, you must also be *hasid*" (*Sifre on Deut.* 49). "My people, children of Israel, as your Father is merciful in Heaven, so must you also be merciful on earth" (*Targum Ps.-Jonathan* on Lev. 22:28). Jesus' instruction is the same: "Be merciful, even as your Father is merciful." "You, therefore, must be perfect, as your heavenly Father is perfect" (Luke 6:36; Matt. 5:48). But also, in his care and love for sinners and outcasts, Jesus displays another aspect of the *imitatio*: imitating the Father, he takes up the role of the father himself towards those who need his comfort and help and expects his disciples to do the same.[675]

Finally, drawing a parallel to an anecdote of Honi as "son of the house," conveying the holy man's intimacy with God, Vermès confirms—as does Flusser—that "a special filial consciousness is manifest in the frequent and emphatic mention of God as his Father, an awareness firmly reflected in the New Testament usage."[676] Further evidence of this filial consciousness may be deduced from Jesus' use of the phrase "Abba" when addressing God the Father.[677]

Vermès concludes his analysis by asserting: "If the reasoning followed in these pages is correct, the earliest use of *son of God* in relation to Jesus derives from his activities as a miracle-worker and exorcist, and from his consciousness of an immediate and intimate contact with the heavenly Father."[678]

The Title "Lord"

Vermès's philological study of the term "Lord" demonstrates the validity of his insistent view that Jewish intertestamental sources are essential and not merely pertinent to the study of the New Testament and Jesus. Vermès's investigation challenges the view that "this title says nothing about the historical Jesus, or even about Palestinian Christianity's understanding of Jesus."[679] This was the dominant view due to the influence of two German scholars, as Vermès affirms: "It is widely held, under the influence of the renowned German scholars Wilhelm Bousset and Rudolf Bultmann, that the New Testament use of 'Lord' originated with the Gentile church, in imitation of the terminology of the mystery cults (the worship of Osiris or Hermes) and of the imperial cult of Rome where the emperor was addressed as 'Lord' (*Kyrios*) or 'our Lord and God' (*Dominus et Deus noster*)."[680]

Vermès determines to correct this "oddity," providing for his readers a discussion of "this title in light of its Semitic and Greek linguistic background."[681] Pointing out that "Hebrew/Aramaic- and Greek-speaking Jews of the intertestamental age were both familiar with the term 'lord' (*'ādôn, mar*[e], or *kyrios*) in various senses, but the precise nuance of the word entirely depends on the context in which it appears,"[682] Vermès provides an outline of the linguistic phenomena to assist the novice:

- In the human context, the title "lord" in the sense of "Master" or "Sir" is regularly used in all the Jewish languages (Hebrew/Aramaic and Greek) of the intertestamental period, as well as in later rabbinic literature.
- In the nonreligious field it denotes persons in authority.
- Moving to the top position in the secular field, we find the king invoked as "Lord."
- In the religious field, the Aramaic *mar/mari* in the sense of "master" regularly refers to a teacher, as do the Hebrew titles *rab* and *rabbi*, as well as *rabbun/rabbuni*.
- However, since among both the Palestinian and the Mesopotamian Jews teachers wielded administrative power, the Patriarch or "chief rabbi" in Galilee was called "Rabban" and the Exilarch, the corresponding dignitary in the Babylonian Jewish community, *Mar*.
- A similar terminology was in use in the Syriac church with bishops, priests, and saints being designated as *Mar*.
- At the summit of the religious ranking, but still in the human sphere, "lord/*mar*" is addressed to the prophet Elijah by a saintly rabbi (*Gen. Rabbah* 94:9) and also to the Messiah (*b. Sanhedrin* 98a).
- Finally, it is well known that in direct continuity from 200 B.C. to A.D. 300 Jews used the title "Lord" in speaking of, or to, God in Hebrew, Aramaic, and Greek.[683]

Affirming that the constant use of "lord" in its various meanings as a deep-seated Jewish linguistic custom that can be traced unchanged over five centuries,[684] Vermès refutes the thesis that "the title 'Lord' entered the Gospels as a loan from Hellenism via Gentile Christianity with no Palestinian Semitic antecedents."[685]

Vermès asserts that "set against its linguistic backcloth, the Synoptic use of 'lord' stands out distinctly."[686] A précis of his historical-philological analysis follows:

- Negatively, there is not a single instance in Mark, Matthew, or Luke in which Jesus as "Lord" is associated with anything to do with divinity. Only in John, and even there only once, are two concepts formally linked by Thomas's invocation of Jesus as "My Lord and my God!" (John 20:28).
- It is therefore beyond doubt that this reverential title, in addition to being applicable to God, possesses a variety of other meanings so that its precise significance cannot be determined without a context any more than, for instance, that of the English "Sir," the title of a schoolmaster in a school, and the form of address of a king in a royal palace.
- It is very important to recognize that the Synoptics never link "lord" to the messianic function of Jesus. The nearest we come to it is in the [Synoptic] interpretation of Psalm 110:1 (Mark 12:35–37; Matt. 22:41–46; Luke 20:41– 44). A passage is presented as an (probably spurious) exegetical debate with the Pharisees, having no direct link to Jesus himself.[687]

Examining the title "Lord" in its various contexts, Vermès confirms that "the largest group of the Synoptics' examples using the invocation 'Lord' comprises miracle stories."[688] Citing several examples of this, Vermès affirms that "after its use in the context of the miraculous, the title 'Lord' most frequently appears as an equivalent of 'Teacher.'"[689] In both contexts, its usage is consistent with Vermès's linguistic backdrop.

Vermès concludes his philological survey of the title "Lord," both affirming his thesis and also imposing a corrective:

> The New Testament career of "lord" reflects the various uses of the term listed in the survey of Aramaic terminology. That it was widely employed will from now on be difficult to contest, for the objections raised against its applicability to the historical Jesus have been shown [to be] specious. The title primarily links Jesus to his dual role of charismatic Hasid and teacher, and if the stress is greater in the earlier strata of the tradition, this is no doubt due to the fact that his impact as a holy man preceded that of teacher and founder of a religious community.[690]

Thus "Lord" is a title, given Vermès's investigation, that Jesus would have well received.

The Title "Prophet"

Typically Vermès prefaces his comments with an explanation of the term in question and a concise overview of the title as conveyed in essential Jewish literature. In this regard, however, Vermès prefaces his comments by citing a bias among New Testament scholars, presumably Christian. From his perspective, some scholars focus their attention upon Jesus as the *final* prophet to his detriment as *a* prophet and then take for granted or explicitly argue "that the role of the prophet, pure and simple is irrelevant in view of his greater function."[691] Their narrow focus upon the prophetic figure "is symptomatic of the difficulty experienced by many a scholar who has to handle the historical evidence on which his religious faith is claimed to rest."[692]

The result, unintentional though it may be, limits one's appreciation of the two kinds of prophetic mission attributed to Jesus in the New Testament: The one represents the Elijah-like wonder-working prophet. The other, *the* Prophet, is conveyed in Jewish expectation of a Moses-like, eschatological prophet as it developed in the Acts of the Apostles and John's Gospel. To remedy this imbalance, both kinds of prophetic mission, Vermès assures the reader, "will be observed equally in the present study."[693]

Returning to his familiar format, Vermès continues. The biblical title "prophet" is not to be confused with the common English idiom "prophet," meaning one who fore-tells the future, as Vermès explains:

> In the biblical language and the Judaeo-Christian terminology of the age of Jesus, the term can relate to a wonder-working prophet like Elijah or Elisha in the Old Testament Books of Kings, or to an inspired messenger of God and revealer of secrets, such as Isaiah, Jeremiah, or the other prophets who left books behind them.
>
> The leading varieties of the prophetic-figure in first-century Palestine, the prophet-teacher, the prophet-eschatologist who announces the events of the final age, and the prophet-thaumaturge, or miracle worker, are familiar representations of Jesus to be found in the Synoptic Gospels. To these we should add a further category, the so-called escha-tological sign prophet who heralds, in a context of miracles, the impending political liberation of the Jewish people. Such sign prophets are well attested in the work of the first-century Jewish historian Flavius Josephus.[694]

Vermès prefaces his survey of the prophetic figure in Jewish literature, citing a dis-crepancy in the chronology of the prophet tradition: "rabbinic tradition suggests that with the death of the prophet Malachi came the cessation of prophecy, replaced by the *bat qôl*—the heavenly daughter of a voice." He asserts that, "nevertheless, intertesta-mental literature, the Dead Sea Scrolls, Josephus in a roundabout way, and the New Testament all seem tacitly to contradict this view."[695] Acknowledging the continued presence of prophecy in the intertestamental age, Vermès observes:

- Biblical prophets, i.e., those communicators between God and the Jewish people may be grouped into two categories: (1) primarily preachers and poets; and (2) primarily doers.
- The political, religious and eschatological message of the former was recorded in the prophetic books of the Bible.
- The historical compositions of the Old Testament, especially Samuel and Kings, testify to the deeds, often miraculous deeds, of the wonder-working prophets, the latter of the two groups mentioned, among whom Elijah and Elisha were the most famous.
- The Bible credits Elijah and Elisha with stopping and starting the rain, making polluted water drinkable, curing the sick, and reviving the dead.

- It is the miraculous aspect of prophecy that is relevant to the Jesus picture in the Synoptic Gospels as well as to popular Palestinian Judaism.
- The continuing speculation surrounding the figure of Elijah, the prophet who having escaped death was believed to have gone to heaven in a chariot of fire, played an important part in the thinking of the evangelists.
- Building on the prediction of the prophet Malachi that Elijah would return (Mal. 4:5), a tradition evolved in which this Elijah was identified as the forerunner of the Messiah who would be sent to prepare the day of the Lord.
- In addition to Elijah, the Jews of the time of Jesus expected another prophet, promised by Moses in Deuteronomy 18:15–18. He, like Moses himself, would be the transmitter of the final message of God.
- This messenger, *the* Prophet, the ultimate mouthpiece of God or messianic Prophet, is identified with Jesus in the Acts of the Apostles and the Fourth Gospel.
- Finally, mention should be made a hybrid prophetic figure—though not pertinent to this inquiry, if it is true that Jesus had no political aspirations—combining the prophet and the political messiah.[696]

Tracing the Elijah typology in the Synoptic memory, Vermès observes: "An unbiased reading of the synoptic evidence reveals that sympathetic witnesses of his Galilean activity recognized Jesus as either John the Baptist, Elijah, or a prophet, a view apparently shared by the entourage of Herod Antipas, with the possible hint at the notion of a prophet *redivivus*. The crowd, on his entry into Jerusalem, also refers to him as 'the prophet Jesus, from Nazareth in Galilee.'"[697]

Yet, it is a view not readily endorsed by others, as Vermès notes:

> The common assumption held by New Testament interpreters appears to be that the prophetic image of Jesus was conceived by friendly outsiders, but that not being good enough, not sufficiently suitable within the circle of his close companions, it was replaced with a more fitting title. That this was not, in fact, the case is shown by the obituary attributed to one of the Emmaus disciples two days after Jesus' death. He was, Cleopas says, "a prophet mighty in deed and word before God and all the people" [Luke 24:19].[698]

Vermès, though concurring with the view that friends and associates perceived Jesus as an Elijah-like prophet, admits:

> In its turn, the Elijah imagery played a central role in the thought of the Synoptists, but the New Testament writers primarily associated Elijah with John the Baptist. . . . A direct connection existed between Jesus and Elijah, the Elijah who was expected to return or the Elijah *redivivus*. This view was not generally embraced by the primitive Christian church, but was one of three opinions held by Jesus' contemporaries, the other two being that Jesus was the reincarnation of some other prophet of the Old Testament, or of John the Baptist (Mark 8:28; Matt. 16:14; Luke 9:19). . . . Fringe opinions though these may have been, they were typical of the mentality of a society which instinctively placed Jesus within the framework of the prophetic tradition.[699]

More important, Jesus apparently saw himself as an Elijah-like prophet, as Vermès observes:

At this point we may venture one step further and note that according to the evangelists Jesus perceived himself explicitly as a miracle-working prophet. The famous Nazareth episode is profoundly revealing: "A prophet is not without honour except in his own country, and among his kin, and in his own house" (Mark 6:4; Matt. 13:57; Luke 4:24). The context of the story makes it plain that Jesus' disillusioned declaration was sparked off by the dislike of the locals for his charismatic teaching and *"mighty works"* (Mark 6:2; Matt. 13:54). Conversely, since the people of his home town had no faith in him, the spiritually paralyzed Jesus was incapable of curing and exorcizing among them.[700]

Given that "the Galilean Jesus and others saw a link between his charismatic deeds and those of Elijah and Elisha, the two foremost wonder-workers active in the northern kingdom of Israel (Luke 4:24–27),"[701] Vermès explores Jesus' Elijah-like self-awareness and the concept of the charismatic Hasid. Citing parallel examples of Hanina ben Dosa and his resemblance to Elijah, he concludes: "In short, it appears to be almost beyond argument that the miracle-working Hasid [Hanina] either modeled himself on Elijah, or was at least seen as another Elijah by men of his generation."[702] Furthermore, as Vermès observes, "it is important to stress that the connection was with the real historical character of the biblical past and not with the Elijah who was to return in the age of the Messiah, which would imply that Hasidic imagery existed—or at least could have existed—without being tied to eschatological speculation of one kind or another."[703]

All this, when juxtaposed with the Synoptic Jesus, leads Vermès to declare:

> Placing the parallel New Testament problem within the framework of charismatic Judaism, it may in consequence be justly held that for references to Jesus as a prophet or Elijah to be meaningful, it is not necessary to fall back on the eschatological concepts of a final mediator or revelation or of a forerunner of the Messiah.
>
> In fact, the belief professed by his contemporaries that Jesus was a charismatic prophet rings so authentic, especially in the light of the Honi-Hanina cycle of traditions, that the correct historical question is not whether such an undogmatic Galilean concept was ever in vogue, but rather how, and under what influence, it was ever given an eschatological twist.[704]

Although a description of himself as a prophet seems to have been acceptable, or even preferred, by Jesus, Vermès is aware that it, the Elijah-like wonder-working man of deeds, is not the dominant New Testament appellation. From his readings of the sources, the explanation for this is due to two elements: (1) There was a rise in pseudo-prophets, meaning self-proclaimed prophets, in 50–70 CE in Palestine. These false prophets deceived the vulnerable, provoking sarcasm and antipathy and eliciting distinctly pejorative overtones in the idiom of Pharisees and Sadducees vis-à-vis the title "prophet." (2) There was a lack of dogmatic adequacy in the Gospels, given the reaction to pseudo-prophets during the period of evangelists and Christian redactors.[705] Nonetheless, it is a title, as Vermès argues, that Jesus himself would have embraced.

Jesus the Celibate

Before concluding his discussion of the title "prophet," Vermès grapples with the apparent celibacy of Jesus, given the "complete silence in the Gospels concerning the marital status of Jesus."[706] The lack of commentary and the presumed celibacy is enigmatic, given both the cultural expectation and the studied tradition. While Vermès recognizes that the Hebrew Bible "prescribes temporary sexual abstinence in certain circumstances, [it] never orders a life of total celibacy."[707] Vermès is aware of the Essenian practice of celibacy and relates this ritual purity vis-à-vis cultic worship—but not misogyny, as Philo and Josephus indicate. He argues that it is "an unlikely source of influence."[708]

Vermès, however, does discern "traditions surviving in rabbinic literature which imply an incompatibility between prophecy and marriage."[709] This leads Vermès to speculate: "Against such a background of first-century AD Jewish opinion, namely, that the prophetic destiny entailed amongst other things a life of continence, Jesus' apparent voluntary embrace of celibacy, at any rate from the time of his reception of the holy spirit, becomes historically meaningful."[710]

We conclude this section, having observed Vermès's adroit use of the "checking mechanism" that secures Jesus more firmly within the charismatic Hasidic tradition. From Vermès's study, the phrase "son of Man" is nontitular in its Hebrew/Aramaic usage. Though Vermès finds this nontitular usage normative in the Synoptics, he accepts that in many parts of the Greek New Testament the phrase conveys a titular meaning.[711] As to the title "Messiah," Vermès, exercising prudential caution—unlike Flusser, who believes Jesus believed that he was the Messiah—finds the evidence ambiguous and inconclusive. Explicitly Jesus avoids the title. Others, such as Peter and the hopeful crowds, saw Jesus as the Messiah, but whether he thought of himself as Messiah remains veiled. As to the remaining titles—"prophet," "lord," and "son of God"—the designation "Hasid" is all the more persuasive, given Vermès's analysis.

Jesus, the Galilean and Charismatic Wonder-Worker

Continuing his investigation of Jesus as a Galilean holy man in the framework of contemporaneous popular, charismatic Judaism, Vermès explores the Hasidic parallels that ultimately confirm his hypothesis. In *The Changing Faces of Jesus*, Vermès recalls for the reader the goal of this juxtaposition and the characters representative therein:

> All these biblical and post-biblical antecedents are highly illuminating in the attempt to understand the real Jesus. They would however, remain somewhat theoretical without the support of more or less contemporary figures with whom Jesus can be compared. The two leading characters, one of them from the first century B.C. and the other from the first century A.D., are known from rabbinic literature, but the story of the earlier is also recorded in Josephus. Studying them will enable us to see traits common to charismatics and the distinguishing marks which give Jesus his characteristic individuality. First we shall review the stories relating to Honi the Circle-Drawer and his two grandsons, and

to Hanina ben Dosa, and then follow this up with a survey of the assessment of these holy men contained in Josephus and in rabbinic literature.[712]

To demonstrate his analysis, it will suffice for us to review succinctly his juxtaposition of Honi the Circle Drawer and Hanina ben Dosa with Jesus of Nazareth.

First, however, it may be helpful to sketch Vermès's portrait of the ancient Hasidim. Their attributes follow:

- In addition to their proverbial humility and unworldliness, poverty was one of their hallmarks.
- They lived frugally and scarcely had enough to eat.
- The Hasidim lived in a state of total detachment from earthly possessions and were ready to share with others the little they had.
- They professed the philosophy, "What is mine is yours, and what is yours is yours" (*m. 'Abot* 5:10).
- They rated piety higher than mere ritual.
- One of them, Rabbi Pinhas ben Yair, extolled sexual abstinence among the Hasidic virtues.
- Above all, the Hasid was famous for his prayer, which was believed to be all-powerful, capable of performing miracles, and revealing his closeness to God, the heavenly Father.[713]

Vermès observes "that many of these traits reflect the Synoptic portrait of Jesus, in particular the absence of anxiety for daily needs, the divesting oneself of riches, even the lack of a home where he could lay his head and the conviction that faith can perform miracles."[714]

Honi the Circle-Drawer

Honi the Circle-Drawer, a first-century-BCE Palestinian wonder-worker, is paradigmatic of the ancient Hasidim that captured Vermès's attention. Vermès emphasizes:

> To understand the figure of Honi [and other Hasidim,] it is necessary to remember that from the time of Elijah, Jews believed that holy men were able to exert their will on natural phenomena. Thus, in addition to offering formal, liturgical prayers for rain, in times of drought people urged persons reputed to be miracle-workers to exercise their infallible intervention on behalf of the community. Such a request for relief from misery is reported to have been addressed to Honi some time before the fall of Jerusalem to Pompey in 63 BC.[715]

Of Honi and Hanina ben Dosa, Vermès writes:

> Of the two, Honi was chronologically the first to appear on the scene. Despite the magical overtones of the title "the Circle-Drawer" which he bears in the Mishnah and the Talmud, he was venerated as a holy Hasid so close to God that his prayer exhibited miraculous efficacy. Therefore people in need came to solicit his help, especially in periods of drought when it was feared that all the crops might fail and a disastrous famine threatened.[716]

Vermès considers an example of Honi's charismatic prowess as a rainmaker, reported in an anecdote from the Mishnah wherein he is depicted "as a spoiled child secure in his knowledge that he can obtain whatever he asks from his heavenly Father."[717] He observes:

> Irony apart, we have here a story that recalls the prophet Elijah starting and stopping rain on Mount Carmel. The Mishnah tells us nothing about Honi as a person, when he lived or where he came from, although we can deduce that the event related above took place around Passover and that the venue was Jerusalem, where in the days of the Temple every pious Jew was duty bound to be at the approach of the festival. Fortunately the historian Josephus comes to our rescue; alluding in passing to the rainmaking episode, he firmly sets our hero in a historical context. Josephus is neither disparaging nor starry-eyed, but respectfully tells his story.[718]

Comparing the similar yet distinct stories, that of the Mishnah and Josephus, Vermès deduces:

> If the pieces of information supplied by the Mishnah and Josephus are combined, we have a man renowned for a rain miracle or for the infallible efficacy of his prayer, of whom the party of Hyrcanus tried to make use in their efforts to defeat Aristobulus. Onias [Honi], however, was unwilling to play their game, and when forced to speak to God he refused to take sides and paid with his life for his courageous act.[719]

Though Josephus says nothing further about Onias, "in rabbinic literature he is presented as if he were the founder of a dynasty of wonder-workers."[720]

Honi the Circle Drawer and Jesus, Elijah-like prophets, share obvious similarities, as shown from Vermès's perusal of the texts: both evidence an intimacy with the Father as favored son—though in Honi's case, a spoiled child; both are perceived by the people as holy men readily accessible; both are known for the efficacy of their prayer; both are wonder-workers, "men of deeds"; both are sought out or caught as "pawns" between powerful politico-religious forces; both die as a consequence of their stance vis-à-vis the established authority. Though this comparison is noteworthy, the similarities between Jesus and Hanina ben Dosa, observed by Vermès, are even more pronounced.

Hanina ben Dosa

Hanina ben Dosa, Jesus' younger contemporary wonder-worker, reportedly "lived in Araba [Garaba/Gabara], a Galilean city in the district of Sepphoris."[721] Vermès, citing supporting evidence to secure Hanina's presence in the first century CE, writes:

> That Hanina lived in the first century AD may be deduced indirectly but convincingly from the fact that the Talmudic sources associate him with three historical figures who definitely belonged to that period: Nehuniah, a Temple official, Rabban Gamaliel and Yohanan ben Zakkai. If, as is likely, the Gamaliel in question is Gamaliel the Elder, a man claimed by the Apostle Paul to have been his master, and not Gamaliel II, the former's grandson, Hanina's activity would appear to have fallen in the period preceding the year of AD 70. In support of this view, it should be underlined that he is nowhere connected with any event occurring after the destruction of Jerusalem.[722]

The following portrait of *Hanina ben Dosa* emerges under Vermès practiced eye:

> Hanina ben Dosa was a first-century Galilean, probably a younger contemporary of Jesus, from the town of Araba or Gabara [or Garaba], about a dozen miles north of Nazareth. Rabbinic sources represent him as a pre-A.D. 70 personality associated with Yohanan ben Zakkai, who is located in the same place before the first Jewish war (A.D. 66–70). The earliest layers of rabbinic tradition depict him not only as a holy man who, like Honi and his grandchildren, could miraculously bring rain and stop it again, but [also] as a person of outstanding devotion who was a famous healer and a master over the demonic powers. He was, in short, rabbinic Judaism's most prominent wonder-worker whose death marked the end of the era of the "men of deeds" (*m. Sotah* 9:15), but he is also remembered as the author of a small number of moral teachings.[723]

Of his public activity, Vermès reports:

> Hanina's fame was primarily based on his charismatic healings, which at the request of the family of the sick person he was able to perform even from a distance. His prayer was seen not simply as an intercession to God, but as directly efficient. In fact he was aware in advance of the efficacy of his words: "If my prayer is fluent in my mouth," he is quoted as saying, "I know that he [the sick man] is favoured" (*m. Berakhot* 5:1).[724]

To further support his hypothesis, Vermès cites several rabbinic stories describing Hanina's charismatic ministry, of which we shall observe, for expedience, but three instances that correspond to Jesus' ministry: healing from a distance, miraculous trans-formation, and influence over forces of evil.

As to the first instance, Vermès writes:

> His two most renowned healings are associated, genuinely or typologically, with the leading Pharisee masters of the first century A.D.: Gamaliel, probably the one mentioned in the Acts of the Apostles (5:34) and claimed by St. Paul as his Jewish teacher, and Yohanan ben Zakkai, allegedly Hanina's own master and leader of the Jews after the fall of Jerusalem. He was much sought after in high places. In the Yohanan story all the actors are located in the town of Araba, but in the case of Gamaliel, the head of the Pharisee confraternity is in Jerusalem and the humble charismatic resides in remote Galilee. Both accounts derive from early traditions from the first or second century A.D., incorporated into the Talmud. The second of these healings . . . is reminiscent of Jesus healing the servant of the centurion from Capernaum.[725]

In both cases, Hanina's prayer was efficacious. As to the second instance, Vermès records three smaller stories, the latter two of which are of interest:

> Of the other two stories, the first relates to the supernatural transformation of vinegar into oil—similar to the changing of water into wine by Jesus. Hanina's daughter in error filled the Sabbath lamp with vinegar and noticed it too late to correct the mistake. Her father told her to light it and the lamp went on burning all day long (*b. Ta'anit* 25a). The second story deals with the miraculous production of bread, and incidentally illustrates Hanina's poverty and the common belief that around him miracles were commonplace [*b. Ta'anit* 24b–25a].[726]

Both anecdotes illustrate a miraculous benefit at the Hasid's intercession, not unlike Jesus' multiplication of bread and fish for the multitudes.

Regarding the third instance, Hanina's influence over evil, Vermès reports:

> Finally, whereas no actual exorcism is attributed to Hanina the healer in rabbinic writings, nevertheless he is hailed there as a master over evil forces. The following story has the form of a folk legend, but seen in the light of parallel accounts, it makes of Hanina an admirable benefactor of his people and of mankind. The anecdote [*b. Pesahim* 112b] is linked to a rule governing Pharisaic-rabbinic proper conduct according to which no respectable Jew was to be seen alone in the street at night, first and foremost to prevent any suspicion of an immoral purpose, but also, deeper down, because of the danger of bumping into demons in the dark. Hanina in his innocence paid no attention to the petit bourgeois regulations of conventional rabbis.[727]

In the story cited wherein Hanina is confronted by the Agrat, the queen of demons, Vermès affirms that "despite his generosity toward the demonic queen, Hanina is shown to be in total control over the forces of hell, and the savior of humankind from their threat."[728]

Both Jesus and Hanina ben Dosa are seen as holy men, men of deeds, who demonstrate similar attributes and sensibilities, among which we may note:

- Both are Galilean, for good or ill, given the Judean negative bias toward Galileans.
- Both were renowned for their healings.
- Both were reported to have healed from a distance, with foreknowledge of the presenting situation.
- Both were humble and embraced poverty.
- Their prayer of intercession was efficacious, exhibiting "direct efficiency."
- As wonder-workers they not only cured the sick but [also] provided for the basic needs, e.g., bread, oil, etc., of many.
- Though no exorcism is directly attributable to Hanina, he and Jesus, who clearly is an exorcist, exercise control of demons.
- Both were teachers, though Jesus was the greater of the two in this regard.
- Neither were recognized as "authorities" in Jewish law.
- Though Hanina does not embrace the title of prophet well, Jesus does. Yet both share a striking resemblance to the prophetic stance and deeds of Elijah.
- Both sense/experience an intimacy with the Father and a preferred status as sons.
- Both show a lack of interest in legal and ritual affairs and a corresponding exclusive concentration on moral questions.
- Both experienced tension with the Pharisees arising from their informal familiarity with God and their charismatic confidence.

Vermès further observes: "Since *halakah* [Jewish law and jurisprudence based on the Talmud] became the corner-stone of rabbinic Judaism, it is not surprising that despite their popular religious appeal, Jesus, Hanina, and the others, were slowly but surely squeezed out beyond the pale of true respectability."[729]

Following a survey of rabbinic praises and quibbles, that is to say, "the broad spectrum of high acclaim to sarcasm and carping,"[730] wherein the rabbinic attitude toward

Honi, Hanina, and Jesus are highlighted so as to "help the reader to grasp the full significance of the comparison with the Synoptic portrait of Jesus,"[731] Vermès asserts: "These are trifling quibbles which do not diminish the genuine veneration in which Hanina and Honi, and the other ancient Hasidim were held by Jews of the intertestamental and rabbinic age."[732]

Finally, having demonstrated a strong parallel between Jesus and the Galilean Hasidim, Vermès ventures:

> Beyond the basic similarities between these charismatic individuals, some features displayed in sources outside the New Testament enable us to bring the Gospel portrait of Jesus into sharper focus. Thus Jesus' harsh utterances and almost uncouth outbursts against non-Jews, which would be hardly appropriate to one whom later Christianity likes to identify as the teacher of the religion of pure love, become understandable when ascribed to the chauvinism of a hot-blooded Galilean. . . . Those who shut their eyes to Jesus' character will find it hard to account for Jesus calling the gravely ill daughter of the Syro-Phoenician woman a "dog." This was no more a term of endearment in the language of the time and place than Jesus' other designation of non-Jews as "swine."[733]

Vermès does, however, note and comment upon a striking difference between Jesus and the ancient Hasidim: Jesus' celibacy. He observes:

> We have seen that the way of life adopted by Jesus as an itinerant preacher is paralleled by the Hasidic style of existence as far as poverty was concerned. The men of God were more concerned with providing for others than with their own well-being. By contrast, Jesus' celibacy—which is implied but nowhere positively stated—has no formal Hasidic counterpart, unless an odd saying of a saintly rabbi of the early second century A.D., Pinhas ben Yair [or Phineas ben Jair], is so understood. The chain of virtues and their consequences drawn up by him lists watchfulness, purity, [sexual] abstinence, holiness, humility, fear of sin, devoutness, holy spirit, resurrection of the dead, and finally Elijah (*m. Soṭah* 9:15). Whatever the meaning of this curious list, it cannot account for the unmarried state of Jesus, which requires a different explanation.[734]

With the exception of this one anomaly, one that both Ben-Chorin and Flusser also find enigmatic, Vermès affirms his hypothesis: "Needless to say, as healer and exorcist Jesus is perfectly at home in Hasidic company."[735]

And yet, Vermès's juxtaposition does not conclude with the similitudes; rather, as Vermès emphasizes "to grasp the real Jesus in his individuality within his historical milieu, the resemblances to his Hasidic contemporaries must be balanced against the factors and features which distinguish them."[736]

"The Shadowy Face of the Real Jesus"

Describing these factors and features[737] as "momentous and many,"[738] Vermès considers only the most essential, observing:

> To begin with, the difference in character needs to be stressed. Even allowing for the lack of historical precision in the portrayals, no one with eyes to see can overlook the

manifest disparity between Jesus and the other Hasidim. To use modern jargon, if Jesus is the star, they are mere supporting actors. Honi is [the] only exception. In spite of his peculiar behavior, when it came to the crunch he showed himself capable of displaying great courage and, like Jesus, sacrificed his life for his convictions. All the others were gentle, kind, well-intentioned, and profoundly saintly, but not particularly significant characters. . . . Even Hanina ben Dosa, perhaps the greatest of those Hasidim, is depicted as a holy man, sweet, benign, always ready to help, and exhibiting the deepest possible devotion to God, but with no great personality and without any popular following.[739]

After juxtaposing and evaluating the pertinent sources, Vermès affirms the Hasidic qualities of the Synoptic Jesus. Emphasizing that "Jesus stood head and shoulders above them [the ancient Hasidim]"[740] yet was not "the meek and mild figure of popular Christian imagination,"[741] Vermès advances a credible, if provocative, description:

- Jesus of Nazareth could be determined, impatient, and angry.
- He inherited the strength, the iron character, and fearlessness of his predecessors, the prophets.
- Like Amos and Jeremiah, Jesus was not afraid to stand up to the powerful.
- He showed love to children, whom he proposed as models for those who sought to enter the kingdom of God.
- He welcomed women and felt pity for the sick and the miserable.
- He surpassed the prophets. They embraced the weak, the poor, the widow, the fatherless; Jesus went further and bravely extended a hand of friendship to the social outcasts, the unclean prostitutes and the despised publicans who were kept at arm's length by his hidebound, pious contemporaries.
- Jesus is depicted as capable of demonstrating extreme emotions. He could be moved by pity and anger; he let his fury fly and strike opponents and critics.
- Slowness in comprehension, let alone lack of understanding, especially on the part of his chosen disciples, often made him indignant.
- He is on one occasion depicted as being quite unreasonable. When hungry, he apparently cursed a fig tree for being without fruit, although it was not the season for figs (Mark 11:12–14). Or maybe as a Galilean, used to the availability of figs ten months out of twelve, he forgot that Jerusalem at 800 meters above sea level had a harsher climate than the lakeside.
- Jesus was a man of steel and warmth at the same time.
- He was a total devotee of God, whose perfection and mercy he set out to imitate.
- Though the Hasidim were all married, with children, Jesus "at least during the public phase of his life" was celibate—"everything points towards a celibate existence."
- Jesus was certainly not a misogynist; neither did he run his life primarily along ceremonial lines. If he chose the unmarried state while preaching the kingdom of God—John the Baptist seems to have done the same—it must have been for some other reason.
- Regarding the question of celibacy, Vermès suggests, having perused the Jewish literature, two possibilities: (1) Jesus qua prophet adopted a celibate lifestyle; (2)

the fuller comprehension of his choice may lie with the eschatological spirit which animated his teaching and life which the other Hasidim did not share.

- Regarding his "otherness" as a teacher, vis-à-vis Honi, Hanina, et al., "not even the prototypes of the charismatic Hasid, Elijah and Elisha, famous for their deeds, have bequeathed ideas and doctrines to later generations to inspire them and oblige them to think."

- Jesus was an exemplary teacher, "a solitary giant among the ancient Hasidim." The gospel preached by him is "fire, power, and poetry, one of the high peaks in the religious creativity of the people of Israel."[742]

And yet, Vermès's Jesus is not yet complete. To conclude, and thereby enhance, his portrait of this Galilean Hasid, Vermès comments on two distinctive elements: Jesus and the Qumran community; and Jesus' eschatological vision and the stimulus of his message.

Jesus and the Qumran Community

Summarizing the similarities between Jesus and the Qumran community, Vermès posits:

> Both Jesus and the Essene teachers used the religious ideas and imagery of their times and shared convictions that the end of the present age was at hand. Both Jesus and the Qumran Teacher of Righteousness sought to hand over to their followers the last divine message. Both the primitive church and the Dead Sea community believed that the scriptural prophecies announcing the events of the last times were being fulfilled before their eyes and in the persons and events associated with them. Both Jesus and the Qumran sectaries emphasized observance of the law.[743]

As to their differences, he writes:

> The principal difference between them consisted in their overall outlook and distinctive emphasis on the Torah. The priestly Essenes, while insisting on inward conversion, laid particular stress on the rigorous performance of the minutiae of the biblical commandments, such as purity, dietary, and cultic regulations. Though asserting the permanent validity of the Torah, Jesus, the Galilean popular preacher, in the footsteps of the prophets gave definite priority to the innermost aspects of Mosaic piety. Whereas the religious system of Qumran was exclusive, keeping out outsiders, Jesus was keen to convey his spiritual insights to all and sundry who honestly approached him inspired by faith. The publicans and sinners, the friends and table-fellows of Jesus, would have received curt treatment from the leaders of the Dead Sea community.[744]

Though allowing for a possible link between the Essenes and Christianity, at its earliest stages, in John the Baptist[745]—if indeed John was at some earlier point influenced by the Essenes or was a member of Qumran—Vermès argues against such improbable, direct influence upon Jesus, emphasizing: "So quite apart from the improbability of contact between Jesus and the Essenes in Galilee, where the presence of the sect is nowhere attested, the profound diversity of their respective religious perspectives renders unlikely that in his public career Jesus had anything to do with the Qumran movement."[746]

Urgency and Actuality of the Kingdom

Vermès, adding the final bits of "glass and stone" to his portrait of Jesus, concludes:

> To add the final distinguishing touch to the portrait of the real Jesus, emphasis should be placed on the eschatological vision and the stimulus of his message which, together with the tragic finale of the cross, invest it with a unique urgency and actuality. Proclaiming not just the nearness, but [also] the virtual and more than once the actual presence of the kingdom of God, he showed himself an incomparable charismatic and religious teacher. His magnetic appeal became more powerful after his death than it could ever have been during his transient ministry in the late twenties of the first century in the Galilee of Herod Antipas and the Jerusalem of Joseph Caiaphas, the high priest, and Pontius Pilate, the imperial legate of Judaea.
>
> The face of this Jesus, truly human, wholly theocentric, passionately faith-inspired, and under the imperative impulse of the here and now, impressed itself so deeply on the minds of his disciples that not even the shattering blow of the cross could arrest its continued real presence. It compelled them to carry on in his name with their mission as healers, exorcists, and preachers of the kingdom of God. It was only a generation or two later, with the increasing delay of the Parousia, that the image of the Jesus familiar from experience began to fade, covered over first by the theological and mystical dreaming of Paul and John, and afterward by the dogmatic speculations of church-centered Gentile-Christianity.[747]

Jesus the Hasidic Jew

Vermès's thirty-year accompaniment of Jesus, beginning with his seminal work, *Jesus the Jew* in 1973, secured for Jesus not only a place as a Jew within Palestinian Judaism but also, and significantly, an honored place within Judaism as one of ancient Hasidim. Not simply as one among many, but rather as *the* one "who stood head and shoulders above them."[748] Far from "reducing [the stature of Jesus] to that of a pale Galilean charismatic,"[749] Vermès, emphasizing Jesus' distinctiveness, affirms that he was "second to none in profundity of insight and grandeur of character."[750]

At the conclusion of his studied journey, Vermès confirms what he first affirmed:

> The positive and constant testimony of the earliest Gospel tradition, considered against its natural background of first-century Galilean charismatic religion, leads not to a Jesus as unrecognizable within the framework of Judaism as by the standard of his own verifiable words and intentions, but to another figure: Jesus the just man, the *zaddik* [*sadîq*], Jesus the helper and healer, Jesus the teacher and leader, venerated by his intimates and less committed admirers alike as prophet, lord and *son of God*.[751]

Summary

Samuel Sandmel, David Flusser, and Géza Vermès each construct a portrait of Jesus from the essential sources or, as in the case of Sandmel, from the cultural influences interpreted intuitively yet reasonably. The Jesus who emerges from their study is similar yet distinctive. Each panel of our mosaic triptych offers a compelling portrait: Jesus *nazir*/cultural icon; Jesus, *naggar*/beloved son; Jesus, *zaddik*/Galilean Hasid.

Sandmel, who determined a modest goal for his inquiry, felt constrained by his inability to get behind the text to Jesus. Given this, we may grasp of his initial efforts the image of the Jewish *nazir*, a person dedicated to God, not unlike Samson or Hillel,[752] yet one who dies as a martyr. However, this Jesus *nazir* is not the Jesus to whom the modern Jewish community is introduced. Rather, as we have seen, it is Jesus, an icon of Western culture whom the Jewish community encounters and to whom they may reasonably relate. Culturally, as if appreciating the art of Monet, or a Mozart symphony, a Jew may appreciate and even be influenced by Jesus as an icon of Western culture. The Jewish apologist and New Testament scholar affirms a positive, if timorous, rendering—an appreciation, an understanding.

Flusser does not share Sandmel's reticence to engage essential sources critically. He optimistically illumines and interprets Jesus within Judaism, within "the framework of his time and people." The portrait of Jesus emanating from his study is that of a Jewish *naggar*, a craftsman. Jesus, *naggar*, the craftsman, the carpenter. Though the Jewish epithet *naggar* is not explicitly used by Flusser, he—as does Vermès— understands that the epithet *carpenter* is often used metaphorically within Judaism, indicating not the skill of a carpenter, but rather that of *a learned person*, not unlike a Jewish sage.[753] Regardless of the validity of the metaphorical claim, from Flusser's perspective Jesus is not "a naive and amiable, simple manual workman,"[754] but rather a faithful, law-observant, learned, Pharisaic-like rabbi. He concurs with Vermès— though independently—and situates Jesus uniquely and distinctly within charismatic Palestinian Hasidim as a *beloved son*. This ancient "learned Jew" has much to teach modernity, and Flusser delights in being his "mouthpiece"[755] to the present age.

Vermès, the boldest of our three, seeks to discern the face of the real Jesus by contemplating *the patterns* conveyed in both the Christian Synoptic Gospels and essential, comparative Jewish sources. It is typology and historical-philological analysis that informs his methodology, clarifying his thought and enhancing the image of Jesus emerging from beneath the Gospel overlay. This innovative, scholarly approach of the historian Vermès is not without critique or commendation. Like Elijah and Elisha in the charismatic tradition of Jewish wonder-working prophets, similar to Honi the Circle-Drawer and Hanina ben Dosa, prayerful, holy men of the ancient Hasidim, Jesus of Nazareth, under Vermès's informed scrutiny, emerges securely within the tradition of the Devout Ones. In Vermès's estimation, Jesus of Nazareth, Galilean Hasid and Jewish *zaddik*, is not merely one among many, but rather is "second to none."[756]

5

Jesus, Jewish Brother

Varying Motifs

> To us Jesus is never more than a man, and deeply as some of us Jews are able to sym-
> pathize with the tragedy of his life and death, we do not see in it any special working of
> the divine.
>
> Samuel Sandmel, *We Jews and Jesus*, 48

Gathered into a convenient category, established in chapter 3 as creative approaches,
the diverse Jewish writers Schalom Ben-Chorin, Pinchas Lapide, Jacob Neusner, and
Eugene Borowitz each offers a perspective of Jesus that is both innovative and provocative. Though having less impact upon the third quest for the historical Jesus than Flusser
or Vermès, their voices are significant. They, as the authors considered in chapter 4,
affirm the Jewishness of Jesus and seek to situate him more securely within Judaism
or, as in Neusner's case, engage him in his Jewish context. Their motives and approaches differ. Ben-Chorin and Lapide are representative of the efforts in the mid-
twentieth century to "reclaim" Jesus for Judaism, whereas Neusner and Borowitz seek
to respond to the Jesus whom they distinctly encounter. Each, either explicitly or implicitly, perceives Jesus as "not only my human brother, but [also] my Jewish
brother."[757]

Jesus, Jewish Brother, Tragic Figure

> His countenance, distorted with pain, is crowned with a diadem of thorns. The martyred
> body bleeds from countless wounds. Thus we see him again, the Jew on the cross. His
> voice carries down through the centuries: Just as you did to one of the least of these my
> brothers, so you did to me.
>
> Schalom Ben-Chorin, *Brother Jesus*, 188

Schalom Ben-Chorin, seeking both to reclaim Jesus as a Jew and to situate
him positively within Judaism, tries to free him from the Christian overpainting,
the Gospels, so as to render plainly what has been hidden or contested. To do

this, Ben-Chorin stakes out a middle ground, as he sees it, between an unverifiable historical position and theological-literary fantasy. This middle ground is intuition. With intuitive interpretation as his point of departure, imbued with kindred empathy, Ben-Chorin confidently maps out the contours of this Jesus, his *Jewish brother*. The Jewish image of Jesus emanates from his perusal of the Synoptic Gospels, "for they are spirit of Israel's spirit, while the Gospel of John breathes a more Hellenistic spirit."[758] We will follow Ben-Chorin's presentation in *Brother Jesus: The Nazarene through Jewish Eyes*, as appropriately citing other sources, especially his article "The Image of Jesus in Modern Judaism."

Jesus of Nazareth

Not surprisingly, Ben-Chorin does not address the apotheosis of Jesus, leaving the question of divinity for someone other than an historian or a Jew. Arguing that "even the question of the messiahship of Jesus must be bracketed here, since it exists apart from historical knowledge and Jewish belief,"[759] Ben-Chorin does see his way clear to speak of Jesus' messianic self-understanding. Concurring with Käsemann that the messianic features in the image of Jesus are "products of kerygmatic revisions of a later hand,"[760] Ben-Chorin concludes that Jesus is not the Messiah, and that he did not think of himself as such. In this latter assertion, he differs with Sandmel, Flusser, Lapide, and Vermès.

Nor is Ben-Chorin prepared to allow Jesus the designation of prophet. Unlike Vermès, who hails this title as the one most acceptable to Jesus, Ben-Chorin finds this designation untenable. Asserting that Jesus was no prophet, no *navi'* (*nābî'*), not in the Old Testament sense of the word, Ben-Chorin explains that "the *navi'* proclaims the utterances of Yahweh; he becomes the mouth of the deity."[761] Jesus obviously does not do this. Jesus' prophetic orations, if they may be deemed such, lack this important distinction since he speaks with personal authority, as indicated by the phrase "But I say to you." Nor is Jesus a seer. This attribute of the Old Testament prophet is lacking in Jesus since no visions are attributed to him such as may be attributed to Isaiah, Jeremiah, or Ezekiel. Finally, Ben-Chorin, in his reading of the Gospels, claims that Old Testament prophetic traits are also lacking in Jesus. Rather, given Jesus' scriptural hermeneutic and use of parables, one finds that "Jesus appears rather to act in the manner of the contemporary teachers of the law, the Tannaim."[762] All this leads Ben-Chorin to suggest that this designation of prophet by Christians is misleading since this distinction creates a rupture with the tradition of Judaism, effectively isolating Jesus from it.[763]

While disavowing Jesus as exalted Lord—a Christian presumption given the re-definition of prophet—Ben-Chorin does see in Jesus of Nazareth a third authority alongside the Pharisaic schools of Hillel and Shammai, respectively. He describes Jesus' interpretation of the law as "a clear tendency toward the *internalization of the law*, whereby *love* constitutes the decisive and motivating element."[764] We shall return to this distinction in the latter part of this chapter when we consider Jesus and his relationship to the law.

Regarding Jesus' education, Ben-Chorin speculates that "it is probable that Jesus was not a *talmid chakham* [*talmîd ḥakîm*], 'scholarly student,' but knew only the Hebrew Bible and interpreted it in his own way."[765] This, though, is conjecture inasmuch as he also admits "to knowing nothing about the teachers and education of Jesus."[766] It is not, however, idle conjecture, given Ben-Chorin's intuitive reading of the Gospels and his sense of first-century Palestine.

Jesus and Palestinian Judaism

Offering an assessment of the competing groups prevalent in first-century Palestine, Ben-Chorin concludes: "In this light, it is probably not wrong to reckon Jesus among the Pharisees, albeit as part of an internal opposition movement within this largest Judaic group of his day. Jesus himself talks like a Pharisaic rabbi, although from a greater position of authority; his extraordinarily forceful manner of speaking is, however, most likely a product of the kerygmatic tradition."[767]

Ben-Chorin concedes that speaking from a sense of full authority is not the prerogative of Jesus alone. The Pharisees, too, were conscious of their own authority, "an authority based on the belief that they, conscious of their succession from Moses, were the fully empowered bearers of revelation."[768] It is doubtless that this Pharisaic sense of authority and succession—imbued with deep seriousness, unconditional devotion to the law of God, and relentlessly consistent logic, attributes that prompt Ben-Chorin to underscore a parallel between Pharisaic Judaism and modern Jewish orthodoxy—is also the flash point where antagonism arose between them and Jesus.

Comparing Jesus to what is known of the other three dominant groups categorized by Josephus, Ben-Chorin discounts Jesus' affiliation with, or affinity for, the Sadducees, Essenes, and Zealots. He affirms: "We may conclude that Jesus cannot be reckoned entirely to have belonged to a single group known to us, although it is to the Pharisees—as peculiar as that may sound—that he has the closest links."[769]

From Ben-Chorin's perspective, Jesus, then, is not a scholarly student nor a prophet nor the Messiah, but rather a Pharisaic-like teacher, an itinerant rabbi, calling for repentance and announcing the presence of the kingdom of God.

Family and Acquaintances

As to Jesus' origins, Ben-Chorin affirms that "the birth of Jesus lies in darkness."[770] This darkness, as Ben-Chorin describes it, refers to the lack of credible biographical information regarding the physical birth of Jesus. Speaking of the dissimilar infancy narratives found in Matthew and Luke, he asserts that here one encounters "typical legend motifs."[771] As to the apocryphal gospels' contribution vis-à-vis Jesus' childhood history, Ben-Chorin posits that "there is of course not a scintilla of biographical worth to any of these narratives."[772] The shroud of darkness remains intact despite the infancy narratives or the apocryphal legends.

This same darkness, according to Ben-Chorin, "led his enemies to the inevitable claim that his birth was out of wedlock."[773] This, then, Jesus' illegitimate birth and his awareness thereof, may explain, as Ben-Chorin suggests, the lack of respect and the subsequent distant relationship between Jesus and his mother, Mary. Though the above is a supposition, Ben-Chorin finds Jesus' relationship with Mary, as evident from the exchange between the two during the wedding at Cana, as shocking. His "hard and completely unjustified rebuke of his mother"[774] prompts Ben-Chorin to regard Jesus' attitude as a "blatant violation of the commandment to honor one's parents."[775] Ben-Chorin is convinced that the relationship between mother and son was disturbed. The cause for that eludes him.

If darkness shrouds Jesus birth, light shines forth at his rebirth at the hands of John the baptizer. Ben-Chorin asserts that questions of "lineage and birth, childhood and education sink into insignificance at the hour of the rebirth,"[776] since the one who enters John's bath of immersion emerges self-consciously aware of his mission. Ben-Chorin affirms this in a curiously poetic manner: "It is the Risen One, the one risen from the watery grave, who carries on into history."[777] According to Ben-Chorin, "the man who facilitates this rebirth with spiritual aid and who can thus claim to be the proper father of Jesus, his father in spirit, is John the Baptist."[778]

John the Baptist and Jesus

Ben-Chorin affirms that "the Jewish view of Jesus takes as its starting point the baptism of Jesus in the Jordan by John, as in the Gospel of Mark, though eliminating Mark 1:10–11—the appearance of the Holy Spirit in the form of a dove."[779] As to the relationship between John and Jesus, Ben-Chorin offers little.[780] He does, however, suggest that after Jesus' rebirth, he continued "to stand in the shadow of John until he [Jesus] separates himself internally by the forty days of solitude."[781] Ben-Chorin further speculates that "after John is taken prisoner, Jesus assumes the leadership of the circles of disciples prepared by John for an eschatological awakening."[782] In light of this, Ben-Chorin concludes: "Now at last Jesus becomes himself; the process of individuation appears to be complete."[783] Jesus begins his public ministry.

Jesus, Healer and Preacher

His debut in the Nazareth synagogue is met with mixed success. Jesus is alternately hailed and condemned, challenged to legitimate his claims that the prophecies of Deutero-Isaiah relate to him personally (Luke 4:16–30). People throughout the region are impressed and astonished, curious and leery. Ben-Chorin asserts that "Jesus legitimates himself not through prophecies but primarily through his miraculous healings,"[784] especially those related to exorcism. As to this latter assertion, he and Vermès are in agreement. Jesus is both physician/healer and teacher in the tradition of the Devout Ones.

Given that Jesus casts out demons, or unclean spirits, Ben-Chorin situates Jesus the physician within the tradition of the *Chassidim* (Hasidim) inasmuch as the authority of Jesus over and against these unclean spirits, the *shedim*, bears great similarity to the Chasidic (Hasidic) rabbi, or *tsaddik*. Ben-Chorin affirms Jesus as a Hasidic physician, a worker of miracles, one who has wide appeal in the face of ubiquitous suffering and sorrow. All of this serves to legitimate Jesus as both a Hasid and a teacher.

As a teacher, Jesus' choice of disciples is quite unusual, given that he chooses the simple folk, such as the fishermen, rather than the learned, such as scribes and Pharisees. Ben-Chorin explains the choice as both intentional and revolutionary. Intentional in that Jesus sought to avoid *pilpul*, the hairsplitting arguments of those learned in the law. Revolutionary, in the sense that he chooses the ordinary folk, the *'am ha-'arets* (*'am hā-'āreṣ*), rather than the learned, the *chaverim* (*ḥăbērîm*, "associates"), between whom there existed hostile opposition born of deep prejudice. Observing that the Pharisees, the learned, constitute the caste of the elect, Ben-Chorin describes Jesus' choice of the *'am ha-'arets* as revolutionary since in so choosing "Jesus breaks through the wall erected by the legal piety of those learned in the law."[785] It is a revolt of popular piety against the institution of scriptural legal experts.

Though he chooses the *'am ha-'arets* as disciples, Jesus himself is not one of the simple folk. Ben-Chorin explains: "We should not, however, imagine that Jesus himself belonged to the *'am ha-'arets*; quite to the contrary. He shows himself, in his disputes with the learned in the law, to be their full equal. Indeed, the numerous passages in the New Testament demonstrate that Jesus' disciples, who did belong to the *'am ha-'arets*, did not understand their rabbi."[786]

Ben-Chorin, hearing in the call of the fishermen to be fishers of men "an echo of the consciousness of martyrdom,"[787] asserts: "Jesus, in calling his followers, knows well that he is leading his disciples down a dangerous path, though he cannot yet predict, in this first phase of his activity, its tragic end; his assumption is that the kingdom of God is at hand."[788]

Jesus as teacher, then, is not one of the simple folk, not simply the Inspired One as the evangelists have cast him, but rather a *self-educated* rabbi conversant with the law, willing to engage others in lively debate, while calling unto himself the least likely to carry forth his message—not without peril.

Jesus the Moschel

As to his message, Ben-Chorin highlights the Sermon on the Mount as evidence, ironically, of both Jesus' *mastery* and *nonoriginality*. Of the Sermon on the Mount, he writes:

> Naturally, it is difficult to reconstruct the Sermon on the Mount in its original form, though in fact there is no reason to do so. The extended version of Matthew contains a

good deal of kerygmatic material, and yet it seems to me that it is precisely here in Matthew that we can ascertain the real voice of the speaker. . . . It is here, if anywhere, that the voice of Jesus is audible as that of a Jewish brother—a Jewish voice whose very inflections we are able to discern.[789]

As to his teaching style, Ben-Chorin, recalling Jesus' rejection of *pilpul,* asserts:

> But in truth, Jesus himself does not hold to the maxim of simple speech. His own speech is very often ambiguous, or enveloped in an opacity that neither the disciples nor his enemies are able to understand. . . .
>
> Jesus was in fact no dogmatic or systematic thinker, for he was—a Jew. He spoke and behaved as dictated by circumstances, and to absolutize individual sentences of Jesus would do violence to him.[790]

As to Jesus' preaching, Ben-Chorin observes: "Jesus' preaching, proceeding from Capernaum, is preaching of the kingdom of God, that is eschatological proclamation. It is produced by that Jewish restlessness which results from the immediate expectation of the last days (*acharith ha-jamim* [*'ahărît ha-yāmîm*]). What distinguished this preaching from similar utterances of that time is that 'He taught forcefully' (Mark 1:22)."[791] This facet of Jesus' confidence, his authoritative teaching, has been addressed above.

As to the question of nonoriginality, it is a nonquestion from a Jewish perspective since "the concept of originality was foreign to antiquity."[792] Ben-Chorin, describing the difference between plagiarism and its opposite, pseudepigraphy, explains:

> Pseudepigraphy represents a type of ancient literature that is no longer conceivable. Unknown authors wrote their works under the name of venerable, usually biblical, personages. The author wished in fact not to be original but to validate his thoughts by the conveyance of a well-known name. Thus, the objection that the Sermon on the Mount contains nothing "original" would appear to Jesus and his contemporaries only as a justification. Jesus did say, to be sure, "But I say to you," but these words themselves belong to a recognized tradition of teaching. What is scattered throughout the Talmud and Midrash is rolled together in the words of Jesus in rhapsodic blocks. That is what gives his words their eternal power.[793]

Finally, regarding Jesus' teaching style, Ben-Chorin agrees that Jesus is a *moschel* (*mōšel*), a speaker of parables in the tradition of Judaism. He affirms:

> The parable, called *maschal* [*māšal*] in Hebrew, belongs to the most essential constituents of the Midrash, the legendary exposition of the Torah. . . . It is especially remarkable that it was the Palestinian rabbis in particular who cultivated the parable, whereas the Babylonian rabbis applied it much more rarely. Jesus, who was a Jew entirely in the tradition of the Jewish homeland, in this respect too remained true to a culture alien to diaspora Judaism; this is readily borne out by comparing Paul's manner of teaching. It is therefore no coincidence that the parables appear predominantly in the synoptic writers but recede in the Gospel of John, which is, despite Qumran, more strongly informed by Greek thought.[794]

As evidenced by his preaching and parables, Jesus, in Ben-Chorin's estimation, deeply understood human nature.

Jesus and Prayer

From parables, Ben-Chorin moves to prayer. "Jesus, the man of prayer," in Ben-Chorin's estimation, "is completely a spirit of Judaism, and the noblest expression of the Hebraic *emunah* [*'ĕmûnāh*, "faithfulness"]."[795] Of this man, who was "deeply convinced of the direct efficacy of prayer,"[796] he writes: "For Jesus, prayer is conversation with the Father in heaven, during which we are made conscious of our childlike position. Three prayers are proper for a human being: the prayer for daily bread, the prayer for forgiveness of sins, and the prayer for the kingdom of God."[797]

Jesus' prayer is a Jewish prayer, so much so, that a Jew may easily join in. Ben-Chorin often did: "On a personal note, whenever I am present when the Our Father is recited, I always pray along, without feeling that I am abandoning or violating my own Jewish faith in the slightest."[798] In Jesus' prayer, especially the prayer that Jesus teaches his disciples (Matt 6:9–13; Luke 11:1–4), he perceives "the brotherly voice of a praying Jew."[799]

Commenting further upon Jesus' model of prayer, Ben-Chorin observes:

> In its simplicity and completeness, however, this prayer is indeed classical. It is timeless, even as it exudes the spirit of the time. From the imminent expectation of the kingdom, of course, a distant expectation arose, but faith always exists in the condition of expectation—the expectation of the unknown, the entirely other. And that is in fact, the kingdom of God. . . . However far away the kingdom of God may be, for the person in prayer—if it is the right kind of prayer—the kingdom in that moment is intimately near. The presence of the kingdom is indeed presupposed within the praying community. As Jesus said, "The kingdom of God is among you" (Luke 17:21).[800]

Jesus and Women

In Ben-Chorin's conversation regarding Jesus and women, he affirms three points: Women were among his disciples. Second, Jesus is not only presented in Christian Scripture as the new Adam, the new Moses, and the legitimate successor of David, but also the new Abraham. Last, Jesus as a rabbi would obviously have been married. A word about each is appropriate.

While having women around is not unusual, their presence customarily tended to be that of a servant or benefactor. What is different in Jesus' case is that these women are not merely servants or benefactors but also disciples. Ben-Chorin narrows his focus upon the three women who are prominent in the life of Jesus. All bear the same name: Mary, or Miriam.

As we have already seen, from Ben-Chorin's perspective, Jesus' relationship with his mother, Mary, is disturbed, untypical, inexplicable, and surprising. Nonetheless Mary is found in the company of Jesus' disciples.

Mary, the sister of Lazarus, is both disciple and friend. It is the memory of this Mary as one, a woman, who sits at the feet of Jesus and listens to the master that distinguishes her from simply a female disciple servant. Not simply a servant or a benefactor or friend, for that matter, but actually a disciple, a student, attending to the word of the master. Ben-Chorin remarks that this "is unusual, if not without parallel."[801]

The third Mary is Mary Magdalene, the prototype of the female sinner whom Jesus accepts into his circle. Though found frequently in the company of disciples, she takes center stage—according to Ben-Chorin—in the story of the anointing at Bethany (Luke 7:36–50). Ben-Chorin observes that this anointing of Jesus by Mary Magdalene is generally understood as a foreshadowing of his death and the subsequent anointing of his corpse in preparation for burial. In this action, however, Ben-Chorin perceives a motif that has gone unnoticed by the evangelists: Jesus as "the new Abraham, the new father of faith, or father of the new faith."[802]

Ben-Chorin sees a parallel between the anointing at Bethany found in the Gospels and a certain pericope concerning Abraham. He posits:

> This motif becomes visible when we view the anointment with precious spikenard within the context of a certain midrash (*Genesis Rabbah* 39:2) in which Abraham is compared to a bottle of precious perfume that has been standing closed in a corner. The bottle is now to be opened and carried from place to place in order to disseminate a lovely aroma. . . . Thus [at God's behest] Abraham is to spread the "aroma of holiness" through his wanderings. Jesus, too, in his own wandering—his pilgrimage to Jerusalem, where he wins many disciples—is anointed with a bottle of precious spikenard in the symbolic act of establishing a great new nation of faith. One must recognize this combination of motifs in order to grasp the anointment scene completely. It seems to me important and typical that gentle female hands should anoint this new Abraham, much as the earlier Abraham was pictured in the company of his exquisitely beautiful wife and half-sister Sarah.[803]

Ben-Chorin's Jesus is not only Jewish brother but also the new Abraham, the *new* father of faith or father of the *new* faith. Ben-Chorin does not elaborate or expand upon the latter appellation. Both epithets, however, signal Ben-Chorin's sympathetic view of the Galilean Jesus and the religion that evolves from his mission and ministry: Christianity.

Continuing to explore Jesus' relationship with certain women, Ben-Chorin considers the woman caught in adultery (John 8:3–11). In Jesus' encounter with the adulteress, as he writes or draws enigmatically on the ground (8:8), Ben-Chorin discerns the actions of a circle-drawer akin to Choni Hame'aggel, Honi the Circle-Drawer.[804] Both he, Flusser, and Vermès would agree, though among the three, Vermès more fully argues and develops this motif.

Jesus, Husband

Focusing his concluding comments upon the question of Jesus' marital status, Ben-Chorin plainly asserts that Jesus was married. Nothing is mentioned of this in the Gospels or extrabiblical texts. Nor does Ben-Chorin seek to support his assertion. From his point of view, Rabbi Jesus was married: obviously, since "an unmarried rabbi is hardly imaginable."[805] The cultural-historical context from which Jesus emerged could hardly support a celibate rabbi. The Talmud condemns celibacy, and Christian Scripture is mute on the topic of Jesus' wife. The lack of information about Jesus' wife in no way diminishes Ben-Chorin's position, given an equal lack of information concerning Mrs. Hillel or Mrs. Shammai and hundreds of other rabbis whose wives go nameless. Not surprisingly, Ben-Chorin concludes that "Jesus of Nazareth, just like every rabbi in Israel, was married."[806] Rabbi Jesus was obviously married though nothing is known about his wife—or family for that matter.

To substantiate his conjecture, Ben-Chorin reviews and comments upon Jesus' use of marital imagery. He states simply that "none of these images would be appropriate to an unmarried Jesus who knew nothing of a bridal night and matrimonial companionship."[807] Finally, he concludes the debate as to whether or not Jesus was celibate or married by affirming that "in none of the writings considered sacred within Judaism at the time of Jesus is celibacy idealized."[808]

Jesus of Galilee

Thus far Ben-Chorin has considered *his* view of Jesus; now he considers Jesus' view of himself. The question of Jesus' self-identity leads Ben-Chorin to explore the three Scripture versions of the episode wherein Jesus poses the question "Who am I?" In Matthew 16:13–20, we hear Jesus asking: "Who do people say that the Son of Man is?" This is Ben-Chorin's point of departure for considering Jesus' self awareness as son of man: a concept not without messianic overtones. But is this what Jesus intends to affirm or subtly communicate, or is this part of the kerygmatic overpainting? To answer this question Ben-Chorin examines the term *bar-'enosh* (*bar-'ĕnoš*), son of man (cf. Dan 7:13–14). There are three possible interpretations of the term: *bar-'enosh*, *ben-'adam* (*ben-'ādām*), and *barnash*: the eschatological, the prophetic, and the purely human, respectively.

The first term, eschatological son of Man, *bar-'enosh*, he dismisses as not viable when applied to Jesus. He suggests that "it is difficult to unify the all-too-human utterances concerning human existence, which encompasses suffering and vagabondage, with the image of the eschatological son of man in Daniel's night vision."[809] As to the second possibility, *ben-'adam*, meaning mortal, Ben-Chorin doubts the effective use of the image to convey a prophetic identity. The third possibility, *barnash*, a vulgar form of *bar-'enosh*, which means everyman or a man such as you or I, is most applicable to Jesus. Ben-Chorin posits: "This is the kind of man Jesus understood himself to be: a man who lives, as man, a typically human life, without possessions and subject to pain. In designating himself 'Son of Man,' Jesus does not stand before us as a prophet or the Messiah but as our brother. And since he is the son of man, the human question erupts within him, 'Who am I?'"[810]

He does, however, provide a caveat lest one think that Daniel's night vision did not play upon Jesus' mind:

But certainly the sublime presentation of the Danielic Son of Man played a decisive role in Jesus' self-understanding; this is later enlarged through the model of the suffering servant of God, the *Ebed* (Isa. 53). Albert Schweitzer pointed out that Jesus developed spiritually in the "shadow of the *Ebed*." Most pertinently the Marburg scholar Rudolf Otto characterized Jesus' self-understanding as a joining of the Son of Man of Daniel and the *Ebed* of Deutero-Isaiah. This view fits organically into the Jewish image of Jesus.[811]

Ben-Chorin, pondering this image of a questioning, reflective Jesus, intuits: "The un-prejudiced eye will see here a confused individual confronting the mystery of his own existence without finding the key to unlock it. Bewildered, Jesus senses that a charisma emanates from him, a power not of himself but one that nevertheless compels others to their knees. This forces him to ask not only 'Who am I?' but also 'Is that who I am?'"[812]

Ben-Chorin passionately defends "his inside perspective":

> The suffering man, the man who suffers over the riddle of his own existence, will not dare to speak the self-confident *I* words of the Johannine Christ (e.g., John 10:24–30). These words belong to a much later community tradition under the influence of Hel-lenistic thought which was foreign to the nature of the bewildered young Jew from Nazareth who himself now becomes the object of questioning. I am well aware that statements of this sort will be dismissed with a superior smile by many New Testament scholars. But no one who has experienced Jesus as his brother—as his human brother and as his Jewish brother—will be able to ignore this inside perspective, however distant it may be from an exact philological methodology.[813]

Concluding, Ben-Chorin affirms: "This questioning Jesus is our brother, not the exalted Christ who has exchanged the human realm for the heights and depths of myth."[814]

Martyr Jesus, Patriot

Ben-Chorin has previously alluded to the politico-religious climate of first-century Palestine that roiled and seethed beneath Roman oppression. It is this milieu that gave rise both to strong nationalistic fervor and heightened messianic speculation. It is this milieu into which the Galilean Jesus was born and that informed his character and a sense of mission, as Ben-Chorin affirms:

> The strong nationalistic character of Jesus is unargued. He is dominated by Israel's idea of chosenness. In accord with the twelve tribes of his people he chose twelve disciples who are to him, as a substitute Israel, the "Salt of the Earth" (Mt. 5:13 and parables). He urged them not to go on the Gentile streets, but only to the lost sheep of the House of Israel. In his harsh words to the Canaanite woman from Tyre and Sidon, he compares the Jews with the children (of God) and the Gentiles with the dogs (Mt. 15:26; Mk.7:27). The nationalist attitude is of course strengthened and made comprehensible by the Roman domination of the land. It is this element which dominates in the Jewish-image of Jesus and places Jesus near the great patriots such as Rabbi Akiba and Simon Bar-Jochai.[815]

Ben-Chorin's Jesus, then, is a Jewish brother, a nationalist patriot, and a tragic figure. Jesus' decision to journey to Jerusalem is a turning point in his life's journey. This journey to Jerusalem is described broadly by Ben-Chorin as a pilgrimage to the central sanctuary as commanded in Deuteronomy 16:16–17; a victory procession—limited in scope but nonetheless cautiously eyed by wary temple authorities; and as a path of martyrdom, which is consistent with Jesus' suffering Son of Man sayings (e.g., Mark 9:12).[816] Of the these three, it is the last, the path of martyrdom, of which Ben-Chorin writes:

> As a clairvoyant man—and that he surely was—Jesus had to have been conscious of the risk involved in his provocation. It was no small thing to challenge all earthly powers simultaneously: the Sadducean priesthood, the Pharisaic legal scholars, the Herodians, and the Roman occupational authority. That appeared to leave the possibility now only of a miraculous victory, which would require the direct intercession of God, or else defeat in an entirely unequal struggle. But a *third* possibility arose that could hardly have been envisioned at the time: *the possibility of victory in defeat.* This third possibility was in fact to become history, albeit outside of the history of Jesus' own life.[817]

Jesus, clairvoyant, sensing a certain charisma emanating from himself, yet being no prophet or Messiah. Jesus, everyman, mortal, yet a new Abraham. Jesus, a human brother, moreover, and significantly, a Jewish brother, yet poignantly a martyr—from Ben-Chorin's perspective—a tragic figure and failure.

Jesus and Jerusalem

Ben-Chorin regards Matthew 21:5–7, Jesus' entry into Jerusalem astride a donkey and a colt—in apparent fulfillment of Zechariah 9:9, "Lo, your king comes to you; . . . on a colt, the foal of a donkey"—as "forced beyond plausibility,"[818] given the unlikelihood that Jesus rode "two" beasts, as Matthew indicates. As to whether Jesus entered Jerusalem anticipating Passover or the Feast of Tabernacles, which seems more likely to Ben-Chorin, he affirms the "possibility that he [Jesus] spent the winter in the environs of Jerusalem, in which case he may have arrived in the city in autumn but did not decide upon his fateful procession until spring"[819]—thus reconciling the Synoptic view of one journey to Jerusalem by Jesus.

Though Jesus' passage into the city may have been among curious onlookers, he was not unaccompanied. Ben-Chorin speculates that Jesus' "little flock" included "pacifists and Zealots, skeptics and female enthusiasts, Hebrew chauvinists and probably also Hellenistic proselytes at the margin."[820] Thus accompanied, Jesus formally entered the city, anticipating the spring's Passover. That he was in Jerusalem with fellow pilgrims and while there provoked the religious authorities is uncontested. However, the provocative event is contested.

Though Ben-Chorin speculates that—like Judas Iscariot, one of Jesus' apostles, who was doubtlessly a Zealot—Jesus may have occasionally fallen under similar influence and considered armed resistance, he dismisses armed insurrection as either Jesus' motive or the provocative event.[821] Unlike most New Testament specialists, such as Flusser and Vermès, who agree that Jesus' violent confrontation with the money changers was the provocative event, the pivotal event that was the catalyst of his demise, Ben-Chorin, influenced by Martin Buber, focuses upon Jesus' statement regarding the coin of tribute (Matt 22:15–22).[822]

Following Buber, who "selected Jesus' statement regarding the coin of tribute as the point of departure for a speech in 1953 ('Geltung and Grenze') on the limits of political authority,"[823] Ben-Chorin argues that "the intent of the original narrative was to diminish the ethical question relative to the eschatological imperative of yielding to the will of God."[824] Given the context in which this "conversation" took place, in the aftermath of Jesus' harsh words concerning the temple, and among whom, the Herodians, Ben-Chorin argues: "We must therefore sharpen our hearing in order to discern the *niggun,* the inflection, with which this fateful statement is uttered [Matt 22:21]."[825] This inflection, which echoes in Ben-Chorin's ears, bespeaks a disdain on the part of the speaker toward his listeners, whom he perceives as among those Jews "who no longer care to know about Israel's commission, who betray Yahweh to Baal and want to be 'like all nations.'"[826]

There is no cool distance here, but rather a pointed belittlement of political influence vis-à-vis the kingdom of God and an implied rebuke to those currying Caesar's favor. Given "the relativity of power, which must eventually yield to a greater power,"[827] Ben-Chorin therefore asserts that "Jesus' declaration concerning Caesar and God must therefore be understood on two levels: it displays both a personal and national dimension."[828] Ben-Chorin explains: "The personal dimension makes it tacitly advisable to answer so as not to fall into the trap of his enemies. The national dimension causes the *foreign* ruler to appear to him from this great—and at the deepest level probably eschatological—distance as the antithesis of God; at the same time, however, it assigns him a lesser relevance."[829]

For Jesus, as with all true Israelites, "Yahweh is king over all. No area can exist outside his dominion."[830] Jesus' dismissal of Caesar's importance vis-à-vis "the indivisibility of the kingdom of God"[831] and his implicit indictment of those Jews complicit with Caesar provoked a fateful response.

Observing that "the curtain of fate continues to close over him,"[832] Ben-Chorin focuses his discussion, given the above, on the third aspect of Jesus' journey to Jerusalem: the path of martyrdom. The tragic climax begins as darkness encroaches.

Jesus' Leil-Shimmurim

Ben-Chorin, at perhaps the zenith of his intuitive prowess, artfully recaptures Jesus' *Leil-Shimmurim*, his Night of Watching, in the garden known as *Gath Shemani*, Gethsemane:

> Jesus steps away from the company and prays. He falls upon his face, as one would pray in the temple, and cries fearfully to his God (Mark 14:35; cf. Luke 22:44). Now, now he knows, with an absolutely certain feeling, that he is lost. Suddenly, it is clear to him that his path to Jerusalem was a path of martyrdom and that standing in the shadow of the

'eved-hashem [*'ebed ha-šēm*, "servant of the Name"], "the servant of God," he must take that suffering into death upon himself in servile obedience.[833]

Ben-Chorin intentionally invokes the *Leil-Shimmurim* of the Exodus, "the night in which the Lord by his strong arm so wondrously proved his faithfulness to his people Israel,"[834] as the parallel to Jesus' night of watchful, fearsome prayer at *Gath Shemani*. Captivated by Jesus' evident humanity, his obvious similitude, this human brother, brother Jesus, Ben-Chorin exclaims:

> He, however, watches, shaken by the creaturely fear of death. One cannot read this report in the Gospels without being moved to tears. This is no hero standing here, no demigod, no myth! This is a man trembling in mortal fear for his very life. And in this hour of fear Jesus is especially close to us. It is inconceivable to me how anyone could interpret this human tragedy in the dogmatic terms of the twofold nature of Christ: true man and true God.[835]

Thus Ben-Chorin affirms "the one who stands before us now, seized by the fear of death, is true man—man who is born with the fear of death—whose life is ever living toward death, and whose thoughts and actions all represent a flight from death."[836] Jesus, son of the Father, prays that this cup of bitterness pass him by, yet "that is not his final word: *Not my will, Father, but yours be done.*"[837]

Ben-Chorin's intuitive comparative analysis of Jesus' *Leil-Shimmurim* provides yet another image, wrestling with God. Of this God and Jesus, he writes:

> The Night God—the night side of God, the demonic, night side of *'Elohim*—is now revealed to Jesus. This is the God who wrestled with Jacob at night (Gen. 32:22–32). This is the God who visited his servant Moses in the night lodging on the road to Egypt, intending to kill him; only blood circumcision could appease the nocturnal demonic Yahweh (Exod. 4:24–26). This is the God who made his terrifying rounds on this night in Egypt, slaying all the firstborn. Only the blood of the lamb smeared with hyssop branches on the doorposts of the Hebrew homes in Goshen, could appease him.
>
> This Unfathomable One thirsts for blood at night. Jesus sweats blood: "His sweat became like great drops of blood falling down on the ground," as Luke reports (22:44). This blood-sweat is not accepted, however. The blood of this man, who has been so horribly elected, must be shed as redemption money for many. Now Jesus realizes that the kingdom of God can be purchased only with blood—his own blood, his own life, which God requires of him.[838]

He concludes his portrayal of Jesus during his *Leil-Shimmurim*, drawing on a complementary image found in the Letter to the Hebrews (5:7):

> The epistle to the Hebrew says candidly, "with loud cries and tears." Jesus' Oriental-Jewish nature, wild and unchained, is depicted realistically here. He does not behave as a servant, with silent submission. He will accept this silent submission and reject active resistance only at the moment of his arrest, shortly after having wrestled in prayer. . . . He drinks the fifth cup [the cup of Elijah]. And that is what is meant by the final words "It is finished" which he utters in dying on the cross (John 19:30), having swallowed the bitter vinegar handed to him on a sponge attached to the hyssop stick (symbol of the first Passover night in Egypt). A terrible caricature of the festive cup. The conclusion to the tragedy.[839]

Grasping this fifth cup, Jesus does not resist arrest.

Jesus, Trial and Execution

Citing several contemporary interpretations of "the night hearing," meaning the trial of Jesus before Caiaphas, the high priest (Mark 14:53–65; Matt 26:57–27:2; Luke 22:54–71; and John 18:12–27), Ben-Chorin argues that "all these interpretations do violence to the sources."[840] Rather than expunge Jewish involvement or culpability, he does the opposite, insisting: "The trial against Jesus of Nazareth was a political trial. At its root lay the question of the right of the threatened Jewish people to survive in a land occupied and oppressed by Romans."[841]

Citing John's Gospel (11:50, on the expedience of one man's death), he continues: "We have only to visualize the situation in which the oppressed Jews were languishing in their occupied homeland. It is altogether reasonable that the authorities should have done everything in their power to neutralize a troublemaker like Jesus of Nazareth, to whom so many of the common people were flocking, including political activists of the likes of Judas Iscariot."[842]

Ben-Chorin ventures that Caiaphas and the members of the Sanhedrin, reeling from the recent murders of the Galilean pilgrims at the hands of the legionnaires of Pilate, who reacted to their presumed provocation, "decided to neutralize this latest rebel from Galilee by taking him into custody."[843] The point of the night hearing, in Ben-Chorin's estimation, "was to find formal grounds on which to justify, both politically and on the basis of Halakha (religious law), handing Jesus over to the Romans."[844]

He is inclined to believe that a preliminary hearing did take place before Annas, the father-law of Caiaphas and member of the Sanhedrin, at Caiaphas's instigation. Annas, then, gave Jesus over to the Sanhedrin for a pretrial in a night session. Given the evidence, Ben-Chorin identifies three complaints brought against Jesus: (1) profanation of the temple, a particular concern of the Sadducees; (2) tax evasion, with respect to the imperial government; (3) presumptive messiahship.[845] Following Mark's Gospel, Ben-Chorin argues that this pretrial is followed by a consultation with the Pharisees, who are summoned the next morning. Jesus, "the rebel considered dangerous to the state,"[846] was remanded to Pilate's authority. The hearing before Pilate is limited to the "question of kingship."

Ben-Chorin, implicating a Sadducean "clique," in stark dissent from the majority Jewish view, which doubts the pre-trial's credibility, captures the rapid escalation of Jesus' peril:

> The entire procedure thus happened in great haste, under pressure of the coming festival and Sabbath. Given the tempo of this proceeding, it was impossible for the scattered Jewish followers of Jesus to be informed. Indeed, the puppet master of the clique intentionally arranged it so. It would have been natural, in fact, for Caiaphas and his company to delay handing over Jesus to Pilate until after the Passover feast and to hold the prisoner in custody through the week of festival. That would likely have been the case if Jesus

had not had so many adherents among the Jewish people. The clique doubtlessly feared that the news of his incarceration would spread rapidly among the people and festival pilgrims, possibly giving rise to resistance groups and counteractions. Such activity was to be prevented by creating a fait accompli. Their haste is therefore understandable, in that "the Jews" involved disagreed on how to handle the situation: in fact, the mass of simple folk, the *'am ha- 'arets* class, stood on the side of Jesus, thus prompting the Jewish collaborators to encourage the Roman Pilate to expedite the case.[847]

Pilate hands Jesus, "the King of the Jews," over to the Roman soldiers for scourging and subsequent crucifixion.

Jesus, the Martyred One, Ben-Chorin sadly affirms as a tragic failure inasmuch as Jesus, from Ben-Chorin's perspective, failed both as the herald and catalyst of God's inbreaking kingdom. And in his failure, Jesus experiences an anguishing sense of abandonment by God.

The Downward Spiral

Ben-Chorin charts this downward spiral as three tragic disappointments in the life of Jesus: *eschatology*, *introversion*, and *passion*.[848]

The first disappointment is the failure or delay of the kingdom of God to appear as Jesus initially expected and announced (cf. Matt 10:23). The disciples return from their mission; apart from their enthusiasm, nothing is altered. The kingdom did not come. This failure causes Jesus to rethink his eschatology in which the anticipated "event of history, the advent of a new age, is now understood as having been attained in completion in the soul."[849] Jesus—in light of Luke 17:21, wherein Jesus announces, "The kingdom of God is among you" (NRSV)—may be suggesting that he is the embodiment of the kingdom of God.

The second disappointment, introversion, refers to Jesus' inability, having interiorized the kingdom, to overcome the disruptive, external forces that have come to bear upon him and his disciples, such as the Sadducean priesthood, the Pharisaic legal scholars, the Herodians, and the Roman occupational authority. This failure leads Jesus "on to the ultimate tribulation: a freely chosen self-sacrifice provoked by the Jewish authorities and Roman authorities."[850]

This ultimate tribulation, this passion, wherein Jesus may hope for victory in defeat, goes horribly wrong. There is no obvious vindication, only a deafening silence and terrifying sense of abandonment. Ben-Chorin aptly describes the debacle:

> This sacrificial path ends with crucifixion and the despairing cry of Jesus, . . . There is every reason to accept the despairing cry, "My God, my God, why have you forsaken me?" as the *true* final words of Jesus. The Martyred One gives up the ghost with the horrifying realization of having been abandoned by God, precisely in this third and final station of his thorn-strewn path toward the kingdom of God.[851]

But in failure there is no ignominy, at least not from a Jewish Chassidic perspective. Ben-Chorin explains:

And thus, in the Jewish historical view, Jesus ends up a tragic failure. That does not, however, belittle his greatness, not even in term of Jewish historical understanding. Rabbi 'Akiva himself, who considered Bar-Kokheva the Messiah, proved to be tragically wrong and ended up a martyr for his faith. Nevertheless, his tragic mistake did not rob him of any of his greatness within the Jewish folk consciousness. Quite the contrary, the Jewish tradition explains this kind of error with the saying, "Out of love for Israel, God sometimes blinds the eyes of the wise."[852]

Ben-Chorin affirms: "Jesus of Nazareth, too, is a tragic, deceived figure whose eyes were blinded out of love for Israel."[853]

Where, then, is the place of Jesus within Judaism, we may ask? Ben-Chorin prefaces his response:

> The uniqueness of Jesus' personality allows him, as already noted, to be numbered within none of the customary categories: he is neither prophet nor priest, neither Pharisee nor Sadducee nor Essene. His personality contains prophetic as well as Pharisaic-Essene characteristics; the priestly Sadducee element retreats completely to the background, although a later Christian tradition wishes to see in Jesus the "high priest" of the new covenant. Jesus most closely approaches the Pharisees and is addressed with the Pharisaical title "Rabbi."[854]

Notwithstanding the ambiguity, Ben-Chorin affirms, in answer to the above question: "Where is the place of Jesus of Nazareth? Not among the prophets, not among the apostates and not among the great teachers of the law. His place is at the side of those who perfect the revolution of the heart in Israel, alongside the Rabbi Israel Baal Schem and the other great leaders of Chassidism. That is the place of the rabbi from Nazareth and those of his disciples who 'knew him in the flesh.'"[855]

Ben-Chorin, evaluating his intuited mosaic, concludes: "Jesus is seen here [in *Brother Jesus*] neither as Messiah nor prophet, but as a revolutionary of the heart."[856]

Jesus, a Pious, God-Fearing Jew and Savior of the Gentiles

> The outer shell of the church's Christology may be thick and gnarled, but the inner kernel that determines its nature and lends it radiance is Jesus, the Jew from Nazareth.
>
> Pinchas Lapide, *Jesus in Two Perspectives*, 117

When asked "the basic question of what separates Jews and Christians from each other, the unavoidable answer is: a Jew."[857] This is Jesus of Nazareth, as Pinchas Lapide poignantly explains: "For almost two millennia, a pious, devoted Jew has stood between us, a Jew who wanted to bring the kingdom of heaven in harmony, concord, and peace—certainly not hatred, schism, let alone bloodshed."[858]

Pinchas Lapide, optimistically and unapologetically, seeks to "bring Jesus home" to Judaism, to reconcile the outcast—*their archenemy*[859]—with his own. Of our authors, he and Ben-Chorin are distinctive in their shared goal: rapprochement between Jew and Christian. Both embrace the process of *modernen Heimholung Jesu in das jüdische*

Volk (the modern repatriation of Jesus into the Jewish people) as the vehicle of rapprochement. In the aftermath of the Shoah, their aims are imperative and ambitious: dialogue and reconciliation, understanding and appreciation, ecumenical and irenic. At issue is Jesus, paradoxically chasm and bridge. Lapide's portrait of Jesus emanates from diverse conversations and shared opinions with his Christian counterparts, Protestant and Roman Catholic. To appreciate Lapide's mosaic of Jesus, *the fifth Jesus*, "who is no lofty, fleshless figure of light but a Jew with deep roots in the faith of his people,"[860] we will eavesdrop, discriminately, upon the various transcripts and books representative of his conversation and opinion.[861]

Jesus

In his book *Three Popes and the Jews*, Lapide begins his commentary on Christianity by querying the "genesis" of Jesus. Asserting Jesus' existence over and against historic skepticism, Lapide writes: "Christianity's central and determinative figure is Yeshua of Nazareth, now known under the Latinized form of his Hebrew name, Jesus, and the Greek translation of the ancient Israelite title, Messiah, that is, Christos (the Anointed)."[862]

While affirming Jesus' existence, he credits little historicity to the infancy narratives of Matthew and Luke or the traditional Christmas story crafted from thence. Following the scholarship of the Roman Catholic H. W. van der Vaart Smit, Lapide ventures: Jesus was born neither in December—the most likely time was the end of August—nor in a stable—"Joseph was comfortably middle class and could easily afford adequate lodgings for his pregnant wife." There was certainly no snow, and the "three kings" who came to worship him are as imaginary as their names.[863]

Lapide is influenced by a growing trend emphasizing Nazareth over Bethlehem as the more likely birthplace of Jesus. Ironically, this unhistoric choice of Nazareth as Jesus' birthplace lends, in Lapide's estimation, greater credibility to his historicity:

> It is this unhistoric choice of the nativity, however, which enhances Jesus' historicity. Had Jesus been a mere myth or a tendentious legend, as some authors would have us believe, it would have been quite plausible to locate his birth and adolescence in Bethlehem. Since, however, his Nazarene origin and youth were generally known, a compromise solution had to be found which tallied with Old Testament prophecy without running counter to contemporary knowledge.[864]

Lapide's biographical sketch of Jesus, gleaned from the Synoptic tradition and personal speculation, follows:

- Jesus was born in Nazareth, the son of a humble and devout Jewish carpenter who had at least five sons and two daughters.
- When, later on, he was regarded as the Messiah, legend shifted his birthplace to Bethlehem, the home of the "son of David."

- His father, Joseph, thus was supplied posthumously with a pedigree going back all the way to King David.
- When, still later, Jesus was elevated to be "the son of God," his human father had to clear the way for the "Holy Spirit" by whom his mother, Mary, conceived him in a miraculous fashion.
- His brothers and sisters, though explicitly mentioned as such in the Gospels, were demoted to the rank of "cousins" in order to safeguard the unique "sonship" of Jesus.
- His rough-hewn peasant tongue was Aramaic, a language akin to classical Hebrew. Unlike Greek and Latin, it can only suggest most abstract ideas by concrete metaphors, which have often been misinterpreted in translation.
- Jesus' parents were devout Jews who probably had a m*ezuzah* on the doorpost of their modest home in Nazareth and kept a *koshe*r kitchen.[865]

As to his education, Lapide cites the Talmud and ventures:

- Joseph taught Jesus the carpenter's trade.
- His parents undoubtedly brought him up to recite the benedictions and prayers prescribed for certain hours of the Hebrew day.
- They sent him to synagogue for the study of Hebrew and the Law.
- Much of the Lord's Prayer paraphrases the old Aramaic prayer, the Kaddish, which Jesus must have learned and absorbed as a youth. Even the Beatitudes and the Sermon on the Mount are a direct reflection of common Jewish beliefs that Jesus could have heard from rabbis at the Nazareth synagogue.
- Jesus most certainly received his scriptural training from the Pharisees, whom he would later criticize. (Flusser and Vermès, who both doubt the sustained presence of the Pharisees in Galilee, would disagree with this speculation.)
- Jesus, like the Pharisees, preached a doctrine of love for all people, Gentile as well as Jew. He, like them, tried to stand aside from Israel's political ferment.
- Pharisees were traditionally of lower-class origin and more likely than other rabbis to receive the son of a carpenter.
- Jesus employed the parable, a favorite method of Pharisaic teaching.[866]

Given the above, Lapide advances a succinct portrait of Jesus:

What emerges from the Gospel accounts, therefore, is the figure of a humble Jewish carpenter, born, circumcised and reared as a Jew, who spent all his life among Jews of what today would be called "the lower classes," living and preaching ethical precepts which were imbued with the Torah of Moses and the teaching of Israel's prophets. In the spirit of Amos and Isaiah, he inveighed against the exploitation of the poor by the rich and the stranglehold that empty formalism seemed to be gaining on genuine religion. He taught the fatherhood of God and human brotherhood, the infinite capacity of repentance to secure God's forgiveness of sins, the attainability of saintliness by the humblest and least learned rather than by the affluent and the sages, the certainty of life everlasting for those of unquestioning faith, the equality of the powerful and lowly before the Divine

Throne. His doctrines were not conspicuously original, but he presented them in a new fashion, enlivened by many parables of haunting beauty.[867]

Lapide offers several other observations, including Jesus' gradual acceptance of himself as the Messiah.[868] All of this led the evangelists "to emphasize his fulfillment of biblical prophecies" when crafting their texts. Lapide, considering Jesus' death on a cross and the affixed *titulus*, "Jesus of Nazareth, King of the Jews," affirms: "The inference is clear. Jesus was killed by the Romans for Messianic pretences which, to non-Jews of his time, could mean only one thing: the wish to replace Roman rule by restoring the Jewish monarchy."[869] Lapide poignantly concludes: "Here ends the life of Jesus—and begins the history of Christianity."[870]

Rabbi Yeshua

Thus far, much of Lapide's portrait of Jesus is discerned from his reading of the evangelists' witness. But what of *Yeshua* sans Christology?

Lapide's remarkable juxtaposition of two great Jewish charismatics—"*Rabbi Yeshua of Nazareth* in Galilee, better known as Jesus Christ"; and "*Rabbi Israel of Mezibezh* in Podolia, better known as the *Besht* (literally, the 'Master of the Good Name')—who lived some seventeen centuries and thousands of miles apart, but were closely akin in their faith, thought and singleminded Godliness,"[871] yields an equally valid, singular portrait. Lapide's portrait of Jesus sans the christological overlay emerges from its Synoptic cloak. His observations follow:

- It was a time of Jewish distress when poverty was as abject and oppression as widespread as hopes for redemption ran high.
- We know but little of the founder of the movement, for he had never committed his sermons and parables to writing.
- His disciples had recorded the essence of his teaching only after his death, whilst tales of his life and miraculous deeds survived for decades primarily by word of mouth.
- He appears to have started out as an itinerant Rabbi who wandered from village to village, teaching people to pray, healing the sick and exorcising evil spirits.
- No mere wonder-worker, he concealed his greatness until he had prepared himself in solitude.[872]

As to the rabbi's reception and effectiveness, Lapide reports:

- When he finally revealed himself to his intimates, he was at once accepted and impressed the mark of his strong personality upon a steadily growing number of followers.
- What he sparked was a burst of deep, religious enthusiasm which drew sufficient strength from the simple countryfolk to start something like a rebellion against the

petrifiers of a living religious code—in the name of a mass return to pristine Bible values.

- He and his school of thought were as harshly ostracized by the Rabbinical establishment, as he was warmly welcomed by the poor, the persecuted and the pariahs.
- He is described as acting with a sense of all-embracing compassion, even when it meant risking his own life; as outraged both by arrogance, hypocrisy and sham-humility, and as ever-conscious of the omnipresence of God in all His creatures.
- Devout prayer, the giving of charity, and love of one's fellow Jews were for him the touchstones of true piety.
- The tales which soon sprang up around his every word and deed are rich in saintly miracles and supernatural touches, but most of them abound in earthy, mundane, wisdom. Just as his birth was removed by pious legend beyond the realm of mortal mankind, so his death was not accepted as a finality: his promised return is still a tenet of faith for his numerous followers.[873]

Lapide concludes: "Humble and full of compassion for human frailty, aflame with a burning sense of the inherent holiness of God's universe, *both Rabbis* have but one desire: To release Israel from sin and the world from its bonds in order to usher in at long last The Kingdom of Heaven."[874]

Jesus, Bright Light of Israel

Significant as the above juxtaposition is, Lapide nonetheless stresses both the distinctiveness of Jesus and his elusiveness: "For me, Jesus is no insignificant person, one of many rabbis in Galilee. For thirty years I have occupied myself with him, his teaching, and the history of his impact. But many riddles remain unanswered, some of his features, I see only in blurred outline, and his precise identity eludes all research. It is certain for me that he is a bright light of Israel and belongs to the great teachers of humankind."[875]

A reprise follows. Lapide is trying to convince the Christian church to amend its position and its rhetoric vis-à-vis Judaism, specifically as this relates to Jewish culpability in the death of Jesus. Succinctly, Lapide asserts, "'Deicide' fathered genocide."[876] To combat "the ancient Christian animosity," Lapide proposes, in *Jesus in Two Perspectives*, to "correct three errors that have served as the roots of that ancient 'Christian' animosity for Jews: Jesus was the Messiah of Israel; Jesus was rejected by the Jews; Jesus has in turn repudiated them."[877] He refutes each thesis in his effort to re-Judaize Jesus.[878] Elements of Lapide's rebuttal inform and clarify his "blurred outline" of Jesus and his place within Judaism. We may now proceed.

Concentrating his scholarship on Jesus rather than the "God-man of Greek alloy,"[879] Lapide asserts: "For me, Jesus is less the founder of Christianity than the instigator of a Christian way of life that has as its great manifesto the Sermon on the Mount: a Christian way of life that at bottom amounts to a Jewish way of life and, like it, unfortunately, finds far too few imitators in either community of faith."[880]

Lapide, trying to clarify the blurred outline of *Rabbi Yeshua*, continues:

> A man comes forth in Israel to make today's prophetic vision tomorrow's agenda; one for whom the teachings of Mount Sinai do not suffice because he wishes to penetrate beyond to the original divine intent; one who, despite war and tyranny, dares to pursue the biblical love of neighbor to its ultimate consequence in order to brand all souls with an ideal of human possibility that no longer allows us to be content with the threadbare, run-of-the-mill persons we are but need not be.[881]

Jesus' Torah

A man comes forth in Israel. Commenting on Jesus' place within Judaism, Lapide emphasizes: "What particularly stands out here is that Jesus' belonging to the people of Israel is not simply a matter of genetics but is revealed especially in his spiritual world and his moral teachings."[882]

Lapide expands his description of this "instigator" and adds:

> If you want it simplified, in a very brief form, I would say that Jesus presented to the Judaism of his time a harmony of contrasts, and both parts of this term make him for me primitively Jewish—I would almost say, only Jewish. You may ask why. It is certain that he was Jewish in spirit in at least six respects: in his hope, in his eschatology, in his Jewish ethos, in his blind trust in God, in his very Jewish messianic impatience and—last but not least—in his Jewish suffering; this we can gather without difficulty from all four Gospels. The fact that he often presented a contrast with his milieu also makes him Jewish, for I know no luminary of Judaism from Moses onwards who did not provoke lively opposition among the Jewish people.[883]

Exploring Jesus' teaching, Lapide asserts:

> Jesus was a Jew and as such was not a theologian. He did his best to provide practical, though at times radical, answers to very human problems. His teachings, even when they were idealistic expression of discontent, never left the plane of earthly reality. Only later did his followers, who were by and large no longer Jews, attempt to squeeze him along with his easily remembered paradoxes into a logical straitjacket. And he is still protesting, "I am no cleverly-thought-out book; I am a human being, with all the inherent contradictions."[884]

As to Jesus' reception by other Jews, Lapide reports: "The list of [Gospel] passages which show Jesus attracted crowds and was accepted positively by the common folk of Galilee as well as Judea is legion."[885] However, not all received him well. Lapide observes that Jesus, as did "every staunch and uncompromising Jew,"[886] had opponents. He observes: "He was certainly rejected by the Sadducees in Jerusalem, that is, by the top level of priesthood who saw their cultic privileges threatened by Jesus' proclamation, and who may also have considered him a dangerous agitator, a disturber of political peace and of the status quo."[887]

Though Pharisaic-like, Jesus had detractors among the Pharisees as well, as Lapide affirms: "Jesus was certainly also rejected by many Pharisees. His liberal interpretation of the Sabbath laws and especially his freedom regarding the regulations governing ritual cleanliness must have appeared problematic to the Pharisees, one of whose chief concerns was the ritual purity of the *whole* people of God (Israel), though it is also true that the points of contact between Jesus and the Pharisees are particularly close."[888]

Debating with Hans Küng concerning Jesus' fidelity, or lack thereof, to the law of Moses, Lapide offers a corrective to a dominant Christian view—a view prompted less by Jesus than by Paul:

> I'm terribly sorry to have to contradict you. But I want to make it crystal clear in one sentence. According to the three Gospels, Matthew, Mark and Luke, the Synoptic Jesus never and nowhere broke the law of Moses, the Torah of Moses, nor did he in any way provoke its infringement—it is entirely false to say that he did. . . . And I must say that you Christians make it too easy for yourselves, because you take only the Pauline image of Jesus and assert that Jesus changed the law, rendered it invalid or even abolished it. This is not true. This is how Paul preached him to the Gentiles, but certainly not to the Jews, because he would otherwise have been thrown out of any synagogue at an early stage.[889]

The Orthodox Jew Lapide adds emphatically: "This Jesus was as faithful to the law as I would hope to be. But I suspect that Jesus was more faithful to the law than I am—and I am an Orthodox Jew."[890] Neither concedes the debate.[891]

However, an explanation from another source may help to clarify Lapide's insistence. In his book *The Sermon on the Mount: Utopia or Program for Action?* Lapide grapples with rabbinic parallels to Jesus' Sermon on the Mount in an effort to demonstrate continuity with Judaism. He asserts that "a Jewish Sermon on the Mount, which would strike the reader as a paraphrase of Matthew 5–7, can be put together without using a single word from Jesus."[892] Lapide thereby proves his point and affirms: "Yet, such a paraphrase is possible because we do possess Jesus' Sermon on the Mount. For the fact that the plaster, the cement, and all the building stones come from Jewish quarries in no way diminishes the greatness of the architect who has used these raw materials to design and erect his own moral code."[893]

Jesus' fidelity and creative nuance are evident in the preface to his Sermon on the Mount, as Lapide affirms: "But Jesus is in no way satisfied with a mere declaration of principle; instead he not only calls attention to his fidelity to the Torah with a triple formulation, but also seeks to disarm any reproaches whatsoever that his daring biblical exegesis is an attempt to annul the original meaning of Scripture: *'Do not think that I have come to destroy the law or the prophets.'*"[894]

This "unequivocal, fiery acknowledgment of Israel's Holy Scripture"[895] prompts Lapide to exclaim: "Jesus is here more radical even than Rabbi Hiyya bar Abba and Rabbi Johanan, both of whom were prepared to renounce a letter—that is, a written character—of the Torah if doing so would publicly sanctify the name of God (see *Yeb.* [*b. Yebamot*] 79a)."[896] Radical, yes; but not anti-Torah or anti-Moses, as Lapide explains: "Here it also becomes clear that Matthew saw his Master not as a new lawgiver but as a legitimate interpreter of God's will as contained in the Torah. Jesus is no anti-Moses to Matthew, but rather one who carries on from Moses, who had begun to expound the teaching of the Torah (Deut. 1:5)."[897]

Therefore, Lapide insists: "Jesus neither destroyed nor misappropriated this Torah. On the contrary, he confirmed and affirmed it. Although he urged its highest fulfillment through the development of its original ethics, he, like many other rabbis, suggested his own exegesis—the radical demand of love, the center of Jesus' ethic."[898]

"A Love That Disarms"

Commenting on Jesus' love ethic, Lapide writes:

> Because Jesus was neither a visionary nor a utopian, but a worldly-wise observer of human nature, he did not demand superhuman selflessness or sentiments that would be overdemanding for almost any human heart, but practical demonstrations of love such as visiting the sick, giving alms in secret, supporting the needy, consoling the sorrowful, sharing bread with the hungry, and all the thousand and one effective good deeds that create trust, demolish enmity, and promote love.[899]

Asserting that "hating one's enemies, rejoicing in their misfortune, and repaying evil with evil are expressly forbidden in Judaism,"[900] Lapide offers his understanding of Jesus' enigmatic command to love one's enemies:

> Love of one's enemies, as Jesus understood it, means far more than covering things up with a smile by tolerating enemies or holding them at a distance with politeness; it entails an honest effort, a campaigning and struggling with them, so that they change, give up their hate, and become reconciled. In short—a theo-politics of little loving steps aimed at making the enemy cease to be an enemy. The same is true of praying for one's own persecutors.[901]

"Jesus' Third Way"

Navigating among the various groups that constitute the theo-politics of first century Palestine, such as Zealots and Sadducees, Lapide confirms: "Jesus was certainly no Zealot, no revolutionary in the usual sense, not even a Galilean gang leader. His statements against violence as a political combat method are too numerous for this to be doubted seriously."[902] Nor was he a Sadducee. Rather, Jesus offered a third way. "For the Jew Jesus," Lapide writes, "there was no cleft between body and spirit, between religion and politics, no bifurcation of competencies, but only one total person under the one God and one dream of an all-encompassing heavenly realm."[903]

Observing the prominence of theo-politics in first-century Palestine, Lapide asserts:

> Just as corporeality and concern for physical well-being are not separated from His Instruction on the Mount, politics cannot be amputated from his good news. *Liberation from the pagan yoke, redemption from faintheartedness, and boundless love of God and fellow humans*—these are the chief goals of his salvation teaching, which he, as a

practical-minded Jew, knew could not be realized on this earth without down-to-earth methods. For if the eschatological peace-vision is to be prepared in an earthly manner—though of course with heavenly authority—then humans as God's collaborators must make use of political means to make it concrete. Moses knew that on Sinai; all the prophets of Israel knew it—and so did Jesus of Nazareth, who never wished to give unto Caesar what belonged to God alone.[904]

Describing Jesus as "a threefold rebel of love,"[905] Lapide writes: "He dared, without weapons, to protest against the cruel Roman domination; he opposed the high clergy of the Sadducees who assumed in their narrow-mindedness that they had a monopoly on God's love; and at the same time he raised an eloquent protest against the faint-heartedness of many of his compatriots who would not credit the God of Abraham, Isaac, and Jacob with a salvation politics of liberation."[906]

Avoiding the violence of the Zealot and the exclusivity of the Sadducee, Jesus charted a third way. Of this third way, Lapide observes:

> And yet Jesus was against naked armed forces—neither out of unworldliness nor out of cowardice, but out of biblical farsightedness and realistic worldly experience. Between quietism of the silent majority and the fanaticism of the despairing minority Jesus found a third way—the golden mean—which promised that "the meek will possess the land," as both the Psalter and the Instruction on the Mount foretell (Matt. 5:5; Ps. 38:11 [37:11]). "Not with power nor with force, but by the spirit of the LORD," preached the prophet Zechariah (4:6). Jesus did not want it otherwise.[907]

Lapide affirms: "Jesus' third way relied neither on passive powerlessness nor on militant counterforce, but on a completely new course of human interaction that would invert all dominant relationships and deprive them of power."[908] The new course is that of service: "Whoever among you will be great should be your servant, and whoever among you would be first should be servant of all" (Mark 10:42–45). Jesus' third way advocates "an ethos of equality, of comradely service and disarming love."[909]

Jesus, Pious God-Fearing Jew

Rabbi Jesus' "multilayered impression" was not without comparison, as Lapide observes:

> It is true: as a Jew among Jews, Jesus was not unique. As teachers of Torah and interpreters of Scripture, other rabbis also contributed their special insights and ideas to the overall wisdom of Israel. Thousands of his fellow Jews died as religious heroes and martyrs on Roman crosses like the one on which he lost his life. As messianic prophets, others called for repentance in the face of the new age which was expected to dawn any day. And more than a dozen messianic contenders were crucified.
>
> Even the debate about Jesus' messiahship within Judaism after Golgotha was not exceptional. Whereas his suffering and ignominious death became the proof of his failure for some, for others the same passion became a clear indication that God had accepted his self-sacrifice.[910]

And yet death did not still the Nazarene, as Lapide observes:

> It is equally true that only in the case of the Nazarene did his disciples experience him as the resurrected One; and as a result, that he would return as Messiah became the certainty of their existence. It is no less true, moreover, that this certainty soon crossed the borders of Israel to become the certainty of salvation which called innumerable Gentiles away from their idols to the living God of Abraham, Isaac, and Jacob.
>
> Last but not least, it is an indisputable fact that Jesus of Nazareth—and he alone—became a person of vital significance for millions of believing Christians whom he has helped, and continues to help, to a better life, an undying hope, and a peaceful death.[911]

Such an influential pious, God-fearing Jew, in Lapide's estimation, "cannot remain irrelevant for Israel."[912]

Certainly, Jesus was not without effect among his contemporaries, as Lapide, considering the various titles associated with Jesus, explains:

> Son of God, Redeemer, Son of David, Lord, Master, Servant of God, and a dozen other titles, which only a few in Israel took literally, are basically nothing more than the spontaneous attempts of the reticent rural folk of Galilee to give expression to their amazement. They simply wanted to express verbally that they believed him, that they regarded him as a person of faith, that they were willing to learn to trust God—blindly and without question, as he did.
>
> A generation later, far from Jesus' homeland, in a totally different religious environment, this confusing polyphony gave rise to a theology which placed its faith in him, intensified Jewish enthusiasm to the point of Greek veneration, and even exalted him to Savior of the world.[913]

Lapide's Jesus: *Rabbi Yeshua*, not the God-man of Greek alloy. Lapide's Jesus: the instigator of a Christian way of life, a discipline imbued with Judaic principles. Jesus: the nontheologian, yet practical, effective human being. Lapide's pious, God-fearing Jew: multifaceted, commonplace, yet controversial. Lapide's Jesus, not the Savior of the world, but rather the "Savior of the Gentiles."

Lest one believe this assessment peculiar to Lapide, he contends:

> Any Jewish scholar who examines the New Testament will find that Jesus was undoubtedly a Jew—not just a marginal Jew, nor a lukewarm, pro forma Jew, but a true Jew, whose spiritual roots rose out of the prophetic core of Israel's faith, that he was closely related to the Pharisees, that he was a Galilean, and that on top of everything else, he was a master in the art of telling parables. But to maintain that he was only a Jew, or only a Pharisee, or nothing but a wandering preacher, would be the height of unbiblical arrogance. Moreover, it would contradict one of the basic principles of those same Pharisees, which asserts that negative testimony is not allowed. . . . Using the sources at our disposal, we can attempt to determine who Jesus was, what he accomplished, and which sayings were most likely his. But what he became after Easter Sunday for believing Jewish Christians and later for the Gentile church in addition to and beyond this remains an untouchable prerogative of faith that belongs to the mystery of the church.[914]

Jesus, the Resurrected One

For Jews and nonbelievers, the light of Easter does little to dispel the darkness of Jesus' empty tomb. Although the evangelists record the disciples' experience of Jesus alive, resurrected, on the third day, little evidence—such as unfurled burial linens, the witness of women—can be garnered to confirm Jesus' appearances after death. The historicity of Jesus' resurrection cannot be firmly ascertained; for most Christians, it is a matter of faith in the witness of others, who presumably and unexpectedly encounter their Master, alive. Of this "stumbling block between the brothers of Jesus and his disciples,"[915] Lapide writes: "For that which happened on the 'third day' in Jerusalem is in the last analysis an experience of God which enters into the realm of things which cannot be proved, just as God himself is unprovable; it can be grasped only by faith."[916]

From Lapide's perceptive, such a lived faith, one that may be "neither refuted nor confirmed," can only be sensed with "empathy."[917] Of this empathy, or lack thereof, vis-à-vis the historicity of the resurrection of Jesus, Lapide asserts:

> There never has been a lack of plausible historical objections which seek to deny any reality of that resurrection. But that which impairs these purely "logical" counter-arguments is the circumstance that they attempt to understand "reality" in a restricted way, exclusively as a physically comprehensible or rationally understandable facticity—a standard which is hostile to all human faith. It is the lack of empathy with the Jewish locus of that original Easter faith whose eyewitnesses and first testifiers were without exceptions sons and daughters of Israel.[918]

Thus far, we have traced the outline of Lapide's sympathetic portrait of Jesus. Now, we concisely follow his empathetic and unique approach to the resurrection of Jesus, an event that "is still controversial, cannot be conceived historically, and has led from the beginning to doubt, discord, and dissension."[919]

Tracing the development of the Jewish doctrine of the resurrection of the dead—highlighting the Maccabean historic belief while suggesting a more-ancient Jewish tradition traceable to Abraham at the sacrifice of Isaac,[920] Lapide proposes: "This certainty of a future resurrection of all and of a possible earlier resurrection of some people especially graced by God was *the precondition* of the Easter faith of the disciples whose faith experience, just as that of their Master, was influenced widely by Pharisaism."[921]

He posits that such a belief, this precondition, is "self-evident," given the disciples' response to Jesus' question, "Who do men say that the Son of Man is?" (Matt 16:13).[922] Moreover, given various hypothetical Good Friday scenarios, such as hypothesizing the outcome of the Jesus movement if the apostles had been Sadducees, or other conjectures, he argues: "Only because they were Jews educated by Pharisees was their solid conviction of resurrection the first step to their later Easter faith. Only because they were Pharisaic Jews was the indispensable foundation of their common confidence that this earthly life, despite all tortures and disappointments, was not meant for meaninglessness and that their master even in death was not deserted by the God of Israel."[923]

Lapide suggests that this precondition, the belief in the resurrection of the dead, and the context, the Passover festival, both lend plausibility to the disciples' belief in Jesus' resurrection. Given the ambiguity surrounding the Easter event, Lapide speculates: "The Passover hope of approaching redemption, the dream of victory over death, the comforting Psalms of the Hallel, and Ezekiel's vision of the resuscitation and resurrection of the dead bones—these four basic elements characterized the mood of the Galilean group of disciples on Good Friday which, without doubt, had to become the most difficult crisis of faith for the Jesus community."[924]

Adding empathy to his assessment, Lapide ponders the disciples' situation, Jesus' enigmatic failure, the ignominy of the cross, the apparent injustice of God, and Jesus' subsequent sense of abandonment.[925] With the anguished cry of the Crucified echoing in his ears—in their ears—Lapide intuits:

> And thus the resurrection of Jesus became for his disciples on that day of ruin a theological imperative which was demanded by their never completely forgotten confidence in God—just as Job had dared to demand an accounting from his God even when it had to be extracted out of the abyss of despair.
>
> Jesus *must* rise in order that the God of Israel could continue to live as their heavenly father in their hearts; and in order that their lives would not become God-less and without meaning.[926]

Lapide explains that this categorical *must* "was based on the Jewish insight that the God who is willing to love and to suffer with human beings cannot be a cruel despotic God like the idols of the Greeks and Romans."[927] Lapide, therefore, argues: "The categorical *must* of the resurrection which can be considered a part of the saving plan of God, therefore, was applicable only and alone to the small group of disciples whose life it was able to change so that they became the founders of the church."[928]

On "the third day," a deed of Israel's God raised Jesus, a righteous Jew, from the dead. Commenting on the significance of "the third day" in Jewish salvation history, Lapide writes: "'On the third day' has nothing to do with the date or with the counting of time but contains for ears which are educated biblically a clear reference to God's mercy and grace which is revealed after two days of affliction and death by way of redemption."[929]

All of this—the empathetic musing, the biblically informed intuition, and kindred spirit—leads Lapide, a twentieth-century, Orthodox Jewish rabbi, to a startling affirmation: "Thus, according to my opinion, *the resurrection belongs to the category of the truly real and effective occurrences,* for without a fact of history there is no act of true faith. A fact which indeed is withheld from objective science, photography, and a conceptual proof, but not from the believing scrutiny of history which more frequently leads to deeper insights."[930]

Clarifying his thought, he continues: "In other words: Without the Sinai experience—no Judaism; without the Easter experience—no Christianity. Both were Jewish faith experiences whose radiating power, in a different way, was meant for the world of nations. For inscrutable reasons the resurrection faith of Golgotha was necessary in order to carry the message of Sinai into the world."[931]

In an enigmatic juxtaposition of two faith experiences, Lapide confirms, not only the historicity of the former, but the latter as well, arguing:

> Both are true faith experiences which—just as the existence of God, courage, or love—escape demonstrable facticity in order to disclose themselves alone in faith. It cannot detract from the kernel of experienced truth that this fact of faith later on—in accordance with the spirit of the epoch—was surrounded by a dense wreath of legends, although doubters of all times say with Faust—or rather sigh—"I hear the message, but faith fails me." Faust has many companions of disbelief who can draw their religious ammunition easily from the New Testament.[932]

Aware of, and despite, the evangelists' contradictory reports, the disbelief of skeptics, scoffing of Gnostics, and the extremely meager evidence, Lapide, nevertheless, affirms: "However, legends *can* also be bearers of truths, which by no means deprive the kernel of the narrative of its historicity, as any scholar of religion will bear out."[933]

Lapide is unique among Jewish scholars in embracing the resurrection of Jesus as a historical occurrence. In his dialogue with Jürgen Moltmann, Lapide states plainly: "I accept the resurrection of Easter Sunday not as an invention of the community of disciples, but as a historical event."[934] Viewing the resurrection of Jesus as a Jewish faith experience—one consistent with Jewish expectation, given their doctrine of the resurrection of the dead as the precondition for Easter faith, Lapide explains:

> I am completely convinced that the Twelve from Galilee, who were all farmers, shepherds, and fishermen—there was not a single theology professor to be found among them—were totally unimpressed by scholarly theologoumena, as Karl Rahner or Rudolf Bultmann writes them. If they, through such a concrete historical event as the crucifixion, were so totally in despair and crushed, as all four evangelists report to us, *then no less concrete a historical event* was needed in order to bring them out of the deep valley of their despair and within a short time to transform them into a community of salvation rejoicing to the high heavens.[935]

Reiterating his position from a rabbinic perspective, Lapide writes:

> From a rabbinic point of view the resurrection is basically a messianic Midrash of the first community of Jesus which grew out of the confidence in God's loving righteousness and of the faith in Jesus as the proclaimer of salvation who was sent by God. It is not difficult to understand historically how this came about. That passover of death with the oppressive fact of the cross must have rested like a curse on the disciples of Jesus from the first day. Their believing survival depended on how they coped with this fact, for the search for meaning and the urge to interpret belong to the very soul of Judaism just as much as circumcision. They *had to* learn to understand the historical events as God's work as Israel has done since the Exodus—in order to master them constructively in an understandable and reflective way.[936]

Observing "that which dawned upon them like a lightning flash of hope was then a new interpretation of the Scripture which combined Isaiah 53 and Ezekiel 37 in an illuminating way,"[937] Lapide advances:

> This was a new, comforting interpretation of the suffering servant of God in the light of the vision of the dead bones. And so they succeeded in illuminating their own experience

of Jesus prophetically in such a way that now sacrificial death, the expiation, and the redemption were fused together into a tremendous experience of God—an experience that helped them to interpret death as transition, the cross as a touchstone, and the resurrection as a down payment for life eternal.[938]

Affirming that "the disciples of Jesus stood solidly within their native Judaism to which belongs also the unequivocal faith in the resurrection,"[939] Lapide, in conversation with Moltmann, posits:

> That Jews and Christians can walk together until Good Friday is in my opinion only a partial truth; I believe we can remain together until Easter Monday and even conceive of the resurrection in Jewish terms, but not as the eschatological watershed, as you do, as the "center of time," as Conzelmann calls it. I see it plainly and simply as a historical event, as a tangible reality, as an indication for the primitive community that this Jesus was not abandoned by God, as a kind of response to the words, troubled unto death, which were spoken on the cross: "My God, my God, why have you forsaken me?" I accept the resurrection in the sense that, I believe, the primitive community understood it. However, I cannot accept it as an eschatological beginning, as an inbreaking of the Reign of Heaven, because unfortunately I am unable to discover a single trace of this Reign of Heaven.[940]

Moltmann's questioning response, "If the resurrection was a historical event, why then did the Jews not react to it?"[941] was anticipated and addressed by Lapide. His standard response follows.

Lapide, addresses the "two circumstances [that] seem to confirm all disbelief, the nonpublic manner and the unoriginality of the resurrection,"[942] and advances two positions. In response to the question of the *nonpublic character of the resurrection*, Lapide argues:

> If Jesus had appeared to all, or to many of his Jewish contemporaries, in that feverish climate of expectation of the imminent advent of the Messiah that permeated all of Israel, then there would have been the possibility that the Jesus movement and the church which followed in its wake would have remained an intra-Jewish institution—as indeed was the case in its initial years—without the message of the one God and his gracious love being carried into the world of the Gentile.[943]

Thus he actually argues that the nonpublic character of Jesus' resurrection facilitates the Jesus movement among the Gentiles. Lapide asserts: "Finally, it was faith alone that enables people to experience what the apostles called resurrection. And faith is not knowledge, but is a certainty which only true faith can grant."[944]

As to *the unoriginality of the resurrection* sustaining disbelief, given the ancient worldview, Lapide cites Moses Maimonides' "pedagogy of God"[945] and responds: "In view of this 'pedagogy of God,' would it not be possible that the Lord of the universe used the myth of the resurrection (which was well known to all pagans) in order 'to eliminate idolatry in the pagan world' through the true resurrection of a just person and to carry 'the knowledge of God' to the four corners of the earth by mean of the Easter faith?"[946]

Finally, Lapide, affirming the resurrection of Jesus as a historical event, suggests three possibilities based upon scientific analysis:

1. The resurrection was a historical event in the framework of this world and in the time of the first century in Jerusalem.
2. The resurrection is a religious myth: a mythically colored legend, lacking any reality.
3. The reports of the resurrection rest on visions of individual persons who experienced them as real experiences but so that they are completely inaccessible to the objective test of the sciences. Most Jewish scholars consider this third possibility as the most likely one.[947]

Lapide affirms the first, rejects the second, and dismisses the third as an inadequate explanation. Emphasizing the metamorphosis of Jesus' disciples from a frightened band of peasants, shepherds, and fishermen into a "confident mission society" sans autosuggestion or self-deception, Lapide asserts: "In a purely logical analysis, the resurrection of Jesus is "the lesser of two evils" for all those who seek a rational explanation of the worldwide consequences of that Easter faith. The true miracle is the fact that this Jewish group of Jesus' followers came to faith, a miracle which, like all miracles, escapes any exact description or scientific proof."[948]

He argues that "something must have happened which we can designate as a historical event since its results were historical—although we are completely unable to comprehend the exact nature of the occurrence"[949] and concludes: "If one removes cautiously all these literary additions, a certain something remains for us which in the apostles' simple manner of expression has been called resurrection."[950] The result of the apostles' metamorphosis from frightened peasants to courageous heralds of salvation, leading to the conversion of the Gentiles to Christianity, informs Lapide's theory of Jesus' role in the *praeparatio messianica*.

Jesus, Savior of the Gentiles

Seeking to understand the significance of the death of yet one more Jewish rebel, Jesus of Nazareth, vis-à-vis the numerous Jewish martyrs, leads Lapide to assert: "The only unique element in the crucifixion of Jesus is for me its *history of effects*, the like of which there is not. In his name, and only in his name, was this world-embracing *Ecclesia Christi* founded, and I would be the last to view that as a side issue."[951] Not a side issue: rather, in Lapide's estimation, "the coming-to-believe of Christendom was without doubt a God-willed messianic act, a messianic event on the way to the conversion of the world to the One God."[952]

Citing Maimonides' medieval precedent of viewing Jesus and the matters pertaining to him as preparation for King Messiah,[953] Lapide endorses a similar role for Jesus, especially given the history of effects that surround him and those who have followed him in Easter's light. Reflecting upon Maimonides' "pedagogy of God" and considering the Hellenistic Gentile world in which the Christian church flourished, Lapide asks: "Is it not conceivable that this pedagogy should enable the post-Easter Nazarene to become in all places the recognized mediator (in Greek dress) in order through him to eradicate idolatry in the Gentile world and by means of the exalted Christ "to bring the knowledge of God to the farthest islands?"[954]

He answers in the affirmative, acclaiming: "Jesus of Nazareth has become, in the inscrutable ways of God, the Savior of the Gentiles."[955]

Rhetorically, Lapide argues:

> Can he who parted the Red Sea to save all Israel not call a pious Jew to be Savior of the Gentiles? If the Persian King Cyrus can be spoken of as the "anointed" of the Lord (Isa. 45:1), because he, as God's instrument, made possible the return of the Jews to their biblical home, why can a rabbi from Nazareth not be designated Savior of the nations— as redeemer from idolatry and faithlessness so that "he might bring . . . to God" (1 Peter 3:18) those "having no hope and without God in the world" (Eph. 2:12) so that "through him [they] have confidence in God" (1 Peter 1:21)?[956]

Lapide thus affirms that Jesus, in God's salvific plan, is the Savior to the Gentiles, and that Christendom is the *praeparatio messianica* of the Gentile world. The evidence is the history of the effects of the resurrection of Jesus.

Moltmann—not without nuance—agrees with Lapide: "Christendom is the *praeparatio messianica* of the Gentile world,"[957] and "through his crucifixion Christ has become the Savior of the Gentiles."[958]

Lapide, given the "experience of a handful of Bible-believing Jews who were able to carry their faith in God into the Gentile world,"[959] nevertheless declares: "Jesus, therefore, without doubt, belongs to the *praeparatio messianica* of the full salvation which is still in the future. He was a 'paver of the way for the King Messiah,' as Maimonides calls him, but this does not mean that his resurrection makes him the Messiah of Israel for the Jewish people."[960]

Neither accepting the messiahship of Jesus nor "striving for any kind of syncretism between Judaism and Christianity,"[961] but rather a dialogue, Lapide concludes his reflection of Jesus as Savior of the Gentiles—and his book *The Resurrection of Jesus* by asserting:

> Two ways of faith such as Judaism and Christianity, which have a common origin and hope for a common messianic goal, should devote their dialogue not only to polite contact at the edges and to the removal of the tensions of the past, but should [also] seek contact from center to center. Without glossing over or bypassing the differences, a dialogue in which both partners take the faith substance of the other as seriously as their own could become a true dialogue—from open faith to open faith, from confidence to confidence, from emphatic searching and finding, and from joy in the duality which knows its ultimate unity in God.[962]

In the end, Lapide offers not one bridge but two. Jesus of Nazareth forms, as it were, an exit ramp—or entrance, depending on one's perspective—from the first span, Judaism, that extends as a second bridge, Christianity, traversing to the Father, while the first continues its initial, parallel trajectory to the same Father. Or put another way, "it was Israel that discovered the One God, but it was a Jewish carpenter's son who gave that God to the world."[963] For the Jews, Jesus—Lapide's *fifth Jesus*—"remains a great teacher of morality as well as a tragic figure of universal human appeal."[964]

Of this *fifth Jesus*, the Savior of the Gentiles, Lapide concedes: "All we can know with reasonable certainty is that at the beginning of Christianity there was a God-struck Jew whose Messianic convictions and prophetic zeal infected a goodly number of his compatriots."[965]

Jesus, Galilean Sage, a Teacher of torah

Nothing I heard from Jesus spoke of covenant, nothing of Israel, nothing of obligation of the whole of Israel, all together and all at once; everything spoke of me, not us; of leaving, not staying; of near-turning, not the long-term state of affairs.

Jacob Neusner, *A Rabbi Talks with Jesus*, 157

Jacob Neusner engages in debate the Jesus that he encounters in Matthew's narrative rather than "the historical Jesus of a scholar's studious imagination."[966] As previously advised, his book *A Rabbi Talks with Jesus* is not about scholarship. Rather, it is about an encounter between two Jewish rabbis meeting across an expanse of two thousand years—both poised at the beginning of two different millennia. Unlike other scholars engaging Rabbi Jesus, Rabbi Neusner chooses a different path. He resists the temptation, "the fabrications of other scholars," both Jew and Christian, to reconstruct Jesus from the confines of the Gospels via historical-critical scholarship, creative intuition, or other hermeneutics. Neusner's path is dialogue and debate, argument, and ultimately, respectful dissent. The medium of their encounter is Jewish literature, specifically the Gospel of Matthew, as presented by a Christian evangelist, and the Torah, the law of God as revealed to Moses.[967] His aim, simple: "By *the truth of the Torah, much that Jesus said is wrong*. By the criterion of the Torah, Israel's religion in the time of Jesus was authentic and faithful, not requiring reform or renewal, demanding only faith and loyalty to God and the sanctification of life through carrying out God's will."[968]

It remains for Neusner to demonstrate his thesis: an effort that conveys not only a portrait of Jesus as teacher but concomitantly also provides a paradigm of religious dialogue.[969]

The Matthean Teacher

Neusner begins with preliminary observations on both Matthew's Gospel and his portrait of Jesus. He observes: "Matthew's Jesus comes closest to an account of Jesus that a believing and practicing Jew can grasp in terms of Judaism. And Matthew's picture of Jesus describes him as a Jew among Jews, an Israelite at home in Israel, unlike the portrait, for instance, given by John, who speaks of 'the Jews' with hatred."[970]

Providing a précis of particulars for the reader of the Gospel of Matthew, the "most Jewish" of the Gospels, Neusner emphasizes: "Among these matters, one is striking: the representation of Jesus as a teacher, with an important message forming part of the evidence that here is the Christ, in whom Israel should believe."[971]

Given that "the content of the message, not only the character of the life and miracles, forms an important component of Jesus' credentials in Matthew,"[972] Neusner
proposes to debate the messenger and in doing so to challenge the message. He writes:

> Today, with so many teachings turned into platitudes and clichés, it is difficult to hear
> his words as challenges, goads, assertions in the face of contrary views. But that is our
> task, too, if we are to have a serious argument about important truths. And it is time, I
> think, for some specific teachings of Matthew's Jesus to receive sustained and serious
> attention as not platitudes and truisms but contentious and vigorous propositions, de-
> manding assent attained through argument. For as you read the stories Matthews tells,
> you cannot avoid the simple fact that Jesus was a man who said things he thought new
> and important, and who claimed that his teaching formed the correct way to carry out
> and to fulfill the Torah, the teachings that God had given to Moses at Mount Sinai.[973]

Neusner explains: "We—eternal Israel, to whom Jesus was sent by God and to whom
Jesus brought his message—are supposed to be persuaded by the character of these
teachings, represented as the fulfillment of the Torah as a matter of fact."[974] Although
"Matthew claims in behalf of Jesus that his is a body of teachings of such obvious
truth that all who hear them must confess the name of the one who said them:
Jesus Christ,"[975] Neusner remains unconvinced and chooses to offer rebuttal and
argumentation.

He suggests: "In response to the message of Matthew's Jesus, a practicing Jew such
as myself, speaking for myself alone of course, but well within the faith of eternal Israel,
can frame an argument."[976] Neusner asserts that "an argument with Matthew's Jesus is
plausible because there really is a shared Torah between us, so we can agree sufficiently
on the main thing [and] . . . disagree on other things."[977]

Neusner does not contest the stories that surround Jesus: "If someone makes a categorical statement to do this, not that, you can argue. But how do you argue a miracle?
Either you believe or you do not believe. . . . Nor would any humane person, and
certainly no Jew, child of a tradition that teaches [that] God prefers the pursued to the
pursuer—the lamb, the sheep, the goat, not the lion or the bear—wish to take issue with
the tragic and disturbing Passion Narrative."[978]

At issue, then, is the validity of Jesus' teachings as conveyed to us by Matthew vis-
à-vis the Torah, as presented by Neusner. As to his position on the Torah, Neusner
could not be clearer: *"We Jews maintain, and I argue here, that the Torah was and is
perfect and beyond improvement, and that Judaism built upon the Torah and the
prophets and writings, the originally oral parts of the Torah written down in the
Mishnah, Talmuds, and Midrash—that Judaism was and remains God's will for
humanity."*[979]

Describing Jesus, then, as "a Torah-teacher teaching his torah to his disciples,"[980]
Neusner engages Jesus on a single subject: "what God wants of me."[981] He explains:

> What God instructed Moses at Mount Sinai and what Moses wrote down in the Torah is
> [are] our shared set of facts. A single problem, an agreed-upon agenda, a shared set of
> facts—these are the requirements for a serious and sustained argument: a dialogue. So
> here I will try to tell the story of the grounds for that dissent, so to frame an account of
> how I should have argued with Jesus and tried to persuade him and those with him that

their view of the Torah—of what God wants for humanity—at important and substantive points was wrong.[982]

This raises the question of a criterion. Addressing this issue of criterion, Neusner argues: "The Torah is a legitimate criterion of truth, since both parties to the argument share the same conviction."[983] Pointedly, Neusner reflects upon this question of criterion and asserts: "And it's an urgent question, because, as we'll see, Matthew's Jesus instructs people to violate at least three of the Ten Commandments. And I am going to ask Jesus to his face: How can you tell the people to violate some of the Ten Commandments and yet claim to teach torah, let alone the Torah of Moses given by God at Sinai?"[984]

It is Jesus' torah[985] with which Neusner takes issue. The Torah of Sinai serves as his criterion of truth.

Galilean Sage

Neusner begins his imaginative encounter with Matthew's Jesus with agreement. He agrees wholeheartedly with what the Matthean Jesus teaches in Matthew 5:17–19:

> *Think not that I have come to abolish the Torah and the prophets; I have come not to abolish them but to fulfill them. For truly I say to you, till heaven and earth pass away, not an iota, not a dot, will pass from the Torah until all is accomplished. Whoever, then relaxes one of the least of these commandments and teaches men so, shall be called least in the kingdom of heaven; but he who does them and teaches them shall be called great in the kingdom of heaven.*[986]

Yet, these words ring hollow as Neusner listens to the Galilean sharing his torah with the crowds gathered around him, "the young man and his students, whom some admired, some hated, but none ignored."[987]

He affirms that "Jesus torah is substantial and, by his own word, controversial, too."[988] Jesus' opening instruction, the Beatitudes, wins Neusner's confidence, yet something is awry. Neusner, leans forward, listening more intently—remembering, "*Think not that I have come to abolish the Torah*"—and observes:

> So I am told to expect something fresh, original, and superior to anything that has gone before—and yet, torah in conformity with the Torah revealed by God to Moses at Sinai. So the sage set for himself a worthy challenge, one that every sage in every generation does well to meet: receive a tradition whole and perfect, hand it on never intact but always unimpaired, so taking a rightful place in the chain of tradition from Sinai."[989]

Sensing in Jesus' use of paraphrase and debate continuity with the Jewish sage tradition, Neusner is nonetheless bothered by the six antitheses[990] of Jesus' teaching: "*You have heard it said, but I say to you.*" Not everything that he hears from Matthew's Jesus "gains such immediate assent: familiar and better."[991] The fourth and fifth statements—"*Do not resist evil*" and "*Love your enemies, . . . pray for your persecutors*" (Matt 5:38–45), coupled with Jesus' instruction on prayer in private vis-à-vis the hypocrites, *"When you pray, go into your inner room"* (6:5–6)—are troubling: the former two, because this is not Torah; and the latter, because this is not Israel at prayer.[992]

Concurring with Montefiore's insight, that "Jesus was not thinking of public justice, . . . but only how members of his religious brotherhood should act toward each other and towards those outside their ranks,"[993] Neusner ventures: "Jesus addresses not eternal Israel, but a group of disciples. His focus, time and again, defines a limited vision."[994] Moreover, he wonders "whether there is not a missed mark here,"[995] writing: "Jesus on the mountain addresses not 'all Israel,' this one and that one, individuals and families. He speaks to our lives, but not to the whole of the world in which we make those lives. For we find ourselves hearing a message for home and hearth, for growing up and growing older—but not for community, state, and ongoing social order, such as eternal Israel comprises in this world."[996]

Neusner affirms that Jesus sees the poor, the mourner, the meek, the merciful, the peacemakers as part of eternal Israel, "perhaps from God's perspective, the best part."[997] Yet, Neusner reports: "I listen for a message to not me alone, or my life and my family but to all of us, eternal Israel, who stood at Sinai not as a motley mob but as God's people, children of Abraham, Isaac, and Jacob. Jesus himself—so Matthew tells me—is son of David son of Abraham. But when he stands on the mountain, that is not the audience he sees."[998]

Of this audience, eternal Israel vis-à-vis Jesus, Neusner writes:

> But it is the audience in which I take my part. That is what I mean by a missed mark. So much for the substance: much with merit, but silences prove ominous. We—eternal Israel—need torah to tell us what God wants of us. But Jesus has only spoken about how I, in particular, can do what God wants of me. In the shift from the "us" of Sinai to the "I" of the torah of the Galilean sage, Jesus takes an important step—in the wrong direction. And if I had been there, I would have wondered what he had to say to not me but to us: all Israel, assembled, that day, in the persons present, before him to hear his torah.[999]

Teacher of torah

Sharing the astonishment of the gathered crowd at the Galilean's audacity, Neusner exclaims: "Here is a Torah-teacher who says in his own name what the Torah says in God's name."[1000] He continues: "I am troubled not so much by the message, though I might take exception to this or that, as I am by the messenger."[1001] Given the striking contrast between *"You have heard it said . . . , but I say to you"*—a contrast between Moses and Jesus, Neusner asks: "So how am I to respond to this 'I,' who pointedly contrasts what I have heard said with what he says?"[1002]

Neusner, realizing the shift in his focus from message to messenger, writes: "At many points in this protracted account of Jesus' specific teachings, we now recognize that at issue is the figure of Jesus, not the teachings at all."[1003] Jesus' statements addressed narrowly to the few and claiming for himself an authority previously reserved to the Torah, is jarring for Neusner. Jesus' torah, though in several ways consistent with the ancient Jewish sages, deviated markedly. Jesus hearkens not to Moses or Torah, but to his own authority as son, unlike other sons of Israel, in teaching Torah.

Amazed at the Galilean's audacity, Neusner observes:

> These statements and many like them address not eternal Israel but only those Israelites (and others) who acknowledge that "me," who refers to "my Father," and who can speak of "these words of mine." All these things are of a single cloth. At Sinai, God spoke through Moses. On this Galilean hill, Jesus speaks for himself. Moses spoke for God to "us," "eternal Israel," and we, Israel, responded as "we": "We shall do, we shall obey." In Galilee, Jesus speaks to the crowds who are astonished at his teaching, identifying in the crowds the special hearers, those revealed on his account, individuals among eternal Israel, hearing this master addressing them, as he says, not as "their" (those others', those outsiders') scribes, "but as one who had authority."[1004]

Jesus, the Galilean sage with limited vision, the torah teacher, who misses a mark, *is* the issue. Neusner, in reaction to this first encounter with Jesus, emphasizes: "By the criterion of the Torah, Jesus has asked for what the Torah does not accord to anyone but God."[1005] "The entire revelation at Sinai is now relegated to 'It was said.' And this in contrast to 'I.'"[1006]

Declining to follow Jesus, if invited by the disciples, Neusner muses: "When God speaks through Moses, it is to all Israel, but your master speaks to you. The rest of us are outsiders. And God does not know outsiders in Israel, only sinners, whom the Torah teaches to repent.[1007]

In his musing he observes a parallel to Jesus: Balaam. Continuing his conversation with Jesus' disciples, Neusner replies: "Jesus reminds me of a prophet, yes, speaking on his own authority—but not an Israelite prophet. He talks like an outsider, or if he is the insider, then much that he says makes the rest of us outsiders."[1008]

A Dividing Sword

Early in his introduction, Neusner promises to demonstrate his critique: Jesus and his torah encourage people to violate at least three of the Ten Commandments. Neusner senses that something is awry: something is missing in Jesus' torah, "ominous silences," thunder. He feels that Jesus neglects certain dimensions of his, Neusner's, existence—community, family and home, individual and private. These dimensions are the hallmarks of the social order of Israel, commandments integral to eternal Israel's identity, commandments that Jesus alters. I present the commandments in question as juxtaposed to Jesus' torah (below), following Neusner's example:

1. "Honor your father and your mother" versus "Do not think that I have come to bring peace on earth."
2. "Remember the Sabbath Day to keep it holy" versus "Look, your disciples are doing what is not lawful to do on the Sabbath."

3. "You shall be holy; for I the LORD your God am holy" versus "If you would be perfect, go, sell all you have, and come, follow me."[1009]

It is beyond our purpose to probe too deeply into Neusner's studied rebuttal to Jesus' torah. On one hand, it suffices to say that, in each case, Neusner does, to his satisfaction, offer conclusive rebuttal. On the other hand, elements of his rebuttal bear presentation so as to clarify his portrait of Jesus. Following Neusner, salient features emerge.

Of Jesus' torah on the Ten Commandments, Neusner observes:

> Jesus begins with fundamental affirmations about life with God. He concludes with teaching about the personal life. In the middle, between the opening, theological commandments and the closing personal ones, I find two commandments, both of them focused on life in community: that is, on the society of the here and now. That is where I live; that is where life flourishes, so these attract my attention.[1010]

Neusner affirms: "One commandment concerns the Sabbath; the other, the home and family in particular: the household."[1011] He considers the latter first.

Honor the Family

Jesus' contradictory teaching about the commandment concerning family—"*I have come to set a man against his father, and a daughter against her mother*"—"startles and alarms" Neusner:

> Eternal Israel holds the land—so the Ten Commandments say—in virtue of honor of father and mother. When God says to Moses, ". . . that your days may be long in the land which the LORD your God gives to you," the stakes are not trivial. Now, in the context of Jesus' own message, a disciple may point out to me that to follow Jesus, I have to place his call above even my love for parents: ". . . He who does not take his cross and follow me is not worthy of me. He who finds his life will lose it, and he who loses his life for my sake will find it" (Matt. 10:38–39). And yet, if I do what he says, I abandon my father and mother, my brothers and sisters, my wife and my children. Then what is to be of Israel? For if all of us do what he wants, then the family disintegrates, the home collapses, and what holds the village and the land together, the body of the family, gives way. To follow him, do I have to violate one of the Ten Commandments?[1012]

At the heart of Neusner's critique is his apprehension that "Jesus' advice runs counter to what and who we [eternal Israel] are, which is everywhere and always "Israel," a whole people, a community of families, all of us with the same parents and grandparents, Abraham and Sarah, Isaac and Rebecca, Jacob and Leah and Rachel, whose God is the God of us all."[1013]

Arguing that the commandment concerning the honoring of parents is "not personal and private, but public, social, and corporate,"[1014] Neusner sees in Jesus' torah, as evidenced by Matthew 12:46–50, a violation of Torah. Jesus' disciples' neglect of their families further troubles Neusner and illustrates his point—though he admits "that in time to come masters would call disciples away from home and family, and they would leave their wives and children for long periods of time, so as to study the Torah."[1015]

This and Jesus' emphasis on himself rather than the Torah vis-à-vis the sage-disciple relationship leads Neusner assert the crux of the issue: "Now we see what is truly at stake: honor of parents form a this-worldly analogy to honor of God. So the issue is not discipleship alone, but the comparison between and among relationships: relationship of disciple to master, relationship of child to parent, relationship of human being to God."[1016]

In light of this, Neusner queries Jesus' disciple: "Is your master God?"[1017] His explanation is his critique: "In the end the master, Jesus, makes a demand that only God makes. . . . Jesus' link of family to master-disciple-circle forms only the first step, leading not to honor of the master like, or more than, honor of parents, but, ultimately, honor of master like, or as much as, honor of God."[1018]

Though approving of Jesus and his pedagogical technique as "a model for the teacher,"[1019] Neusner takes issue with Jesus' narrow focus: on the "I" and the "me" vis-à-vis eternal Israel. Speaking to Jesus, he asks: "But then, is everything in your torah's fulfillment of the Torah to speak only to my conduct as one person? Is there no torah for me as part of a family, as part of that Israel that existed before Sinai and assembled at the foot of Sinai: children of Abraham and Sarah, Isaac and Rebecca, Jacob and Leah and Rachel? I am of the family of Israel. What have you to say to me in that family?"[1020]

Continuing in this vein, he asks:

Master, is there an Israel in your "You"?—not an "Israel" out there, in the abstract, but an "Israel" in here, in my village, in my family? . . .

Master, do you speak only to me, not to my family? only to your family of disciples, not to your family after the flesh? . . .

So, master, where is there place, and space, in your "you" for that "us" that makes up Israel?[1021]

Though the master does not answer him directly, Neusner finds an answer to his response in Matthew 6:25–27, 31–33—"*Do not be anxious about your life, what you shall eat or drink. . . . Seek first his kingdom and his righteousness*"—wherein Jesus contrasts "this 'you' with the Gentiles; so the Gentiles seek these things, but 'your heavenly Father' knows you need them."[1022] Neusner concludes:

So Jesus does have a message for me in Israel. But the Israel here is not family and village; the concerns of family and village, that Israel of the here and now, for food and drink and clothing and shelter—these God of course will attend to. But then, if what should concern me is his kingdom and his righteousness, where I live, with whom I live—these really bear no consequences. Once more we find a message in the silence, as much as in the speech, we hear from the top of the mountain. This "Israel" is then something other than, different from, that Israel of home and family that I know. And my argument consists in only one "but":

"But, Sir, the Israel of home and family is where I am."[1023]

All of this prompts Neusner's final question: "*What of Israel where it is, what of Israel when it takes place.*"[1024] What of "Israel in the here and now of home and village?"[1025]

The Sabbath: Imitatio Dei

Neusner, focusing on what the Galilean master says *and* does in relationship to the Sabbath, draws a similar conclusion. Neusner affirms that in fidelity to God's command, Israel rests and keeps holy the seventh day, the Sabbath. In imitation of God, Israel keeps holy the Sabbath and refrains from work: "We do on the Seventh Day what God did on the Seventh Day of creation."[1026]

Of Jesus' torah of the Sabbath, Neusner observes:

> Jesus treats the Sabbath in two statements, which stand side by side. The two statements, appropriately, deal with the Sabbath first in the setting of our relationship with God, and only second, in the context of the things we do and do not do. So Jesus stands well within the framework of the Torah in his presentation of what he wishes to say about the Sabbath: a this other-worldly moment that bespeaks eternity. The Sabbath forms the centerpiece of our life with God, and Jesus treats it as the centerpiece of his teaching; only as a second thought do the do's and the don't's matter.[1027]

Neusner's reflection on Jesus' invitation to those still outside his circle of disciples, Matthew 11:27–30—"*Come to me, find rest, for my yoke is easy and my burden is light*"—prompts him to initially affirm Jesus' torah: "Since, on the Sabbath, I rest as God rested, . . . I find entirely appropriate the focus here: How do I come to God? And how do I find rest?"[1028] Juxtaposing Jesus' invitation with two events that follow, the unlawful gathering of grain and healing on the Sabbath (Matt 12:1–14), Neusner is jarred by what he sees, but more so by what he hears: "*It is lawful to do good on the Sabbath*" (Matt 12:12). Why is he jarred? Because "the Sabbath is not about doing good or not doing good; the issue of the Sabbath is holiness, and in the Torah, to be holy is to be like God."[1029]

Regarding this *imitatio Dei* and Jesus' torah, Neusner observes:

> In addressing the issue of the Sabbath, therefore, Jesus and his disciples strike squarely at the critical issue: What do we do to imitate God? How do we so live as to make ourselves into that "eternal Israel" that God through the Torah has brought into being? Like honor owing to father and mother, therefore, the celebration of the Sabbath defines what makes Israel Israel. The entire way of life of the community centers on that day.[1030]

Neusner provides a discussion of the significance of the Sabbath Day as "the defining moment in the life of eternal Israel."[1031] He affirms: "In this law of the Torah, therefore, we are told about a day that defines Israel in time and place. Accordingly, the Torah lays the foundation for the construction of the holy life of eternal Israel on the Sabbath Day."[1032]

Observing Jesus and his disciples and listening to Jesus' torah concerning these commandments that undergird the social order of Israel, Neusner takes issue with the liberal Jesus. The issue is Jesus, self-proclaimed "lord of the Sabbath," and promoter of good deeds on the Sabbath as Neusner explains: "Jesus' claim to authority is at issue, not the more lenient, or less lenient, character of his rulings on what we do on the holy day. These counsels simply express in a concrete way a much deeper conviction, and if, as for the purpose of this argument we must concede, he really said these things, then through them he meant to declare himself and his disciples to form a new entity in place of the old."[1033]

Pointedly Neusner argues:

> At issue in the Sabbath is neither keeping or breaking this one of the Ten Commandments. At issue here as everywhere else is the person of Jesus himself, in Christian language, Jesus Christ. What matters most of all is the simple statement that no one knows the Father except the Son and anyone to whom the Son chooses to reveal him. There, startling and scarcely a consequence of anything said before or afterward, stand the centerpiece of the Sabbath-teaching: my yoke is easy, I give you rest, the son of man is lord of the Sabbath indeed, because the son of man is now Israel's Sabbath: how we act like God.[1034]

Expanding upon this insight, Neusner asserts:

> In the very context of the Sabbath, when in sacred space and holy time, Israel acts like God, we grasp that Jesus addresses that very issue—what does it mean to know God?—and does so in precisely the context in which Israel, from Sinai, knows God and acts like God: the Sabbath. Jesus has chosen with great precision the message he wishes to set forth with regard to the Sabbath, both the main point which comes first, and then the details and consequences of that same point, which follow.[1035]

Over against Jesus, Neusner affirms: "From the perspective of the Torah as I understand it, only God is lord of the Sabbath."[1036] Of his argument, he writes:

> What is God's stake in remembering the Sabbath Day? The Torah teaches me that it is my celebrating creation, acting on the Sabbath Day as God acts on the day when creation ceases: blessing the Sabbath Day and sanctifying it. Jesus, too, teaches that the Sabbath Day brings the gift of rest—but it is a rest that God gives through the son. So we find ourselves precisely where we were when we wondered what is at stake in honor of father and mother: keeping the Sabbath forms [a] this-worldly act of imitation of God.[1037]

Neusner concludes with a familiar challenge: "Is your master God?"[1038]

Holy or Perfect

Neusner describes the preceding as "the sideshow": concerns, important though they may be, "merely illustrate the fundamental issue that Jesus comes to address."[1039] The "main event," the most fundamental issue, "the heart of Jesus' teaching," in Neusner's estimation is: "What does God want of me?"[1040]

Continuing his imaginative encounter, Neusner eavesdrops on the conversation between Jesus and a young man in Matthew 19:16: *"What must I do to have eternal life?"* Again, Neusner approves Jesus' reply: Observe the Ten Commandments and the Great Commandment (Lev 19:18): *"You shall love your neighbor as yourself."* If the conversation had but ended there, muses Neusner, it would be acceptable. But, in Neusner's hearing, the conversation, after a slight pause, a moment wherein the young man found Jesus' answer wanting, continues: *"Go, sell your possessions, give to the poor, and follow me."*

Startled by the rapid exchange, Neusner observes: "Here is a profound turn. Jesus grasped the question the young man really wanted to ask, which was not merely about eternal life but about 'perfection'—something else altogether."[1041]

Perfection! Neusner exclaims, as if in soliloquy: "Given the frailty of humanity, none can expect perfection as the price for eternal life."[1042] Later, overhearing Jesus answering a similar question in a different setting, "*Teacher, which is the great[est] commandment in the law?*" (Matt 22:36–40), Neusner debates Jesus concerning the intrusion of the concept of "perfection" into his torah. To this reply of Jesus, Neusner approves, but to rebut the insertion of perfection, previously affirmed, Neusner adds a third commandment that is like it: "You shall be holy; for I the LORD your God am holy." (Lev 19:2).[1043]

Neusner argues: "Here, after all, is a commandment that addresses not me personally and how I love God, or not me in relationship to someone else, but to all of us, all Israel together."[1044] Of Jesus' torah, he declares: "Once more, therefore, I am struck by the dimensions of the world that Jesus addresses: the individual in search of salvation, the private person in quest of God."[1045] Neusner underscores what is lacking: "And all due honor for the Torah-teaching that he [Jesus] cites, but the Torah says something about a dimension of human existence that, in these sayings, Jesus does not discern: the community as a whole, all of us together, what in today's language we should call the social order."[1046]

In light of this, Neusner wonders: "Is there no relationship of us all before God?"[1047] The Torah is his firm affirmation of God's love for "all at once and all together."

Of Jesus' silence, he continues:

> That is why in my mind, what Jesus has not said takes on profound weight; he has spoken to me, but not to us; there is no dimension of holy and eternal Israel in his reading of the Torah's fundamental teaching. He has said that I should sell all I have, give to the poor, and follow him; Aqiba [Akiba ben Joseph] in context told Tarfon no less. But he has not said that we—not I, but we, Israel—are to be; how are we, eternal Israel, to strive to be like God. After all, "loving your neighbor as yourself" (Lev. 19:18) comes at the end of the very passage that commences with, "You shall be holy; for I . . . am holy." Since Jesus knows the Torah at least as well as anybody else, he has made choices, selecting what counts and silently what does not. . . . Here the thought passes my mind: he might have said, "You have heard it said, . . . but I don't say that to you."[1048]

Jesus' failure to connect Leviticus 19:18 to 19:2—which in Neusner's studied estimation is the main point: "Why should I love my neighbor as myself? Because, as Moses taught us, 'You shall be holy, for I the Lord your God am holy'"[1049]—illustrates an ominous silence.

Neusner confronts Jesus with his deliberate omission of the Torah's commentary on holiness: "'Sir,' I ask, 'how about 'You shall be holy'? What does the Torah want me to be when it tells me to be holy?'"[1050] In Neusner's opinion, in the exchange between Jesus and the young man, Jesus has taught that being holy is *not enough*. Though the young man has fulfilled the Torah's expectation, Jesus has suggested that something was lacking, something more was required: *"Go, sell, give, follow me."* Neusner challenges Jesus and his torah: "What I hear you saying is, the Ten Commandments are not enough, the Great Commandment, the Golden rule—these, too, are not enough. Perfection consists in poverty and obedience to Christ."[1051]

More troubling than Jesus' contrast of Christ and wealth, with which Neusner would not argue—later Akiba would contrast the Torah and wealth[1052]—was Jesus' call to be like him:

Sell all I have and

- Study Torah.
- Follow Christ.
- Which?[1053]

Neusner realizes that to argue this point with Jesus, given that he engages only the Matthean Jesus and not the Christ, is beyond the scope of his intention,[1054] yet he does find ground upon which to challenge Jesus: "If we examine what our sages teach we must do in order to be holy, like God, the beginning of a fair exchange may be discerned."[1055]

Neusner's single point of difference between the Torah and Jesus is familiar: "If I had to point to the single difference between the message of the Torah, at least as our sages mediate that message, and the message of Jesus as Matthew quotes and portrays that message, it is a simple fact: The message of the Torah always concerns eternal Israel. The message of Jesus Christ always concerns those who follow him."[1056]

Neusner argues:

The Torah always speaks to the community and concerns itself with the formation of a social order worthy of God who called Israel into being. Jesus Christ in Matthew's account speaks of everything but the social order of the here and now; here he speaks of himself and his circle; then, in time to come, he speaks of the kingdom of heaven.

Lost in between the man and the coming kingdom is the everyday of the common life. But it is that everyday, common life that the Torah commands Israel to sanctify. And at stake in that life of a social order aimed at sanctification is nothing less than the sanctification of God on high.[1057]

The issue is holiness; the pattern is God; the guide, for Neusner, is the Torah of Moses —not Jesus, the Galilean sage with limited vision, the torah teacher, who misses a mark.

Jesus poses a choice to those gathered near: choose between Jesus and God, imitate the grace and mercy of Christ or imitate the grace and mercy of God. Neusner, like most of the Jews that heard Jesus' torah, chooses God.

The Kingdom of Heaven

That Neusner takes issue with Jesus' torah, his limited vision, is evident; so too, though perhaps less emphatic, is his critique of Jesus' eschatology. For Neusner and for most religious Jews, the kingdom of heaven, the reign of God, is immanent, not imminent—eternal Israel of the here and now, of family and village. This is all the more certain when Neusner, reacting to Jesus' severe critique of the scribes and the Pharisees (Matt 23:1–36), writes:

> What bothers me in Jesus' harsh judgments about the scribes and the Pharisees is that *I'm one of those people who do the things that the scribes and Pharisees observe.* That is to say, I really do believe that God wants me to carry out the Torah; I believe that God wants me to strive to be holy. Jesus lays down so vigorous a barrage of criticisms of people like me that, from that time to our own day, Pharisee loses its capital *P*, and a pharisee is a hypocrite: "They do all their deeds to be seen by men." And that judgment about Judaism (not to mention the forms of Christianity, and they are very many, who also do deeds to serve God, and believe God is pleased by those deeds) concerns not only hypocrites or people who do it all for show. It concerns everybody who carries out the religious duties, the mitzvoth [*miṣwôt*] or commandments, that the Torah teaches.[1058]

Juxtaposing Jesus and the Pharisees, Neusner begins his closing argument with Jesus. He points to the one thing that Jesus offers to those gathered near instead of a life of holiness like God, namely, the kingdom of heaven:

> Over and over again, Jesus tried to explain what was at stake: "Repent, for the kingdom of heaven is at hand" was Jesus' first message (Matt. 4:17). So at stake is overcoming sin, so as to enter God's kingdom. Jesus preached the gospel of the kingdom and healed every disease and infirmity (Matt. 9:35). Over and over again, he explained what was on his mind in parables, and these, time and again, concerned the kingdom of heaven, what it is like, how it is to be understood.[1059]

Jesus' vision of the kingdom of heaven is the key—the catalyst of cohesion, in Neusner's estimation—to his enigmatic and jarring torah.[1060] A perceptive Neusner, given the divergent torahs of Jesus and the Pharisees, observes: "But it [Jesus' message] is a message the Pharisees are not hearing, because they have a different message. And it is one that scarcely intersects with the teaching of Jesus. His is a message of forgiveness of sin in the here and now, in preparation for the coming of the kingdom of heaven in the on-rushing future. The Pharisees' is a message of purification for a life of holiness in the here and now."[1061]

Neusner, "faced with a choice . . . would have honored the one, but followed the other."[1062] He explains:

> I would honor Jesus, but I would follow the Pharisees, and I do that even now: it's why I wrote this book. For the Torah had defined Israel as a kingdom of priests and a holy people. That is the way taken by the Pharisees. Their Israel found commonality in a shared, holy way of life, required of all Israelites—so Scripture held. The Mosaic Torah defined that way of life in both cultic and moral terms, and the prophets laid great stress on the latter. What made Israel holy—its way of life, its moral character—depended primarily on how people lived. And that was in the here and now. What the Pharisees had to say about what would happen later on, Jesus never suggests; that is not a point on which he had an argument with them.[1063]

He observes one more fact, one that also underlies why he wrote his book *A Rabbi Talks with Jesus*: "But in retrospect, we wonder how much of an argument the two sides had anyhow. For Pharisees were a group shaped by the holy way of life of Israel, talking about sanctification. Jesus and his disciples were a group concerned with sin and atonement in preparation for the near-term coming of God's kingdom. The two neither converse nor argue."[1064] One speaks of sanctification, the other of salvation. One speaks of eternal Israel here and now, the other of the imminent kingdom of heaven.

Jesus within Judaism

Neusner goes on to explore briefly Jesus' silences and what Jesus does not say regarding ritual purity vis-à-vis the Pharisees.[1065] Yet it will suffice for us to consider one last issue. Neusner frames it appropriately: "Just because I could not follow Jesus, did that mean I had to suppose not that I'd walked away from him, but that he's walked out on Israel's Torah?"[1066] His answer: "Well, that depends."[1067]

Conceding that Israel with the Torah, "had room for three kinds of teachers: priests, sages, and prophets,"[1068] Neusner conceivably could situate Jesus more comfortably within the sage-prophetic tradition. In the end, however, especially in light of Jesus' healing of the centurion's servant (Matt 8:5–13), although Neusner finds much of Jesus' torah compelling, "exalted, encountering the sublime,"[1069] he also finds it insufficient and confronts Jesus' ominous silence. Jesus fails, in Neusner's observation, to speak of three things: "First, you do not tell me the story of the Torah, which tells about beginnings and endings, where we come from, who we are. Second, you do not tell me about us, Israel. Third, you do not account for the unfaith of the Gentiles."[1070]

The fact that the centurion believed *in Jesus*, which Jesus found praiseworthy, only confounds Neusner, who fails to see how the centurion's belief *in* Jesus made "him us, Israel, and has that faith fulfilled the requirement of the Torah?" The implicit juxtaposition of Jesus as a New Moses and Moses of Sinai is more than strained. Neusner, grappling with tradition and innovation, with Pharisee and Galilean sage, with ritual cleanliness and virtuous ethic, with eternal Israel here and now and Jesus' imminent kingdom of heaven, concedes: "God will settle all these questions—eventually."[1071] And of himself and rabbi Jesus and their encounter?

The answer is in an echo of an earlier assertion: "A great master is not the one who says what is new, but one who says what is true, and the master I seek is the one who speaks to me, who wants to be found by me—so that I, too, may learn what God through the Torah has asked of me."[1072]

Their last meeting was on the road to Jerusalem: Rabbi Jesus poised, resolute, to go forward, and Rabbi Neusner determined otherwise. Of his parting from the Matthean Jesus on the road to Jerusalem, Neusner writes: "I called after him: 'Go in peace— *lekh be-Shalom.*' I wished him well, but I went home."[1073]

With eyes turned homeward, Neusner reflects:

The Torah had told me things about God's kingdom that Jesus neglected, and Jesus had told me things about God's kingdom that the Torah had not affirmed. Jesus' account of God's rule drew my eyes on high, to heaven. But I lived, and now live, in the here and now of goring oxen and quarreling families. The kingdom of heaven may come, perhaps not even soon enough, but until it is upon us, the Torah tells me what it means to live in God's kingdom—in the here and now.[1074]

Grappling, not with the essential sources or modern hermeneutics, but rather with the singular figure emerging from the text of Matthew, Neusner argues, debates, rebuts the Galilean preacher, Jesus. Neusner's mosaic is largely a Matthean composite, critically arranged to bring the face of Jesus into sharper relief. Set against the Torah and evidentiary rabbinic literature, Matthew's Jesus is applauded by Neusner and criticized, debated and decried from a halakic Jew's perspective.

Neusner's studied dissent frames his mosaic. The portrait that emerges is not that of a New Moses bearing a new Torah. Instead, Neusner's Jesus, similar to Matthew's but distinct, emerges as a Galilean sage of limited vision, the teacher of torah, who misses the mark, one whose "elegance in speech found its match in silence."[1075]

Jesus, Light and Shadow

We remain fearful of that Jesus, the one who is the only way to the Father, the son who comes to supersede all prior covenants, the Lord whom everyone should and one day will come to serve. If you do not see the shadow, you won't appreciate the light.

> Eugene Borowitz, "Jesus the Jew in the Light of the
> Jewish-Christian Dialogue," 17

Eugene Borowitz views the historical Jesus as an elusive figure, one not readily or convincingly retrieved from the essential sources: the New Testament. Borowitz, creatively, chooses to describe, from his perspective, the Jesus whom he encounters in his Christian dialogue partner. His subjective rendering, though brief when juxtaposed with our other authors, offers both affirmation and challenge. Reflecting upon "the Jesus mediated to me and communicated to me by this dialogue partner,"[1076] Borowitz writes of his unique perspective: "I can hope to recognize the Jewishness of this [figure] because, in fact, I am being asked to recognize something about myself which the other has seen in me and the faith I bear and identified with the Jesus of his or her Christian faith."[1077]

Though his first effort, "Jesus the Jew in Light of the Jewish-Christian Dialogue," is creative and subjective, his second lecture, "The Challenge of Jesus the Jew for the Church," is indicative of his facility with both the biblical figure of Jesus and Judaism, ancient and modern. Since the latter enhances the former, our task is to discern from both efforts Borowitz's portrait of Jesus.

Jesus, Light

In the refracted light of religious dialogue, Borowitz perceives this "mediated" Jesus fundamentally as a lover of God, whom he recognizes as "the God of Israel, of Abraham and Sarah, of Isaac and Rebecca, of Jacob and Leah and Rachel."[1078] This Jesus is a Jew, bound by Jewish heritage and tradition, by the Torah and the Prophets, expressing his fidelity to God. Of "his peculiar Jewish intimacy with God,"[1079] Borowitz observes:

> That is to say, Jesus turns to God directly and immediately. He has no difficulty in the field, in the synagogue, wherever he is, addressing God, knowing that God will at once be available to him. He does not feel that to speak to God he needs the help of any of the priests of the Temple or of the Temple rites. He is not even concerned with any particular ritual of address. He feels that he can, whenever he wishes to, address God immediately, that he can turn to God personally, in his own language and his own way, and establish communication. Or, to put it the other way around, the God of Jesus is directly accessible and is ever-present.[1080]

This Jesus, who senses the immediacy of God, expresses his love of God in service, "in ways which I find quite familiar for they are the ways commanded to the people of Israel, of which I am a part."[1081] Moreover, "this Jesus understands serving God primarily as loving people and reaching out to them."[1082] This Jesus, continually involved with diverse people, carries out his service to God "in a wonderful old Jewish style."[1083]

On Jesus' style, Borowitz observes:

> He is mostly a teacher, one involved with instruction. He has quite a familiar pedagogical style. Sometimes he cites familiar texts from the Torah like, "Thou shalt love the LORD thy God with all thy heart, with all thy soul and with all thy might," a citation from the book of Deuteronomy (6:5). I know it well, for we recite it regularly. . . . He also cites the prophets, my prophets. Though probably people spoke Aramaic in his day rather than Aramaic translation, he almost certainly cited them in the original Hebrew which, to this day, we still read in synagogue on Saturday mornings or on holidays.[1084]

This Jewish teacher, though familiar, has at least two distinctive qualities. First, Jesus teaches in parables, "not an unfamiliar method,"[1085] as Borowitz explains: "It is an old Jewish way of teaching but one that he utilizes with extraordinary creativity, insight, and compassion. Jesus has a quite admirable genius for telling a quick little story which touches the hearer's heart and soul."[1086]

Second, Jesus is somewhat unusual "because he is often quite concerned with people on the fringe."[1087] Though this in itself is not unique, since "in his outreach I hear echoes of that old biblical refrain that we must have special regard for the widow, the stranger, and orphan."[1088] In Jesus, Borowitz encounters "a person of some special yet nonetheless not uncommon Jewish concern,"[1089] a Jewish teacher "who is interested in sinners and publicans,"[1090] one "who likes to go to synagogues, not just synagogues for outcasts, [but also] synagogues for ordinary Jews."[1091]

On Jesus and the people of Israel, Borowitz affirms:

> Jesus is part of this daring folk. He seems primarily concerned with his fellow Jews. He spends his life with Jews and addresses himself to his ethnic kin. He could easily have traveled across the Mediterranean to talk to other people—but he didn't. And I don't need to remind you of those passages where Jesus seems to restrict his message to his own religio-ethnic community. Besides, he is as much a part of its culture as he is native to its land. He knows his people's literature; he speaks its language; he utilizes its distinctive style of instruction.[1092]

Jesus is "a popular preacher, speaker, religious type,"[1093] whose message of repentance is familiar. Borowitz explains:

> The daily prayers of the Jews include prayers for not only insight and understanding but [also] prayers of forgiveness and for God's help in carrying through our work of repentance. So when I hear this Jewish preacher exhorting his fellow Jews to repent, I hear him echoing a Jewish tradition sounding strongly in the law and climaxed in the prophets in Ezekiel's marvelous sermon (chapter 18) on individual responsibility.[1094]

Here again, Borowitz enhances the mediated Jesus' portrait, explaining:

> He says to them, "Repent, for the Kingdom of God is at hand." He does not tell them, "Go to the temple and participate in the rites of the Day of Atonement." He does not advise them, "Have one of the priestly class lead you through the established rites of repentance." He doesn't say such things because he takes it for granted that Galileans or Jerusalemites to whom he is speaking can, in fact, carry out *teshuvah* [*těšûbāh*], repentance, entirely on their own. His preaching, in this respect, reflects, as I understand it, his ancestral Jewish faith.[1095]

Borowitz, recognizing in Jesus' preaching on the imminence of God's kingdom "a dialectic typically Jewish,"[1096] comments:

> What at first seems like such a pessimistic message, "You're a sinner; repent," is also incredibly optimistic. God will rule! The power of evil will be overthrown! History can be utterly transformed! It might happen now—get ready by repenting your sins. This theme is not as fully and immediately developed in the prophets who say it in their own way and for their own time. But it is only unfamiliar in urgency, not in substantive content.[1097]

Finding "particularly attractive"[1098] Jesus' activism, reminiscent of Nathan's and Amos's faith, "one that confronts and seeks to change real people facing real situations,"[1099] Borowitz affirms:

> This Jesus is a Jewish type that I can easily place. He's Galilean pietist, an itinerant preacher and teacher who wants Jews to be more Jewish, who wants them to take their religion more seriously, to express its inner belief in their lives, to add sanctity to their day-by-day affairs as part of the people dedicated to God and pledged to see that God's rule ultimately triumphs in history. When I meet this Jesus, the Jesus I find in the eyes of someone who meets me in honest dialogue, I recognize [that] I have come across something particularly precious.[1100]

This Jesus is particularly precious, in Borowitz's estimation, because "this is such a new Jesus for Jews to confront."[1101]

Borowitz explains:

> It is only 20 years or so since serious dialogue has been taking place between Jews and Roman Catholics, and not much longer between Jews and Protestants. After 1,600 years, that is, ever since the Edict of Tolerance made Judaism a permitted but a degraded religion in the Roman Empire, after 1,600 years of discrimination, oppression and outright hatred, to encounter a radically changed attitude and therefore to see the possibility of *another Jesus*, one I recognize, is quite an extraordinary experience.[1102]

Paradoxically, this *new* Jesus, this possibility of another Jesus, *is* the *first* Jesus, albeit a portrait thereof mediated through a dialogue partner. This first Jesus—and his positive place within Judaism—was usurped, or overshadowed, by a *second* Jesus, one whom the Jews, suffering at the hands of their Christian contemporaries, learned to despise and fear. It is the first Jesus and not the second that Borowitz finds precious.

Jesus, Shadow

Borowitz is not naive. He knows well that in the absence of authentic religious dialogue, the Jesus who might gain ascendancy (again) is the second Jesus, Jesus of the shadow. Borowitz fears this Jesus whom he encounters "when dialogue is not fully present;"[1103] as do all Jews, lest "the old Jewish-Christian animosities [should] some-how reassert themselves."[1104] Borowitz describes poignantly the Shadow's darkness: "This Jesus is the one who validated the hatred and oppression of his own people. He is the Jesus who stands for crusades, inquisitions, ritual murder charges and forced conversions. He is the Jesus who did not protest the Holocaust. That Jesus may not hate his kinfolk in his heart, but he has stood idly by while his kinfolk bleed."[1105]

Given the past animosities, Borowitz, though appreciative of the renewed efforts at authentic dialogue, affirms: "We remain fearful of that Jesus, the one who is the only way to the Father, the son who comes to supersede all prior covenants, the Lord whom everyone should and one day will come to serve. If you do not see the shadow, you won't appreciate the light".[1106]

Darkness does not have the final word. Confident in the "extraordinary step" taken by the Roman Catholic Church in its call for genuine dialogue "to reverse an old and painful relationship"[1107]—the firstfruits of which appeared in the unprecedented Vatican II document *Nostra Aetate, Declaration on the Relation of the Church to Non-Christian Religions*—Borowitz, though wary of the Shadow, welcomes this new openness and engages the Light.

Summary

Schalom Ben-Chorin, Pinchas Lapide, Jacob Neusner, and to a lesser extent Eugene Borowitz engage creatively, albeit unconventionally, either pertinent literature or, as in the case of Borowitz, persons; their goal is to intuitively or imaginatively construct or retrieve from "glass and stone" their respective portraits of Jesus. Though all situate Jesus securely and, with the exception of Neusner, positively within Judaism, distinctive portraits emerge.

Given their shared irenical efforts among Jews and Christians, Israelis and Germans, it is not surprising to discern parallel emphases in the efforts of Ben-Chorin and Lapide. Both retrieve Jesus from the Christian overlay or overpainting and centuries of Jewish taboo and defamation in their embrace of a Jewish rapprochement: *modernen Heimholung Jesu in das jüdische Volk.* Ben-Chorin, a kindred spirit, with intuitive interpretation, perceives Jesus as a Jewish brother, a Pharisaic-like, itinerant preacher—though married, and a rabbi—and not a *talmid chakham* (*talmîd ḥakîm*). Ben-Chorin, at times inconsistent, both disallows and then enigmatically affirms Jesus as charismatic and clairvoyant, not in a popular sense but rather in the Jewish sense of the ancient Hasidim—though he and Lapide both perceive parallels between Jesus and the rabbis of the eighteenth-century Eastern European Hasidim. Ben-Chorin views Jesus as both *moschel* (*mōšel*) and martyr in a long tradition of Jewish nationalists. Jesus: Jewish brother, tragic figure—*a revolutionary of the heart.*

Lapide also perceives the Galilean Jesus as a revolutionary of sorts, "a threefold rebel of love," charting his "third way," the way of service. He endorses the Jewish rapprochement vis-à-vis Jesus and in doing so underscores Jesus the Galilean's role in the *praeparatio messianica.* Lapide's Jesus, *the fifth Jesus,* the one disguised and yet emanating from the essential sources and diverse conversations, is not the Messiah, but rather one who prepares the way for King Messiah. Jesus—*Rabbi Yeshua*—from the apologist Lapide's perspective, is both a pious Jew, likened to Rabbi Israel Baal Shem, the *Besht,* founder of the modern Hasidim, and the Savior of the Gentiles, by virtue of the missionary activity of his followers emboldened by Easter's light.

Lapide is singular, perhaps idiosyncratic, in his acceptance of the historicity of the resurrection of Jesus, given his observation of the *history of effects.* Lapide's *fifth Jesus* is an "incorrigible optimist and hero of the faith," a great Jewish teacher of morality and yet a tragic figure: a Jewish brother whose tragic end is transfigured into a providential beginning.

Lapide's—and Ben-Chorin's—affirmation of Jesus' fidelity and creative nuance vis-à-vis the Torah stands in stark contradiction to Jacob Neusner's dissent. Jacob Neusner, no less creative, engages the Matthean Jesus, the one the Christian knows from reading the Gospels, in an imaginative debate wherein he grapples with Jesus' innovation and aberration of the Torah. Jesus, in Neusner's estimation, is a Galilean sage of limited vision and a teacher of torah who misses the mark. Set against the Torah and evidentiary rabbinic literature, Matthew's Jesus is applauded by Neusner and criticized, debated, and decried from a halakic Jew's perspective. Neusner's dissent is unique among the authors of this study. From his perspective, and as is discernible to the cognoscenti, his "talk" with Rabbi Jesus, rabbi to rabbi, not only competently defends his thesis—and thus his dissent—but also provides concomitantly a paradigm for authentic religious dialogue. What is unclear, however, is whether the Jesus of history, the Galilean teacher of Torah, is guilty of the aberrations with which Neusner indicts the Matthean Jesus.

Eugene Borowitz, a minor yet significant voice in this conversation, embraces Jesus as Light. This light is both illuminating and illumined in Borowitz's candid, albeit overtly subjective, encounter with the Jesus mediated to him through his Christian dialogue partner. This "mediated" Jesus is a *new* Jesus, one whom Borowitz finds "particularly precious," especially given the alternative, the shadowy Jesus. Borowitz is singular in his candid warning vis-à-vis the *second* Jesus, the Jesus of Jewish taboo and Christian zealotry. Though wary of this second Jesus, the *Shadow Jesus*, Borowitz affirms and welcomes the emerging openness and engages this new Jesus as Light.

6

"Novelty and Originality"

Novelty and originality usually consist in looking at familiar issues from an unfamiliar angle, in giving a new slant to classic ideas, in shedding fresh light on problems discussed since time immemorial.

Géza Vermès, *The Authentic Gospel of Jesus*, 373

Throughout this presentation we have occupied ourselves with the perspectives of others: select Jewish authors' perspectives of Jesus, post-Holocaust. Reflecting upon a thesis gleaned from Maurice Merleau-Ponty's *Phenomenology of Perception*, "to focus on a particular is to become blind to the whole,"[1108] James H. Charlesworth, while pondering a final perspective on Jesus research, observes: "That caveat means we must focus in order to see, but we must also step back, take a general overview, refocus, correct the distortion caused by myopia, and then attempt to obtain a representative perception from multiple attempts at focusing, absorbing the view, and refocusing again to grasp the correct perception."[1109]

This phenomenon of focusing and refocusing provides us an insight into the essential challenge and subsequent effort of the scholars under consideration. Each author vies with the tension between object and background, probability and certitude, ambiguity and historicity. Each tries to focus upon the figure of Jesus from a different, unfamiliar angle, while appreciating, discriminately, the context, the milieu that animates the figure under study.

This phenomenon of refocusing to grasp the correct perception also succinctly captures the task at hand. In this closing chapter, we will consider the response of select New Testament and rabbinic specialists and others to the provocative—though currently axiomatic—Jesus portraits discerned from Jewish perspectives. I will also comment on the contribution of the authors in question to the advancement of Jesus research and Jewish-Christian relations, as applicable. Third, we will examine the authors' critiques of each other's work, where available. Given our task, we will return to the pattern established in chapter 1 and consider our Jewish authors chronologically and the responses elicited. This effort may prove uneven since not all authors have elicited or provoked an equal or weighty response. In addition, a retrospective spanning forty years of research and commentary, often conveyed in lecture or book or hypothesis, finds some authors with scant reviews or consistent critique. What has been gleaned follows. Convergence and divergence inherent in these various critiques of the authors studied will be obvious to the reader. I will reserve final observations for the conclusion, which follows this last chapter.

Samuel Sandmel

Though Sandmel provided only one book on Jesus, his contribution to the study of the Jewish origins of Christianity has proved invaluable, not only to the Jewish community but to the Christian community as well. Sandmel's New Testament scholarship, implicit in *We Jews and Jesus* and clearly evident in *A Jewish Understanding of the New Testament*, exemplifies an effort to educate Jews about the literature held sacred by Christians—much of which was Jewish in origins or style—and also the enigmatic Jewish figure, Jesus, emanating from those documents.[1110]

In his review of *We Jews and Jesus*—an early review, July 1965—the Roman Catholic Silas Musholt, OFM, finding the rabbi's partisanship (chap. 1) "most depressing," nonetheless offers tentative praise:

> Sandmel has written effectively. For anyone well acquainted with recent Gospel scholarship, this book will be useful for its clear, sincere presentation of the difficulties encountered in the Gospel materials. Its appearance is certainly timely in view of our ecumenical age, and the spirit of ecumenism should be very much a part of the approach in reading this book. The Catholic reader will marvel over and over again at the effectiveness of his own God-given faith and will appreciate more profoundly that his faith is fundamental to an understanding of the Gospel of our Lord Jesus Christ.[1111]

The Jewish New Testament scholar, Paul Winter, writing in September of 1965, found Sandmel's *We Jews and Jesus* praiseworthy: "To clarify the borderlines between the two communities, without exacerbating differences, and to state his own position, Rabbi Sandmel, Provost of the Hebrew Union College in Cincinnati, has written an attractive book, informative yet unpolemical, forthright but courteous."[1112] Winter, aware of Sandmel's nontechnical aim, observes however that Sandmel is "too modest" in his presentation of New Testament scholarship; "unduly skeptical" with regard to some New Testament narratives, such as Jesus' baptism at John's hand; and "unnecessarily reserved," as in his reference to Josephus's passage about Jesus.[1113]

In assessing Sandmel's perspective, he affirms:

> Sandmel never allows the reader any doubts as to his own position. Without a hint of arrogance, he writes with a calm, sober dignity, stressing his Jewishness even in such minor matters as using the term *"Tanakh"* instead of "Old Testament." Yet his pronounced Jewishness does not prevent him from a fair assessment of the moral values that lie in Christianity. He is equally free from pathological aversion with which some Jews traditionally regard Jesus and from the false romanticism that characterizes the works of certain Jewish novelists when they write of the man from Nazareth. . . . By virtue of his personal tone as well as his ideas, Sandmel argues eloquently for the possibilities of better understanding and better relations between Jews and Christians, without either of them sacrificing the beliefs they individually hold.[1114]

Isaac Jacob, OSB, also providing an early review of *We Jews and Jesus*, applauds Sandmel's efforts: "One cannot fail to be impressed with Rabbi Sandmel's latest book. . . . The work not only shows a masterful grasp of vast factual knowledge, but also reveals a thoughtful, penetrating, and fair analysis of the data about him who binds and, at the same time, separates the Jew and the Christian."[1115] Acclaiming the first three chapters of the book "a great boon,"[1116] Jacob is equally impressed with Sandmel's mastery of "the bewildering labyrinth of 175 years of New Testament scholarship"[1117] as evidenced by the trail he blazes in chapter 4. Sandmel's effort is not without criticism, as Jacob observes: "There are indeed not a few sections of the book with which the Christian reader might take exception."[1118]

Susannah Heschel, in her 1998 book *Abraham Geiger and the Jewish Jesus*, is assessing the postwar effort in Jewish scholarship on the New Testament and writes of Sandmel: "Samuel Sandmel is striking for his disinterest in reclaiming Jesus for Judaism and his caution in drawing parallels between the Gospels and rabbinic literature. According to Sandmel, while Jesus was a loyal Jew, and unoriginal in his specific teachings, he believed himself to be the Messiah, and thereby exerted an extraordinary influence on Western civilization."[1119]

Clinton Bennett, in his book *In Search of Jesus*, senses in Sandmel's separate but equally valid approach to Judaism and Christianity an implicit endorsement of Franz Rosenzweig's two-covenant theory of salvation.[1120] Pinchas Lapide not only endorses, though not explicitly, Bennett's assessment but also shares Sandmel's embrace of the Rosenzweig two-covenant theory of salvation—though Sandmel does not participate in the *modernen Heimholung Jesu in das jüdische Volk.*

Lapide, commenting on rabbis' impressions of Jesus in *Israelis, Jews, and Jesus*, writes of Sandmel's "no" to Jesus but implicit "yes" to two-covenant theology: "Christians and Jews may possibly be united by the Messiah, but until he comes, they remain divided. And even Jesus, newly evaluated and demythologized, is not able, not yet anyway, to bridge the gap between his brothers and his disciples. That is what Rabbi Samuel Sandmel seeks to make emphatically clear in his book *We Jews and Jesus*— however much it may distress some ecumenists."[1121]

Schalom Ben-Chorin affirms, with Lapide, that Sandmel's *A Jewish Understanding of the New Testament* sheds light on these Christian texts from a Jewish perspective— though Ben-Chorin emphasizes that this perspective is "from the standpoint of Liberal Jewish theology."[1122] He also affirms that in this same text, Sandmel provides " a clear Jewish view of the figure of Jesus."[1123]

Donald A. Hagner, in his 1997 book *The Jewish Reclamation of Jesus*, describes Sandmel's efforts in *We Jews and Jesus*:

> In this helpful volume Sandmel briefly reviews the history of the Jewish study of Jesus and presents his view of a "reasoned and reasonable" Jewish approach to Jesus. He writes from the standpoint of a Liberal Jew in the lineage of Montefiore and Abrahams but, much more than they, Sandmel assumes and builds on the substructure of modern critical scholarship. Sandmel is a classical liberal in the very best sense of that word.[1124]

Commenting upon Jewish authors and their use of Gospel criticism, Hagner confirms Sandmel's own diffidence, actually skepticism, vis-à-vis the "sources": "By far the most pessimistic of Jewish scholars on this question is Sandmel who, by no coincidence, is also the Jewish scholar most influenced by radical Protestant Gospel criticism."[1125]

Of the Jewish authors considered in his study, Hagner found Sandmel extreme in his skepticism; in Hagner's estimation, David Flusser represents the opposite. Nonetheless, Hagner credits Sandmel with calling attention to the "paradox" that one encounters in the Jewish approach to the Gospels. Hagner is referring to the tendency among some Jewish authors to utilize the criterion of dissimilarity in only one direction, flagging anything overtly Christian as less historically viable than that which is truly Jewish.[1126] Hagner observes that "Sandmel is also dubious about the confident assigning of authenticity on the basis of 'Jewishness': 'The broad congruency of some item in the Gospels with Jewish practice does not in itself establish historical reliability.'"[1127] In addition, Hagner affirms that Sandmel "has appropriately criticized form criticism and 'its supposedly objective method by which to differentiate between [items] historical and [items] unhistorical.'"[1128]

Hagner also sees Sandmel as a "maverick" when juxtaposed with other Jewish scholars, such as Ben-Chorin, Flusser, and Lapide, and their belief that a kind of Hebrew Ur-Evangelium underlies the present form of the Christian Gospels. Sandmel's critique of Lapide's optimism vis-à-vis a discernible Hebrew version of the Gospels is an example of his dissent and distinctiveness.[1129] Hagner correctly identifies Sandmel as a Reform Jew, a member of the liberal wing of Judaism. As such, Sandmel and other similar Jewish scholars generally do not focus on Jesus' eschatology but rather on his ethics since ethics occupies pride of place in Reform Judaism.

G. David Schwartz, in his critique of Hagner's *The Jewish Reclamation of Jesus*, brings us greater clarity regarding Liberal Judaism and Sandmel, an adherent thereof, as well as several other Jewish scholars with whom we are already familiar. Given this, it is beneficial to permit Schwartz a larger voice so the reader may better appreciate the perspectives of the above authors:

> I suspect that the Liberal Jewish concern with Jesus has a specific intention. Considering that the Reform movement in general began in the early nineteenth century, the works of Klausner and Montefiore in the early-to-mid-twentieth century cannot be said to be a dramatic leap. Further, the real explosion of interest is less than twenty years old. The names of Vermès, Flusser, Sandmel, and perhaps Lapide represent a literal doubling of the earlier authors (Lapide, it should be noted, is an Orthodox Jew). Along with the interest in Jesus comes a critical stance toward Jewish ritual. As Judaism became no longer a national assembly but a religious fellowship, ethics was proposed as the spiritual exemplar of the Jews. If so, the scholarly presentation of Jesus is not the intellectual act of following an ethical teacher, or of discovering a predecessor. Rather, it seems [to be] an act of justifying Reform Judaism in the eyes of the world court (which in the West is Christianity). No non-Western Jew has written at all extensively on Jesus.[1130]

Schwartz's thesis, that Liberal Jews write about Jesus in defense of Reform Judaism, will be revisited. That his thesis finds merit, or parallel, in *We Jews and Jesus*, is obvious from Sandmel's own explanations, caveats, and emphases. As we have seen, Sandmel is most reluctant to deduce anything critically from the sources, given his perspective of recognizing the ambiguity and lack of objectivity that pervade historical Jesus study. Skepticism and pessimism influence his reasoning vis-à-vis historical critical analysis. Faith and familiarity undergird his confidence in Judaism. Though he may understand and appreciate the efforts to construct a positive Jewish theology of Jesus, Sandmel remains unswayed.

Commenting upon Sandmel, Jacob Neusner observes that "Sandmel was much earlier [than Vermès] and, for all his warnings on parallelomania, looked for parallels, Hillelizing Jesus."[1131] Even so, Neusner, in describing the Judaic Christology emanating from modern Jewish-Christian "dual monologues"[1132] in his book *Telling Tales*, finds Sandmel's presentation in *We Jews and Jesus* to be noteworthy:

> Perhaps the most articulate Judaic theology of Jesus derives from Samuel Sandmel, who explained "where Jews can reasonably stand with respect to Jesus." Of course a view of Jesus "as more than a man" is "uncongenial to Jews, inconsistent with Judaism."
>
> The other view, that "those virtues ascribed to Jesus the man, the 'Jewish Jesus,' are characteristically Jewish virtues, expressed in Judaism and integrally a part of it," yields the Christology of "a good and great man—a prophet, a rabbi, or a patriotic leader—but he was not better or greater. . .than other great Jews." And, Sandmel judges, "These two points probably reflect responsibly the essence of what there is to be said."[1133]

Equally significant is Neusner's appreciation of Sandmel's candid grasp of the crux of the matter in the modern Jewish-Christian dialogue, an absence of understanding: "Sandmel here points to the critical dilemma of dialogue: an absence of understanding, in our terms, of what Christians mean by their terms, and that is the case whether these are terms we use or do not use."[1134]

In Neusner's estimation, authentic religious dialogue is required, focused not upon "trivializing Judaic Christology,"[1135] but rather upon "Jesus Christ God Incarnate."[1136] Sandmel would concur.[1137]

Schalom Ben-Chorin

Ben-Chorin consistently portrays Jesus as "a tragic but guiding Jewish figure."[1138] Reaction to Ben-Chorin's *Brother Jesus* presents a bit of a challenge. Written in German in 1967, the text is outdated, lacking the emphases and nuances of recent historical Jesus research. However, Ben-Chorin's work, though written primarily for Christians, was widely received in Europe, especially in Germany and Italy. Since the text was not translated into English until 2001, it lacked a wide English readership. Ben-Chorin was both aware of the Klein-Reinhart translation and "filled with joy that it has at last been translated into English and that it can now find its way in the New World."[1139] The previous lack of an English translation was not the only difficulty in citing responses to the work. Search for critical reviews in general proved elusive, no doubt due to the age of the book. Fortunately, mention of Ben-Chorin by Jewish contemporaries, such as Lapide, and recent reviews of the English translation, as in Amy-Jill Levine's review in the *Journal of the American Academy of Religion*, will serve as a measure of Ben-Chorin's reception.

In the afterword of the German edition, *Bruder Jesus*, Ben-Chorin acknowledges that his book is "not a technical work,"[1140] not a work intended for scholars. Rather, he describes it as *Stückwerk*, piecework, due to its lack of full presentation because of the nature of the sources, with the kerygmatic Greek overlay.[1141] This limitation is not his alone. Nonetheless, he hopes that his efforts contribute to the ongoing Jewish-Christian dialogue.[1142]

Pinchas Lapide, commenting Ben-Chorin's *Bruder Jesus*, observes:

> To Schalom Ben-Chorin, "Brother Jesus" is the prodigal son of the House of Israel to whose return and rehabilitation he dedicates his book of the same title. Digging cautiously through mountainous layers of mythology, legend and mystification, Ben-Chorin attempts to retrieve for his readers the God-struck carpenter whose messianic zeal infected the Western world. . . . Taking his cue from Martin Buber, Ben-Chorin warns that "alienation, diffidence and hatred" between Christianity and Judaism cannot be removed or transformed by "mutual illusions of the other's creed, but only by a clear recognition of the two religious positions." Whereupon he proceeds to offer edifying sidelights on the "last supper," the Sermon on the Mount, the wedding at Cana and other New Testament scenes—scenes where significance is greatly enhanced when seen against the background of Jewish customs, Rabbinic law and Galilean lore.[1143]

Hagner is conversant with Ben-Chorin's intuitive encounters with Jesus and writes: "In *Bruder Jesus*, he carefully roots his study in the texts of the Gospels as well as in the Jewish background of the first century. The conclusion that emerges is that Jesus was neither Messiah nor a prophet but a 'revolutionary of the heart.' Ben-Chorin's writings are both perceptive and sensitive, and when he speaks of his own struggles with, and even his closeness to, Jesus, his eloquence is moving."[1144]

Yet Hagner also notes the disagreement that exists between Ben-Chorin and Flusser regarding Jesus' messianic self-consciousness. Although Ben-Chorin views this messianic consciousness as unhistorical, Flusser yields to a gradual acceptance, vis-à-vis Jesus' sense of sonship, that Jesus probably did see himself as Messiah.[1145]

Puzzling over the religious or moral significance of Jesus for Jews in an atmosphere of *Heimholung Jesu*, Harvey Cox observes:

> Ben-Chorin opens the door for conversation but also sets the limits of the Jewish appreciation for the religious significance of Jesus: "I feel," he says, "his brotherly hand which grasps mine so that I can follow him, . . .but it is *not* the hand of the Messiah. This hand is marked with scars. It is not a *divine* but a *human* hand in the lines of which is engraved the most profound suffering." Then Ben-Chorin, pouring a lot into a few words, goes on to make the statement. . .that "The faith *of* Jesus" (emphasizing "of") unites us but faith *in* Jesus divides us."[1146]

Géza Vermès, reviewing the Klein-Reinhart translation of *Brother Jesus,* captures both the essence of Ben-Chorin's perspective and the efforts, mirrored therein, of Liberal Judaism in its reclamation of Jesus:

> Inspired by Martin Buber, the English translation of the well-known German work by Ben-Chorin (1913–1999) is a splendid example of the reconstruction of the picture of the historical Jesus by a Jewish sympathiser totally opposed to the historico-theological approach of German New Testament scholarship. The book is more useful for the understanding of a certain type of twentieth-century German-Jewish mind-set than for the rediscovery of the real Jesus.[1147]

Though the above observations are episodic, Amy-Jill Levine, an American New Testament scholar and Jewish feminist, provides us with a significant critical assessment of the Klein-Reinhart translation of *Brother Jesus.* In this "elegant translation," she discerns Ben-Chorin's purpose:

> Drawing upon Rabbinic literature, Jewish folk-tradition, and Semitic philology, Schalom Ben-Chorin (1913–1999) presents for an intended Christian readership a Jewish Jesus whom, he believes, can mend the breach between Synagogue and Church. This elegant translation of the 1967 German original . . . offers a positivistic romanticized "brother Jesus" (the expression is from Martin Buber), an "eternal brother" (this term borrowed from Stefan Zweig) located within an equally romanticized eternal Judaism.[1148]

Of his portrayal of Jesus, she observes:

> Ben-Chorin's Jesus emphasizes the relationship between radical orthopraxy prompted by eschatological speculation and *kavanna* (intention) [he] promotes the internalization of Torah fulfilled through love [and] teaches a robust, simple trust in G-d the Father. . . . Coming "to full consciousness of his tragic mission as a suffering servant of G-d" (127) at his final Seder, brother Jesus "continues to live . . . in his Jewish people, whose martyrdom he embodies" (19).[1149]

As to his style, composition, and argument, Levine writes:

> Frequent citations from the Talmud and Midrash not only correct the image of Rabbinic Judaism as aridly focused on legal *minutiae*, they [also] offer intriguing if often highly speculative suggestions: . . . Making the Jewish tradition both more familiar and more appealing are numerous lexical observations (e.g., the term *mikve's* double connotations of hope and immersion) and thematic connections (e.g., Rashi's notice that the Divine Spirit hovers like a dove). Readers interested in the historical Jesus will appreciate Ben-Chorin's list of dialogue partners, including Leo Baeck and Joseph Klausner along with Rudolf Bultmann and Robert Eisler.[1150]

The irony of Ben-Chorin's irenical effort is not missed by Levine who asks rhetorically: "What's not to like? Unfortunately, highly conjectural historiography creates an infirm foundation for interfaith dialogue, and the lovely apologetic threatens to confirm the very negative stereotypes of Judaism it seeks to redress for its Christian audience."[1151]

Sharpening her focus, she observes assertions in his narrative that provoke blunt rebuttal. Reacting to Ben-Chorin's criterion of authenticity, that intuition can proceed from a "deep kindred empathy," Levine retorts candidly: "Nonsense. 'Deep kindred empathy' is no substitute for historical rigor; the focus on 'belief and doctrine' casts Judaism in Christian terms even as it anachronistically fails to recognize major elements of Second-Temple praxis such as pervasive familiarity with the sacrificial cult and the importance of quotidian purity practices."[1152]

Warning that "deep empathy degenerates occasionally into pop psychologizing,"[1153] which distorts rather than focuses, Levine next challenges Ben-Chorin's outdated stereotypes of first-century women, "regarded as absent from active participation in community life."[1154] She reacts to Ben-Chorin's assertion that Jesus' refusal to respond to the Canaanite woman (Matt 15:21–28) "is entirely in keeping with those learned in the law, who refused extended conversations with women" (42) and retorts: "Nonsense again: silence in response to maternal desperation is not a Rabbinic ideal."[1155]

Continuing her critique of Ben-Chorin's stereotypes of first-century women, Levine counters a third time: "Conversely, Ben-Chorin claims that Jesus' conversations with the Canaanite (Matthew 15) and the Samaritan (John 4) women offer 'a clear rejection' of the Jewish liturgy wherein the Deity is praised for not having made the one praying either a pagan or a woman (82). Nonsense again: a conversation with a woman and a foreigner says nothing about matters for which one praises G-d."[1156]

She agrees with Ben-Chorin's assertion that "up to this day in observant Jewish circles the idea continues to exist that a woman who truly serves a man learned in the Scriptures will share eternally in the merits that he gains for himself through study" (97). However, she criticizes his omission, failing to mention the diverse roles of women in the Jesus movement and in early Judaism and that "even in 'observant circles' women are doctors, lawyers and business executives."[1157]

Levine finds Ben-Chorin naïve at times, as in his assertion that if Jesus were unmarried then, how could one account for the bridegroom imagery in his teachings (103)?[1158] Yet she observes more deliberate license: "To make his case, Ben-Chorin will sometimes freely rewrite the Gospels."[1159] Expanding upon this observation, she asserts: "Additionally compromising its usefulness are unfortunate terms, equations, and errors, only some of which are noted by the translators, and a reading of the Gospels that, with no critical explication, either ignores material antithetical to the construct of 'brother Jesus' or dismisses it as misreadings of the Church."[1160]

Finally she assesses the current value of Ben-Chorin's efforts:

> Ben-Chorin emigrated from Germany to Israel in 1935, where he spent the next six decades promoting interfaith understanding. Used cautiously, *Brother Jesus* still has potential to continue this mission, but *not* because of what it says about Jesus. Rather, the values and the knowledge that Ben-Chorin himself expresses, and the elegance with which he does so, reveal that the fraternal connections to the Christian are more with this German Jew than with the first-century Mediterranean Rabbi.[1161]

One cannot miss the sympathetic view expressed by Lapide when juxtaposed with Levine's candid, critical assessment of Ben-Chorin's efforts in *Brother Jesus*. Lapide's lack of criticism, though his evaluation is brief, is perhaps indicative of their shared efforts. Both he and Ben-Chorin seek to retrieve Jesus for Judaism from Christian accretions. Both, too, perhaps can be forgiven for their lack of a feminist perspective, given their gender and worldview.

David Flusser

Flusser provides Jewish scholarship with several precedents. He is the first to introduce the study of Christianity and the Jewish origins thereof to Hebrew University in Jerusalem. He is the first among Israeli scholars to occupy the position of Professor of New Testament and Early Judaism at Hebrew University, where he taught Judaism in the Second Temple Period and Early Christianity. Flusser is the first among Jewish authors who write about Jesus and have a priority that is not primarily Jesus' Jewishness.

Though Flusser also wrote only one book on Jesus, the breadth of his scholarship on the New Testament, Early Christianity, and Early Judaism and his interest in and focus upon Jesus and his message are evident in his numerous books and articles. Flusser's *Jesus in Selbstzeugnissen und Bilddokumenten*, written in German in 1968, was widely translated and well received. The German text and other translations fared well, but not the English translation thereof. Flusser himself, in his recent 2001 corrected and augmented version of the 1968 text, acknowledges that the initial 1969 English translation was not widely read: "Not being widely read, this translation was never reprinted, and is no longer available."[1162]

On the 1968 German text's reception, Flusser writes: "The German edition of my book was very well received in Europe, and encountered only slight opposition from some excessively conservative Christian circles. Their American counterparts should understand that, because of my Jewish background, I cannot be more Christian than the majority of believers in Jesus."[1163]

Lapide, a contemporary of Flusser at Hebrew University, reviews *Jesus: In Selbstzeugnissen und Bilddokumenten* and observes:

> The uniqueness of Jesus in the history of Jewish thought, the supremacy of his message of love and the relevance of that message for our nuclear age constitute the triple concern of David Flusser, whose "Jesus" was written, as he says in the preface, "primarily in order to prove the possibility of writing a biography of Jesus." Flusser . . .utilizes insights gained from the Dead Sea Scrolls, Rabbinic literature and the Apocrypha in order to de-Hellenize and re-Judaize "the great preacher" whom he rates with Socrates among the world's illuminaries."[1164]

Comparing Flusser's Jesus with a predecessor's reconstruction, Lapide affirms: "Compared with Klausner's Nazarene, Flusser's Jesus is not only more plausible in his attitude toward the Torah and in his radical concepts of morality, but his Jewish message concerning 'The Kingdom of Heaven' [also] makes historic sense—in both the religious and the secular plane."[1165]

Ben-Chorin, in his survey of modern Jewish books on Jesus, observes:

Somewhat later, Professor David Flusser's *Jesus* (Hamburg, 1968) appeared: here testimonies and documents according to the author, are supposed to prove "that it is still possible to write a life history of Jesus." But proof is still lacking. Quite properly this book has been included in the Rowohlts monographs—note that these are indeed monographs and not biographies, for Flusser, too, does not progress beyond a piecemeal presentation of the figure of Jesus.[1166]

Of Flusser's efforts, he writes:

Flusser is the first Jewish author to present the figure and teaching of Jesus for the general public without having the author's Jewishness especially stressed in the book. . . . The book sees Jesus within the matrix of contemporaneous Judaism, yet Flusser stresses much more strongly than do other writers the connection with Hellenic-Jewish literature, especially the apocalyptic. Flusser's work shows how Jewish authors today participate fully in the scholarship centered on the life of Jesus.[1167]

Hagner hails Flusser as "the most optimistic" of all the Liberal Jews writing on Jesus.[1168] Commenting upon Flusser's enigmatic embrace of the Synoptic Jesus as "the historical Jesus," not the kerygmatic Christ, Hagner observes:

Flusser, who in this conclusion parts radically with critical scholarship, explains the historical character of the Synoptic Gospels as the result of their having been written after A.D. 70, when the influence of Paul had declined and therefore was less likely to have had an effect on the writing down of the tradition. Flusser, indeed, makes a valiant effort to interpret the Synoptic Gospels as they are with almost no appeal to the church's alteration of the tradition. He succeeds to the extent that he does, however, only by ignoring much of the problematic material in the Gospels.[1169]

" By definition the Jewish Jesus," in Hagner's estimation, given Flusser's reconstruction—and the reconstructions of a Jewish Jesus by other Liberal Jews, such as Ben-Chorin, Lapide, and Vermès—"is the Jesus of history."[1170] "It is presupposed, of course, that the historical Jesus must fit into the contours of his Jewish environment and that he could not have broken out of the limited perspective of his contemporaries."[1171] Hagner observes a similar premise in the work of Flusser—and Vermès: "For Flusser, the Jewishness of Jesus, if not the key to determining the authentic material in the Synoptic Gospels, is at least the key to correct interpretation."[1172]

Interestingly, Flusser argues conversely: he claims that his is not the study of the Jewish Jesus, but rather the Jesus of history.[1173]

Hagner, discerning the optimistic and ambitious claims of those modern Jewish authors re-Judaizing Jesus, comments upon their collective position vis-à-vis Jesus and the Torah. He observes that this group discerns no essential difference when Jesus and his pedagogy are juxtaposed with rabbinic Judaism.[1174] Hagner includes Ben-Chorin, Flusser, Lapide, and Vermès in this group of Jewish scholars. Of the four, Flusser, in his estimation, "has taken one of the strongest stands against the suggestion that Jesus violated the law in any sense at all—whether written or oral."[1175] Hagner finds Lapide's view identical with Flusser's: "According to Lapide, 'Jesus was and remained a Torah-true Jew, who never and nowhere (in Matthew, Mark and Luke) transgressed against the Mosaic and rabbinic legislation.'"[1176]

Craig A. Evans offers a cogent review of Flusser's newly revised *Jesus* and affirms that it "touches many aspects of Jesus research and Gospel interpretation."[1177] Evans's particular focus, however, is Flusser's inclusion in the new edition of fresh insights drawn from both rabbinic literature and the Dead Sea Scrolls. Before focusing on Flusser's use of these sources, Evans observes Flusser's "unconventional" solution to the Synoptic Problem, investing Luke's Gospel with primacy, given his belief that it preserves the earliest Gospel tradition retaining primitive Semitic traditions. Evans deems this presumption a "scholarly curiosity."[1178] Evans further observes: "The assumption of putative Hebrew sources underlying Luke and Matthew sometimes leads Flusser to propose underlying mistranslations or misunderstandings. Getting 'behind' the Greek Gospels to their Hebrew sources, he thinks, often solves historical, cultural, and exegetical conundra. In most cases, however, these efforts are unconvincing and unnecessary."[1179]

Examining Flusser's frequent appeals to rabbinic literature and "proposed retroversions into Hebrew," Evans discerns "a number of problems here."[1180] For example, Flusser claims that the night meeting of the Sanhedrin (Mark 14:53–65) is a Markan invention because of the amicable caricatures of Nicodemus (John 7:50–52) and Joseph of Arimathea (Matt 27:57–61) preserved in the Christian narratives. Flusser comes to this decision, in Evans's estimation, "because of the tension with mishnaic tradition and because of Lukan priority."[1181] Evans counters:

> Many Gospel scholars suspect that apologetics are at work with respect to the stories of Joseph of Arimathea and Nicodemus. But Flusser takes all this very seriously and tries to trace the history of Nicodemus in rabbinic and other sources. Even if we accept Flusser's point about the friendly Joseph and Nicodemus, that still does not necessarily discount Mark's nocturnal proceedings. Indeed Flusser himself suspects that Caiaphas called together only those who would support his plans to do away with Jesus.[1182]

Advancing his critique, he continues, "I think Flusser has attached too much technical significance to the word 'sanhedrin' (or 'council'), as well as too much credence to later mishnaic traditions. Surely Mark does not mean to imply a formal convening of the full body of the Sanhedrin. He probably has in mind only some members, who, as Flusser sensibly suggests, were in essential agreement with the ruling priests."[1183]

Evans finds Flusser's use of the Qumran Scrolls both speculative, though often reasonably so, and inexplicable. Evans observes that omissions and selective foci seem to characterize Flusser's Qumran juxtapositions. A few examples of his critique will suffice:

> The plethora of references to God's kingdom in the *Song of the Sabbath Sacrifice* contradicts Flusser's claim that this "concept did not appear among the Essenes." Since these texts have been known since 1986, Flusser's failure to make use of them is hard to explain. . . .
>
> Ignoring these important texts from Qumran, Flusser instead speaks of late and probably spurious rabbinic tradition in which we are told that a heavenly voice address Hanina ben Dosa as "my son" (*b. Ta'an.* 24b). . . .

In chap. 9 ("Son of Man") Flusser rightly directs our attention to Daniel 7, eschewing the unnecessary skepticism of much modern criticism. However, he is caught in a bind [while] trying to explain why the Hebrew-speaking Jesus [Flusser's contention] would make use of an Aramaic epithet drawn from an Aramaic book in the Bible. His solution, based on the reference to Abel as the "son of Adam" who sits on a throne and will come in judgment according to the *Testament of Abraham*, is convoluted and unconvincing. . . .

Finally, regarding what Flusser says about messianism and the factors leading up to Jesus' death (chaps. 8, 9, and 11), it is odd that he makes no mention of 4Q285, one of the *War Scroll* texts. This composition vividly attests the expectation of a militant Messiah. . . . Proclamation of the kingdom of God, seen through the lens of the *War Scroll* texts, could easily have been perceived by the Roman authorities as a declaration of holy war.[1184]

Examining Flusser's quixotic analysis of *11QMelchizedek*, Evans concedes: "Flusser rightly suspects that Jesus did see himself as the eschatological son of man."[1185]

Evans concludes his critique by writing:

It is only fair to conclude this review by mentioning features of Jesus where in my judgment Flusser is persuasive. In chap. 12 ("Epilogue") he concludes that Jesus' messianic consciousness is probable. In chap. 10 ("Jerusalem") Flusser concludes that Jesus spoke of a new Temple, and in doing so hinted that he was the Messiah (as in all probability would have been inferred from a passage like Zech. 6:12, which in the Targum is explicitly messianic). At the Last Supper, which is a Passover meal, Jesus hints at his impending martyrdom, "This is my body, " and tells his disciples that he expects to eat his next Passover lamb and drink his next cup in the world to come (not the "kingdom of God," as in the Gospels). And finally, in chap. 11 ("Death") Flusser believes that Jesus' affirmation of the messianic question put to him by the High Priest resulted in his being handed over to the Romans and crucified as "king of the Jews."[1186]

Evan's final comments are affirming: "Although it is disappointing that Flusser's *Jesus* is not more current, especially with regard to the recently published Scrolls and the lively scholarly discussion concerned with them, the book is not without points of interest and insight. It is also refreshing—though sometimes frustrating—to read a book whose author is not bound by critical orthodoxy or theological dogmas, be they Christian or Jewish."[1187]

Pinchas Lapide

Lapide wrote and coauthored numerous books in German, many of them transcribed conversations of radio broadcasts or verbatim of interfaith dialogues. Lapide's arena of dialogue, and therefore influence, was primarily Germany and German-speaking populations. Since Lapide's irenical aim is consistent, his perspective is oftentimes repetitious. His focus is not primarily the historical Jesus but a renewed and efficacious interfaith dialogue between Jews and Christians—of which Jesus serves as bridge. Therefore, his portrait of Jesus is discernible in rebuttal and rapprochement, in praise and critique, in scholarly speech and speculation.

Orthodox and irenical, paradoxical and enigmatic, controversial and cordial—these are but a few descriptive phrases that come to mind when considering Lapide and his efforts to span the chasm between Jew and Christian in a post-Holocaust world. In Lapide's Jesus, we encounter a prodigal Jesus, not a lost squanderer of heritage and despoiler of tradition, but rather one previously lost to antiquity, disguised by myth, yet now restored to his rightful place among the sages of Judaism. Lapide's efforts exemplify the *modernen Heimholung Jesu in das jüdische Volk.* An episodic survey of critiques or responses follows.

Hagner, affirms the above assessment, echoing: "Lapide's approach is solidly within the modern trend to reclaim Jesus by affirming his genuine Jewishness and finds its primary motivation in the desire to bring Jews and Christians closer together."[1188]

Samuel Sandmel penned the foreword of the 1979 English translation of Lapide's *Ist das nicht Josephs Sohn? Jesus im heutigen Judentum* (1976) entitled, curiously, *Israelis, Jews, and Jesus*. Complimenting Lapide's initiative and irenical effort in pro-viding a timely survey of the image of Jesus in the modern State of Israel, Sandmel affirms:

> There is one additional service that Dr. Lapide renders. All too often the Jewish side of the Christian-Jewish controversy has rested on the hostility of the Middle Ages and on the folklore among Jews about Christians (which balances the folklore among Christians about Jews). In the Jewish folklore, Christians are guilty of illiteracy, stupidity, drunk-enness, and a glorying in personal physical power, not in the power of the mind. A contrary viewpoint expressed by great Jewish sages and philosophers, has usually gone ignored. . . . Dr. Lapide, however, provides many examples and it is wonderful to have this material brought together and presented so well.[1189]

Ever the consummate scholar, Sandmel is compelled to offer a disclaimer:

> I think that I should, in all honesty, issue a very quiet academic disclaimer about some of the passages in the book. One in particular I must advert to—namely, Lapide's ex-cessive certainty that there was a Hebrew version of some of the Gospel material. I think this is incorrect, and I regard it a legendary development from the view of the second-century Bishop Papias, quoted in Eusebius, that Matthew had written his Gospel in Hebrew.[1190]

Nonetheless, he affirms Lapide's overall efforts in *Israelis, Jews, and Jesus*: "The im-portant thing is that Dr. Lapide has written an enlightening book that ought to be of great interest to American Jews and Christians."[1191]

David P. Scaer, commenting on Lapide's *Ist das nicht Josephs Sohn? Jesus im heutigen Judentum*, writes:

> The title "Is This Not Joseph's Son?" (a citation from. . .[Luke 4:22]) is appropriate for the contents. Those who did not accept Jesus as God's Son could advance no further than acknowledging his alleged human father, Joseph. The Israelis (Jews) have come no further.
> The need for this kind of research only became necessary when the nation of Israel had to provide for its own schoolchildren an explanatory biography about their land's most famous son. At first, Jesus could be ignored but, with the influx of Christian

tourists, the luxury of ignorance was no longer affordable. . . . To be sure this is no Christology, at least in the traditional sense. Much of what is said about Jesus is fabricated, i.e., it has no support from the Gospels, but it is not necessarily negative. For those engaged in missions among the Jews, this book should be made available. The person of Jesus has to be the starting point for any meaningful discussion with the Jews. Lapide has extended his hand to the Christian community.[1192]

Affirming Lapide's positive Jewish theology of the Christianity, Paul M. van Buren provides a review of three of Lapide's books: *The Resurrection of Jesus*, *Jesus in Two Perspectives*, and *The Sermon on the Mount*. Van Buren hails Lapide as a "rather unorthodox Jewish ecumenist"[1193] and explains his enigmatic epithet: "What is unorthodox about him is that as a committed, believing, Orthodox Jew, he is determined to move out from under Christianity's horrible past history of hatred for the Jews and build the foundations for a new positive relationship between the church and the Jewish people. . . . Here is ecumenism at a daring level."[1194]

Describing Lapide's book on Jesus' resurrection as "surely his most provocative," van Buren enthusiastically provides more of a précis than a critique. Turning to *Jesus in Two Perspectives*, van Buren assesses Lapide's theses vis-à-vis Jesus, Judaism, and the Christian tradition regarding both; he affirms: "These theses, rebutting staples of the anti-Judaic tradition of the church, however, are now shared by most Christian scholars."[1195] Even so, van Buren contends: "Many so-called educated Christians might well profit from reading Lapide's clear refutation of long-held beliefs, not least because he is critically much more conservative than his Christian respondent, who is Professor of New Testament at the University of Bern."[1196]

Focusing upon *The Sermon on the Mount: Utopia or Program for Action?* van Buren offers a sympathetic, if uncritical, review. Affirming that "Lapide makes a thought-provoking case for the latter," he further asserts: "There could scarcely be a Christian preacher, pastor, or layperson who would not learn from Lapide's book a new respect for this text and for its original author. The original author having been a Jew speaking only to Jews, it should not be surprising if a Jewish interpreter could open up the text for Christians."[1197]

The Christian ecumenist van Buren and his Jewish contemporary Rabbi Neusner could not disagree more!

Though van Buren concedes Lapide's "misunderstandings" of Christianity, he overlooks them as "first of all misunderstandings of the Christian church."[1198] Undaunted, he claims with palpable zeal: "In reading him, we are on the cutting edge of the so-called Jewish-Christian dialogue."[1199] Expanding upon this acclamation, he asserts:

Lapide is surely correct theologically in seeing in Jesus the bond between the church and the Jewish people, because he is correct historically in seeing him as a Jew in a Jewish context. More daringly, he has advanced beyond any Jewish author with whom I am familiar, including even Franz Rosenzweig, in seeing the church as a vital piece of the history of God's covenant and so a matter for Jewish prayer and concern. He is building a positive Jewish theology of the Christian church which challenges the church to come up with a positive Christian theology of the Jewish people.[1200]

James H. Charlesworth is more balanced in his critique of Lapide. In an annotated bibliographical note describing *Jesus in Two Perspectives*, Charlesworth writes:

> Lapide, a Jew, posits three arguments: Jesus did not claim to be the Messiah, he was not rejected by Israel but was warmly received by the majority of Jews, and he did not reject Israel. Luz, the Christian, tends to agree with Lapide's conclusions; but he wisely points out that the main insightful questions that are important for a "Jewish-Christian discussion concerning Jesus are not raised . . ." (p. 123). He astutely points out that such a discussion cannot begin in a vacuum; and he sees far better than Lapide the diversity and complexity of such issues in first-century Palestine.[1201]

Most startling and controversial is Lapide's provocative affirmation of the resurrection of Jesus as a historical event. In his 1975 conversation with Hans Küng (*Jesus im Widerstreit: Ein jüdisch-christlicher Dialog*), Lapide responds to Küng's pointed question regarding Lapide's view of Jesus' resurrection:

> Up to a short time ago I thought that anything like a self-abasement of God—*kenōsis* [self-emptying; Phil 2:7]—and incarnation in the Christian sense were alien to Judaism. To my astonishment, I have learned in the meantime that there were germinal traces of both ideas among marginal groups in Judaism as early as the first century before Christ, and still more in the first and second Christian centuries, so that even these things entered later Christianity not from Hellenism, but in fact from certain Jewish circles. With utmost seriousness, as an Orthodox Jew, I must say that I cannot accept what you call resurrection, *kenōsis* and *apokatastasis* [restoration; Acts 3:21], since this is not suggested by our Jewish experience of God. But neither can I deny it, for who am I as a devout Jew to define a priori God's saving action?[1202]

Lapide expresses his mature reflections on this question in his book *Auferstehung: Ein jüdisches Glaubenserlebnis*, translated as *The Resurrection of Jesus: A Jewish Faith Experience.* Cullen I. K. Story, of Princeton Seminary, observes:

> Lapide's book registers a strong demurral to abstract paraphrases on the resurrection by modern theologians (e.g., Bultmann, Rahner, Marxsen) who are "ashamed of the material facticity of the resurrection." The writer cites the remarkable change of "the solid hillbillies from Galilee" into a "jubilant community of believers," and then claims, "Jesus *must* rise" so that the God of Israel could continue to live in the hearts of his disciples. Though risen, Jesus is not the Messiah but prepares the way. Yet the experience of his resurrection is the foundation of the church. Thereby, faith in Israel's God has reached the Western world, an experience which "must belong to God's plan of salvation." So the writer pleads for dialogue between Judaism and Christianity where common origins and basic differences will allow conversation to proceed "from open faith to open faith."[1203]

Wendell W. Frerichs, of Luther-Northwestern Seminaries, citing the translator of Lapide's dialogue with Jürgen Moltmann, *Jewish Monotheism and Christian Trinitarian Doctrine: A Dialogue*, discerns a possible explanation of Lapide's unorthodox position vis-à-vis the resurrection of Jesus:

> Some other matters not directly related to the main topic are also worth discovering in the book. For instance, the translator, Leonard Swidler, in his preface shows that such

interfaith dialogue was not possible for earlier generations of believers. Even now, only a minority—those who hold to a non-absolutized, dynamic view of truth—dare really able to participate in such an encounter. This makes the event recorded in the book all the more valuable. It also explains how Lapide can speak of the Church as a God-willed community of salvation or of Jesus' resurrection as an historical event.[1204]

Whether the above explanation is valid or not, there is no doubt that Lapide's idiosyncratic perspective met with discordant reaction, soliciting praise, consternation, outrage, and rebuttal. An episodic survey follows.

Describing Lapide's *The Resurrection of Jesus* as "a fascinating book devoted to the Jewish-Christian dialogue,"[1205] Gerald O'Collins, SJ, of the Gregorian University, Rome, observes: "Like Maimonides, Lapide holds that the Christian Church must be part of God's plan, a *praeparatio messianica*. Lapide goes further to argue that Jesus' role as Saviour of Gentiles came about through his resurrection from the dead."[1206]

Joseph Sievers, Professor of Judaic studies and a colleague of O'Collins at the Gregorian University, scrutinizes Lapide's hermeneutics vis-à-vis the Jewish literary sources and asserts:

> Unfortunately, here [in *The Resurrection of Jesus*] we are dealing with a tendentious interpretation of Jewish sources which leads to an apparent closeness to Christian positions. It seems that such an affirmation does not serve the better understanding of the historic Jesus, nor does it serve in the deepening of the dialogue between Jews and Christians. Even if Lapide did and continues to do much to sensitize a vast Christian public to the essential relationship between Christianity and Judaism, it is necessary to distinguish between affirmations based on good conscience and sources and understandings which contribute to a better comprehension of them and other affirmations made mostly for their public effect.[1207]

Clinton Bennett, in assessing Lapide's *The Resurrection of Jesus*, writes:

> The publication of *The Resurrection of Jesus* (1979) by the German Orthodox Jew, Pinchas Lapide, has been described as "an event without precedent in the long history of Jewish-Christian relations." Like Rosenzweig, Lapide argues in favour of Christianity's need of Jewish witness. . . . Lapide rejects the idea, suggested by Reimarus and others, that the resurrection was purely a fiction invented by the disciples. Rather, he believes that the resurrection of Jesus *really happened.* As an event, it retains certain ambiguities, but its effect on the disciples was unambiguous.[1208]

On Lapide's *Resurrection of Jesus*, United Methodist theologian Albert Outler affirms that the book's value lies in its "illumination of the Jewish perspective on resurrection, its critique of Christian demythologizing of the Resurrection of Jesus, [and] its refocusing of the crucial issue of kinship and alienation between Jews and Christians."[1209]

The "Religion" section of *Time* magazine reported both the unprecedented "event" and Jewish reaction:

> West Germany's Jews have excoriated Lapide's view as outrageous. Some scholars complain that he has made highly selective use of Jewish sources, including the medieval sage Maimonides. It is "a terrible shock. He has overstepped the bounds of Jewish

theology," snaps liberal German Rabbi Peter Levinson. "If I believed in Jesus' Resurrection I would be baptized tomorrow."

Among German Christians, even those who express doubts about Jesus' Resurrection, Lapide's ideas have been welcomed.[1210]

Géza Vermès

Vermès, uniquely equipped as historian and distinguished Dead Sea Scrolls scholar—though not a New Testament scholar per se—navigates a distinctive course. He asserts the "inalienable rights of the historian to pursue a course independent of beliefs,"[1211] "despite widespread academic skepticism,"[1212] vis-à-vis "our increased knowledge of the Palestinian-Jewish realities of the time of Jesus."[1213] Vermès scrutinizes both historical and nonhistorical sources, meaning the Gospels, to glean from them historically reliable evidence concerning both the person of Jesus and first-century Palestine. In doing so, he provides a paradigm for future investigation, thus, unwittingly, becoming the forerunner of what emerged as a third quest for the historical Jesus.[1214]

It would be imprudent to assume that Vermès intended to spark such a resurgence of inquiry or that his impetus, unlike Ben-Chorin or Lapide, was a Jewish reclamation of Jesus, irenic or otherwise. Vermès, the historian, sets out to discern Jesus of Galilee from the evidence, old and new. What began as a distraction from his Qumran studies evolved into a major study and the impetus for a renewed effort to retrieve the historical Jesus from the christological overlay.

Vermès himself provides us an episodic survey of the initial reaction to his nascent inquiry. In the opening address to a 1987 ecumenical conference in Birmingham, England, entitled "The Parting of the Ways," Vermès provides his audience both précis and critique of his early works: *Jesus the Jew* (1973) and *Jesus and the World of Judaism* (1983). Rather than focusing his comments upon "objections that are essentially academic in nature, such as those querying my way of handling the Jewish sources,"[1215] Vermès focuses his survey upon "reactions prompted by religious attitudes."[1216] Since he provides numerous citations as evidence of the diverse reactions, the reader is referred to the article. Some selected citations from the published, revised version of the lecture will suffice to illustrate the reaction of Jews and Christians.[1217]

Juxtaposing Jewish and Christian reactions, Vermès reports that "on the Jewish side, I have not come across strongly worded hostility"[1218] and writes:

By contrast, among the Christian ranks there have been outbursts on a few occasions. What happened behind closed doors, I cannot say, although rumour has it that the Catholic publishers of the French *Jésus le Juif* were severely reprimanded in private by angry episcopal voices. An outraged French writer in the extreme right-wing *La pensée catholique* has qualified the book as scandalous and blaspheming. Intermittently, even scholars have allowed free expression to their bad temper, such as the Protestant professor L. A. Keck: "Jesus the Jew deserves better that this"; or the Jesuit J. A. Fitzmyer: "I am always immediately put off by those who claim to write about the Gospels as 'historians'; that immediately means that an axe is being ground."[1219]

Describing these as "exceptions," Vermès affirms the majority view: "Indeed, the majority of reviewers, even those who have major reservations concerning some of my chief conclusions, seem to find in this 'historian's approach' worthwhile openings for a fuller understanding of the real Jesus and, on the Christian side, a firmer basis for theology and belief."[1220]

As to the initial reaction among Jews to his efforts, Vermès reports:

> As has been noted, Jewish reactions, perhaps for understandable reasons—Jesus is not indispensable for an understanding of Judaism—are sporadic, but generally hopeful. Thus David Daube concludes his review of *Jesus the Jew*: "Whether it will do much towards removing ill-will and distrust may be doubted. These attitudes are largely independent of scholarly data. Still, with luck, it may do a little. The present climate gives some ground for hope." Likewise, David Flusser, of the Hebrew University, himself an author of a book on Jesus, sees *Jesus the Jew* and *Jesus and the World of Judaism* as valuable illuminations of both "the progress in Judaic Studies and of the Jewish roots of Christianity."[1221]

Leaving the published address, we find Vermès in *Jesus in His Jewish Context* (2003), the revised version of *Jesus and the World of Judaism*, commenting upon the reception of the third book of his Jesus trilogy, *The Religion of Jesus the Jew* (1993). He writes:

> Always foreseeing the worst, I was amazed by the warm reception granted to *The Religion of Jesus the Jew* in all shades of public opinion. On 2 March 1993, the day after its publication, in a full page piece in the *Evening Standard* headed "The scholar who found the real Jesus," A. N. Wilson wrote: "Of Jesus the man, perhaps we still know little—but of the kind of teacher and healer he was, the kind of religion he preached, the kind of audience he addressed, we now know infinitely more, thanks to Vermès."[1222]

After citing similar reviews, Vermès concedes:

> As could be expected, there were some dissenting voices in the confraternity of transatlantic New Testament scholars, particularly quibbling with my lack of "methodology" in the use of rabbinic literature in the interpretation of the Gospels. Missing the humoristic tone in the characterization of my approach to the issue as "true British pragmatism," with a distinct preference for "muddling through," because "innovative [research] should not be bound by fixed, predetermined rules" (*Religion*, 7), a recent critic of the trilogy, John P. Meier, felt entitled to deliver a little sermon in my direction and for my benefit: "Any scholarly investigation that is not totally erratic operates by certain rules." If Meier had taken the trouble to glance at "Jewish Studies and New Testament Interpretation," referred to on the same page as an account of my method in Gospel exegesis, his readers could have been spared such a pompous remark.[1223]

We shall consider Meier's critique and the critique of Bruce Chilton, both of whom exemplify the "the dissenting voices of the confraternity of transatlantic scholars," following the entries from Vermès regarding the Jewish reaction to *The Religion of Jesus the Jew*.

Vermès, perhaps in light of Meier's "harsh words," cites Tessa Rajak, "a friend and former pupil," who describes his efforts as "the low-key, meticulous, fair-minded—positively British—investigations of the now emeritus professor of Jewish studies at Oxford."[1224] Lastly, he adds: "A powerful revolutionary echo came from Israel, too. Reviewing *The Religion of Jesus the Jew* in the country's leading newspaper, *Ha'aretz*, Magen Broshi, director of the Shrine of the Book, called the age-old ban by virtue of which the name of the Nazarene was never to pass through Jewish lips 'patently absurd.'"[1225]

As Vermès indicates, John P. Meier, Bruce Chilton, and others—whom he contends harbor a "German-based North-American methodological dogmatism"[1226]—take exception to his "muddling through"[1227] the sources, referring to Vermès's pragmatic methodology. Since Meier's critique is paradigmatic of the "confraternity," we will follow, judiciously, his lengthy rebuttal.

"Muddling through," the phrase that evoked little humor, though such was the intention,[1228] sparked a severe rebuke by Meier of those scholars, such as Vermès, who in his estimation "brush aside the whole question of method and criteria."[1229] Meier warns: "The danger in 'muddling through' is that one easily begins to draw from the data the conclusions one wants rather than the conclusions the data warrants."[1230]

Expanding upon his rebuke, Meier pointedly criticizes Vermès:

> Géza Vermès proclaims his disdain for "methodology" and his preference for "muddling through" in *The Religion of Jesus the Jew* (Minneapolis: Fortress, 1993), 7. The problem is, though, that any scholarly investigation that is not totally erratic operates by certain rules, whether or not they are acknowledged, labeled, and thought through. The danger of not thinking through one's method and criteria becomes evident almost immediately in Vermès' work. (1) He implicitly works with the criterion of multiple attestation of sources, but does not use the criterion properly. For example, to show that Jesus was observant of the cultic law, Vermès (p. 18) states that "all three Synoptic Gospels report that after curing a leper, he [Jesus] enjoined him to appear before a priest for examination"; Mark 1:44 is cited as evidence. Yet, in the judgment of most commentators, the Matthean and Lucan versions of the story are simply their theological adaptations of the Marcan story. There is, then, only one independent source attesting to the historical event. . . . (2) Vermès also uses something like a combination of the criteria of embarrassment and discontinuity (p. 17). However, when using such a criterion, one must be very careful in appealing to rabbinic material. Unfortunately, Vermès is disconcertingly free and easy in using not only the Mishnah (redacted ca. A.D. 200) but also the Tosefta, the various midrashim and targums, and even the Jerusalem Talmud (redacted in the first half of the fifth century) and the Babylonian Talmud (redacted in the first half of the sixth century), achieving its final form in the eighth century. The problem of using rabbinic material to understand Judaism(s) in the early first century A.D., a problem highlighted by the works of Jacob Neusner in particular, is not taken seriously (pp. 7–10).[1231]

Refuting Vermès's assertion that his inquiry is "untendentious," meaning sans theological preconception, and his "analysis of the available evidence [is] without fear [anger] or favor, *sine ira et studio*,"[1232] Meier—while arguing a similar case, one that reflects a "rethinking" of the project—challenges Vermès's objectivity:

The problem is that, despite loud protestations about a purely historical approach, most authors of books about the historical Jesus mesh their historical agenda with a theological one. This was true of Reimarus; it remains true of post-Bultmannian portraits from Bornkamm and Käsemann—and, I would add, of portraits from supposedly neutral historians like Géza Vermès. One should note, for instance, how Vermès begins his book *Jesus the Jew: A Historian's Reading of the Gospels* (Philadelphia: Fortress, 1973) with a polemic against the Nicene Creed and a lament for Jesus as "this man, so distorted by Christian and Jewish myth alike . . ." (p. 17). This does not augur well for a cool, objective reading of the evidence by a historian. Claims to purely historical scholarship notwithstanding, the quest for the historical Jesus is usually part of a theological program that seeks either to replace the Christ of faith with the historical Jesus (Reimarus and Vermès) or to show how the historical Jesus is relevant to present-day concerns (Sobrino, Segundo).[1233]

Though Meier is critical of Vermès's objectivity, he does find merit in his hypothesis—but not without critique:

Géza Vermès has made the intriguing suggestion that Jesus of Nazareth should be understood as one of a number of popular Galilean holy men or *ḥăsîdîm* who were noted for their powerful spontaneous prayers, the miracles that often answered their prayers, and the practical acts of kindness. They were not, however, famous for either their teaching on the Mosaic law or their punctilious observance of the finer points of the law. Hence, as freewheeling possessors of special power not transmitted by the usual conduits of religious authority, they stood in tension vis-à-vis both the temple officials in Jerusalem and the Pharisees zealous for the law.[1234]

Vermès's juxtaposition of Jesus with Honi the Circle-Drawer and Hanina ben Dosa, two charismatic Jewish figures emanating from rabbinic texts, confirms Vermès's hypothesis, from Vermès's perspective. Meier, however, is not convinced. He argues:

If we did have reliable access to the "historical" Honi or Hanina, the typology suggested by Vermès would indeed be valuable. However, as with Apollonius [of Tyana], so with Honi and Hanina, the devil is in the details of the sources. Despite the attempts of Vermès and others to sift the sources carefully, in the end one must admit that all written sources are later than Jesus, and almost all of them centuries later. I would venture to claim that, beyond the fact that around the turn of the era there existed two Jews in Palestine named Honi and Hanina, both of whom were famous for having their prayers answered in extraordinary ways, nothing definite can be said.[1235]

Reviewing the evidence himself, Meier, admittedly influenced by Sean Freyne's perspective on Hanina ben Dosa in his essay "The Charismatic," asserts that what is true regarding Honi—and of Apollonius of Tyana and of Jesus of Nazareth—holds true for Hanina ben Dosa: the dubious use of sources that postdate the persons and events under consideration. Meier asserts: "I realize [that] this flies in the face of two detailed studies on the Hanina tradition by Géza Vermès, but the critique of Vermès's work by Sean Freyne emboldened me to demur."[1236]

Vermès is aware of the potential difficulties inherent in an attempt to confirm the Hasidic typology from rabbinic sources, as Meier notes: "Despite his own warnings, Vermès does attempt to create a profile of the historical Hanina from the various rabbinic reports, some of which are quite late."[1237] Reviewing the evidence gleaned from Jewish sources, with "the lack of explicit and unambiguous reference to real miracle-working in the Mishnah's portrait of Hanina ben Dosa"[1238] and Vermès's assertions thereof, Meier exclaims:

> Despite the fact that many of the traditions about Hanina ben Dosa do not find any literary attestation earlier than the two Talmuds, Vermès suggests that in some of the statements attributed to Hanina we may possess genuine sayings of "a remarkable personality living in first-century Palestine," sayings that "constitute the most direct insight we possess into the Hasidic mind and outlook." That Vermès can make this claim when discussing sayings attributed to Hanina in the *Pirqe Rabbi Eliezer* (*Pirqe R. El.* 29, 31) leaves one speechless. This work apparently originated in the eighth or ninth century A.D.; while it uses older tradition, it is not basically "a compilation like other midrashim, but . . . the creative achievement of a personal author."[1239]

Meier concludes: "Ultimately, Vermès' acritical use of the sources undermines his whole argument."[1240]

Before yielding space to Bruce Chilton and Larry W. Hurtado, we should allow Sean Freyne a correlative observation. Scrutinizing Vermès's artificial distribution of the Hanina traditions into convenient categories—healer, teacher, miracle-worker, and a fourth category of Hanina's praises, Freyne asserts: "In fact this principle of arrangement can easily lead to treating the material as potentially biographical, a trap Vermès falls into only too often in his apparent desire to establish good parallels between the historical Jesus and the historical Hanina."[1241] Speaking of his own perspective, Freyne does, however, concede: "We have made no attempt to date the historical Hanina, though the pre-70 date suggested by both Vermès and Neusner does seem to be a more plausible context for his activity as a man of deed."[1242]

Bruce Chilton, in a survey of the figure Jesus within Judaism, highlights George Foot Moore's attraction to two teachers emanating from the rabbinic corpus: Honi, called Circler, and Hanina ben Dosa. Having provided this preface, Chilton next describes Vermès's efforts: "In his popular work, *Jesus the Jew*, Géza Vermès takes up just these two examples within his portrait of Jesus as a 'charismatic' or 'Hasid.' Vermès differs from Moore, however, in presenting that category as an alternative to that of a rabbi. His argument is nothing if not elastic, since he even concludes that Eliezer ben Hyrcanus was a charismatic!"[1243]

Asserting that "Vermès does not explain the sources of his thought (nor, indeed, his debt to Moore), but they are plain enough,"[1244] Chilton attempts an explanation: "The neo-orthodox mode of Protestant thought (and, in its wake, Catholic thought) after the Second World War made Martin Buber a companion saint with Karl Barth, and the image of the prayerful Hasid appealed both to theologians such as Reinhold Niebuhr and to historians such as Roland de Vaux and André Dupont-Sommer in their work on the Dead Sea Scrolls."[1245]

Recognizing that "the picture of the sectarians of Qumran as monastic Hasidim has since drawn considerable criticism,"[1246] Chilton continues: "Vermès, at first active within the French-speaking Catholic circles which propagated the Hasidic/Essene hypothesis worked on the scrolls during the period in which the hypothesis was most in vogue, and he has recently been described as having 'reiterated it without any essential modification ever since.'"[1247]

As to Vermès's use of the Hasidic typology vis-à-vis Jesus, Chilton observes: "The adjective 'charismatic' serves in Vermès' reading to distinguish Jesus (with Honi and Hanina) from any communal structure. . . . It remains an unresolved issue within critical study, however, whether that paradigm of charismatic heroism can appropriately be applied to Honi, Hanina, or Jesus."[1248]

He pointedly continues: "As if in compensation for the lack of direct evidence for a portrait of Jesus as such a self-consciously heroic figure, Vermès pushed the discussion of the Aramaic locution 'son of man' (בר אנש [*bar-'ĕnoš*, Dan 7:13]) in a new and interesting direction. . . . Vermès suggested that a speaker might refer to himself as 'son of man' as a circumlocution for his own personal existence, rather than as belonging to humanity as a whole."[1249]

Chilton concludes his review of Vermès by asserting:

> In three respects, Vermès' portrait of the charismatic Hasid has been weakened since the publication of *Jesus the Jew*. First, William Scott Green has shown that Honi and Hanina were both claimed by rabbis of a later period as of their own, so that any bifurcation of "Hasidim" from rabbis within the first century would not seem to be recommended. . . . Second, the notion of the isolation of Galilee from Judea (and from the Graeco-Roman world), which is asserted several times by Vermès without supporting evidence, has effectively been disproved by subsequent study. Third, it has been demonstrated that "son of man" in Aramaic is a generic form of language in which a speaker includes himself within the realm of humanity, rather than the heroic designation of oneself as distinct from others, which Vermès claimed it was.[1250]

Nonetheless, Chilton concedes: "Despite the weakness of its own argument, *Jesus the Jew* has brought about a renewal of interest in the Judaic matrix of Jesus and Christianity."[1251]

Concluding this section of academic critique, Larry W. Hurtado, in his essay "A Taxonomy of Recent Historical-Jesus Work," echoes and thereby summarizes "significant objections to major features of his [Vermès's] Jesus work."[1252] Hurtado asks: "Is Vermès correct to attach so much importance to rabbinic sources and traditions? Is the Jesus of individual piety really borne out in the Jesus tradition, or is there not in the most assured material indication of a more collective vision of the divine purpose (as reflected, e.g., in the calling of the Twelve)? Is the Hasid model really adequate, given the several qualifications Vermès himself has to recognize?"[1253]

Hurtado also concedes: "We could continue with other objections, but one must grant that Vermès has provided us with distinctive and sometimes valuable material for the current quest. With Sanders, he is especially salutary in insisting on the need for any portrait of Jesus to be credible within an informed picture of first-century Jewish religiosity."[1254]

Discerning in Vermès's "rescue" of Jesus from Christianity a tendentious aim, Hurtado asserts a final observation:

From his earliest book onward, Vermès has presented himself as a "historian," who, because he is not a Christian theologian, is able to give a more objective portrait of Jesus. All along, however, the careful reader has been able to detect in Vermès his own hermeneutical aims and concerns, and in his most recent volume these come out quite explicitly, especially in the concluding chapter. Vermès is clearly concerned to deny Jesus any role as "founder" of Christianity, and seeks "to re-instate him among the ancient Hasidim," toward fulfillment of Buber's prophecy": "A great place belongs to him in Israel's history of faith." In short, Vermès would rescue Jesus from Christianity, and make the Hasidic Jesus a fixture in Jewish spiritual history. It is surely not too difficult to detect a hermeneutical and religio-political aim here.[1255]

Echoing Meier's earlier concern, Hurtado brings this segment full circle.

Since Meier's critique, now augmented by others, is paradigmatic of the basic objections to Vermès's Jesus work, Vermès's response to Meier will suffice as a response to all. We are fortunate to have the response to Meier because Vermès usually does "not respond to criticism and leave[s] it to the readers to form their own judgment."[1256] Given the "open hostility in the United States especially in the wake of some harsh words said about my method by Professor John P. Meier,"[1257] Vermès was "persuaded by friends and colleagues to make an exception."[1258] Following his response—found largely in the preface to *Jesus in His Jewish Context*, we will provide an episodic survey of more favorable, critical reviews of his trilogy and more recent works.

Acknowledging Meier's "two serious objections against my way of portraying Jesus,"[1259] namely, the lack of methodology and an "acritical" use of the rabbinic sources, Vermès issues a cogent rebuttal. Above, we have indicated Vermès initial response to Meier's rebuke of Vermès's habit of "muddling through." Vermès's more precise response follows.

Vermès accepts that Meier misunderstood his remarks: "Professor Meier interpreted it *à la lettre* although it appeared in the context of a jocular piece of self-mockery."[1260] Taken aback at Meier's affront, his lecturing of Vermès as to the need of certain rules lest a scholarly investigation become erratic, Vermès responds: "It does indeed. Yet if this otherwise so meticulous researcher had taken the trouble to read, or even glance at my essay, 'Jewish Studies and New Testament Interpretation: *Reflections on Methodology*,' deliberately cited on the same page as the quotation which so upset him, he might have realized that I am not as unprincipled as he seems to imagine."[1261]

That being said, Vermès pointedly continues:

Instead of analysing the documents, Meier adopts a simplistic stand in his dealing with rabbinic literature. For him the date of a tradition is determined by the date of the literary source, which transmits it. So he simply declares the Mishnah, Midrash, Talmud and Targum unfit for use in the study of Jesus because their redaction occurred after the composition of the New Testament (late first–early second century AD), namely, between, say, AD 200 and 500. But scholars familiar with the works of the rabbis are well aware that a rabbinic anthology often contains teachings and interpretations, which are centuries older than the final compilation in which they are housed. They also know that it is possible to distinguish ancient elements from more recent material.[1262]

As to Meier's charge of an acritical use of rabbinic literature, Vermès retorts:

> The issue arises from my application to Jesus of the concept "charismatic Hasid," which I have modeled mostly on the Mishnaic-Talmudic, but also partly on the Josephan, portrayal of two Jewish "miracle-workers," Honi (first century BC) and Hanina ben Dosa (first century AD). My approach to the figure of the charismatic Hasid was typological. I argued from features, which are attested and verifiable in *all the historical periods* of ancient Judaism from the age of the eighth-century-BC Old Testament prophets down to the Tannaitic and Amoraic rabbis in the early centuries of the Christian era. Anyone acquainted with my publications, which now stretch over more than fifty years, can see that I am fully aware of the time factor affecting the rabbinic sources and of the evolutionary process characteristic of them. After all, I spent more than twenty years on rewriting and re-editing *The History of the Jewish People in the Age of Jesus Christ*, Emil Schürer's monumental classic, *the* textbook on the period of the Gospels.[1263]

Vermès disassembles Meier's "speechless" dismay, given Vermès's speculative assertions regarding Hanina ben Dosa, by asserting: "Indeed, I have explicitly called the two texts in question 'spurious' (ibid., p. 49). In the light of these correct facts, I invite the readers to decide whose argument, Professor Meier's or mine, is undermined by an 'acritical' handling of the evidence."[1264]

Concluding his refutation of Meier's critique, Vermès focuses his critical eye upon Meier's Jesus research:

> Meier has strongly objected to my way of employing the model of the charismatic prophet and the Elijah-like miracle-worker in the study of the historical Jesus. Therefore let us now inquire how his "*marginal Jew*" is defined. Jesus, according to Professor Meier, is an "eschatological prophet" and a "charismatic" similar to "Elijah." In other words, the "marginal Jew" is the mirror image of the "charismatic Hasid" delineated by me in *Jesus the Jew* twenty-one years before Father Meier. Thus unwittingly he vindicates my cynical remark published prior to the appearance of volume II of *A Marginal Jew* (1994). "Methodology," I wrote, "makes me see red perhaps because more than once I have been rebuked by transatlantic dogmatists for illegitimately arriving at the *right* conclusion, following a path not sanctioned by [their] sacrosanct rule book."[1265]

Vermès is not singular in defense of his approach and the efficacy of his typology. Two Jewish contemporaries of Vermès share initial, affirming critiques. The rabbinic scholar Jacob Neusner, writing in late 1974 a review of *Jesus the Jew*, affirms:

> The comparison of the figure of Jesus represented fairly consistently in the Gospels to have done wonders and signs (magic in the eye of the outsider) with Honi or Hanina, men of grace, seems to me [to be] apt and accurate. The claim, at the end, that the titles later assigned to Jesus in general were remote from his conception of himself, as evidenced in the more reliable sayings, is well founded. The argument is a sound one, carefully worked out, with full and requisite attention to the varieties of Judaism, the strata of the rabbinic literature, the entire range of critical problems important in contemporary New Testament and rabbinic scholarship.[1266]

While approving Vermès's figure of Jesus, Neusner does, however, make an important observation—one that seemingly vindicates Vermès's "guarded optimism" while appreciating the reserve of New Testament scholars:

Any historian would be satisfied, given the state of the evidence and of the art of interpreting it, with these results. But the New Testament scholars have a second, entirely unhistorical agendum, and that is a search, with a historical map, for theological truths not . . . included in the cartography of historical studies. For them, merely interpreting the evidence along the lines followed by Vermès is unsatisfying. . . . I think Bultmann is entirely right in holding that we shall never know what the sources . . . do not contain. These are not letters written by Jesus himself, nor are they stories composed by witnesses to the events for the purposes of a newspaper account or archival record. But I think Vermès is correct in maintaining that historical studies are nonetheless feasible.[1267]

Though Neusner's initial critique of Vermès was affirming, his support for Vermès and his Hasidic typology waned. In 1991, having perhaps reflected upon the weaknesses inherent in the historical Jesus quest—and concomitantly the Jewish-Christian dialogues—Neusner, in his book *Jews and Christians: The Myth of a Common Tradition*, pointedly dismisses—without naming him—not only the validity of Vermès's innovative approach, but also the entire enterprise that tries to recover the historical Jesus:

The representation of Jesus in the Gospels constantly surprises, even amazes one familiar with other reports of the Judaism of the time—just as the authors of the Gospels said. But then what is a Judaic believer to make of Christianity? When Jesus contrasted his teaching with what others had been saying, he underlined this simple point: the Christ of theology begins with the Jesus of history. Jesus was Jesus Christ in the Gospels and to the evangelists as much as he was Christ Jesus to Paul; any distinction between the Jesus of history and the Christ of faith, whether invidious or favorable, ignores not only the explicit claims of the Gospels themselves but also the genuinely surprising character of the representation of Jesus in the context of any Judaism known to us today. The characterization of Jesus as a Galilean wonder-worker like Honi the Circle-Drawer, for example, is *a total fabrication, a deliberate misreading* of the Gospels, and *a distortion* of the very character of the rabbinic evidence adduced in behalf of the proposition.[1268]

Neusner's shift from initial affirmation to harsh critique is inexplicable. Vermès is aware of Neusner's critique and provides the following response:

Jack Neusner's present attitude to the New Testament and to the historical Jesus curiously resembles that of a fundamentalist Christian. For a fundamentalist Christian there is no distinction between the Christ of faith and the Jesus of the Gospels or indeed of the Christ of the rest of the New Testament. For me and for the historically minded students of the Gospels (and of the Hebrew Bible, rabbinic literature, Josephus and Philo . . .), there is. This is not "fabrication," but the outcome of a painstaking analysis and reconstruction, bearing in mind the nature or the sources, the character of the authors and the aim pursued by them in producing their accounts. Jack and I used to be in agreement on these basics and considered ourselves for twenty years comrades in arms in the great fight for the historical truth. While still rating very highly many of his achievements, on the question of the historical Jesus, I beg to differ and am happy to leave it to the enlightened reader to make his choice between two irreconcilable positions.[1269]

Vermès remains firm in his approach and perspective. Neusner remains consistent in his critique, writing: "I am fond of Géza Vermès, but his Galilean wonder-worker is not Jesus Christ."[1270]

Another contemporary, David Flusser, writes favorably in his 1986 review of *Jesus and the World of Judaism*:

> As to Jesus himself and his message, the present volume contains very valuable insights, and I hope that the third part of this trilogy will be finished as possible, though I imagine that to write about Jesus' message will . . . be no easy task, even for such a gifted writer as Vermès. Already, in the present volume, the picture of Jesus as teacher is very attractive. I confess that, independently of the author, I came to the conclusion that Jesus was a Galilean "Hasid" and wonder-worker, as Honi was before him and Rabbi Hanina ben Dosa was some years later, though I did not compare them thoroughly enough, possibly because I hinted at this idea in a small German booklet. I am happy that Vermès also discovered this side of Jesus' personality and developed his insight in a fruitful way.[1271]

Vermès has been consistent in his insistence that, though certain procedures and hermeneutical techniques are necessary, they are hardly de rigueur. Instead, he advocates—as he reiterated recently during our conversation at Wolfson College, Oxford, in late January 2005—the premise introducing this chapter: "Novelty and originality usually consist in looking at familiar issues from an unfamiliar angle, in giving a new slant to classic ideas, in shedding fresh light on problems discussed since time immemorial."[1272]

As promised, before concluding this section on Vermès, we will consider, episodically, additional academic critiques. Vermès himself introduces two other American contemporary scholars, Paula Fredriksen and E. P. Sanders, and a British colleague Nicholas King, who—unlike Meier and Chilton—find considerable merit in his efforts.

Nicholas King, SJ, in his review of *Jesus and the World of Judaism*, expresses a "little disappointment" that the book, essentially a collection of ten papers, is not what was anticipated. Though "only prolegomenal to the long expected work"[1273] he nonetheless affirms:

> The main thrust of his work is to locate Jesus in his background as a Galilean Hasid, and to that end he repeatedly draws our attention to the vast tracts of material in Hebrew and Aramaic which remain so foreign (and even, alas, so unsympathetic) to so many NT scholars, but which have nevertheless so much to tell us of the world in which Jesus lived. "Pure history," without dogmatic preconceptions, is what Vermès is about, and though we may have our doubts whether such a thing is possible, the attempt is praiseworthy, and those of us who *do* have dogmatic preconceptions about the significance of Jesus cannot fail to learn from the attempt, if we listen calmly and with an open mind.[1274]

He concludes his review by asserting:

> Any collection of papers has unevennesses and repetitions that would not be found in a book that is a literary unit, but Vermès' admirers will find plenty to relish in this tome. It will however increase rather than slake their desire, . . . and even those who do not expect to agree with very much of it, can at least hope to be thoroughly stimulated by

this distinguished scholar's *impish delight* in questioning all established orthodoxies within both Jewish and Christian scholarship. We can all learn in the process how closely the two partners of Judaeo-Christianity belong together, and how much we depend on each other.[1275]

Paula Fredriksen, Jewish patrologist and author, reviews *The Religion of Jesus the Jew* and provides a balanced critique. Affirmingly, she writes:

> Twenty years ago, Géza Vermès worked a small revolution in New Testament studies with the publication of his now-classic *Jesus the Jew*. Placing Gospel traditions in a religiously Jewish and linguistically Semitic context, he put forward a compelling portrait of a Galilean Hasid and charismatic holy man whose practice and piety were firmly rooted in strata of Second Temple Judaism still visible in later rabbinic texts. Now, drawing on more recent work in both Christian origins and late Second Temple Judaism, Vermès enhances and refines his earlier reconstruction in *The Religion of Jesus the Jew*.[1276]

Describing the work as "a vigorous and self-confident study, its picture of Jesus and his religious convictions clear and appealing,"[1277] she nevertheless expresses two concerns:

> My two chief criticisms are linked: I think Vermès' emphasis on Jesus as an "existential teacher" (p. 137 and passim) concerned with individual ethical efforts sits poorly with other factors that we have about him, especially the Temple tantrum (which I, as Vermès, take to be historical) and his death at Rome's hand. It also obscures the trajectory of Jewish apocalyptic eschatology which passes through Jesus and Paul to the Christian communities of antiquity.[1278]

Addressing both of her concerns, she concludes by asserting:

> But these are the objections of an enthusiast. Vermès has produced an erudite and elegant essay whose value, especially in light of the author's *peerless command* of Scrolls material and Aramaic and Hebrew sources, will enrich and aid the serious student in quest of the Jesus of history. And I can only hope that the authority with which he states his judgment that Jesus' Judaism stands closer to that of the ancient Hasidim and rabbis of the Mishnah than to that of his nearer contemporaries, the covenanters of Qumran, will spare us all further silliness about Jesus and the Scrolls.[1279]

E. P. Sanders, reviewing *The Changing Faces of Jesus* (2001), prefaces his critique with praise for the "enormously successful," *Jesus the Jew*:

> One of the other principal contributions [the first, Galilean Hasidic typology] of Vermès' work was a meticulous study of the titles of Jesus: . . . Vermès concluded that Jesus preferred thinking of himself as a "prophet," while Christians assigned him the other titles for diverse reasons. By 1993 Professor Vermès could note with justified satisfaction that his campaign, in which he had been joined by others, to fit the life of Jesus convincingly into other evidence from first-century Palestine, and especially Galilee, seemed to be widely accepted.[1280]

Refocusing his gaze upon Vermès's 2001 book *The Changing Faces of Jesus*, Sanders affirms:

In fact, those who want to understand the historical Jesus and the evolving ways in which he was perceived in the following decades can do no better than to read his book. It is the masterly statement of a great scholar who has spent decades considering his topic, and whose work is gentle, irenic, relatively unargumentative, and written with exceptional skill. Although firmly insistent that Christianity has substantially disguised the historical Jesus, Vermès is not stinting in his praise of Jesus. . . . *In Vermès, Jesus has found his best Jewish interpreter.*[1281]

Jacob Neusner

Among the authors considered in this study, Neusner is singular in his criticisms of Jesus as a Jewish teacher. But so also his approach is singular: to argue, to debate—but not to offend, as he clearly states:

> So my intent is not to give offense, only to take issue. That again explains why I isolate for debate only the this-worldly component of a wholly supernatural figure—and no one can encounter Matthew's Jesus without concurring that before us in the evangelist's mind is God incarnate. In every line of these pages I realize I am writing about somebody else's God, to whom prayer and devotion and lives of service are sanctified, not a man but God incarnate, to whom vast masses of humanity turn with their hope for life eternal.[1282]

After demonstrating his thesis, an effort that conveys not merely a portrait of Jesus as an erroneous teacher of the Torah of Moses but concomitantly also provides a paradigm of authentic religious dialogue, it remains for us to measure Neusner's effect. This is no easy task.

Neusner presents us with a dilemma. As Neusner indicates, this is not a book on scholarship—nor is it a book on the historical Jesus per se; nor a book on Jesus the Jew similar to those of Jesus researchers, Vermès, Sanders, and others. Rather, Neusner, who is not a Jesus scholar per se, engages the Matthean Jesus whom he encounters in the pages of the Christian text. The debate, the argument, that transpires between the two rabbis—separated by two millennia, yet united in Neusner's imagination—is a literary device, a vehicle, for Neusner's paradigm of authentic religious dialogue. Ultimately the book is less about Jesus and more about modern Jews and modern Christians and the need of a better paradigm for interfaith dialogue, given the obvious diffidence in grappling with difficult, distinctive interfaith issues.

Reviews of the book reflect this tension. Moreover, as Donald H. Akenson observes in his foreword to the revised 2000 edition, the initial text "appeared fairly recently (1993) and disappeared quickly, though not before attracting some fervent admirers."[1283] This was due, in Akenson's estimation, to a "rebarbative subtitle appended on the otherwise lively work—'an intermillenial exchange'—and this repelled all but the most determined book buyers."[1284] The book did not fare well. Thus, the revised and expanded "second-effort."

Ironically, most of the reviews, popular or critical, found in library or online searches are reviews of the 1993 text. Reviews of the 2000 revised and expanded edition prove elusive. If the lack of current reviews, popular or critical, is any measure, then

Neusner's 2000 edition, seemingly, experienced a fate similar to the first edition. Since we have followed Neusner's 2000 edition in this study, we will begin with Akenson's foreword in the same edition and then continue with episodic reviews of the 1993 text.

Akenson describes the newly revised and expanded version as "an example of a genre that we have seen only rarely since the High Middle Ages. . . . Those rare moments of respectful and erudite encounter flicker in the past's long blackness of intolerance and intentional misunderstanding."[1285] Applauding Neusner's restoration of this classic form of Jewish-Christian encounter, he writes: "Professor Neusner reanimates the ancient form and does so with an amiability that is contagious. I imagine that many Christians and Jews will wish to argue with him; but I also expect that they will wish to do so with the same mixture of friendliness and respect for the other person's faith that he so clearly evinces."[1286]

On the encounter, the debate, between the two rabbis, Akenson observes:

> Rabbi Neusner's gentle discussion avoids the intellectual sterility and the acrimony of such [previous] engagements. He simply presents a case that the Jesus who is depicted in the Christian Scriptures . . . did not understand the Torah very well. This procedure elegantly elides the question of whether or not the historical Jesus (the "real" figure behind Jesus-the-Christ, as found in the Gospels) made these same errors. Instead, it leads ineluctably to an inference that all believers, Christians and Jews alike, should ponder: that the Jewish and Christian faiths are really distinct entities, operating on different premises and incapable of being melded together, save through indifference and ignorance. And thus, a friendly and respectful definition of irreducible difference is a mitzvah or, perhaps, a work of supererogation.[1287]

Describing Neusner's 1993 book as "one of the most honest and moving religious books of recent years,"[1288] Rabbi Jeffrey Salkin asserts: "Professor Neusner, formerly of Brown University, the most prolific Jewish writer of our generation, renews and revitalizes the discussion of how the essential message of Jesus differs from normative Judaism."[1289]

Commenting upon the lively debate's pastoral usefulness, Salkin suggests: "Jews and Christians will be able to refer to it in dialogue and joint study. It sharpens the debate on the problematic nature of syncretistic groups such as Jews for Jesus. It will also teach intermarried families why it is impossible to raise children with dual theological identities. Once again, Jacob Neusner moves the Jewish-Christian dialogue to its next level."[1290]

Mark Daniel Napack—in 1993 a doctoral (STD) candidate—writes generously: "The Christian reader of *A Rabbi Talks with Jesus* can see that in profound ways Rabbi Neusner has his finger on the Christological pulse of Matthew's Gospel. Indeed, I expect that this book will take its place beside Martin Buber's *Two Types of Faith* as one of the most perceptive Jewish accounts of Jesus."[1291]

Commenting on Neusner' critiques of the Jesus questers, he observes: "Rabbi Neusner insists that the various revisions of Jesus as merely righteous teacher and prophet are not at all true to the warp and woof of Matthew's text, and efforts to get behind the text are hopeless. 'Jesus makes sense . . . only in the setting of the Christ of faith' (p. 54)."[1292]

Not all Christian voices are as affirming. Describing Neusner's "frank criticism" as "for the most part . . . a highly repetitive stream of consciousness,"[1293] William E. Phipps, of Davis and Elkins College, demurs: "From the title we might expect a dialogue; rather we are given a soliloquy justifying traditional Judaism. Neusner finds virtually nothing good in Jesus' teaching that is not contained in the Torah as interpreted by the Mishnah and Talmud. In this regard, he is less generous than Claude Montefiore and Martin Buber, whom he admires."[1294] Aware that Neusner's book is deliberately not a book of scholarship, Phipps nonetheless counters: "This book displays the need for interfaith exchange that is understandable but [one that] displays a careful consideration of the position of scholars of other faiths."[1295]

More balanced in his critique, Philip A. Cunningham, Executive Director of the Center for Christian-Jewish Learning at Boston College, is pointed in his astute observations of Neusner's inconsistencies, given Neusner's aim and the parameters of inquiry and debate. Cunningham, conversant with Neusner's previous work, frames his response to Neusner's *A Rabbi Talks with Jesus* around one question: "Is Neusner actually interacting with the teachings of Jesus of Nazareth?"[1296]

Expecting to find the exegetical analysis necessary "to distinguish what Jesus might have said during his ministry (stage 1) from Matthew's adaptation and portrayal of those words fifty years later (stage 3),"[1297] Cunningham is surprised "that Neusner eschews scholarly portraits of the historical Jesus, but will read the Gospels as most people do: 'They assume that they are hearing the Jesus Christ of Christianity' (p. xv)."[1298] He finds "this tension between the proposed setting of the book in the stage 1 ministry of Jesus and Neusner's actual dialogue with stage 3 preaching about Jesus is often jarring."[1299]

Discerning "a parallel problem" arising in Neusner's juxtaposition of the Matthean Jesus' teaching with the Torah as interpreted by later rabbis, Cunningham asserts: "It seems anachronistic to gauge the 'Jewishness' of Jesus by contrasting it with an understanding of Judaism that was not normative during Jesus' lifetime. It is puzzling that a scholar who has often stressed the pluriformity of first-century Judaisms . . . has in fact produced not so much a conversation between Jesus and a first-century proto-rabbi as a dialogue between a modern rabbi and a modern Christian."[1300]

Stressing that the book "does not necessarily help readers to know Jesus better," Cunningham affirms its usefulness for grasping a better understanding of normative Judaism. He concludes his review by asserting: "In short, this book represents an approach to the modern Jewish-Christian dialogue that focuses on the differences between the two faiths. This has the comforting effect of enhancing group boundaries and religious self-identity, but one wonders whether Jesus of Nazareth, seen in his own historical and social context, really deviated from the Torah tradition as much as Neusner would like us to believe."[1301]

New Testament scholar Daniel J. Harrington, SJ, describing Neusner as a "publishing legend," whose "many books and articles [have] revolutionized the study of formative and rabbinic Judaism,"[1302] provides a straightforward abstract of the 1993 text. He affirms: "Readers will learn much about both Judaism and Matthew from what Cardinal Joseph Ratzinger has called 'by far the most important book for the Jewish-Christian dialogue to have been published in the last decade.'"[1303]

Joseph Cardinal Ratzinger (in 2005 elected as Pope Benedict XVI), in response to a request by Neusner's publisher (Doubleday, in 1993), offers a commendable first impression: "By far the most important book for the Jewish-Christian dialogue in the last decade. The absolute honesty, the precision of analysis, the union of respect for the other party with carefully grounded loyalty to one's own position characterizes the book and makes it a challenge especially to Christians, who will have to ponder the analysis of the contrast between Moses and Jesus."[1304]

How are we to understand these diverse reactions? The answer may lie in yet another critique—our last. Ruth Graf, RSM, of Xavier University, Cincinnati, observing in Neusner's analytical debate with the Matthean Jesus "no hint of accusation, hatred, or resentment,"[1305] discerns an implicit or prerequisite expectation of the reader—which, in my estimate, resolves the dilemma:

> Since the Holocaust and Vatican II, scholars have been talking with each other about Jewish-Christian relations. Much of the work has remained on a scholarly level, and too few attempts have been made to help Christians at large to see the deadly memories which are present in an uncritical reading of the Gospels. Hatred and suspicion of Jews are spread unwittingly every time the stories of the Gospels are presented and taken literally. Neusner's debates with the text presuppose a critical reading. Neusner has made a great contribution to mutual understanding by the very way in which he has presented Jesus. Unfortunately, the very style and substance of this book put it in the category of scholars talking with each other. This is not a work that could be understood easily by the average person.[1306]

Yet, she, too, sees pastoral applications for it and thus asserts: "This does not mean, however, that the book is not recommended. It could be read and discussed by groups that want to understand the situation of first-century Jews and Christians as well as the ongoing dialogue between Jews and Christians."[1307]

Neusner's respectful debate and dissent, his tentative approval and diffidence, are reflected in the reviews of the scholars cited—so too, his scholarly acumen and creative style. The success of his endeavor, to make Christians better Christians and Jews better Jews, notwithstanding the above critiques, is difficult to gauge.[1308]

Eugene Borowitz

Since Borowitz's published contributions were initially lectures, there are neither reviews nor critiques.

Summary

The similarities and differences of our authors, their innovation and argumentation, emanate from the various critiques garnered above. Sandmel as the critical maverick and Neusner as the contentious legend are justifiably companions in their discernment and dissent. On the other hand, Flusser as the eminent optimist and Vermès as the distinguished innovator are found more comfortably—though not without diffidence, given their embrace of *Heimholung Jesu*—in the company of Ben-Chorin as the fraternal ecumenist and Lapide as the unorthodox irenicist. The first pair is forthright and compelling in their apologia of Judaism vis-à-vis Christianity and Jesus' departure therefrom. The latter four consistently and convincingly—if at times enigmatically—situate Jesus well within the Judaism(s) of first-century Palestine.

What was novel thirty-five years ago—paradoxically provoking outrage and enthusiasm—is today axiomatic: Jesus of Galilee is best grasped and affirmed as a Jew, retrieved and reconstructed within the matrix of first-century Palestinian Judaism as discerned from the Jewish literary corpus of the Second Temple period, the extant pre-70-CE Palestinian archaeological evidence, and the Christian Scriptures that are constituent parts of that Jewish evidence and not extraneous to it. The converse, perceptively and insistently argued by Vermès, and approvingly and subsequently by other scholars—Jewish and Christian, is also true: first-century Palestinian Judaism is constituent of, and not extraneous to, any effort to understand and appreciate the person of Jesus the Nazarene, who after all emerges from within its milieu and paradoxically provides us greater insight into that same period and culture. Argued hypothetically and demonstrated convincingly—initially and significantly—by modern Jewish scholars, the premise has become de rigueur, as evidenced by the burgeoning field of Jesus research.

Borowitz's effort, his imaginative depiction of Jesus, seemingly epitomizes the dialogue that Neusner would correct. And yet Borowitz's perspective is generous, offering enlightened hope as well as sober caution.

Conclusion

"Theology's Masquerade"

Why do I maintain that in the works on "the historical Jesus" we deal with theology, not history at all? Because, with the best will in the world, these apologia strike me as nothing other than constructive theology masquerading as history and in the name of a healthy religious intellect claiming the authority of reasoned, historical scholarship.

Jacob Neusner, *Rabbinic Literature and The New Testament*, 176

The above citation refers specifically to Neusner's critique of the works of John P. Meier, *A Marginal Jew: Rethinking the Historical Jesus*, and John Dominic Crossan, *The Historical Jesus: The Life of a Mediterranean Peasant*. One could expect that his assessment would extend to other, contemporary Jesus researchers, such as E. P. Sanders, James D. G. Dunn, and James H. Charlesworth, to mention but a few. Obliquely, Neusner's analysis of these two Christian scholars indicates the difficulty inherent in any reconstruction—Jewish or Christian, scholarly or popular—of the historical Jesus: objectivity. The areas of convergence and divergence highlighted in chapter 6 (above) reflect this tension. Clearly, this is true of the sharp exchange between John P. Meier and Géza Vermès. Neusner himself echoes, though not explicitly, much of Meier's concerns vis-à-vis Vermès's approach to the sources. Though not a Jesus scholar, Neusner in his critique of various "questers" implicitly shares a sentiment expressed earlier by Albert Schweitzer and echoed by the modernist George Tyrrell, who in describing the presence of bias observed that many scholars *peering down the well of history* encountered *their own reflection*.

This penchant to reduce Jesus to a mirror image of the reconstructor is a constant hazard and dogged critique of the historical Jesus quest. Forewarned, Jesus scholars strive to limit the effect of their own bias, their subjectivity, as they struggle to retrieve the historical Jesus objectively from the kergymatic Christian overlay. To do otherwise would be to embrace either the polemics of fantasy, as opposed to intuition, or skepticism, as opposed to legitimate historical criticism. This need to temper one's subjectivity vis-à-vis the historical Jesus quest is readily acknowledged, as evidenced in both Vermès's and Meier's works—though, as we have seen, the latter accused the former of an acritical approach to the sources.[1309] Inherent in the quest for the historical Jesus is the unresolved debate concerning the essential, legitimate sources and the valid criteria applied thereto in order to approximate the earliest historical evidence. Diverse motives, historical or theological, ecumenical or sociological certainly undergird, obscure, clarify, and sustain the quest for the historical Jesus. The venture is not without tension and critique. Scholars, Jewish and Christian, debate the efficacy of the historical Jesus quest per se.[1310] Thus, its ebb and flow; its swell and decrescendo. The debate continues, as evidenced by our epigraph opening this conclusion.

Our Jewish authors are not immune from such subjectivity or critique. Nonetheless, without their contribution, the Jesus we speak of today would be but a shadow of his authentic self. Without the clear emphasis on his Jewishness and all that implies, our perception of the historical Jesus would be limited, seen primarily through Christian lens, refracted by kerygma and controversy. Under the scrutiny of twentieth-century Jewish and Christian scholars peering through Jewish lens, enhanced by recent biblical and archaeological scholarship, Jesus the Christ emerges more clearly defined as a robust first-century Jewish figure, similar to and yet markedly distinct from his Galilean peers and Pharisaic adversaries.

The sustained conversation and scholarship stimulated by an investigation into the person of Jesus of Nazareth by serious, if often sympathetic, Jewish writers in the twentieth century bears witness to the efficacy of their efforts. Both the initial conversation and the contemporary scholarship arose in the aftermath of a period that had produced European anti-Semitism, the climax of which was the Shoah. Numerous Jewish authors were motivated by the desire to bridge the ever-widening gulf between these two historic monotheistic faith communities, kindred though estranged, while at the same time affirming the uniqueness of Judaism; they joined the consideration of Jesus anew, from a decidedly Jewish perceptive.

Before this Jewish endeavor, Jesus, depending on one's perceptive, was either the villain or the victor, the betrayer or the victim, the taboo or the testament. He had either rejected Judaism or had been rejected by Judaism. Jesus' Jewishness, if acknowledged at all by either Christian or Jew, was but a patina cloaking an already-elusive figure. In the wake of the Holocaust, the Jesus who was formerly the obstacle, the taboo, the name not spoken, became—for some intrepid Jewish authors—the bridge, the brother, and the catalyst for a renewed rapprochement and interfaith dialogue between Jews and Christians. This twentieth-century Jewish effort to seriously engage with the person of Jesus—to analyze, evaluate, and critique this itinerant Galilean preacher figure emanating from the Christian Gospels—was both apologetic and irenic. Their aim was humble and expansive. In 1922, Joseph Klausner, in his Hebrew text *Yeshu ha-Notsri* (translated by 1925 as *Jesus of Nazareth*)—the catalyst of subsequent twentieth-century Jewish inquiry—sought to convey to the Hebrew reader a "truer idea of the *historic* Jesus," different from the portrayal in Christian as well as Jewish theology, and as far as possible, "objective and scientific."[1311] If successful, he hoped that he would be allowed to claim to have covered a page in the history of Israel that had hitherto been written, almost exclusively, by Christians.[1312] A half century later, teaching at the same university as Klausner, Jerusalem's Hebrew University, David Flusser would endorse and initiate the study of Christianity as a means of deepening one's appreciation of Judaism and the Jewish origins of Christianity. As a consequence of his work and the efforts of his Jewish contemporaries, more than a page concerning Jesus and nascent Christianity has been contributed to the history of Israel, penned by Jewish hands.

From the "objective and scientific" efforts of Klausner emerged similar efforts to apprehend Jesus from a Jewish perceptive. Our seven authors are representative of an effort emerging in the aftermath of the Second World War: an effort whose motivation, in some measure, was not merely scientific. Before Auschwitz-Birkenau, Treblinka, Sobibor, and the like, most European Jews encountered Jesus in the recriminations of Christians or as a figure suspended upon the wooden crossbeams of Christian way-side shrines. Both such matters encountered were to be avoided. In the aftermath of Hitler's genocide, diffidence yielded to confrontation, avoidance to scrutiny, silence to dialogue.

Lapide, cognizant of this, conveys succinctly four ways in which the figure of Jesus, seen from a Jewish perceptive, was affected by Hilter's genocide; three of them undergird the irenic and scholarly endeavors of our seven select authors:

- As a counterpoise to the sea of tears from Auschwitz, people sought refuge in a factual, scientific image of the Nazarene, beyond passions and emotions.
- Jewish authors sought neither the gospel Son of God nor the Talmud's heretic and perverter of the people but the human brother who lived an exemplary Jewish life in a world full of inhumanity.
- We find, too, the antithesis of brother Jesus, among those survivors of the "final solution" who cannot separate Christ from [the] Christendom that committed or tolerated the murder of six million Jews. Their caricature often borders on hatred of Christ.
- But on the whole we are dealing with the process of the Jewish recovery of Jesus, of bringing him home. This inscribes his name, with the honor due a hero, on the mass graves of the victims of Nazism or in the ranks of the resistance fighters. The faith and zeal of the Nazarene, the unshakable power of his hope, the deep love which he cherished for Israel, and his tragic death have made him dear to many thinkers and poets in Israel today, beyond all walls and graves.[1313]

The initial efforts to re-Judaize Jesus, to bring him home, as typified by Ben-Chorin and Lapide—in contradistinction to the de-Judaizing efforts of European, "pseudo-Christian" anti-Semites of the 1930s—though effective in engendering and sustaining renewed dialogue among Christians and Jews, has yielded to an emerging multidisciplined approach, stimulated by modern scholarly inquiry and debate, typified by Sandmel, Flusser, and Vermès.

This joint, though unorchestrated, Jewish and Christian approach, situating Jesus securely within Judaism while seeking objectivity and assessing historical probability, was supplemented by recently discovered archaeological evidence, imbued with scholarly optimism and modern technique, and characterized by rapprochement and renewed Christian-Jewish dialogue. Furthermore, it both influenced and contributed to the emerging late twentieth-century scholarship characterized as Jesus research and focusing on the body of pre-70-CE Palestinian evidence—archaeological, historical, and philological—that enhances our perspective of first-century Palestine and concomitantly our perception of Jesus.

Throughout this retrospective on Jewish perspectives of Jesus, post-Holocaust, I have been aware of a twofold dilemma confronting me as a Christian author grappling with Jewish perspectives. Representing their perspectives, though challenging, was not part of the dilemma. Rather, the twofold dilemma lay, on the one hand, in capturing and conveying primarily to Christians, and perhaps to secular Jews, the chasm that first had to be bridged by each Jewish author before any affirmation of Jesus as a venerable Jewish brother: the centuries-old animosities and atrocities that Christians have afflicted upon Jews under the banner of *Yeshu* the Christ. This psychological chasm, if it may be described as such, had to be surmounted first, even if not consciously acknowledged. Not all were successful; not all tried the catharsis. On the other hand, I was faced with what may be called, for lack of adequate expression, our Christian presupposition.

We Christians often presuppose to know Jesus: we assume to know Christ, as mediated in and through Christian Scripture and tradition and apprehended in our religious conviction and experience. The validity of Christian doctrine and religious experience is not in question. The presupposition that we truly know Jesus, however, is a limitation. This is not a pejorative critique. It is a simple, empirical fact. Presupposition may hinder our willingness to widen our appreciation of Jesus from a perspective other than our own, which may actually be parochial. Bias may cloud our perspective and limit our vision. We are not accustomed to having our faith perspective, not to mention the iconic figures of our faith, critiqued and enhanced by someone not of our faith. It seems to be counterintuitive. And yet, we may certainly benefit since Jesus the Jew, representative of first-century Palestinian Judaism, is someone, I would venture to say, with whom the average Christian is not well acquainted.

We grant that twentieth-century Jewish scholars, as well as Christian scholars, grapple with various sources and evidence in an effort to reconstruct first-century Palestine and Second Temple Judaism. Nonetheless, I am convinced of the efficacy of their efforts. The experience of studying these Jewish authors and their perspectives is reminiscent of my first visit to the Holy Land. Afterward, my reading of the Gospels was enhanced, deepened, clarified. The same is true of my image of the Jesus of Nazareth, informed, as it now is, by insights gleaned from these Jewish perspectives. Clearly as a Christian, I am not in complete agreement with their diverse and somewhat controversial positions. However, much of what they offer bears consideration, clarifies what was enigmatic, and fires the imagination. I can only encourage Christians to explore this studied, kindred perspective.

As to the Jewish aspect of my dilemma, Pinchas Lapide, in his survey of Jesus in Hebrew literature, provides me with the possibility of conveying, however inadequately, their inner struggles. Aware of "a growing sympathy for the life and death of the Galilean, a feeling often indistinguishable from love, and a consciousness, evident even in the writings hostile to Christ, of sharing as brothers in a common fate,"[1314]

Lapide includes in his survey the anguish of one such hostile, contemporary Israeli writer, Shin Shalom (1904–73). We can but eavesdrop upon his soliloquy and in this way apprehend, as best as one may, his anguished rebuke:

> I know Galilee the way a man knows his own soul. I know its wild rocky gorges, its hidden springs, its vast, clear skies, . . . but there is a man in Galilee whom I know nothing about, whom I have never asked after. His existence is for me an open wound, which no one touches, which one tries *not* to think about. Quiet! Just don't remind me of it. . . . When I was in that menacing mountain range called Nazareth and I thought I saw his eyebrows wrinkled in pain, I closed my eyes. I would not let his name cross my lips. I did not curse, I did not bless. I said nothing. . . . But sometimes a voice came up out of the silence, the voice of a lost brother, the voice of a man who has gone off course, has gone astray among strangers, who at the same time confesses his guilt and points an accusing finger, who wants to come back, if you'll go out to meet him lovingly and whisper only one word in his ear: brother! In that hour I mustered all my support troops—all the bitter memories of my life and all the terrible experiences in the history of my people—lest this man clear himself before me by his confession. Out of the abyss of oblivion I brought up all the tortures of the Inquisition, all the butchery of the pogroms, all the murders of the holy crusades, all the blows which we suffer from the bearers of his name, all the outrage we had to endure from the guardians of his teaching. The endless chain of the generations of tortured martyrs, the armies of Jewish brothers wandering restlessly around, despised, hunted and hounded from prison to prison, from atrocity to atrocity—I had to make them all march up in a broad front against him, to force him to silence, to make him keep to himself, to push him away from me with both hands—this one-time brother, the carpenter's son from Galilee.[1315]

Perhaps this captures and conveys the enormity of the effort of these modern Jewish authors, who, risking disdain and rejection from both Christian and Jew—the former for their presumption, the latter for their betrayal—have ventured forth, giving rise to contemporary Jewish voices and perspectives on Jesus. Some modern Jews may sense solidarity with the martyred Nazarene; others revile such efforts, forbidding empathy. Shin Shalom pushed the Galilean away, banishing him to silence. Yet, out of the silence rose contemporary, twentieth-century Jewish voices offering favorable, often critically and controversially rendered, portraits of the Galilean preacher from Nazareth: Jesus.

Another aspect that confronts the modern reader of these and similar perspectives of Jesus reconstructed, or retrieved from the sources, is the debate or the confusion over which Jesus is being re-presented: the Jesus of history, meaning the *real* Jesus, or the historical Jesus, the *figure reconstructed* from a historical-critical investigation of the sources. Throughout this study of Jewish writers, several of our authors presume, unsurprisingly, to retrieve the *real* Jesus, *Jesus the Jew*, from beneath the "Christian overpainting." The exceptions to this assertion are Sandmel, Neusner, and Borowitz, respectively. Yet Ben-Chorin, Lapide, Flusser, and Vermès strive and claim to deliver—to their satisfaction—a Jesus retrieved from Christian kerygmatic accretions. These are praiseworthy efforts that miss the mark, albeit in varying degrees. The fault lies less in intent and more in their optimism vis-à-vis their ability to adduce, deduce, or intuit from the sources and discernible data an authentic portrait of Jesus. It is a confidence shared by fellow questers.

Like the portraits of previous questers, these Jewish portraits are fragmentary. To borrow from Meier, speaking of the historical Jesus quest in general: "Of its very nature, this quest can reconstruct only fragments of a mosaic, the faint outline of a faded fresco that allows of many interpretations."[1316] This does not diminish the importance of the modern Jewish contribution to an emerging Jesus mosaic, fragmentary though it may be.

Like all similar efforts to retrieve the Jesus of history, meaning the *real* Jesus, from the sources, scholars are limited in what they may adduce from those sources, regardless of motive and methodology, since the sources themselves are not historical, biographical records per se. Recent scholars concede as much. James D. G. Dunn has recently affirmed this, explaining succinctly the confusion inherent in the quest for the "historical" Jesus:

> An important factor in all this has been the confusion injected into the quest by the key phrase itself—"historical Jesus." It is true that whenever a definition is offered for the phrase, the person offering the definition is clear that the "historical Jesus" is *the Jesus constructed by historical research*. Despite that, however, the phrase is used again and again in a casual way to refer to the Jesus of Nazareth who walked the hills of Galilee, and it is that sense which predominates overall. Or to be more precise, the phrase "the historical Jesus" as typically used is something of an amalgam of the two senses. The quest has generally assumed its capacity to construct (from the available data) a Jesus who will be the real Jesus: the historical Jesus (reconstructed) will be the historical Jesus (actual); again and again the one sense elides indistinguishably into the other. It is this confusion which largely lies behind the surprising confidence of the nineteenth- and late-twentieth-century questers that a Jesus reconstructed from the sources available would be a sound base (the actual Jesus) for a critique of the Jesus of the sources. It needs to be said once again, then, that the "historical Jesus" is properly speaking a nineteenth- and twentieth-century construction using the data supplied by the Synoptic tradition, *not* Jesus back then and *not* a figure in history whom we can realistically use to critique the portrayal of Jesus in the Synoptic tradition.[1317]

One can imagine Vermès bristling at Dunn's assertion. Dunn's is not a solitary voice. Invoking Martin Kähler's previous observation,[1318] Dunn, expands upon it:

> The idea that a Jesus *reconstructed from the Gospel traditions* (the so-called "historical Jesus"), *yet significantly different from the Jesus of the Gospels*, is the Jesus who taught in Galilee (the historical Jesus!) is an illusion. The idea that we can see through the faith perspective of the NT writings to a Jesus who did *not* inspire faith or who inspired faith in a *different* way is an illusion. There is no such Jesus. That there *was* a Jesus who *did* inspire the faith which in due course found expression in the Gospels is not in question. But that we can somehow hope to strip out the theological impact which he actually had on his disciples, to uncover a different Jesus (the real Jesus!), is at best fanciful. It is not simply that "we reach Jesus only through the picture his disciples made of him," it is also that the only Jesus we reach through that picture is the Jesus who inspired that picture.[1319]

Dunn is aware of the invocation of external sources vis-à-vis the Jesus study, concomitant with the Synoptic traditions, and specifically the use of rabbinic literature, of which he writes:

> Of the possible references to Jesus in *Jewish* rabbinic sources, the most plausible echo of early pre-rabbinic (Pharisaic) reaction to Jesus is *b. Sanhedrin* 43a, referring to Yeshu (Jesus) who was hanged on the eve of Passover and describing him as a magician who beguiled Israel and led it astray. But the whole enterprise of reading first-century details from often much later rabbinic traditions is too fraught with difficulty for us to put too much weight on them.[1320]

Obviously, this latter assertion puts him at odds with Vermès in this regard and in agreement with John P. Meier and Jacob Neusner, to mention but a few. Yet Dunn does not despair of the effort to reconstruct the figure of Jesus, meaning the *historical* Jesus (not the *real* Jesus), from the Synoptic discourse. Nor does Vermès or Meier.[1321]

I point this out and risk a digression, inasmuch as Vermès is singular, among our authors, in his staunch enlistment of rabbinic sources to confirm the validity of his Hasidic typology vis-à-vis the Synoptic Jesus. Moreover, the Hasidic Jew emanating from the Synoptic corpus, as adduced from the rabbinic sources, is *the* Jesus of history, the *real* Jesus, in Vermès's estimate—inasmuch as Vermès is *not* bound, as a historian and a Jew to abide by the faith perspective of the Synoptics, nor to preclude the use of external sources, specifically rabbinic sources and typologies, that others find sparse or spurious.

That much of New Testament scholarship weighs heavily against his persistent, consistent hypothesis does not sway Vermès. He is obstinate in his defense of his premise, methodology, and erudite optimism. This persistence also is not surprising when one realizes that Vermès's studied technique of arguing from later rabbinic sources to support a position or hypothesis, historical or philological, finds its *precedent* in his innovative contribution to the "son of man" debate of the 1960s. His unconventional position—that the phrase *bar naša* could also be used as a circumlocution for "I"—has garnered for him the now-familiar rebuke from diverse colleagues.[1322] Vermès currently, forty years later, is unlikely to change his stance or practice. From Vermès's scholarly perspective, no doubt, his portrait of Jesus the Hasidic Jew is as valid as other similar attempts to capture the figure of Jesus from among the Synoptic currents, if not more so. His methodology remains a point of controversy among scholars, as we have certainly seen.

Controversy seems to accompany the quest for the historical Jesus, not surprisingly. It is difficult for us, forty year later, to grasp the initial significance of Vermès's thesis, a position that has become prerequisite for both questers and Jesus researchers: for any serious study of Jesus to be efficacious, the author of the study must situate Jesus securely within his first-century Jewish Palestinian milieu. An appreciation of Second Temple Judaism becomes prerequisite or concomitant to the quest for the historical Jesus. This is confirmed in the recent works of Christian Jesus researchers: E. P. Sanders, *Jesus and Judaism* (1985); John P. Meier, *A Marginal Jew*, vol. 1 (1991); James H. Charlesworth, *Jesus' Jewishness* (1991); N. T. Wright, *Jesus and the Victory of God* (1996); and James D. G. Dunn, *Jesus Remembered* (2003). The fact that we may distinguish between questers and Jesus researchers is also indicative of the influence of pre-70-CE Jewish Palestinian data gleaned from various disciplines.

As we have seen, this enthusiasm—sparked by Vermès' *Jesus the Jew* and coupled with the work of his colleagues Ben-Chorin, Lapide, and Flusser, all of whom had ventured into Jesus study, ecumenically or academically, before Vermès did—reinvigorated Jewish-Christian relations. It is difficult to assess qualitatively the impact that the modern Jewish assessment of Jesus has had upon the Jewish-Christian relations. Yet the following weigh heavily in favor of an overall positive effect: (1) the "explosion" of interest in Jesus' Jewishness, as evidenced by the numerous books reflecting the topic; (2) the historic declarations, such as the Roman Catholic Conciliar Declaration *Nostra Aetate* (1965) and a second and equally significant Catholic document *Bible et Christologie* (1984), translated into English as *Scripture and Christology* (1986), which stresses the importance of studying Judaism for a correct understanding of the person of Jesus; (3) recent statements of individual faith communities, such as "Guidelines and Suggestions for Implementing the Conciliar Declaration *Nostra Aetate*" (1974) and "Notes on the Correct Way to Present the Jews and Judaism in Preaching and Catechesis in the Roman Catholic Church" (1985), both documents issued by the Vatican Commission for Religious Relations with the Jews; as well as, in September of 2000, "*Dabru Emet* [Speak the Truth]," a modern Jewish statement on Christianity published in the *New York Times* and *Baltimore Sun* newspapers and signed by Jewish rabbis and scholars from the United States, Canada, the United Kingdom, and Israel; (4) various agreements among select interfaith dialogue groups, such as The World Council of Churches' 1968 consultation document "The Church and the Jewish People"; (5) as well as nascent attempts to construct a more positive Christian theology of Judaism and a Jewish theology of Christianity by each respective community, as evidenced by the 2004 establishment of the Interfaith Theological Forum at the Pope John Paul II Cultural Center in Washington, DC.

Expanding upon two documents mentioned above provides further evidence of this ecumenical harvest. *Nostra Aetate* is the historic, conciliar declaration of the Roman Catholic Church addressing the Church's relationship with non-Christian religions. Speaking of the Church's relationship with Judaism, the council fathers affirmed our shared spiritual heritage:

> As the sacred synod searches into the mystery of the Church, it remembers the bond that spiritually ties the people of the New Covenant to Abraham's stock.
>
> Since the spiritual patrimony common to Christians and Jews is thus so great, this sacred synod wants to foster and recommend that mutual understanding and respect which is the fruit, above all, of biblical and theological studies as well as fraternal dialogues.
>
> Furthermore, in her rejection of every persecution against man, the Church, mindful of the patrimony she shares with the Jews and moved not by political reasons but by the Gospel's spiritual love, decries hatred, persecutions, displays of anti-Semitism, directed against Jews at any time and by anyone.[1323]

These are fledgling steps toward unprecedented declarations and accords.

His Holiness, Pope Benedict XVI, the second Roman pontiff in history to visit a Jewish synagogue formally (John Paul II, Benedict's predecessor, visited the Great Synagogue of Rome in 1986[1324]), during his address to those gathered in Cologne's synagogue, emphasized the progress in Jewish-Christian relations. Speaking of *Nostra Aetate*, the Holy Father remarked:

> This year also marks the fortieth anniversary of the promulgation of the Second Vatican Council's Declaration *Nostra Aetate*, which opened up new prospects for Jewish-Christian relations in terms of dialogue and solidarity. This Declaration, in the fourth chapter, recalls the common roots and the immensely rich spiritual heritage that Jews and Christians share. Both Jews and Christians recognize in Abraham their father in faith (cf. *Gal* 3:7, *Rom* 4:11ff.) and they look to the teachings of Moses and the prophets. Jewish spirituality, like its Christian counterpart, draws nourishment from the psalms. With Saint Paul, Christians are convinced that "the gifts and the call of God are irrevocable" (*Rom* 11:29; cf. 9:6, 11; 11:1ff.). In considering the Jewish roots of Christianity (cf. *Rom* 11: 16–24), my venerable Predecessor, quoting a statement by the German Bishops, affirmed that: "whoever meets Jesus Christ meets Judaism" (*Insegnamenti*, vol. III/2, 1980, p. 1272).
>
> The conciliar Declaration *Nostra Aetate* therefore "deplores feelings of hatred, persecutions and demonstrations of antisemitism directed against the Jews at whatever time and by whomsoever" (No. 4). God created us all "in his image" (cf. *Gen* 1:27) and thus honoured us with a transcendent dignity. Before God, all men and women have the same dignity, whatever their nation, culture or religion. Hence the Declaration *Nostra Aetate* also speaks with great esteem of Muslims (cf. No. 3) and of the followers of other religions (cf. No. 2). On the basis of our shared human dignity the Catholic Church "condemns as foreign to the mind of Christ any kind of discrimination whatsoever between people, or harassment of them, done by reason of race or colour, class or religion" (No. 5). The Church is conscious of her duty to transmit this teaching, in her catechesis and in every aspect of her life, to the younger generations which did not witness the terrible events that took place before and during the Second World War. It is a particularly important task, since today, sadly, we are witnessing the rise of new signs of antisemitism and various forms of a general hostility towards foreigners. How can we fail to see in this a reason for concern and vigilance? The Catholic Church is committed—I reaffirm this again today—to tolerance, respect, friendship and peace between all peoples, cultures and religions.
>
> In the forty years that have passed since the conciliar Declaration *Nostra Aetate*, much progress has been made, in Germany and throughout the world, towards better and closer relations between Jews and Christians. Alongside official relationships, due above all to cooperation between specialists in the biblical sciences, many friendships have been born. In this regard, I would mention the various declarations by the German Episcopal Conference and the charitable work done by the "Society for Jewish-Christian Cooperation in Cologne," which since 1945 have enabled the Jewish community to feel once again "at home" here in Cologne and to establish good relations with the Christian communities. Yet much still remains to be done. We must come to know one another much more and much better. Consequently I would encourage sincere and trustful dialogue between Jews and Christians, for only in this way will it be possible to arrive at a shared interpretation of disputed historical questions, and, above all, to make progress

towards a theological evaluation of the relationship between Judaism and Christianity. This dialogue, if it is to be sincere, must not gloss over or underestimate the existing differences: in those areas in which, due to our profound convictions in faith, we diverge, and indeed precisely in those areas, we need to show respect for one another.[1325]

"*Dabru Emet* [Speak the Truth]"[1326] is another remarkable, modern document, signed by more than 170 Jewish scholars: Dr. Eugene B. Borowitz; Rabbi David Sandmel, Samuel Sandmel's son; and Dr. Géza Vermès are among the signatories. It was issued in September 2000 in an effort to inform the public of the "dramatic and unprecedented shift" in Jewish and Christian relations. The preface clearly reflects the momentum:

> In recent years, there has been a dramatic and unprecedented shift in Jewish and Christian relations. Throughout the nearly two millennia of Jewish exile, Christians have tended to characterize Judaism as a failed religion or, at best, a religion that prepared the way for, and is completed in, Christianity. In the decades since the Holocaust, however, Christianity has changed dramatically. An increasing number of official Church bodies, both Roman Catholic and Protestant, have made public statements of their remorse about Christian mistreatment of Jews and Judaism. These statements have declared, further-more, that Christian teaching and preaching can and must be reformed so that they acknowledge God's enduring covenant with the Jewish people and celebrate the contri-bution of Judaism to world civilization and to Christian faith itself.
>
> We believe these changes merit a thoughtful Jewish response. Speaking only for ourselves—an interdenominational group of Jewish scholars—we believe it is time for Jews to learn about the efforts of Christians to honor Judaism. We believe it is time for Jews to reflect on what Judaism may now say about Christianity.[1327]

Added to the above, one could cite the modern work of Clemens Thoma, *A Christian Theology of Judaism*, the foreword of which was written by David Flusser; as well as the recent Jewish text *Christianity in Jewish Terms*, edited by Tikva Frymer-Kensky, David Novak, Peter Ochs, David Fox Sandmel, and Michael A. Signer. Add to these the Pontifical Biblical Commission's 2001 document "The Jewish People and Their Sacred Scripture in the Christian Bible." Each, in some measure, is evidence of the modern effort to formulate within each respective faith community appropriate, con-temporary approaches to the other's tradition.

The above body of evidence speaks well of the sincere, shared interest among modern Jews and Christians to deepen their understanding and appreciation for each other's unique traditions, cultures and contributions to civilization. We can assign to our seven Jewish authors a modest role in this achievement. With diverse motives and methodologies, our authors, critically or intuitively, wrestled with the essential sources to craft from the various "bits of glass and stone" a mosaic of Jesus from Jewish per-spectives, i.e., a Judaic reading of the Jesus sources.

A Judaic reading of the Gospels (i.e., a Judaic hermeneutic) informs, nuances, and challenges Jesus research—and vice versa. Jesus research, a burgeoning field of study echoing select Jewish voices, focuses upon first-century Palestinian Judaism, recent archaeological discoveries, and scholarly inquiry and debate.[1328] It is not a perfect sci-ence. Diverse voices, Jew and Christian, challenge the venture, trivialize its efficacy. Neither the momentum waivers nor the interest falters. Emanating more clearly from

the sacred Christian texts, the man of Galilee, securely situated within a Jewish Palestinian milieu, ventures forth into the third millennium. A *reverse* metamorphosis of
sorts has occurred.

Diverse twentieth-century currents converged in the aftermath of the Shoah, facilitating a modern investigation of Jesus of Nazareth from modern Jewish perspectives
and giving voice to a "third quest" for the historical Jesus.[1329] Arguably, select Jewish
perspectives, nuanced and developed further, gave momentum to an emerging "third
quest" for the historical Jesus. This concept, this Judaic hermeneutic, seemingly counterintuitive, has become *axiomatic* in contemporary Jesus study. This third quest, then,
yielded yet a more comprehensive field of study, Jesus research, which in turn gave a
wider voice to this nascent *Judaic* hermeneutic. At each stage, a Galilean figure
emerges, more clearly discernible, more compelling: Jesus, *nazir*; Jesus, *naggar*; Jesus,
zaddik.

In his masterful conclusion to *The Changing Faces of Jesus*, Vermès describes the
metamorphosis of "Jesus, the religious man with an irresistible charismatic charm,"
into "Jesus the Christ, the transcendent object of the Christian faith."[1330] That such a
complete metamorphosis—wherein "the existential religious manifesto of the real Jesus advocating repentance, instant readiness, and submission to God" was replaced by
"a program steeped in metaphysical speculation on the incarnate Christ's person and
nature, on his relation to the eternal Son of God, and on the mutual tie between the
divine persons of the Holy Trinity"[1331]—went substantially unchallenged was due, in
Vermès's estimate, to the lack of Jewish voices. As Vermès asserts: "And they [the
church fathers] could do so freely since by that time there was no longer any Jewish
voice in Christendom to sound the alarm."[1332]

Vermès and his Jewish colleagues have soundly raised the alarm, diminishing the
halo but not the aura of the Galilean of Nazareth. Modern Judaism and Christianity
have responded in "dramatic and unprecedented" ways. Jesus' patina of Jewishness
has been burnished, yielding a more clearly discernible figure steeped in the tradition
of the Jewish sages, imbued with the Elijah-like charismatic attributes: the fiery
Galilean prophet, the *nazir*, a tragic martyr and Jewish brother, *Yeshu ha-Notsri*—Jesus
of Nazareth.

We started with *Jesus the Jew*. It is appropriate to give Géza Vermès the final word.
Reflecting upon the *real* Jesus, "For there was a real Jesus, without any doubt,"[1333]
Vermès writes:

> Over the space of months, or perhaps even of two or three years, this Jesus of flesh and
> blood was seen and heard around the countryside of Galilee and in Jerusalem, an un-
> compromising, single-minded lover of God and his fellow-beings, convinced that by
> means of his example and teaching he could infect them with his own passionate sense
> of relation with the Father in heaven. And he did so. The magnetism of this real Jesus
> was such that not even the shame and humiliation of the cross, and not even the collapse
> of his ministry, could extinguish the faith of the men and women of his company. But it
> is a long time now since he was thought of. Very many ages have passed since the simple
> Jewish person of the gospels stepped back and gave way to the rich and majestic figure
> of the church's Christ.

Yet it occurs to the historian, as he reaches the end of his presentation of the gospel of Jesus the Jew, that the world may not have heard the last of the holy Galilean. In this so-called post-Christian era, when Christ as a divine form seems to ever-increasing numbers not to correspond, either to the age's notion of reality, or to the exigencies of the contemporary human predicament, is it not possible that Jesus the healer, teacher and helper may yet be invited to emerge from the shadows of his long exile? And not by Christians alone? If, above all, his lesson on reciprocal, loving and direct relation with the Father in heaven is recalled and found universally valid, may not the sons of God on earth stand a better chance of ensuring that the ideal human brotherhood becomes something more than a pipe-dream?[1334]

———————

And who knows, perhaps this fresh understanding will express itself in a reorientation of minds and a renewal of religious spirit inspired by the real Jesus among the heirs of the Judeao-Christian civilization and beyond in the third millennium.

Géza Vermès, *The Changing Faces of Jesus*, 286

We must come to know one another much more and much better.

Benedict XVI, Cologne, Germany, August 2005

Notes

Introduction: Convergence

1. James D. G. Dunn, *Jesus Remembered*, vol. 1 of *Christianity in the Making* (Grand Rapids: Eerdmans, 2003), 885.

2. Géza Vermès, *Jesus in His Jewish Context* (Minneapolis: Fortress, 2003), 1. This text is meant to replace and further enrich Vermès's earlier work *Jesus and the World of Judaism* (London: SCM, 1983). To gain some perception of a Jewish view of Jesus before the modern appreciative stance, see Samuel Sandmel, *We Jews and You Christians: An Inquiry into Attitudes* (New York: Lippincott, 1967), 66–67. To appreciate "the Jewish debater's initial advantage," given a historical approach to Jesus, see Eugene Borowitz, *Contemporary Christologies: A Jewish Response* (New York: Paulist Press, 1981), 4.

3. David Flusser, "Jesus and Judaism: Jewish Perspectives," in *Eusebius, Christianity, and Judaism*, ed. Harold Attridge and Gohei Hata (Detroit: Wayne State University Press, 1992), 103.

4. Vermès, *Jesus in His Jewish Context*, 60.

5. Pinchas Lapide, *The Resurrection of Jesus*, trans. Wilhelm C. Linss (Minneapolis: Augsburg, 1982; repr., Eugene, OR: Wipf & Stock, 2002), 7.

6. Raymond E. Brown, *Jesus, God and Man: Modern Biblical Reflections* (New York: Macmillan, 1967), ix–x.

7. Larry W. Hurtado, "A Taxonomy of Recent Historical-Jesus Work," in *Whose Historical Jesus?* ed. William E. Arnal and Michel R. Desjardins (Waterloo, ON: Wilfrid Laurier University Press, 1997), 272–95, esp. 272–73.

8. Schalom Ben-Chorin, "The Image of Jesus in Modern Judaism," *Journal of Ecumenical Studies* 11 (Summer 1974): 202.

9. Pinchas Lapide and Hans Küng, *Brother or Lord? A Jew and a Christian Talk Together about Jesus / Hans Küng and Pinchas Lapide*, trans. E. Quinn (London: Fount Paperbacks, 1977), 21.

10. Ibid., 44. On this "unprecedented" opportunity to study together, see also Jacob Neusner, *Judaism in the Beginning of Christianity* (Philadelphia: Fortress, 1984), 10–11.

11. Professor Borowitz confirms this in a recent e-mail to me, writing: "I wish I were able to be of help with your inquiry as I understand it, but except for sporadic involvement, I have not been actively involved in the area nor am I

sufficiently involved with the colleagues who are to give you some sense of reliance on the work of Sandmel, Flusser, or Vermès" (September 20, 2005).

1. "From a Different Angle"

12. Sandmel credits Branscomb with encouraging him toward New Testament studies. See Samuel Sandmel, *A Jewish Understanding of the New Testament*, augmented ed. (London: SPCK, 1977), xix; idem, *The First Christian Century in Judaism and Christianity* (New York: Oxford University Press, 1969), x.

13. Samuel Sandmel, "The Trial of Jesus," *Judaism* 20, no. 3 (Summer 1971): 69–74.

14. Samuel Sandmel, *We Jews and Jesus* (New York: Oxford University Press, 1965), vii. This book was written in 1964 and first published in 1965 before the promulgation on October 28, 1965, of the Second Vatican Council's "Declaration on the Relations of the Church to Non-Christian Religions," *Nostra Aetate*, as the declaration is generally known, which in part expressed the Catholic Church's attitude toward the Jews. Sandmel acknowledges this in the preface to his 1973 edition of *We Jews and Jesus*. In this book, Sandmel provides an overview of Jewish attitudes toward Jesus; a useful survey of the historical Jesus study; and a critical assessment of the Gospels as both primary sources for historical Jesus research and Christian literature. Prompted by *Nostra Aetate*, in 1967 Sandmel wrote *We Jews and You Christians: An Inquiry into Attitudes*. As the title suggests, the author concerns himself with questions pertaining to relations between Jews and Christians and not specifically the person of Jesus.

15. Sandmel, *We Jews and Jesus*, 14.

16. Ibid., 3.

17. Ibid., 3–4.

18. Ibid., 107.

19. Ibid., 107–8.

20. Ibid., 108; throughout the book, brackets enclose added clarification except as otherwise stated.

21. Ibid.

22. Ibid., 124.

23. Ibid., 108.

24. As a Reform Jew and therefore heir of the Liberal Jewish scholarship that gave rise to Jewish Jesus research of the nineteenth century and early twentieth century, Sandmel's following self-description may be helpful in appreciating his approach to this topic: "I am writing on the significant religious content of the book [the New Testament], as a scholar of it, not as one religiously committed to it. In the sense that I am a Reform Jew it is undeniable that the modernism and rationalism of Reform Judaism shape my approach, as such factors shape the approach of anyone to a traditional literature. A Reform Jew is selective in what he accepts as valid in the ancient Jewish traditions; it is to be expected then, that he will exercise similar selectivity in his approach to Christianity, and that an earnestly sympathetic understanding, therefore, of one facet or another

of that tradition is not to be equated with a doctrinal acceptance of it" (*A Jewish Understanding of the New Testament*, xvi).

25. Sandmel, *We Jews and Jesus*, 108–9.
26. Ibid., 109.
27. Samuel Sandmel, *Judaism and Christian Beginnings* (New York: Oxford University Press, 1978), 398.
28. Sandmel, *We Jews and Jesus*, 111.
29. Ibid.
30. Ibid., 112.
31. In 1970, Ben-Chorin followed *Bruder Jesus* (Munich: List, 1967) with a smaller book (79 pages), *Jesus im Judentum*, which is a collection of radio talks and essays on different occasions. This smaller book provides a survey of the Jewish attitude toward Jesus through the centuries. Though *Jesus im Judentum* is not yet translated into English, the essay "The Image of Jesus in Modern Judaism" is a translation of Ben-Chorin's 1953 essay "Das Jesusbild im modernen Judentum," *Zeitschrift für Religions- und Geistesgeschichte* 5 (1953): 231–57, and offers similar observations.
32. Schalom Ben-Chorin, *Brother Jesus: The Nazarene through Jewish Eyes*, trans. and ed. Jared S. Klein and Max Reinhart (Athens, GA: University of Georgia Press, 2001), vii.
33. Ibid., 7.
34. Ben-Chorin, "The Image of Jesus in Modern Judaism," 411.
35. Ben-Chorin, *Brother Jesus*, 5.
36. Ibid.
37. Ben-Chorin, "The Image of Jesus in Modern Judaism," 411.
38. Ben-Chorin, *Brother Jesus*, 4–5.
39. Ben-Chorin, a student and friend of Martin Buber, was profoundly influenced by Buber's consideration of Jesus as "my great brother." See Martin Buber, *Two Types of Faith*, trans. Norman P. Goldhawk (New York: Harper, 1961), 12–13. See also Ben-Chorin, *Brother Jesus*, 5.
40. Ben-Chorin, *Brother Jesus*, 5.
41. Ibid.
42. Ibid., 6.
43. Ibid., 7.
44. Ibid., 6.
45. For pertinent Josephus texts and Dead Sea Scroll texts, see C. K. Barrett, *The New Testament Background: Selected Documents* (San Francisco: Harper & Row, 1995).
46. Ben-Chorin, *Brother Jesus*, 8–9.
47. Ibid.
48. Ibid., 10.
49. Ibid., 11.
50. Ibid., 16.
51. Ibid., 91.
52. Ibid., 124.

53. Ibid., 17.
54. Ibid.
55. Ibid., 18.
56. Ben-Chorin, "The Image of Jesus in Modern Judaism," 408; Ben-Chorin is quoting Rabbi Leo Baeck, *Harnacks Vorlesungen über das Wesen des Christentums*, enlarged ed. (Breslau: W. Koebner, 1902), an offprint based on Baeck's book review in *Monatschrift für Geschichte und Wissenschaft des Judentums* 45 (1901).
57. Ben-Chorin, *Brother Jesus*, 19.
58. David Flusser, *Jesus in Selbstzeugnissen und Bilddokumenten* (Hamburg: Rowohlt, 1968). See also the reprint, David Flusser, *Jesus* (Hamburg: Rowohlt, 1999), 7.
59. David Flusser in collaboration with R. Steven Notley, *Jesus* (Jerusalem: Magnes, 2001), 21–22; all further references in the notes are to this edition unless otherwise stated. See also Robert L. Lindsey, "A Modified Two-Document Theory of the Synoptic Dependence and Interdependence," *Novum Testamentum* 6 (1963): 239–63. For Flusser's explanation of this approach, see Flusser's foreword in Robert L. Lindsey, *A Hebrew Translation of the Gospel of Mark* (Jerusalem: Dugith, 1969).
60. Flusser, *Jesus* (2001), 10.
61. Ibid., 15.
62. Ibid.
63. Ibid., 11.
64. Ibid., 177.
65. Ibid., 16. Flusser credits his childhood experience of life in a predominantly Catholic, Bohemian town of Czechoslovakia, specifically his encounter with Josef Perl, a pastor and member of the Unity of Bohemian Brethren and his lack of encounter among the townspeople of anti-Jewish sentiments, as the influences that led him "to occupy myself with the person and message of Jesus." Later, Flusser would become acquainted with the Mennonites of Canada and the United States, who are spiritual heirs of the Bohemian Brethren.
66. Ibid.
67. Ibid.
68. Ibid., 13.
69. Ibid., 51.
70. Ibid., 58.
71. Ibid.
72. Ibid., 60, 63, and 81, respectively.
73. Ibid., 92.
74. David Flusser, "Hillel's Self-Awareness and Jesus," *Immanuel*, 4 (Summer 1974): 35.
75. Flusser, *Jesus* (2001), 266.
76. Ibid., 277. For a more detailed explanation of the messianic timetables, see ibid. chap. 20, "The Stages of Redemption History according to John the Baptist and Jesus," 255–75.

77. Ibid., 176.
78. Pinchas Lapide, *Encountering Jesus—Encountering Judaism: A Dialogue*, trans. Davis Perkins (New York: Crossroad, 1987), 104.
79. Pinchas Lapide, *Jesus in Two Perspectives: A Jewish-Christian Dialog / Pinchas Lapide and Ulrich Luz*, trans. L. W. Denef (Minneapolis: Augsburg, 1985), 10.
80. Ibid.
81. Ibid., 24. See also, Lapide in *Brother or Lord?* 13–14, wherein Lapide describes five bonds that he, as a Jew, possesses that better facilitate his study vis-à-vis a Christian contemporary. Pinchas Lapide further argues in *The Sermon on the Mount: Utopia or Program for Action?* (trans. A. Swidler [Maryknoll, NY: Orbis Books, 1986], 8) that "Jesus' Jewishness and the fundamentally Hebraic quality of his glad tidings should be the two-fold guide in getting behind the translation-Greek of the evangelist and as close as possible to the original meaning of the masterpiece of Jesus' ethical teachings."
82. Lapide, *Jesus in Two Perspectives*, 10.
83. Ibid.
84. Ibid., 25.
85. Ibid., 26, with emphasis added.
86. Ibid., 77.
87. Ibid., 25.
88. For Lapide's explanation, see his *Jesus in Two Perspectives*, 117–18.
89. See Lapide, *The Resurrection of Jesus*, 152–54.
90. Pinchas Lapide, *Israelis, Jews, and Jesus*, trans. Peter Heinegg (Garden City, NY: Doubleday & Company, 1979), 33. The image of the *fifth Jesus*, this Jewish Jesus, is provided to Lapide by a young Israeli poet, whom Lapide does not identify. This fifth Jesus is the object of Lapide's quest and reconstruction.
91. Lapide, *Jesus in Two Perspectives*, 114–15.
92. Ibid., 115.
93. Ibid., 117.
94. Ibid., 83. It is commonly asserted by Jewish scholars that the Easter Jesus emerges primarily as the synthesis of Pauline and Johannine interpretation, a Hellenic hybrid, markedly dissimilar to the Jesus of history. Therefore, Jewish scholars concentrate their efforts on recovering the Galilean rabbi of Nazareth and do not generally delve into the Christ of Pauline and Johannine interpretation.
95. Ibid., 114.
96. Lapide, *The Sermon on the Mount*, 7.
97. Lapide in *Brother or Lord?* 25.
98. Lapide, *Jesus in Two Perspectives*, 112.
99. Ibid.
100. Ibid., 113.
101. Ibid.
102. Though his family was Jewish at his birth, he and his family later converted to Catholicism. In 1928 his family resettled in Gyula, Hungary. When he was six years old, Vermès's parents, seeking to provide an advantage for him, sent him

to a local Roman Catholic school. In June of 1931, he and his family were baptized. Whether this was due to the influence of a teacher or the possibility of their son's advancement is unclear. What is clear is that, at eighteen, Vermès decided that the Roman Catholic priesthood offered him the best possibility for continued education. Having survived the Nazi occupation of Hungary, Vermès eventually joined the order of Notre-Dame de Sion and was ordained a priest on December 27, 1950. Within seven years, he would leave the priesthood to marry; in ten, he would reclaim his roots as a Jew by joining a Progressive Jewish synagogue in England. See Géza Vermès, *Providential Accidents: An Autobiography* (London: SCM, 1998).

103. Ironically, in his fifth book on Jesus, Vermès offers for the first time "a critical interpretation of the Gospel text itself" wherein he seeks to "discover new principles and devise a fresh procedure." See Géza Vermès, *The Authentic Gospel of Jesus* (London: Penguin Books, 2003), viii and 374, respectively. The portrait of Jesus that emerges at the conclusion of Vermès's critical analysis is shaped by his "approximation of the real teaching" (viii) of Jesus. This approximation is derived from Vermès's formulation of the principles for determining authenticity, "the principles which allow the determination of the parameters of authenticity" (ix). Vermès's critique of the standard criteria to arrive at such a determination lies less in the criteria itself and more "in the manner in which they have been formulated" (373). For a brief overview of the standard criteria, Vermès's critique, and alternative proposal, see 373ff. This most recent rendering of Jesus, though consistent with Vermès's previous depictions, accents diverse features of Jesus that reflect "a colourful, complex and rich human personality" (405). It may be suggested that this work was precipitated as a response to critics who question the criteria that Vermès employs to determine authenticity, as in Géza Vermès, *The Changing Faces of Jesus* (New York: Viking Press, 2001). See Judith Lieu's review in *Journal of Jewish Studies* 52, no. 2 (Autumn 2001): 375–76, raising that criticism and discerning a "familiar hermeneutical circle" where "presuppositions and end result are integrally linked."

104. Géza Vermès, "Jesus the Jew," in *Jesus' Jewishness: Exploring the Place of Jesus in Early Judaism*, ed. James H. Charlesworth (New York: Crossroads, 1991), 108.

105. Ibid., 108–9.

106. Ibid., 109–10.

107. Géza Vermès, *Jesus the Jew: A Historian's Reading of the Gospels* (Philadelphia: Fortress, 1981), 42.

108. Ibid., 19–20.

109. Vermès, *The Changing Faces of Jesus*, 221.

110. Vermès, *Jesus the Jew*, 69.

111. Ibid. See Vermès's footnote 53, in which he credits as "the most important book on this topic" Adolf Büchler's *Types of Jewish-Palestinian Piety from 70 B.C.E. to 70 C.E.* (London: Jews' College, 1922). Vermès informs us that Büchler's text is "a rich mine of information rather than a valid historico-critical assessment

of the data." As Büchler demonstrates, these Hasidim should not be confused with later Hasidic Jews.

112. Ibid., 69.

113. Ibid., 72. "The central rabbinic tradition about Hanina describes him as a very pious man with an extraordinary power to enact healings." See Nils Martola, "Vermès's *Jesus the Jew* after Twenty-Five Years," *Approaches to Ancient Judaism* 7 (1995).

114. Ibid.

115. Ibid., 74.

116. Ibid., 78.

117. Ibid., 79.

118. Ibid., 79–80.

119. Ibid., 79.

120. Ibid., 83

121. Jacob Neusner, *Jews and Christians: The Myth of a Common Tradition*, expanded ed. (Binghamton, NY: Global Publications, 2001), xi–xii.

122. Ibid., xii. Italics added. Having provided the fundamental reasons for the lack of dialogue, Neusner in chapters 7 and 8 points the way forward: "Only when we recognize difference can we appreciate points shared in common" (Preface, lv).

123. Jacob Neusner, *A Rabbi Talks with Jesus* (Montreal: McQueen's University Press, 2000), 4.

124. For Neusner's explanation of Torah and torah, see *A Rabbi Talks with Jesus*, 21. It is Jesus' torah, the instruction of a master, with which Neusner will take issue.

125. Ibid., 6.

126. Ibid., 20.

127. Ibid., 20–21.

128. Borowitz describes himself as "one of a tiny number identifying themselves as Jewish theologians and, rarer still, one with postrabbinic training in Christian theology." Eugene Borowitz, "Recent Historic Events: Jewish and Christian Interpretations," *Theological Studies* 44, no. 2 (June 1983): 221.

129. Eugene Borowitz, "Jesus the Jew in the Light of the Jewish-Christian Dialogue," in *Proceedings of the Center for Jewish-Christian Learning*, ed. A. E. Zannoni, vol. 2 (St. Paul, MN: University of St. Thomas, Jay Phillips Center for Jewish-Christian Learning, Spring 1987), 16.

130. Ibid.

131. Ibid.

132. Ibid., 16–17.

133. Ibid., 17.

134. Ibid.

135. Ibid.

136. Ibid.

137. Ibid.

138. Ibid.

139. Ibid.

2. Of Glass and Stone

140. In this same book, Vermès comments on Bultmann's influence. Géza Vermès, *The Religion of Jesus the Jew* (Minneapolis: Fortress Press, 1993), 1–2. For a more detailed presentation of Bultmann's position, form criticism, and the subsequent debate sparked by both, see also Dunn, *Jesus Remembered*, 73–85, 193–95; James H. Charlesworth, "The Foreground of Christian Origins and the Commencement of Jesus Research," in *Jesus' Jewishness*, 78–81.

141. Vermès, *The Religion of Jesus the Jew*, 3.

142. Ibid., 3–4.

143. Who or what is the historical Jesus? See Dunn, *Jesus Remembered*, 125–26; "'the historical Jesus' is properly speaking a nineteenth- and twentieth-century construction using the data provided by the Synoptic tradition, *not* Jesus back then and *not* a figure in history whom we can realistically use to critique the portrayal of Jesus in the Synoptic tradition" (126). See also John P. Meier, *A Marginal Jew: Rethinking the Historical Jesus*, 3 vols. (New York: Doubleday, 1991–2001), 1:21–31.

144. Charlesworth, "The Foreground of Christian Origins," 82–83.

145. The grouping is an artificial construct so as to facilitate comparative analysis. Given that these authors have admittedly opted, creatively, to loosen or deny the benefits of employing normative, critical methodology, I have described them as creative. However, it would be an egregious distortion to suggest, for example, that Jacob Neusner is not a critical scholar. Similarly, one could argue perhaps that Samuel Sandmel, who disparaged his historical-critical effort to get behind the Gospels, nonetheless offered his particular interpretation of Jesus. Having so argued, one could assert that Sandmel, too, qualifies to be admitted to this creative group. To this I would counter that though Sandmel does indeed present a portrait of Jesus apart from the normative criteria, he does so after seriously engaging with the data and then despairing of the effort; only then does he opt to venture an opinion. Ben-Chorin, Lapide, and Borowitz, in my estimation, are conveniently placed within this "creative" category, given the manner in which they have advanced their perspectives. Regarding Neusner and his use of historical-critical methodologies in his study of Judaism and rabbinic literature, see Meier, *A Marginal Jew*, 1:94n38.

146. Vermès, *The Religion of Jesus the Jew*, 4. However, Meier disagrees with the tendency to succumb to the "tyranny of the Synoptic Jesus." He writes: "The question of historical value plagues the material from the Fourth Gospel even more, and some critics simply ignore John. Nevertheless, contrary to the tendency of Bultmann and his followers, John's Gospel, in my opinion, is not to be rejected en masse and a priori as a source for the historical Jesus. To be sure, the rewriting of narratives for symbolic purposes and the reformulation of sayings for theological programs reach their high point in John. Yet such tendencies are not totally absent from the Synoptics, and at times (e.g., in such questions

as the nature of the Last Supper and the date of Jesus' death) John rather than the Synoptics may be historically correct" (*A Marginal Jew*, 1:45).

147. Josephus's contribution is deemed monumental by John Meier in that such extrabiblical evidence may quell the doubting, such as in the secular media. See Meier's comments on Josephus's *Testimonium* on Jesus (*Jewish Antiquities* 18.63–64), in *A Marginal Jew*, 1:59–69.

148. For an explanation of midrashim, see Jacob Neusner, *What Is Midrash? and, A Midrash Reader* (Atlanta: Scholars Press, 1994).

149. See Meier's section on "Jewish Sources besides Josephus," in *A Marginal Jew*, 1:93–98.

150. On the question as to whether or not one may use later rabbinic material to explain earlier Gospels, see Vermès, *The Religion of Jesus the Jew*, 7–10, esp. 8. For an example of Vermès's methodology regarding the comparative study of rabbinic literature and the Gospels, see his *Jesus in His Jewish Context*, 74–80. On the significance of the Jewish perspective, see Dunn, *Jesus Remembered*, 88–92.

151. For a detailed account of the sources, see Meier, *A Marginal Jew*, 1:40–166; Dunn, *Jesus Remembered*, 139–72.

152. Norman Perrin advances the criteria in his book *Rediscovering the Teaching of Jesus* (New York: Harper & Row, 1967). For a detailed explanation of the current criteria, see Meier, *A Marginal Jew*, 1:167–95. For a brief summary of the various criteria, see Dunn, *Jesus Remembered*, 81–85, 102–5. Also, Dunn has offered a different approach to the criteria vis-à-vis the question of transmission. See Dunn's challenge to change the "default setting" of the literary paradigm, in *Jesus Remembered*, 336. See also James D. G. Dunn, "Altering the Default Setting: Re-envisaging the Early Transmission of the Jesus Tradition," *NTS* 49, no. 2 (April 2003): 139–75.

153. Sandmel, *We Jews and Jesus*, viii.

154. Ibid.

155. Ibid., viii–ix.

156. Sandmel devotes but a dozen pages in *We Jews and Jesus* to the sources, in chap. 2, "Early Christianity and Its Jewish Background." Given that his task is markedly different (not to mention much earlier) than Meier or Dunn, a comparison of the three would be untenable. However, for decisive evidence of Sandmel's facility with the sources, see *The First Christian Century* and *A Jewish Understanding of the New Testament*.

157. Sandmel, *Judaism and Christian Beginnings*, viii.

158. Sandmel, *A Jewish Understanding of the New Testament*, xvi.

159. Ibid. For a stronger statement, see Sandmel, *The First Christian Century*, 147. Though Sandmel owns an indebtedness to Protestant biblical scholarship, he is not unappreciative of Catholic biblical scholarship of the same period. Cf. Sandmel, *The First Christian Century*, 198n3.

160. Sandmel, *We Jews and Jesus*, 5.

161. Ibid.

162. Ibid., 13.

163. Ibid., 6–15, passim.

164. Ibid, 13. See also Sandmel's description of the consequences imposed on American rabbi Stephen S. Wise because of his presumptive zeal regarding the Jewish reclamation of Jesus, in *We Jews and Jesus*, 102–3.

165. For Sandmel's description, see *We Jews and Jesus*, 17–18. For more detailed comments by Sandmel on Josephus, see also *Judaism and Christian Beginnings*, chap. 3, esp. 44–50.

166. For a more detailed discussion of the three passages in question, see Sandmel, *Judaism and Christian Beginnings*, 395–96.

167. Ibid., 55–56.

168. Ibid., 397.

169. Sandmel, *We Jews and Jesus*, 106. For more detailed explanation of the Dead Sea Scrolls by Sandmel, see *Judaism and Christian Beginnings*, chap. 3, esp. 92–102.

170. Ibid., 17. Regarding the Talmud, see Sandmel, *We Jews and Jesus*, 28n1; elsewhere Sandmel more adequately treats this question of rabbinic and nonbiblical sources, as in *Judaism and Christian Beginnings*, chap. 3, especially 50–55, 103–28.

171. Sandmel, *A Jewish Understanding of the New Testament*, xi.

172. Ibid., 18.

173. Ibid., xxiii.

174. Sandmel, *The First Christian Century*, 144.

175. Sandmel, *A Jewish Understanding of the New Testament*, 32.

176. Ibid., 33.

177. Ibid., 38.

178. Sandmel, *We Jews and Jesus*, 132.

179. Ibid., 26.

180. Sandmel, *A Jewish Understanding of the New Testament*, 50–51.

181. Ibid., 51.

182. Ibid. For Sandmel's description of Pauline Christianity as "a completely Grecian phenomenon," see *A Jewish Understanding of the New Testament*, 104.

183. Ibid., 52.

184. Sandmel, *We Jews and Jesus*, 26.

185. Sandmel expands upon his understanding of this distinction and its ramifications for Jesus research in *The First Christian Century*, 147–58, 188–96.

186. Ibid. For Sandmel's defense of the Gospels as "potentially historical," see *The First Christian Century*, 191.

187. Ibid., 148.

188. Ibid., 153.

189. Ibid., 154. Sandmel asserts elsewhere that predisposition and partisanship continue to prejudice Jesus scholarship. See *A Jewish Understanding of the New Testament*, 202.

190. Ibid., 155.

191. Sandmel, *We Jews and Jesus*, 124.

192. Sandmel, *The First Christian Century*, 155–56.

193. Ibid., 156.
194. Sandmel grapples at length with his growing suspicion of and disillusionment with form criticism given its tendencies toward overprecision and subjectivity; *The First Christian Century*, 143–58.
195. Ibid., 188; cf. 118n35. For a more recent explanation of midrash, see Jacob Neusner, *What Is Midrash? and, A Midrash Reader*. In the Preface of book 1 Neusner argues that the Hebrew word "midrash" should not be confused with the English word "exegesis," described as interpretation and explanation. Rather, "midrash," defined as biblical exegesis by ancient Judaic authorities, is better understood as prophecy, paraphrase, and parable.
196. Ibid., 189. Sandmel argues earlier that "the nature of midrashic expansion is such that we should never be able from the aggregate of midrashic expansions alone to re-create securely the scriptural Abraham of Genesis."
197. Sandmel, *We Jews and Jesus*, 126.
198. Ibid., 128. A difficulty may arise here for the reader. Sandmel is writing *We Jews and Jesus* for a Jewish audience. In chap. 5, "The Jewish Reader and the Gospels," Sandmel assists the Jew in approaching the Christian religious texts, especially the Gospels. He endorses an approach that views the Christian texts as literature, which then may be compared to other types of literature. The Gospels as literature he finds ordinary. The Gospels as objects of study are his life's work.
199. Ibid., 107.
200. Sandmel, *A Jewish Understanding of the New Testament*, 207.
201. Ibid., 208–9.
202. Ibid., 209.
203. Sandmel, *The First Christian Century*, 191–92.
204. Sandmel, *Judaism and Christian Beginnings*, 398. This is all the more curious since in this same book, Sandmel writes that he "personally subscribes to the view that Jesus was indeed a political rebel" (394).
205. Sandmel, *We Jews and Jesus*, 124.
206. Sandmel, *The First Christian Century*, 195.
207. Ibid.
208. Ibid., 195–96.
209. Ibid., 196.
210. Sandmel, *We Jews and Jesus*, 108.
211. Ibid.
212. Flusser, *Jesus*, 18.
213. Ibid., 22.
214. Ibid., 22–23.
215. Ibid., 19.
216. Ibid., 22.
217. Ibid.
218. Ibid.
219. Ibid., 177.

220. Though Flusser is conversant with archaeology's fledging contribution to a better understanding of this period, such evidence did not substantially advance Flusser's biography of Jesus. Though not prominent, Flusser does, however, intersperse within the text of his book *Jesus* some photographs of archaeological evidence that corroborate the historicity of Jesus and the cult of his followers. Beyond this, little use of archaeological evidence is discernible.

221. David Flusser, *Jewish Sources in Early Christianity* (New York: Adama Books, 1987), 13.

222. Ibid., 58–59.

223. Ibid., 9–10.

224. Ibid., 10.

225. David Flusser, "The Dead Sea Sect and Pre-Pauline Christianity," in *Judaism and the Origins of Christianity* (Jerusalem: Magnes, 1988), 24.

226. For Flusser's explanation of this new sensitivity as precondition to Judaism's openness to Jesus' message, see David Flusser, "A New Sensitivity in Judaism and the Christian Message," in *Judaism and the Origins of Christianity*, 469–89. As to the "germ of revolution in Jesus' preaching," see Flusser, *Jesus*, 81, 86–87.

227. Flusser, *Jewish Sources in Early Christianity*, 58.

228. Ibid.

229. Ibid.

230. Ibid., 59.

231. Ibid.

232. Flusser himself argues that the literary process cited above, the process whereby New Testament writers create Christian midrashim from Jewish midrashim to portray the image of Jesus as Messiah, "is evidence for the fact that such midrashim had existed in a very early period (ibid., 65).

233. Flusser describes midrash as "a creative exegesis and understanding of the text of the Bible and its stories, an attempt to discover all the various senses implicit in the biblical verse" (ibid., 61).

234. Ibid., 61–62.

235. Ibid., 14. Flusser is quoting from the Shlomo Pines's tenth-century Arabic text of Josephus.

236. Ibid., 68. Here Flusser's assessment of a second-stratum affinity to the Dead Sea Scrolls agrees with Bultmann's position regarding "two theological strata in the early Church" ("The Dead Sea Sect and Pre-Pauline Christianity," 24–25).

237. This position is more cogently argued in Flusser, "The Dead Sea Sect and Pre-Pauline Christianity," 23–74.

238. Ibid., 23–24.

239. Flusser modified his position regarding Essenian influence upon Jesus: "Meanwhile my later study has somewhat modified this position as it relates to the message of Jesus. By no means would I deny the essentially 'rabbinic' character of Jesus' teaching. In fact, I have even tried to show (in no. 9) that Jesus rejected the sectarian separation of the Essene sons of light. But, on the other hand, an indirect influence of the Essene approach to Jesus' ethics is palpable. . . . While

the Essene anthropological and ecclesiological concepts were not accepted by Jesus, he showed sympathy towards other Essene tendencies like their positive evaluation of poverty and their opinion that wealth is a danger to faith (see no. 10). Also we were able to show that the first three Beatitudes are connected with Essene poetry (see nos. 6 and 7)" (*Judaism and the Origins of Christianity*, xviii).

240. Flusser, "Jesus and Judaism: Jewish Perspectives," 80–109.
241. David Flusser, "The Jewish-Christian Schism," in *Judaism and the Origins of Christianity*, 621–22.
242. Flusser, *Jesus*, 20.
243. Ibid.
244. Ibid.
245. Ibid.
246. Ibid., 21.
247. Ibid.
248. Ibid.
249. Ibid., 22. Flusser contends that during this period most people were fluent in Hebrew, which was "the daily language and language of study." He argues: "This question of spoken language is especially important for understanding the doctrines of Jesus. There are sayings of Jesus which can be rendered both into Hebrew and Aramaic; but there are some which can only be rendered into Hebrew, and none of them can be rendered only into Aramaic. One can thus demonstrate the Hebrew origins of the Gospels by retranslating them into Hebrew" (*Jewish Sources in Early Christianity*, 11).
250. Ibid. 22–23.
251. Vermès, *The Changing Faces of Jesus*, 2.
252. Ibid.
253. Ibid.
254. Vermès, *Jesus the Jew*, 16; for an example of this distinction between the task of theologian and historian, see Vermès's presentation on the Gospels' titles of Jesus (84).
255. Vermès, "Jesus the Jew," 110. The illustrations to which Vermès refers are (#1) *"yšú,"* the name of "Jesus," as inscribed on an ostracon; (#11) a Caesarian inscription with the name of Pontius Pilate; (#19) at Jerusalem, an ossuary inscription: *šlby dwd;* and (#21) at Qumran, Cave IV.
256. Ibid.
257. Vermès, *The Changing Faces of Jesus*, 2.
258. Ibid., 2–3.
259. Ibid., 3.
260. Ibid.
261. Ibid.
262. Vermès, *The Authentic Gospel of Jesus*, 375. See also idem, *Jesus in His Jewish Context*, 74. In *The Authentic Gospel of Jesus*, Vermès uses the term "gospel" spelled in lower case to distinguish the message of Jesus from the later redacted

texts, the Gospels. Cf. Meier's discussion of "uniqueness" and the criterion of discontinuity as applied to the ipsissima verba, in *A Marginal Jew*, 1:173–74.

263. Vermès, *The Religion of Jesus the Jew*, 7.

264. This contentious relationship will be explored more appropriately in chap. 6, where we juxtapose Meier's critique of Vermès's "methodology" alongside Vermès's sharp rebuke.

265. For an explanation of typology and rabbinic literature, see Vermès, *The Changing Faces of Jesus*, 254–55.

266. Vermès, *Jesus the Jew*, 26.

267. For a full explanation, see Vermès, *The Religion of Jesus the Jew*, 7.

268. For Vermès's explanation, see *The Authentic Gospel of Jesus*, 373ff.

269. Vermès, *The Religion of Jesus the Jew*, 4.

270. Vermès asserts, as does Flusser, that rabbinic literature, though dated later than the Christian Gospels (of ca. 70–100 CE), nonetheless conveys within it some Jewish traditions that are contemporary with the Gospels. See Vermès, *Jesus in His Jewish Context*, chaps. 5 and 6; also idem, *The Religion of Jesus the Jew*, 8; and idem, *The Authentic Gospel of Jesus*, xvii. Flusser sees the study of the New Testament and primitive Christianity as an opportunity to enrich Judaism's understanding of itself, specifically during this period (*Jewish Sources in Early Christianity*).

271. Vermès, *The Changing Faces of Jesus*, 4. An example of this, the Gospels as midrash, may be found in Vermès's *The Religion of Jesus the Jew*, 66.

272. Charlesworth, "The Foreground of Christian Origins," 83.

273. Vermès, "Jesus the Jew," 112–13.

274. In the third book of his trilogy, *The Religion of Jesus the Jew* (5), Vermès reaffirms this chief assertion he had made in *Jesus the Jew*, of Jesus as Galilean Hasid.

275. Vermès views the major works of the Jewish writer Flavius Josephus as "our most precious source of Jewish history, religion and culture of the intertestamental age and of the first century AD in particular"; and "a priceless mine of information for the interpreters of the sayings of Jesus"; see Géza Vermès, *The Complete Dead Sea Scrolls in English* (New York: Penguin Press., 1997), xvi, with added emphasis.

276. Vermès, *The Authentic Gospel of Jesus*, xiv.

277. Vermès, *Jesus in His Jewish Context*, 68.

278. Ibid. Cf. Martin Hengel, *Judaism and Hellenism*, 2 vols. (London: SCM, 1974), 1:65.

279. Ibid.

280. Here Vermès (*The Religion of Jesus the Jew*, 7–8) is referring to John Lightfoot's *Horae Hebraicae et Talmudiae* (1658–78) and the "notorious" four-volume work *Kommentar zum Neuen Testament aus Talmud und Midrasch* (Munich: Beck, 1922–28) by Hermann Strack and Paul Billerbeck. Vermès also offers his defense for the inclusion of rabbinic literature as primary sources, not as merely an ancillary source to the New Testament, even after the discovery of the Dead Sea manuscripts (*The Religion of Jesus the Jew*, 8–9).

281. See Vermès, *Jesus in His Jewish Context*, 70–72, for his critique of Joseph Fitzmyer's thesis (found in "The Aramaic Language and the Study of the New Testament," *Journal of Biblical Literature* 99 [1980]: 5–21) wherein he regards the contribution of rabbinic literature as "neglible," given the discovery and study of the Dead Sea Scrolls, which give evidence of the "latest Aramaic" for comparison with New Testament sources. See also Sandmel's appraisal of rabbinic literature's impotence in this regard (*Judaism and Christian Beginnings*, 56).

282. Vermès, *Jesus and the World of Judaism*, 81. This effort comprises the latter half of *Jesus the Jew*.

283. Vermès, *The Religion of Jesus the Jew*, 4.

284. Ibid.

285. Vermès, *Jesus the Jew*, 42.

286. Ibid., 43–44.

287. Most of the scrolls, which number about 800, are written in Hebrew, a smaller portion in Aramaic, and only a few attest the ancient Greek or Septuagint version of the Bible. The Qumran Scrolls date ca. 200 BCE–70 CE. Most existed during the lifetime of Jesus.

288. Vermès's first article on the Dead Sea Scrolls appeared in 1949 and his first book, *Les manuscrits du désert de Juda* (Tournai: Desclée), in 1953. It was translated into English in 1956 as *Discovery in the Judean Desert* (New York: Desclée). By 1962 he had translated and published *The Complete Dead Sea Scrolls in English* (Oxford: Oxford University Press), and in 1977 *The Dead Sea Scrolls: Qumran in Perspective* (London: Collins).

289. Vermès, *The Complete Dead Sea Scrolls*, 7th ed. (New York: Penguin, 1997), 24.

290. Ibid.

291. Ibid., 25.

292. Ibid. Cf. Vermès, *The Religion of Jesus the Jew*.

293. Vermès, *The Complete Dead Sea Scrolls*, 22–23, giving a more detailed explanation of this threefold heading.

294. Vermès observes that "thus instead of restricting the boundaries of the Jewish background to the New Testament, the Dead Sea Scrolls have enlarged them: they are additional to the pre-existing material" (*Jesus in His Jewish Context*, 63; cf. also 60–64, 70–71).

295. For Vermès's explanation of his double conviction, see *The Religion of Jesus the Jew*, 4. See also, idem, "Jesus the Jew," 109–10.

296. Vermès, *The Religion of Jesus the Jew*, 6.

297. Ibid., 8.

298. Ibid.

299. Ibid.

300. Cf. Joseph Fitzmyer, "The Aramaic Language and the Study of the New Testament," *Journal of Biblical Literature* 99 (1980): 5–21.

301. Vermès, *The Religion of Jesus the Jew*, 6.

302. Ibid.

303. Ibid., 9.
304. Ibid.
305. Ibid.
306. Ibid.
307. Ibid.
308. For Vermès's discussion of this proposal and his subsequent challenge to New Testament scholars, see *Jesus in His Jewish Context*, 75–80, esp. 78–79.
309. Ibid., 79. For Vermès's description of rabbinic literature, such as the Mishnah, Tosefta, etc., see *The Authentic Gospel of Jesus*, xvi.
310. Vermès, *Jesus in His Jewish Context*, 79.
311. Ibid., 74–75. Vermès discusses this at length in the second half of *Jesus the Jew*.
312. Vermès, *The Changing Faces of Jesus*, 237. For Vermès's observations on "The Christ of Paul," see *The Changing Faces of Jesus*, 83–124: "For him [Paul], the history of Christ began with 'the night of his betrayal' (1 Cor. 11:23) and ended three days later with his resurrection. The term 'Jesus' on its own appears only about ten times in the letters of Paul . . . and is invariably connected with the only aspects of the earthly Jesus which were significant to Paul: his death and resurrection" (83–84). Pointedly, Vermès writes: "There is little concrete about the Jesus of Paul" (109).
313. Vermès, *The Changing Faces of Jesus*, 238.
314. Ibid.
315. Vermès, *Jesus in His Jewish Context*, 17.
316. Ibid., 18.
317. Ibid. Vermès will restrict his analysis of the Gospels to the Synoptic texts: Mark, Matthew, and Luke. The exclusion of John is due to the text's high christological assertions and questionable historicity. See Vermès, *The Religion of Jesus the Jew*, 4.
318. Ibid.
319. Vermès, *The Authentic Gospel of Jesus*, x.
320. Vermès, *Jesus in His Jewish Context*, 18.
321. Vermès, *The Authentic Gospel of Jesus*, x.
322. Vermès, *Jesus in His Jewish Context*, 18.
323. Ibid. Jacob Neusner, though he disagrees with Vermès's methodology and conclusions, offers a similar view regarding the lack of the genre in comparative rabbinic literature: "Yet, for the study of biography in antiquity, before the church fathers with their voluminous writings well preserved, we have few figures nearly so well documented as is Jesus. Take Judaism, for instance. Not a single rabbi represented in talmudic literature is given anything like a biography, let alone four of them; no rabbi left anything like "Q." All rabbis' statements are reworked into documents representing a consensus of their framers. Excluding only a handful, those who flourished at the end of the second century and are represented in the Mishnah ca. 200, not a single rabbi of antiquity is attested in a document that (we suppose) reached closure within so close a span of time after his death as is Jesus by the Gospels" (Jacob Neusner, *Rabbinic*

Literature and the New Testament [Valley Forge, PA: Trinity Press, 1994], 177n5).

324. Vermès, *The Authentic Gospel of Jesus*, 370; for Vermès's explanation as to why these irreconcilable variations may not be attributed to one man, much less to Jesus, see 370–72.
325. Ibid., 19.
326. Ibid., Vermès quoting Bultmann, *Jesus and the Word* (London: Scribner, 1934), 14.
327. Vermès, *The Authentic Gospel of Jesus*, 374.
328. Ibid., 375. For Vermès's register of authentic and inauthentic sayings, see ibid., "Appendix: A Classification of the Sayings of Jesus," 419–36.

3. Creative Variations

329. Neusner, among others, has applied a similar critique to both Flusser and Vermès, as we shall see in chap. 5 (below).
330. Ben-Chorin, *Brother Jesus*, 6.
331. Ibid.
332. Ibid., 5.
333. Ben-Chorin, "The Image of Jesus in Modern Judaism," 411.
334. Ben-Chorin, *Brother Jesus*, 5.
335. Ibid., 4.
336. Ibid., 2. Ben-Chorin affirms this elsewhere in *Brother Jesus*, emphasizing that the New Testament "has no interest in offering either a biography of Jesus or a description of Jewish antiquities" (126).
337. Ibid., 18.
338. Ibid.
339. Ibid., 3.
340. Ibid., 18–19.
341. Ibid.
342. Ben-Chorin, "The Image of Jesus in Modern Judaism," 412.
343. Lapide, *Jesus in Two Perspectives*, 25–26.
344. Lapide, *The Resurrection of Jesus*, 30.
345. Ibid., 10.
346. Ibid., 6–7.
347. Lapide, *Jesus in Two Perspectives*, 9.
348. Ibid., 25.
349. Pinchas Lapide, *Israelis, Jews, and Jesus*, trans. Peter Heinegg (Garden City, NY: Doubleday, 1979), 33.
350. Ibid. The image of this *fifth Jesus*, this Jewish Jesus, is provided to Lapide by a young Israeli poet, whom Lapide does not identify. The full citation attributed to this unidentified poet may be found in *Israelis, Jews, and Jesus*, 33. This fifth Jesus is the object of Lapide's quest and reconstruction.
351. Lapide in *Brother or Lord?* 13.

352. Ibid., 14, emphasis added. This paragraph paraphrases Lapide's description of the five bonds that bring Jesus closer to him (than to a non-Jew). For the complete text, see 13–14.
353. Lapide, *The Resurrection of Jesus*, 9.
354. Lapide, *Israelis, Jews, and Jesus*, 3. Lapide, Flusser, and Ben-Chorin concur that underlying the Greek Synoptic Gospel texts is a Hebrew version. Once ascertained, this Hebrew stratum would give obvious evidence as to the Jewishness of Jesus inasmuch as it would be free of Christian accretions. Sandmel does not concur. He regards this preoccupation with a Hebrew stratum as stemming from "a legendary development from the view of the second-century Bishop Papias, quoted in Eusebius, that Matthew had written his Gospel in Hebrew." See Sandmel's introduction to Lapide's book, *Israelis, Jews, and Jesus*, ix–x. In the same text, Lapide himself, given his confidence that a Hebrew stratum underlies the Synoptic Gospels, charges that "the entire Christology of the churches—and the same goes for Jewish research on Jesus—is based on secondary sources" (32–33).
355. Ibid.
356. As an example of Christian texts "read by Jewish eyes through Hebrew lens," see Lapide, *The Sermon on the Mount* (1986), originally published in German as *Die Bergpredigt—Utopie oder Programm?* (Mainz: Matthias-Grünewald, 1982).
357. Lapide, *Jesus in Two Perspectives*, 26.
358. Neusner explains this crucial difference between Torah and torah: "Torah with a capital *T* stands for God's revelation to Moses at Mount Sinai. When we write 'torah' with a small *t*, we mean, 'the instruction of a master—in the context of the teaching of the Torah.' It is a somewhat odd shift; what Jesus does is teach the Torah, and what he teaches also is torah. . . . He is a teacher of the Torah, so in the framework of the Torah, he teaches the Torah and he himself adds to the Torah: so his is a labor of torah too" (*A Rabbi Talks with Jesus*, 21).
359. Ibid., 6.
360. Ibid., with emphasis added.
361. Ibid.
362. Ibid., 7.
363. Ibid.
364. Ibid.
365. Ibid., 6. Neusner, having provided a précis of the essentials regarding Matthew's Gospel and Jesus' portrait, informs the reader: "From here on, I dispense with the proper acknowledgement of scholarship. . . . This is a book about faith meeting faith, . . . [and] Matthew's road is just one" (33).
366. Ibid., 24–25.
367. Ibid., 8.
368. Ibid.
369. Ibid., 31–32.
370. Ibid., 8.
371. Ibid., 9.

372. Ibid., 22.
373. Ibid., 23; see also Matt 5:17–20.
374. Ibid., 10.
375. Ibid. It is essential to recognize that Neusner is confronting Jesus as a religious Jew, not as a scholar, but rather as a practicing Jew responding to a teacher of torah. Therefore, true to his schema, he chooses not to question the historical veracity of Matthew's text.
376. To appreciate his request, see Borowitz, *Contemporary Christologies*, 8.
377. Jacob Neusner gives Borowitz's achievement high praise: "So far as I know, in two thousand years, only one Judaic theologian has ever written in an objective, informed, sympathetic, and constructive way about the issues of Christology" (*Telling Tales*, 67n3).
378. Borowitz, "Jesus the Jew in the Light of the Jewish-Christian Dialogue," 16.
379. Ibid.
380. A halakic Jew is one "who believes that the only authentic way to live in Covenant is to observe the discipline laid down in the Bible, the Talmud and the classic Jewish codes as interpreted by the Orthodox sages of our generation" (Borowitz, *Contemporary Christologies*, 7).

4. Jesus within Judaism

381. Dunn, *Jesus Remembered*, 88. What may seem curious to Dunn may reflect both a bias against Judaism and Jewish scholarship in this regard, coupled with criticisms concerning methodologies, hermeneutics, and the lack or inadequacies thereof.
382. Ibid. Dunn mentions the Jewish authors Joseph Klausner, Ben-Chorin, Flusser, and Sandmel (88n114). The latter three are among the authors considered in this study. Both Flusser and Vermès, as previously identified, may be described as Jesus researchers. They, then, not only precede and influence but also contribute to the third quest. Also see Dunn's comments concerning Sanders and Wright (88–89).
383. Ibid., 88.
384. Ibid., with emphasis added.
385. Sandmel, *We Jews and Jesus*, 15.
386. I say "timorously rendered" to remind readers of Sandmel's conviction that Jesus the man cannot not be retrieved from the sources. Sandmel's conundrum was discussed thoroughly in chap. 2 (above). Paradoxically, he sets aside his scholarly dilemma and creatively intuits from the pertinent milieu a Jewish sketch of the elusive Jesus. His familiarity and facility with both Judaism and New Testament scholarship inform his effort.
387. Sandmel, *We Jews and Jesus*, 20
388. Ibid., 20–24, and passim.
389. Sandmel, *The First Christian Century*, 191.
390. For Sandmel's survey of Christian titles of Jesus, see *We Jews and Jesus*, 30–50. Also see Sandmel, "Christology, Judaism, and Jews," in *Christological*

Perspectives: Essays in Honor of Harvey K. McArthur, ed. R. F. Berkley and S. A. Edwards, 170–78 (New York: Pilgrim, 1982).

391. Sandmel, *We Jews and Jesus*, 44.
392. Ibid., 24.
393. Ibid., 25.
394. Sandmel, *The First Christian Century*, 195.
395. Ibid., 196.
396. Sandmel, *We Jews and Jesus*, 51–52. This period, the end of the eighteenth century and beginning of the nineteenth century, embraced the definition of history made by Leopold von Ranke, a leading German historian: "The task of history is to tell exactly what happened." The consequences of accepting such a definition, according to Sandmel, "reflected a rejection of supernatural faith and the scorn of miracles." The Protestant scholarship of the day "held that myth, legend and true history could be distinguished from each other in general." These consequences were far-reaching, as we have seen (ibid., 52).
397. For a detailed explanation, see ibid., 73–75.
398. Ibid., 75.
399. Ibid.
400. Ibid.
401. Ibid.
402. Ibid. Abraham Geiger, in Sandmel's view, "expected what he should never have expected," a lack of reverence vis-à-vis Jesus on the part of critical Christian scholars. See Sandmel's comments on Christian iconoclastic scholarship (74–75).
403. Ibid., with emphasis added.
404. Ibid., 108.
405. Ibid., 108–9.
406. Ibid., 109.
407. Ibid.
408. Ibid.
409. Ibid., 109–10.
410. Ibid., 110.
411. Ibid.
412. Ibid.
413. Ibid. Sandmel suggests that Jesus may have been regarded as a *nazir* (121–22).
414. Ibid., 110.
415. Ibid., 110–11.
416. Ibid., 111. The inadequacies of which Sandmel speaks pertain to inadequacies discernible, from Sandmel's perspective as qualified above, in Jewish culture and not in the Jewish religion per se.
417. Ibid.
418. Ibid., 112.
419. Ibid.
420. Ibid.

421. Ibid., 121–22. Sandmel suggests that a confusion over this term accounts for the mistaken view, in his opinion, that Jesus was from Nazareth. "The word *nazir* . . . has led to the opinion that the passage Matthew 2:23 means not that Jesus was really from Nazareth but only that he was a *Nazir*." Ben-Chorin views John the Baptist as a *nazir*, but not Jesus (*Brother Jesus*, 28).

422. Sandmel, *We Jews and Jesus*, 108. Sandmel sees the use of "Rabbi" as a title as anachronistic, though he concedes that, when referring to Jesus, it could simply be a term indicating a teacher.

423. Flusser, *Jesus*, 26. To substantiate his claims as to the presence of Davidic descendants at the time of Jesus, Flusser cites Joachim Jeremias's *Jerusalem in the Time of Jesus* (London: SCM Press, 1969).

424. Flusser, *Jesus*, 27.

425. Ibid., 28.

426. Ibid. Flusser is aware that some scholars are of the view that Jesus' brothers and sisters were, in fact, his cousins, or children of Joseph by a previous marriage. See Josef Blinzler, *Die Brüder und Schwestern Jesu* (Stuttgart: Katholisches Bibelwerk, 1967).

427. Flusser, *Jesus*, 29.

428. Ibid.

429. Ibid., 30.

430. Ibid.

431. Ibid., 32.

432. Ibid.

433. Ibid.

434. Ibid., 33. Regarding this sense of "carpenter," see also Vermès, *Jesus the Jew*, 21–22.

435. Flusser, *Jesus*, 34.

436. Ibid., 35.

437. Ibid., 40.

438. Ibid., 38.

439. Ibid.

440. Ibid.

441. Ibid., 42.

442. Ibid., 41.

443. Ibid., 42.

444. Ibid., 53. Flusser also believes that Jesus apparently viewed John the Baptist as a "type of second Moses" (261n8).

445. Ibid., 55.

446. Ibid., 83.

447. For Flusser's explanation of this new sensitivity and the Pharisaic debate that gave rise to it, see "A New Sensitivity in Judaism," 469–89, esp. 471–73.

448. Ibid., 473. Antiginos of Sokho lived in the second century BCE, but before the Maccabean revolt.

449. Ibid.

450. Ibid., 481.

451. Ibid., 476.
452. Flusser, *Jesus*, 83.
453. Flusser, "A New Sensitivity in Judaism," 475.
454. Ibid., 482.
455. Flusser, "Jesus and Judaism: Jewish Perspectives," 80.
456. Flusser, "A New Sensitivity in Judaism," 483.
457. Ibid.; also see 485–86.
458. Ibid., 487.
459. Flusser, "Jesus and Judaism: Jewish Perspectives," 98.
460. Flusser, "A New Sensitivity in Judaism," 488.
461. Flusser, *Jesus*, 81.
462. Ibid., 58.
463. David Flusser, in the foreword to Clemens Thoma, *A Christian Theology of Judaism* (New York: Paulist Press, 1980), 16.
464. Flusser, *Jesus*, 58. For this single incident, Flusser favors Luke 6:1–5 as being closest to the original account. He also dismisses its significance in two ways: (1) According to some interpreters, "on the Sabbath it was permissible to pick up fallen heads of grain and rub them between the fingers." (2) This practice may have been a Galilean custom with which some Pharisees found fault.
465. Ibid., 59–60.
466. Ibid., 60.
467. Ibid., 62. The healing on the Sabbath was that of the man with a withered hand (cf. Luke 6:6–11). The implications of this healing are threefold, from Flusser's perspective: (1) It demonstrates that Jesus did not transgress the Law in healing the man since he used a verbal command, "Stretch out your hand," which was allowed. There were, then, no legitimate grounds for condemnation. (2) The action of Jesus and the response of some bystanders demonstrate the tension that existed between the Pharisees and the wonder-workers, the Hasidim, like Jesus. (3) A leitmotif of the plot that finally lead to Jesus' destruction appears in Mark and Matthew for the first time. A Hebrew reading of these texts reveals that the bystanders "discussed with one another what they might do *to* Jesus." Cf. "Jesus and Judaism: Jewish Perspectives," 95.
468. Flusser, *Jesus*, 62.
469. Ibid.
470. Flusser, "Jesus and Judaism: Jewish Perspectives," 96. Flusser enlists scriptural citations from Paul to underscore his point (Gal 4:4–5; Rom 15:8).
471. Ibid.
472. Ibid.
473. Ibid.
474. Ibid., 97–98, with added emphasis.
475. Ibid.
476. Flusser, *Jesus*, 72.
477. The Pharisees were not a homogenous group. Both Schalom Ben-Chorin and David Flusser, citing the Talmud, mention the seven types of Pharisees that constituted Pharisaic Judaism in the time of Jesus. Of the seven, the first

five, broadly described as "hypocrites," are the negative types, drawing the most criticism. The remaining two types—the fearing Pharisees (with fear or awe of God), like Job; and the loving Pharisees, like Abraham—are the positive types. (Hillel and Jesus would be numbered among loving Pharisees.) These two types are viewed favorably in rabbinic literature. See ibid., 70, wherein Flusser mentions the list and makes a brief point. For the list, which he derives from the Palestinian Talmud, and his comments, see Flusser's "Jesus and Judaism: Jewish Perspectives," 91–92. For a detailed list from the Jerusalem Talmud and explanation, see Ben-Chorin, *Brother Jesus*, 13ff. Both Flusser and Ben-Chorin situate Jesus as a Pharisaic rabbi in Pharisaic Judaism, and as part of an internal opposition movement.

478. Flusser, *Jesus*, 72. Because of the detectable heightening of tensions by the evangelists, Flusser doubts the existence of genuine hostility between Jesus on one hand and the scribes and the Pharisees on the other hand. However, he acknowledges that some petty-minded Pharisees, suspicious of this wonder-worker, Jesus, hoped to entrap him. Flusser maintains that an orthodox Jesus eluded their snares.

479. Ibid., 81.

480. Ibid., 110.

481. Ibid.

482. Ibid., 111.

483. Ibid.

484. Ibid., 112.

485. Ibid., 102.

486. See Paul Winter, *On the Trial of Jesus* (Berlin: de Gruyter, 1961), 148. According to Winter, who typifies this trend, Jesus "was a normal person—he was the norm of normality."

487. Flusser, "Hillel's Self-Awareness and Jesus," 31.

488. Ibid., 34–35.

489. Ibid., 35.

490. Flusser, *Jesus*, 266.

491. Flusser, "Hillel's Self-Awareness and Jesus," 36. In his book *Jesus*, Flusser asserts that "the high self-awareness of the 'historical' Jesus began evolving into the Christology of the Christian faith" (175). He thus confirms his premise and his critique of other scholars who "see little connection between Jesus' understanding of his task in the divine economy and the 'kerygma' of the Church." From Flusser's perspective, this high self-awareness, recalled by the fledging Christian community during its first crisis—the death of Jesus—leads them to stress "the divine character of Christ and the cosmic significance of his task" (*Jesus*, 175). A metahistorical drama evolves.

492. Flusser, "Jesus and Judaism: Jewish Perspectives," 81.

493. Ibid., 82.

494. Ibid.

495. Ibid.

496. Ibid., 82–83. Flusser is conversant—and apparently in agreement—with Géza Vermès's work regarding this Hasidic typology; this is confirmed implicitly by his content and, where appropriate, explicitly in footnotes or endnotes. Though Flusser here embraces the aptness of the Hasidic typology, his previous assertion in his book *Jesus* that Jesus was a scholar, almost a "young talmudist" (see n. 46 above) would seem to make the Hasidic typology ill-suited. In "Jesus and Judaism: Jewish Perspectives," Flusser makes no mention of the incongruence.
497. Ibid., 83.
498. Flusser describes both Abba Hilkia and Hanina ben Dosa as Galileans, like Jesus. Vermès is more cautious and regards such assertions about Hilkia, Hana, and Honi himself as "purely conjectural." However, he does find the Galilean background of Hanina ben Dosa as "incontestable" (*Jesus the Jew*, 71–78).
499. Flusser, "Jesus and Judaism: Jewish Perspectives," 83.
500. Ibid., 84–85.
501. Ibid., 86.
502. Flusser, *Jesus*, 118.
503. Flusser, "Jesus and Judaism: Jewish Perspectives," 87.
504. Ibid.
505. Ibid.
506. Ibid., 88.
507. Ibid.
508. Ibid.
509. Ibid.
510. Flusser, *Jewish Sources in Early Christianity*, 22–25.
511. Ibid., 23–24.
512. Flusser, "Jesus and Judaism: Jewish Perspectives," 88.
513. Ibid.
514. Ibid., 93.
515. Flusser, *Jesus*, 92.
516. Ibid., 118.
517. Ibid., 120.
518. Ibid., 121.
519. Ibid., 122.
520. Ibid.
521. Ibid.
522. Ibid., 123.
523. Ibid.
524. Ibid.
525. Ibid., 125.
526. Ibid.
527. Ibid., 126.
528. Ibid., 128.
529. Ibid, 128–29. Flusser is aware that Dan 7 was written in Aramaic. Yet, he contends that Jesus, teaching in Hebrew, would have used the phrase *ben-'ādām* rather than the Aramaic *bar-'ĕnoš*.

530. Ibid., 129.
531. Ibid., 130.
532. David Flusser, "Jesus and the Sign of the Son of Man," in *Judaism and the Origins of Christianity*, 534.
533. Ibid.
534. Ibid.
535. Flusser, *Jesus*, 130. Cf. Flusser, "Melchizedek and the Son of Man," in *Judaism and the Origins of Christianity*, 186–92.
536. Flusser, *Jesus*, 131.
537. Ibid.
538. Ibid., 132.
539. Ibid.
540. Ibid. For Flusser's comparative messianic timetables, see 272.
541. Ibid., 273.
542. Ibid., 274.
543. This point—that the coming of the Son of Man and his last judgment would be postponed to the distant future and preceded by the present realization of the kingdom of heaven—"this change," according to Flusser, "was the crux of the conflict between the Baptist and Jesus" (ibid., 273). It was this change that gave distinction to Jesus' messianic timetable.
544. Ibid., 274–75.
545. Ibid., 132.
546. Ibid.
547. Ibid., 133.
548. For a concise presentation of Jesus research, see Hurtado, "A Taxonomy of Recent Historical-Jesus Work," 272–95.
549. Vermès, *Jesus and His Jewish Context* (2003), 127. This text "updates and enriches further" his *Jesus and the World of Judaism* (1983).
550. Vermès recognizes that each author's impetus in writing their respective Gospel was kergymatic, theological, and not primarily biographical or historical per se. That historical facts, however, may be gleaned from these Jewish documents forms the basis of his inquiry.
551. Vermès, *Jesus the Jew*, 19. The phrase "echoing primitive tradition" should not be underestimated. These traditions, Jewish in their origin and orientation, form the basis for Vermès's Synoptic reconstruction when juxtaposed with contemporary, comparative Jewish literature.
552. Ibid., 20.
553. Ibid., passim. For an explanation of Vermès's Synoptic focus vis-à-vis the Johannine and Pauline texts, see his *Jesus in His Jewish Context*, 126–27.
554. Vermès, *Jesus the Jew*, 20–22, passim. Regarding Jesus as carpenter or carpenter's son, Flusser was also aware of this metaphorical use of "carpenter" to refer to a scholar or learned man. Neither, however, suggest that Joseph "the carpenter" may have been Jesus' teacher.
555. Vermès, *Jesus in His Jewish Context*, 6.

556. Ibid., 8.
557. Ibid., 6. Here Vermès cites Jesus curing in absentia and compares this Matthean account to a similar story of Hanina ben Dosa, Jesus' younger contemporary, found in the Talmud (*b. Ber.* 34b). This is but one of many parallels that Vermès discerns between Jesus and the charismatic Hasidim.
558. Vermès, *Jesus in His Jewish Context*, 8. Here too Vermès cites a parallel between a Markan episode (5:15) and Hanina ben Dosa (*b. Pesaḥ.* 122b).
559. Vermès, *Jesus in His Jewish Context*, 9.
560. Ibid., 9–10. Regarding Jesus as prophet and the appellation "Elijah redivivus," see also Vermès, *The Changing Faces of Jesus*, 205.
561. Vermès, *Jesus in His Jewish Context*, 10; see Luke 4:23–26.
562. Vermès, *Jesus the Jew*, 26–29, passim. In this book, Vermès chooses not to investigate or debate the authenticity of the sayings attributed to Jesus, observing that "some of these may have been handed down intact, but others are reformulations of the originals made by the early Church, and still others are actual interpolations devised to secure the authority deriving from the 'words of the lord' for beliefs in vogue at a subsequent stage of doctrinal development" (26). Instead, Vermès focuses on the *kind* of teacher Jesus was according to the evangelists. His inquiry is concerned not "so much with the contents as with the *mode* of his preaching and the *impression* it left on sympathetic listeners" (26, emphasis added). This focus upon the mode and impression, or *patterns*, is both the hallmark of Vermès's approach and his Achilles' heel, at least according to some critics, such as Bruce Chilton and Seán Freyne.
563. Vermès, *The Religion of Jesus the Jew*, 46. Vermès clashes with Flusser's portrait of Jesus in at least two ways: (1) Vermès sees Jesus as "not a particular [sic] useful guide for the world and its problems" and more of an existential teacher "for the individual and not the collectivity," whereas Flusser see him as "the" moral exemplar for this twentieth century; (2) Vermès's Jesus is itinerant, but Flusser's is scholarly, akin to a young Talmudist. See Peter Stanford, "Géza Vermès: A Child of his Time," *The Independent* (UK), December 19, 2003, http://arts.independent.co.uk/books/features/article72504.ece (accessed September 29, 2007).
564. Vermès, *The Religion of Jesus the Jew*, 46.
565. Ibid., 47.
566. Ibid.
567. Ibid.
568. Ibid., 70. For Vermès's above-mentioned survey, see *The Religion of Jesus the Jew*, 50–70.
569. Vermès, *The Religion of Jesus the Jew*, 70.
570. Ibid., 71.
571. Ibid., 73.
572. Ibid., 73–74.
573. Ibid., 74, with added emphasis. Jesus as prophet will be considered in the later section of this chapter that explores Vermès's presentation of the New Testament titles of Jesus. Regarding Vermès's reference to Otto, see Rudolf

Otto, *The Kingdom of God and the Son of Man* (London: Lutterworth, 1938), 333–76, wherein Otto expressly applies the charismatic concept to Jesus. E. P. Sanders concurs with Vermès in describing Jesus as a "charismatic" or "charismatic prophet" (*Jewish Law from Jesus to the Mishnah: Five Studies* [London: SCM, 1990], 3).

574. Vermès, *The Changing Faces of Jesus*, 208.
575. Ibid. For a more detailed presentation, see *The Religion of Jesus the Jew*, 11–45.
576. Vermès, *The Changing Faces of Jesus*, 209.
577. Vermès observes for his reader that Jesus' teaching regarding the permanent validity of the Torah is authentic. He argues this given "its very survival in the New Testament in the face of the deep embarrassment caused by it in the antinomian Gentile church, which provided the Gospels of Matthew and Luke with a permanent home" (ibid., 209).
578. Ibid.
579. Ibid., 207.
580. Ibid., 209–10.
581. Ibid., 210–11.
582. Ibid., 211.
583. Ibid., 211–12. Regarding the antitheses, see also his *The Religion of Jesus the Jew*, 30–37.
584. Vermès, *The Religion of Jesus the Jew*, 47, with added emphasis.
585. Ibid., 45.
586. Vermès, *The Changing Faces of Jesus*, 212.
587. Ibid.
588. Ibid.
589. Ibid., 212–13, passim. Of this latter quality, love for an enemy, Vermès adds: "The idea is startling and is often thought to be exclusive to Jesus. However, in a less spectacular fashion Flavius Josephus attributes a similar outlook to Moses" (213; Josephus, *Contra Apionem* 2.211). Elsewhere Vermès sees in Jesus' ethical imperatives hyperbole and exaggeration consistent with his ethnicity and distinct religiousness (*Jesus and the World of Judaism*, 53).
590. Vermès, *The Changing Faces of Jesus*, 214.
591. Ibid., 214–15, passim. For Vermès's presentation of *Abba*, see "'Abba Father': The God of Jesus," in *The Religion of Jesus the Jew*, 152–83.
592. Vermès, *The Changing Faces of Jesus*, 215. For his presentation on the development of primitive Christian eschatology, see 145, 76, 19.
593. Ibid., 215–16.
594. Ibid., 216, passim.
595. Ibid. For a more detailed presentation of Jesus and the kingdom of God, see Vermès, *The Religion of Jesus the Jew*, 120–51.
596. Ibid., 217.
597. Ibid., 146.
598. Ibid.
599. Ibid.

600. Vermès, *The Changing Faces of Jesus*, 217. Vermès asserts that the "so-called" eschatological discourse (Mark 13:5–20; Matt 24:5–22; Luke 21:8–24) was composed by the primitive church since it is uncharacteristic of Jesus (217).

601. Vermès, *The Religion of Jesus the Jew*, 147.

602. Ibid., 148.

603. Vermès, *The Changing Faces of Jesus*, 217–18.

604. Géza Vermès, "The Gospels without Christology," in *God Incarnate: Story and Belief*, ed. A. E. Harvey (London: SPCK, 1981), 67, with added emphasis.

605. Vermès, *The Changing Faces of Jesus*, 218–19, passim.

606. Ibid., 219. Vermès goes on to suggest that "such a perspective has no room for the idea of an organized society, a church, destined to last until heaven and earth pass away in a far-distant age to come (219). Regarding Jesus' eschatology, Vermès is conversant with Albert Schweitzer's "consistent" (*konsequente*) eschatology, C. H. Dodd's "realized" eschatology, and Joachim Jeremias's "process of realization" (*sich realisierende Eschatolgie*). See Vermès, *The Religion of Jesus the Jew*, 147; also 148n27, giving his critique of the positions of both E. P. Sanders and Paula Frederiksen regarding the Jesus' concept of the kingdom of God.

607. Vermès, *The Religion of Jesus the Jew*, 200; see 196–200 for his explanation of *těšûbāh* and *'ěmûnāh*. Vermès's Riddell Lectures, delivered at the University of Newcastle upon Tyne in 1981, were later published under the title of *The Gospel of Jesus the Jew* (Newcastle-on-Tyne: University of Newcastle-on-Tyne, 1981). These lectures, slightly revised, were included in Verme's book *Jesus and the World of Judaism* (1983).

608. Vermès, *The Changing Faces of Jesus*, 220.

609. Ibid. In the estimate of one critic, this view of Jesus' eschatology, as Vermès perceives it, advances an understanding of the outlook of Jesus as "doom and gloom." (Jack Dominian, *One Like Us: A Psychological Interpretation of Jesus* [London: Darton, Longman & Todd, 1998], 5). Vermès rejects Dominian's appraisal (*The Changing Faces of Jesus*, 220).

610. Vermès, *Jesus in His Jewish Context*, 10.

611. Ibid., 3. For Vermès's initial presentation of Jesus and Galilee, see his *Jesus the Jew*, 42–57.

612. Vermès, *Jesus in His Jewish Context*, 4.

613. Ibid. This conviction is axiomatic today, as is the affirmation of the Jewishness of Jesus. Neither was the case when Vermès wrote in 1973.

614. Ibid. For Vermès's more recent assessment of Galilee, see his *The Changing Faces of Jesus*, 238–40.

615. Vermès, *Jesus in His Jewish Context*, 4–5. For a more recent description of Galilean culture at the time of Jesus, especially as this relates to Jerusalem antagonists toward Galileans, see Vermès's *The Changing Faces of Jesus*, 240–46. Cf. Seán Freyne, *Galilee, Jesus, and the Gospels: Literary Approaches and Historical Investigations* (Philadelphia: Fortress, 1988).

616. Vermès, *The Religion of Jesus the Jew*, 5.

617. Vermès, *Jesus the Jew*, 29.

618. Ibid., 30, passim.

619. Ibid., 30–31, passim.

620. Ibid., 31.

621. Ibid., 31–33, passim.

622. Ibid., 33. Vermès finds it interesting that "Mark is satisfied with a straightfor-ward presentation of Jesus as John's successor" (33).

623. Ibid.

624. Ibid.

625. Ibid. Vermès goes on to suggest that the absence of this Markan retort in Syn-optic parallels is "no doubt due to an early 'censorship' tendency in the evolving Christian tradition" (34).

626. Vermès, observing that James, the brother of Jesus, became head of the Jerusalem church, does allow that the family may have had a change of heart (ibid., 34).

627. See Luke 4:28–30. Vermès doubts the historicity of the purported threat of lynching and sees it as a Lukan exaggeration (*Jesus the Jew*, 34).

628. Ibid., 35.

629. Ibid.

630. Ibid.

631. Ibid. Vermès contends that prior to 70 CE there was little Pharisaic presence outside of Judea. There was, however, a well-defined group in Jerusalem and its environs. He concludes that "Pharisaic opposition to Jesus was mostly foreign and not local" (57). See his *Jesus the Jew*, 56–57; and *The Religion of Jesus the Jew*, 70.

632. Vermès, *Jesus the Jew*, 36.

633. Vermès, *Jesus in His Jewish Context*, 10–11.

634. Ibid., 11.

635. Ibid.

636. Ibid.

637. Ibid.

638. Ibid.

639. Ibid., 12. Vermès says surprisingly little about the arrest and execution of Jesus. In the preface to *The Religion of Jesus the Jew*, his comments are relegated to the preface: "The arrest and execution of Jesus were due, not directly to his words and deeds, but to their possible insurrectionary consequences feared by nervous authorities in charge of law and order in that powder-keg of first-century Jerusalem, overcrowded with pilgrims. Had Jesus not caused an affray in the Temple by overturning the tables of the merchants and money-changers, or had even chosen to do so at a time other than Passover—the moment when the hoped-for Messiah, the final liberator of the Jews, was expected to reveal himself—he would most probably have escaped with his life. He died on the cross for having done the wrong thing (caused a commotion) in the wrong place (the Temple) at the wrong time (just before Passover). Here lies the real tragedy of Jesus the Jew" (ix–x.).

640. Vermès, *Jesus the Jew*, 36.

641. Ibid., 36–37. See also, Winter, *On the Trial of Jesus*.

642. Vermès, *Jesus in His Jewish Context*, 12. Regarding "this perplexed cry from the cross"—*Elōi, elōi, lema sebachthani?*—Vermès, in his more recent effort, *The Changing Faces of Jesus*, suggests an alternate explanation to that given by some New Testament interpreters. Given that, if a prayer, it lacks the original Hebrew form one would expected to find, Vermès surmises that "the Aramaic sentence was a proverbial exclamation of a man in despair" (*The Changing Faces of Jesus*, 297n5).

643. Vermès, *Jesus the Jew*, 37. Vermès admits that both Mark and Matthew cite Jesus as predicting his death and following resurrection, but he asserts, in keeping with the above position, "It is generally held even by academic orthodoxy that the references to the resurrection at least constitute prophecy after the event" (37). In the same vein, he writes in *The Changing Faces of Jesus*, 183: "This most significant prophecy of Jesus appears to have fallen on deaf ears or to have sunk straight into oblivion, with not a single apostle or disciple recalling it during the crucial hours between Friday and Sunday."

644. Vermès, *Jesus the Jew*, 38.

645. Ibid., 41.

646. Ibid. For parallel of Vermès's example of the resurrection, interpreted from a liberal historian's point of view, see Lapide, *The Resurrection of Jesus*. Winter, *On the Trial of Jesus*, asserts, "Crucified, dead and buried, [Jesus] yet rose in the hearts of his disciples who had loved him and felt he was near" (208).

647. Vermès, *Jesus the Jew*, 41.

648. Ibid.

649. Vermès, *Jesus in His Jewish Context*, 127. Vermès in *Jesus the Jew* advises: "Four dependent epithets are discussed with the principal ones: 'rabbi' and 'teacher' with 'lord'; 'son of David' with 'the Messiah'; and 'the son' with 'son of God'" (85).

650. Vermès, *Jesus the Jew*, 84.

651. Vermès, *The Changing Faces of Jesus*, 42–44, passim. For Vermès's philological discussion of the phrase "son of man," Joseph A. Fitzmyer's reply, and Vermès's rebuttal, see Vermès, "'The Son of Man' Debate," *Journal for the Study of the New Testament* 1 (1978): 19–32; Fitzmyer, "Another View of 'the Son of Man' Debate," *JSNT* 4 (1979): 58–68; and Vermès, *Jesus and the World of Judaism*, 77–80. Vermès's discussion is also reproduced in *Jesus and the World of Judaism*, 89–99.

652. Vermès, *The Changing Faces of Jesus*, 188.

653. Ibid., 189. Vermès adds: "The same remark applies to the excerpts containing implicit references to Daniel 7 (Mark 8:38; Matt. 16:27; Luke 9:26, etc.)."

654. Vermès, *Jesus the Jew*, 185–86. As to how his conclusion is so radically difference from other contemporary New Testament scholars, Vermès quips: "If a problem is approached wrongly, wrong answers are bound to multiply" (186).

655. Vermès, *The Changing Faces of Jesus*, 189.

656. Ibid.

657. Ibid., 190–91, passim.

658. Ibid., 193.
659. Ibid., 193–94, passim.
660. Ibid., 194.
661. Ibid.
662. Ibid., 194–96, passim.
663. Ibid., 196.
664. Vermès, *Jesus the Jew*, 149.
665. Ibid., 152–53. As to why the early church embraced the title "the Christ," given Jesus' reticence to do so, see Vermès's tentative suggestions (154–56).
666. Ibid., 192.
667. Ibid., 200.
668. Ibid., 205.
669. Ibid., 206.
670. Ibid.
671. Ibid.
672. Ibid., 208–9.
673. Ibid., 209.
674. Ibid.
675. Vermès, "The Gospels without Christology," 65–66.
676. Vermès, *Jesus the Jew*, 210.
677. For Vermès's comments on Jesus' use of *Abba*, see ibid., 210–11; *The Changing Faces of Jesus*, 214.
678. Vermès, *Jesus the Jew*, 211.
679. Vermès, *The Changing Faces of Jesus*, 198. Vermès does recognize that "only a minority of them [New Testament scholars] concede authenticity to the application of this mode of address to Jesus during his lifetime" (*Jesus the Jew*, 103).
680. Vermès, *The Changing Faces of Jesus*, 198–99.
681. Ibid., 199. For his analysis of the philological background, see *Jesus the Jew*, 111–22.
682. Vermès, *The Changing Faces of Jesus*, 169.
683. Ibid., 199–200.
684. Ibid., 201.
685. Ibid.
686. Ibid. For his presentation of the use of "Lord" in the Gospels, see also *Jesus the Jew*, 122–27.
687. Vermès, *The Changing Faces of Jesus*, 201.
688. Ibid.
689. Ibid., 202.
690. Vermès, *Jesus the Jew*, 127.
691. Ibid., 86.
692. Ibid.
693. Ibid.
694. Vermès, *The Changing Faces of Jesus*, 30–31.
695. Ibid., 203.

696. Ibid., 204–5, passim.
697. Vermès, *Jesus the Jew*, 87.
698. Ibid., 88.
699. Vermès, *The Changing Faces of Jesus*, 205.
700. Ibid., 206. Vermès acknowledges: "It is impossible to prove the verbal authenticity of these sayings, but as far as their substance is concerned I have no doubt that it was not in the interests of the evangelists or of the primitive church [given the focus on Jesus as *the* Prophet] to invent them. They [Jesus' sayings] definitely went against the grain" (207).
701. Ibid., 206–7.
702. Vermès, *Jesus the Jew*, 90.
703. Ibid.
704. Ibid.
705. Ibid., 98–99.
706. Ibid., 99.
707. Ibid. Examples of those embracing temporary sexual abstinence are soldiers on campaign and those, such as temple ministers, participating in an act of worship.
708. Ibid., 99–100.
709. Ibid., 100. Vermès cites a talmudic tradition relating Moses' decision to remain chaste permanently after receiving his call from God. This example would tend, it seems, to lend support to the view that Jesus may be better perceived as *the* Prophet in the line of Moses, rather than Elijah. One may observe the continued interchange of the words "celibacy," "chastity," and "sexual abstinence." The Christian tradition maintains that Jesus was chaste and presumably unmarried.
710. Ibid., 101. The evidence is scant. Noteworthy, as Vermès also reports, at the end of the first century AD, Rabbi Eliezer ben Hyrcanus and Simeon ben Azzai both compared "deliberate abstention from procreation to murder." John Meier points out that in the Old Testament Jeremiah (Jer 16) was celibate, and so too, possibly, were Elijah and Elisha (as well as, in the New Testament, John the Baptist—from indirection and inference, and presumably Jesus). See John Meier, *A Marginal Jew*, 339–40.
711. Given Vermès's emphasis on the nontitular usage of the phrase "son of Man," he has been criticized as "unorthodox." His latter point, the Greek New Testament's titular evidence, he clarified with me in an e-mail communication, June 16, 2005. Professor Vermès maintains that the original usage of the phrase was "nontitular."
712. Vermès, *The Changing Faces of Jesus*, 254. Given that these written sources, the Mishnah and the Talmud, postdate the figures in question, Vermès does not "argue on the basis of details, but from *typology* that is verifiable in all periods from the age of the prophets down to that of the rabbis (emphasis added)."
713. Ibid., 257, passim.
714. Ibid., 258.
715. Vermès, *Jesus the Jew*, 69.

716. Vermès, *The Chaging Faces of Jesus*, 254. Rabbinic literature refers to this first-century BCE holy man as Honi the Circle-Drawer; Josephus refers to him as Onias the Righteous (69).

717. Vermès, Ibid., 255. The anecdote is found in *m. Ta'anit* 3:8.

718. Vermès, *Jesus the Jew*, 255; the story is found in Josephus, *Ant.* 14.22–24.

719. Vermès, *Jesus the Jew*, 256; Josephus records the story of warring Jewish brothers Aristobulus II, the high priest, and Hyrcanus II during Passover, probably in April 65 BCE. *Ant.* 14:22–24.

720. Ibid. Vermès reports further that "two of Honi's grandsons also had a reputation as charismatic rainmakers with the difference being that they were exceedingly modest, unworldly, and humble, unlike their petulant grandfather."

721. Vermès, *Jesus the Jew*, 72.

722. Ibid., 73.

723. Vermès, *The Changing Faces of Jesus*, 258. Vermès further notes that "to understand the title 'man of deed' one should remember that the miracles of Jesus were also designated as 'deeds' (Luke 24:19; Matt 11:20; Acts 2:22). As to the teaching of Hanina, Vermès writes that he "was better known in rabbinic tradition for his marvels of benevolence than for his teaching, of which precious little has survived" (263).

724. Ibid.

725. Ibid., 259. Rabbinic writings include further examples of a Hasidic lack of enthusiasm about purity regulations; see, for example, "Hanina and the Snake" (ibid., 261). See also *t. Berakot* 3:20 and *b. Berakot* 33a.

726. Ibid., 262.

727. Ibid.

728. Ibid.

729. Vermès, *Jesus the Jew*, 82.

730. Vermès, *The Changing Faces of Jesus*, 264.

731. Ibid.

732. Ibid., 266. For Vermès's survey of "rabbinic praises and quibbles" see 262–66.

733. Ibid., 267–68.

734. Ibid., 269.

735. Ibid.

736. Ibid., 271.

737. The subhead is Vermès's phrase (ibid., 266–80).

738. Ibid., 271.

739. Ibid.

740. Ibid.

741. Ibid.

742. Ibid., 271–74, passim.

743. Ibid., 274.

744. Ibid.

745. Ibid., 275.

746. Ibid.

747. Ibid., 275–76. Vermès, in reply to why Jesus was executed, after considering the pertinent sources, responds: "Had he not been responsible for a fracas in the Temple of Jerusalem at Passover time when Jewish authorities expected the Messiah to reveal himself, very likely Jesus would have escaped with his life. *Doing the wrong thing in the wrong place and in the wrong season resulted in the tragic death of Jesus on the Roman cross*" (ibid., 280, with emphasis added).

748. Ibid., 271.

749. Ibid., 270.

750. Vermès, *Jesus the Jew*, 224.

751. Ibid., 225. For confirmation of continuity, compare this citation with his description of the metamorphosis of Jesus into "the otherworldly Christ" in his more recent text *The Changing Faces of Jesus*, 281–82.

752. Sandmel, *We Jews and Jesus*, 121.

753. Flusser, *Jesus*, 33. Flusser observes also that Luke omits any mention of the profession of carpentry in connection with Joseph or Jesus. The Jewish usage of the term *naggar* is not dependent upon Luke. It is significant that Matthew posits that Jesus was a "carpenter's son" (Matt 13:55), which may imply that Jesus in his early hidden life was also. Though we may not make too much of this, the metaphorical implications of "the carpenter" are thought-provoking.

754. Ibid.

755. Ibid., 16.

756. Vermès, *Jesus the Jew*, 224.

5. Jesus, Jewish Brother

757. Ben-Chorin, *Brother Jesus*, 5.

758. Ben-Chorin, "The Image of Jesus in Modern Judaism," 425.

759. Ben-Chorin, *Brother Jesus*, 8.

760. Ibid.

761. Ibid.

762. Ibid., 9.

763. Ibid.

764. Ibid., 10.

765. Ibid. In this, Ben-Chorin differs with Flusser, who saw Jesus as a young Talmudist. Vermès, on the other hand, is less optimistic than Flusser. Though hailing Jesus as an influential teacher, Vermès does not believe him to be an expert in Jewish law.

766. Ibid., 11. Ben-Chorin does mention a few dubious references found in the Talmud that suggest various teachers of Jesus, such as Yehoshua Ben-Perachia. See also Joseph Klausner, *Jesus of Nazareth: His Life, Times and Teaching*, trans. Herbert Danby (New York: Macmillan, 1925), 24–26. The evidence is unreliable.

767. Ben-Chorin, *Brother Jesus*, 14. Vermès and Flusser would see Jesus' authority as stemming from his charisma as a wonder-working prophet. It is this source

of authority apart from "established authority" that is both a hallmark of the Hasidim and the crux of the tension between Jesus and the Jewish "authorities."

768. Ibid.
769. Ibid., 16.
770. Ibid., 20.
771. Ibid., 24.
772. Ibid., 25.
773. Ibid., 23.
774. Ibid., 66. Ben-Chorin asserts that if any statement of Jesus is authentic, then this arguably is. "For what writer would have made up such a statement?"
775. Ibid. It is also worth mentioning that in describing the lack of wine at the Cana wedding, Ben-Chorin takes the opportunity to comment upon the Essenes and Rechabites, both of whom refused the enjoyment of wine. This being so, Ben-Chorin concludes that Jesus was neither Essene or Rechabite since he enjoyed wine (68).
776. Ibid., 26.
777. Ibid., 27.
778. Ibid. Ben-Chorin describes John "as a type of *shaliach [šālîaḥ]*, an apostle of the sect of Qumran, who pursued an inner mission even as he directed his service to those outside of the community" (33). Though John apparently lived alone, Ben-Chorin posits a close relationship between him and Qumran.
779. Ben-Chorin, "The Image of Jesus in Modern Judaism," 425.
780. Ben-Chorin does, however, observe the differences in John's and Jesus' styles of teaching as similar to that found between the schools of the brusque Shammai and the gentle Hillel (*Brother Jesus*, 38).
781. Ibid., 37.
782. Ibid.
783. Ibid.
784. Ibid., 43.
785. Ibid., 47.
786. Ibid.
787. Ibid.
788. Ibid.
789. Ibid., 52.
790. Ibid., 58.
791. Ben-Chorin, "The Image of Jesus in Modern Judaism," 425.
792. Ben-Chorin, *Brother Jesus*, 62.
793. Ibid., 63. Given this tradition of pseudepigraphy, Ben-Chorin observes, "It is striking that Jesus never mentions an author, but we have reason to assume that the Evangelists, who propagate the undiluted authority of Jesus, consciously or unconsciously repress such references" (62).
794. Ibid., 72.
795. Ben-Chorin, "The Image of Jesus in Modern Judaism," 426. Also see Ben-Chorin's presentation of Jesus and the Seder night, wherein he demonstrates

Jesus' familiarity with sacred Jewish ritual and his creative renewal (*Brother Jesus*, 125–45, chap. 10).

796. Ben-Chorin, *Brother Jesus*, 88.
797. Ibid.
798. Ibid., 89.
799. Ibid., 91. Even so, Ben-Chorin does find it "striking that Jesus does not mention Israel—or make any national reference at all [in his prayers]" (93).
800. Ibid., 94.
801. Ibid., 97.
802. Ibid., 99.
803. Ibid.
804. Ibid., 100.
805. Ibid., 101.
806. Ibid., 102.
807. Ibid., 103.
808. Ibid.
809. Ibid., 106.
810. Ibid., 107.
811. Ben-Chorin, "The Image of Jesus in Modern Judaism," 427.
812. Ben-Chorin, *Brother Jesus*, 109.
813. Ibid.
814. Ibid., 111.
815. Ben-Chorin, "The Image of Jesus in Modern Judaism," 428.
816. Ben-Chorin introduces these three pilgrimages in chap. 9 of *Brother Jesus*, 112—24.
817. Ibid., 123.
818. Ibid., 114.
819. Ibid., 115. Ben-Chorin accepts that the entry into Jerusalem by some "prophet" from Nazareth might catch the attention of onlookers, but he contends it would have been less a victory procession as passage among curious onlookers—under the alert, wary eyes of the temple authorities (116).
820. Ibid., 116.
821. Ibid., 118.
822. Ibid., 119. One might see, or expect Ben-Chorin to agree, that both events, the confrontation with the money changers in the temple area *and* the coin of tribute, would constitute more than sufficient provocation, given the authorities' para-noia. However, Ben-Chorin *denies* the historicity of the Jesus' confrontation with the money changers. He argues that "the story that Jesus, armed with a whip of cords, overturned tables of the money changers and drove out the clerks of the temple bench is *too adventurous to be true*." He adds, curiously, "It is hard to believe that a disturbance of public order (or disorder) of this magnitude would not have provoked arrest." He sees the Gospel account as fulfillment legend (cf. Zech 14:21; ibid., 119, with added emphasis). And yet, just before his assertion, he seems to give credence to Jesus' "outrage" over the condition of the temple (Matt 21:13; ibid., 118). Cf. Jacob Neusner: "The overturning of

the money-changers' table, as we have seen, represents an act of the rejection of the most important rite of the Israelite cult, the daily whole offering, and therefore, a statement that there is a means of atonement other than the daily whole offering, which is null" (*Jews and Christians*, 101).

823. Ben-Chorin, *Brother Jesus*, 120.
824. Ibid.
825. Ibid., 121.
826. Ibid.
827. Ibid., 122.
828. Ibid.
829. Ibid.
830. Ibid.
831. Ibid.
832. Ibid., 123.
833. Ibid., 148.
834. Ibid.
835. Ibid., 149.
836. Ibid.
837. Ibid., 150.
838. Ibid., 150–51.
839. Ibid., 153. For his reference to the fifth cup, see 149–50. His use of an image from the Letter to the Hebrews as an image of Jesus coincides with Sandmel's suggestion that the Letter to the Hebrews forms a "Fifth Gospel," one "calculated by its author to avoid the difficulties encountered by the four existing Gospels" (*We Jews and Jesus*, 127).
840. Ben-Chorin, *Brother Jesus*, 158.
841. Ibid. Ben-Chorin also does not believe, as some argue, that one may dismiss the possibility of this pretrial or night hearing inasmuch as the Gospel record contradicts Jewish trial procedure. He cites contemporary abuses to drive home his point that political trials, like Jesus', "are not always conducted in harmony with every paragraph of legal protocol" (162).
842. Ibid., 159.
843. Ibid.
844. Ibid., 160.
845. Ibid., 160–61.
846. Ibid., 164.
847. Ibid., 172. Ben-Chorin even allows for the possibility of the self-cursing of the Jewish mob (Matt 27:25), saying that it was at least possible and citing a similar formulation in the oath of David (2 Sam 1:16; ibid., 170).
848. Ibid., 17. See also Ben-Chorin, "The Image of Jesus in Modern Judaism," 428–29.
849. Ben-Chorin, *Brother Jesus*, 17.
850. Ibid.
851. Ibid.

852. Ibid. 'Akiva (Akiba) Ben-Yosef (ca. 50–135 CE) was considered to be the greatest scholar of his generation. The Bar-Kokhba Rebellion (132 CE) is today viewed as one of the greatest catastrophes in Jewish history. Rabbi 'Akiva was subsequently executed by the Romans for refusing to comply with their ban on the study of the Torah. To this day he is considered to be one of the greatest of Jewish martyrs. For detailed editor's note, see ibid., 191n9. The hasidic quotation "Out of love . . . " is found in Martin Buber's text *Die chassidischen Bücher* (Hellerau: Hegner, 1928), 460. Cf. Ben-Chorin, "The Image of Jesus in Modern Judaism," 429.

853. Ben-Chorin, "The Image of Jesus in Modern Judaism," 429.

854. Ibid., 427–28.

855. Ibid., 424. Rabbi Israel Baal Shem (the Besht) is the founder of modern Hasidim, an influential eighteen-century Jewish mystical movement as a reaction to the rigid academicism of rabbinic Judaism. This group is not to be confused with Vermès's Hasidim, the ancient Devout Ones.

856. Ibid., 412.

857. Lapide, *The Resurrection of Jesus*, 30.

858. Ibid.

859. For reference, see Lapide, *Jesus in Two Perspectives*, 14.

860. Lapide, *Israelis, Jews, and Jesus*, 33, with emphasis added.

861. Apart from the transcripts of ecumenical conversation, Pinchas Lapide wrote several small books on Jesus, including *Der Rabbi von Nazaret: Wandlungen des jüdischen Jesusbildes* (Trier: Spee, 1974) and *Wurde Gott Jude? Vom Menschsein Jesu* (Munich: Kösel, 1987); neither has been translated into English. His position in these books, however, is consistent with his translated publications.

862. Pinchas Lapide, *Three Popes and the Jews* (New York: Hawthorn Books, 1967), 14.

863. Ibid., 15.

864. Ibid., 16. Ben-Chorin is content to say regarding Jesus' origins: "The birth of Jesus lies in darkness" (16).

865. Ibid.,16–17, passim.

866. Ibid., 17–18, passim. Lapide apparently is unaware of the metaphorical sense of "carpenter," meaning a learned person, previously mentioned by Flusser and Vermès.

867. Ibid., 18.

868. Ibid., 19.

869. Ibid., 21.

870. Ibid., 22.

871. Pinchas Lapide, "Two Famous Rabbis," *Annual of the Swedish Theological Institutes*, vol. 10, ed. B. Knutson (Leiden: Brill, 1976), 97, with punctuation adapted. Lapide, as does Ben-Chorin, draws a strong parallel between Jesus and the eighteenth-century Rabbi Israel Baal Shem of Mezibezh (the Besht). Both Lapide and Ben-Chorin emphasize the eighteenth-century Hasidim in comparison to Jesus, whereas Flusser and certainly Vermès stress Jesus' affinity with

the ancient Hasidim of Palestinian charismatic Judaism. There is no explanation for the distinction; it may have to do with what is more familiar to the author.

872. Ibid.

873. Ibid.

874. Ibid., 109.

875. Lapide, *Encountering Jesus—Encountering Judaism*, 82–83.

876. Lapide, *Jesus in Two Perspectives*, 24.

877. Ibid.

878. For the essentials of his rebuttal, see ibid., 45–46, 78–79, 85, and 108–9, respectively.

879. Ibid., 83.

880. Lapide, *The Sermon on the Mount*, 7.

881. Ibid., 7–8.

882. Ibid., 8.

883. Lapide in *Brother or Lord?* 25.

884. Lapide, *Jesus in Two Perspectives*, 18–19. Regarding Jewish "nontheology," which typified Jesus' teaching, see 19. For Lapide's defense of Jesus' pedagogical style as Jewish, see *Israelis, Jews, and Jesus*, 80–81.

885. Lapide, *Jesus in Two Perspectives*, 140, which also gives a précis of the Jews' positive acceptance of Jesus.

886. Ibid., 141.

887. Ibid.

888. Ibid.

889. Lapide in *Brother or Lord?* 26–27.

890. Ibid., 27.

891. Küng and Lapide fail to resolve their differences on this point. See Küng's response in *Brother or Lord?* 28, 30, 32–33. "In brief, precepts exist for men and not men for precepts." Such a position placed Jesus' life in peril.

892. Lapide, *The Sermon on the Mount*, 10.

893. Ibid. Underscoring his point, he adds: "After all, Beethoven did not invent a single new note to compose the Ninth Symphony, his immortal masterpiece."

894. Ibid., 13–14. Lapide emphasizes: "Jesus did not say 'law' but 'torah,' which means 'directive' or 'teaching.' The word has more of a sense of promise, fulfillment, salvation history, and ethos about it than of actual law and rule" (15).

895. Ibid., 14.

896. Ibid.

897. Ibid.

898. Ibid. Lapide, in his defense of Jesus' fidelity to Torah, explains the word "radical" as coming from "*radix*—source, stem, or root; Jesus wishes to penetrate to the roots of the Torah" (15). For Lapide's reaction to those who insist otherwise, see also 42–43. For his insistence that Jesus never abandoned the ground of his pluralistic Judaism, see 44–45.

899. Ibid., 97.

900. Ibid., 96.

901. Ibid., 98. Accompanying this latter assertion, Lapide offers a parallel episode from the Talmud: *t. Ber.* 10a.
902. Ibid., 100–101.
903. Ibid., 102.
904. Ibid., 102–3, with added emphasis.
905. Ibid., 103.
906. Ibid.
907. Ibid., 103–4.
908. Ibid., 104.
909. Ibid.
910. Lapide, *Jesus in Two Perspectives*, 112. Though Lapide attributes Jesus' death, at the hands of the Romans, to sedition and not blasphemy, Küng asserts the involvement of some Jewish authorities, such as the Sadducees, who feared Jesus' interpretation of Jewish law and his emphasis on ethics over cultic worship. Here, in Küng, we find echoes of the evangelists' memories. Profanation of the temple, an echo of Ben-Chorin's assessment, leads some Jews to silence Jesus. Their plot escalates and reaches its climax before Pontius Pilate, the Roman procurator. In Küng's estimation, Pilate condemns Jesus to death as a political rebel—though the action was religiously and politically motivated. Lapide does not yield. See *Brother or Lord?* 33–37. Ben-Chorin differs with Lapide on this point.
911. Lapide, *Jesus in Two Perspectives*, 112.
912. Ibid., 113.
913. Ibid., 114.
914. Ibid., 114–15.
915. Lapide, *The Resurrection of Jesus*, 30.
916. Ibid., 31.
917. Ibid.
918. Ibid., 43.
919. Ibid., 32. Lapide, in light of the New Testament witness, affirms: "Resurrection, exaltation, and glorification are understood not as Jesus' own deed but, in good Jewish manner, as a raising by God, as a gracious deed of God on the crucified Jesus" (33).
920. For this explanation, see ibid., 55.
921. Ibid., 64, with emphasis added.
922. Ibid., 65.
923. Ibid.
924. Ibid., 83–84.
925. Ibid., 88.
926. Ibid., 88–89.
927. Ibid., 89.
928. Ibid., 90. Lapide sees a modern parallel of this categorical *must* in the creed scrawled upon a wall by an unknown Jew caught in the "inferno of genocide," the besieged Warsaw ghetto.
929. Ibid., 92.

930. Ibid., with emphasis added. Flusser describes the resurrection of Jesus as part of a metahistorical drama (*Jesus*, 175–76).
931. Ibid.
932. Ibid., 93.
933. Ibid.
934. Lapide, in Pinchas Lapide and Jürgen Moltmann, *Jewish Monotheism and Christian Trinitarian Doctrine: A Dialogue by Pinchas Lapide and Jürgen Moltmann*, trans. Leonard Swidler (Philadelphia: Fortress, 1981), 59. Lapide, however, does not explain the "how" of the appearances: "The manner in which the resurrection took place is today just as uncertain as it was in Hillel's time, when controversy concerning the general resurrection of the dead occupied rabbis (*Genesis Rabbah* 14 and *Leviticus Rabbah* 14) but wisely was left open." Citing the Jesuit, F. Lentzen-Deis, "The whole *how* of the appearances remains closed to us," Lapide concurs (*The Resurrection of Jesus*, 127).
935. Lapide, in *Jewish Monotheism and Christian Trinitarian Doctrine*, 60, with emphasis added. Though Vermès does not embrace Lapide's thesis vis-à-vis the resurrection of Jesus, he does affirm: "His [Jesus'] magnetic appeal became more powerful after his death than it could ever have been during his transient ministry in the late twenties of the first century in Galilee of Herod Antipas and the Jerusalem of Joseph Caiaphas, the high priest, and Pontius Pilate, the imperial legate of Judea" (*The Changing Faces of Jesus*, 275). Cf. Sandmel's comments on "an initial significant alteration in the Messianic pattern" vis-à-vis Jesus' death (*We Jews and Jesus*, 33). These authors, with different emphases, acknowledge the subsequent effects of Jesus' death upon the fledging community of believers.
936. Lapide, *The Resurrection of Jesus*, 135.
937. Ibid.
938. Ibid., 136.
939. Ibid.
940. Lapide, in *Jewish Monotheism and Christian Trinitarian Doctrine*, 68.
941. Ibid.
942. Lapide, *The Resurrection of Jesus*, 116.
943. Ibid., 117–18.
944. Ibid., 118. He also argues in this vein: "True faith experience has never been a mass phenomenon but the special gift of a few, of the clairaudient, of the metaphysically gifted, and of the sensitive"—among whom he includes Abraham and Moses (119).
945. In *Jesus in Two Perspectives*, Lapide explains: "God's pedagogy, as the medieval Jewish scholar Maimonides taught, made use of trusted thought-patterns and traditional practices gradually to lead humanity to higher insights" (116).
946. Lapide, *The Resurrection of Jesus*, 122.
947. Ibid., 123–25.
948. Ibid., 126.
949. Ibid., 128.

950. Ibid. Lapide, given the survival-after-martyrdom theme, also draws a parallel between the resurrection of Jesus and the creation of the modern State of Israel: "The same abyss yawns between cross and resurrection as between the mass Golgotha of the Hitler years and the national resurrection in the year 1948" (ibid., 149).

951. Lapide, in *Jewish Monotheism and Christian Trinitarian Doctrine*, 71, with emphasis added. Lapide, referring to emerging Christianity, states in *The Resurrection of Jesus*: "The resurrection of Jesus was ambiguous as an event, but unambiguous in the history of its effect" (144).

952. Lapide, in *Jewish Monotheism and Christian Trinitarian Doctrine*, 71.

953. Lapide, *The Resurrection of Jesus*, 142–43.

954. Lapide, *Jesus in Two Perspectives*, 116–17.

955. Ibid., 117.

956. Ibid., 117–18.

957. Lapide, in *Jewish Monotheism and Christian Trinitarian Doctrine*, 74.

958. Ibid., 79. Here Lapide is quoting Moltmann, *The Church in the Power of the Spirit* (New York: Harper & Row, 1977), 139. See Moltmann's nuanced response in *Jewish Monotheism and Christian Trinitarian Doctrine*, 74.

959. Lapide, *The Resurrection of Jesus*, 146.

960. Ibid., 152.

961. Ibid., 153.

962. Ibid., 153–54. Lapide's thesis, that there are at least two paths to the Father, meaning Judaism and Christianity, is influenced by Franz Rosenzweig (*The Star of Redemption*, trans. Barbara E. Galli [Madison: University of Wisconsin Press, 2005]; and *Briefe* (Berlin: Schocken, 1935). Lapide's comment regarding multiple paths of salvation is in *Jewish Monotheism and Christian Trinitarian Doctrine*, 59. Also see Martin Buber, *Two Types of Faith*, trans. Norman Goldhawk with an afterword by David Flusser (Syracuse, NY: Syracuse University Press, 2003).

963. Lapide, *Three Popes and the Jews*, 32.

964. Ibid., 31. Apropos of Jesus as tragic figure, Lapide shares Ben-Chorin's assessment of Jesus' downward spiral (31–32). Also see Ben-Chorin, "The Image of Jesus in Modern Judaism," 428–29.

965. Lapide, *Three Popes and the Jews*, 33.

966. Neusner, *A Rabbi Talks with Jesus*, 7. Though Neusner agrees that the historical Jesus is a presence within and behind the Gospels, he chooses to engage the Jesus known through the Gospels—in this case, Matthew's Gospel. He does so because this is the Jesus the readers of the Gospel encounter when they read the text.

967. For the Gospel of Matthew as Jewish literature, see Daniel J. Harrington, *The Gospel of Matthew* (Collegeville, MN: Liturgical Press, 1991), 1–20, esp. 17–18.

968. Neusner, *A Rabbi Talks with Jesus*, 5, with his emphasis. Flusser and Vermès would disagree with Neusner. Cf. David Flusser, in the foreword to Thoma, *A Christian Theology of Judaism*, 16: "Even though he [Jesus] gave his own

personal bent on Jewish ideas, selected from among them, purged and reinterpreted them, I cannot honestly find a single word of Jesus that could seriously exasperate a well-intentioned Jew." Cf. Vermès, *The Religion of Jesus the Jew*, 47, 70–75, speaking of Jesus' elasticity vis-à-vis the Torah.

969. Neusner offers a new point of departure, of which the above is paradigmatic, for the Jewish-Christian dialogue/relations: complementarity. See Neusner, *Jews and Christians*, 105–16; for examples of Neusner's approach, see 120ff.

970. Neusner, *A Rabbi Talks with Jesus*, 8. On Jesus as Jewish teacher, see also Harrington, *The Gospel of Matthew*, 17–18.

971. Neusner, *A Rabbi Talks with Jesus*, 8.

972. Ibid.

973. Ibid., 19.

974. Ibid., 8. For his explanation of eternal Israel, meaning Israel, see 58.

975. Ibid., 9.

976. Ibid. Neusner reminds the reader: "Once again, in Judaism, argument forms a principal means of religious discourse: it is how we talk with one another, the way in which we show our esteem and respect for the other" (29).

977. Ibid., 7. In his 1974 review of Géza Vermès's *Jesus the Jew*, Neusner, digressing, compares Jesus with other Jewish teachers, not simply with Honi and Hanina, and deems the rabbinic sages greater than Jesus. Though he affirms Jesus as a Jewish teacher, a contemporary among others, Neusner, at least not in the review, does not yet charge him with violating Torah and teaching erroneously—as he does twenty years later in *A Rabbi Talks with Jesus*. See Jacob Neusner, "Jesus as Jew," review of *Jesus the Jew*, by Géza Vermès, *Mainstream*, December 1974, 72.

978. Neusner, *A Rabbi Talks with Jesus*, 9.

979. Ibid., 4, with his emphasis.

980. Ibid., 22.

981. Ibid.

982. Ibid. Neusner will challenge at least three teachings that Jesus makes, calling them erroneous and misleading. Vermès differs with Neusner. Of Jesus' torah and the Torah, Vermès asserts, given the "antitheses" (Matt 5:21–48) in question: "However, when objectively analyzed, his [Jesus] declarations strengthen and clarify, rather than contradict, the Torah" (*The Changing Faces of Jesus*, 211).

983. Neusner, *A Rabbi Talks with Jesus*, 23. See also Matt 5:17–20.

984. Ibid.

985. Neusner explains this crucial difference between Torah and torah: "Torah with a capital *T* stands for God's revelation to Moses at Mount Sinai. When we write 'torah' with a small *t*, we mean, 'the instruction of a master—in the context of the teaching of the Torah.' It is a somewhat odd shift; what Jesus does is teach the Torah, and what he teaches also is torah. . . . He is a teacher of the Torah, so in the framework of the Torah, he teaches the Torah and he himself adds to the Torah: so his is a labor of torah too" (ibid., 21).

986. Ibid., 7, with his emphasis. I have placed Jesus' words or passages from Matthew in italics to differentiate them from Neusner's dialogue with Jesus. Neusner's debate is presented in normal block style or within quotation marks for concise responses, as he does. Finally, Neusner chooses to place in italics certain quotes from Jewish literature. I follow his pattern in that regard also, so as to show *his* emphasis.

987. Ibid., 20.

988. Ibid., 36.

989. Ibid., 38.

990. For a list and explanation of the six antitheses, see Harrington, *The Gospel of Matthew*, 85–93.

991. Neusner, *A Rabbi Talks with Jesus*, 43.

992. At issue here is Jesus' focus on individual, private prayer over against hypocritical, public piety. Neusner points out that though the Torah recognizes prayer offered by individuals, "the Torah also calls upon Israel to serve God in community, in the Temple, for example, and the notion that the only valid prayer is offered up in secret is something the Torah surely will find difficult to sustain" (50).

993. C. G. Montefiore, *The Synoptic Gospels* (1927; repr., New York: Ktav, 1968), 71.

994. Neusner, *A Rabbi Talks with Jesus*, 44.

995. Ibid., 45.

996. Ibid.

997. Ibid.

998. Ibid.

999. Ibid., 45–46.

1000. Ibid., 46.

1001. Ibid., 47.

1002. Ibid.

1003. Ibid.

1004. Ibid., 48.

1005. Ibid., 49.

1006. Ibid., 50.

1007. Ibid., 52.

1008. Ibid.

1009. Ibid., chaps. 4, 5, and 6, respectively. The third violation involves God's instruction preserved in Lev 19:1–5. Leviticus 19:1–37 represents a blending of cultic requirements and ethical obligations, as expressed classically in the Ten Commandments. See also Exod 20:2–17.

1010. Ibid., 56.

1011. Ibid., 57.

1012. Ibid., 58.

1013. Ibid., 54.

1014. Ibid., 58.

1015. Ibid., 60.

1016. Ibid., 67–68.
1017. Ibid., 68.
1018. Ibid.
1019. Ibid., 70.
1020. Ibid.
1021. Ibid., 71.
1022. Ibid., 71–72.
1023. Ibid., 72.
1024. Ibid., with his emphasis.
1025. Ibid.
1026. Ibid., 75. Neusner builds his argument on the Sabbath commandment as a re-membrance of creation, following Exod 20:8–11. However, in Deut 15:5, as Harrington points out, "it is a remembrance of the exodus from Egypt" (*The Gospel of Matthew*, 175).
1027. Neusner, *A Rabbi Talks with Jesus*, 75.
1028. Ibid., 76.
1029. Ibid., 77.
1030. Ibid., 78.
1031. Ibid., 79–82.
1032. Ibid., 81.
1033. Ibid., 85.
1034. Ibid., 86.
1035. Ibid.
1036. Ibid., 87.
1037. Ibid., 87–88.
1038. Ibid., 88.
1039. Ibid., 90.
1040. Ibid.
1041. Ibid., 91.
1042. Ibid.
1043. Ibid., 95–96.
1044. Ibid., 96.
1045. Ibid.
1046. Ibid.
1047. Ibid.
1048. Ibid., 96–97.
1049. Ibid., 97.
1050. Ibid.
1051. Ibid., 99.
1052. Ibid., 100.
1053. Ibid.
1054. Ibid., 100–102.
1055. Ibid., 102.
1056. Ibid., 102–3.
1057. Ibid., 103.

1058. Ibid., 112, with emphasis added in the first sentence.

1059. Ibid., 121.

1060. Ibid., 121–22.

1061. Ibid., 122.

1062. Ibid.

1063. Ibid.

1064. Ibid. In this latter assessment resides Neusner's critique of modern ecumenical dialogue. Implicit in his "argument" with Jesus is his paradigm for true dialogue among religions (122–23).

1065. Ibid., 134–50, esp. 145–46. "For the Pharisees, uncleanliness functioned on a different framework from ethics" (145).

1066. Ibid., 123.

1067. Ibid.

1068. Ibid.

1069. Ibid., 127–28.

1070. Ibid., 130.

1071. Ibid., 150.

1072. Ibid., 91.

1073. Ibid., 156.

1074. Ibid.

1075. Ibid., 129. Although nearly all the Jewish scholars embracing *Heimholung* fault Paul for the aberration, a departure from the expected, which resulted in Christianity, Neusner credits Jesus with the distortion of the Torah and thus the lack of continuity or common origin between Judaism and Christianity (*Jews and Christians*, 120).

1076. Borowitz, "Jesus the Jew in the Light of the Jewish-Christian Dialogue," 17.

1077. Ibid.

1078. Ibid.

1079. Eugene Borowitz, "The Challenge of Jesus the Jew for the Church," in *Proceedings of the Center for Jewish-Christian Learning*, vol. 2 (Spring 1987), 24.

1080. Ibid.

1081. Borowitz, "Jesus the Jew in the Light of the Jewish-Christian Dialogue," 17.

1082. Ibid.

1083. Ibid.

1084. Ibid.

1085. Ibid.

1086. Ibid.

1087. Ibid.

1088. Ibid.

1089. Ibid.

1090. Ibid.

1091. Ibid.

1092. Borowitz, "The Challenge of Jesus the Jew for the Church," 24.

1093. Borowitz, "Jesus the Jew in the Light of the Jewish-Christian Dialogue," 17.

1094. Ibid.

1095. Borowitz, "The Challenge of Jesus the Jew for the Church," 24.

1096. Borowitz, "Jesus the Jew in the Light of the Jewish-Christian Dialogue," 17.

1097. Ibid.

1098. Ibid.

1099. Ibid.

1100. Ibid.

1101. Ibid.

1102. Ibid., with added emphasis.

1103. Ibid.

1104. Ibid.

1105. Ibid.

1106. Ibid.

1107. Ibid.

6. "Novelty and Originality"

1108. James H. Charlesworth, in *Images of Jesus Today*, ed. James H. Charlesworth and Walter P. Weaver (Valley Forge, PA: Trinity International Press, 1994), 27. See also, Maurice Merleau-Ponty, *Phenomenology of Perception*, trans. Colin Smith (New York: Routledge, 1962), 67–68: "It is necessary to put the surroundings in abeyance the better to see the object, and to lose in background what one gains in focal figure. . . . Objects form a system in which one cannot show itself without concealing others."

1109. Charlesworth, in *Images of Jesus Today*, 27.

1110. One need only peruse the jacket cover of the second printing of *We Jews and Jesus* in June 1965 to gain an appreciation of its praiseworthy acceptance among Jews—to whom the text was addressed. Sandmel's *A Jewish Understanding of the New Testament* has appeared in a new printing (Woodstock, VT: SkyLight Paths, 2004); his son, Rabbi David Sandmel, has written the preface for this classic.

1111. Silas Musholt, review of *We Jews and Jesus*, by Samuel Sandmel, *Catholic Biblical Quarterly* 27 (July 1965): 290–91.

1112. Paul Winter, "The Person of Jesus," review of *We Jews and Jesus*, by Samuel Sandmel, *Commentary* 40, no. 3 (September 1965): 108.

1113. Ibid.

1114. Ibid., 110.

1115. Isaac Jacob, review of *We Jews and Jesus*, by Samuel Sandmel, *Journal of Ecumenical Studies* 3 (Winter 1966): 169.

1116. Ibid.

1117. Ibid.

1118. Ibid.

1119. Susannah Heschel, *Abraham Geiger and the Jewish Jesus* (Chicago: University of Chicago Press, 1998), 237.

1120. Clinton Bennett, *In Search of Jesus: Insider and Outsider Images* (New York: Continuum, 2001), 265. Also see Rosenzweig, *The Star of Redemption*.

1121. Lapide, *Israelis, Jews, and Jesus*, 153. Lapide, commenting on Sandmel's *A Jewish Understanding of the New Testament*, also credits Sandmel with providing "the first purely scientific study undertaken by a rabbi of the Christian Scriptures" (146).

1122. Ben-Chorin, "The Image of Jesus in Modern Judaism," 411.

1123. Ibid.

1124. Donald A. Hagner, *The Jewish Reclamation of Jesus* (Eugene, OR: Wipf & Stock, 1997), 32. Hagner's text provides a survey of select Jewish authors and cogent criticisms thereof—from an evangelical Christian perspective. Though a "useful bibliographical tool," Brad Young, a former student of Flusser, finds that Hagner "fails to grasp the significance of the contribution of the Jewish writers." Young views Hagner's efforts as a "digression" rather than a contribution ("Jewish Scholarship and Jesus," *Immanuel*, no. 19 [Winter 1984/85]: 102–6).

1125. Hagner, *The Jewish Reclamation of Jesus*, 75.

1126. Ibid., 80.

1127. Ibid., 82.

1128. Ibid., 83.

1129. Ibid., 81–82.

1130. G. David Schwartz, "Explorations and Responses: Is There a Jewish Reclamation of Jesus?" *Journal of Ecumenical Studies* 24, no. 1 (Winter 1987): 106–7.

1131. Jacob Neusner in a personal e-mail to me, December 5, 2004. Commenting in this same e-mail on my list of Jewish authors, he adds: "I have a very high opinion of Borowitz's Jewish Christology [referring to *Contemporary Christologies: A Jewish Response*]; the others on your list are looking for a Jewish position that mediates between Judaism and Christianity by Judaizing Jesus and Christianizing Judaism." Reaffirmed, September 18, 2005.

1132. Neusner, *Telling Tales*, 84. Judaic Christology is a phrase used pejoritvely to describe the legitimacy in which modern Judaism has cloaked Jesus, endowing Rabbi Jesus, in Neusner's estimation, "with a valid pedigree and vocation" (85). For an appreciation of Judaic Christology, see also 86–88. The phrase "dual monologues" captures the essence of Neusner's critique of the modern Jewish-Christian dialogue. See, 81–86, esp. 86.

1133. Ibid., 86–87.

1134. Ibid., 89.

1135. Ibid., 88. Though Neusner finds Sandmel's nuanced Judaic Christology praiseworthy, he finds the Jewish designation of Jesus as Rabbi (Reform Rabbi) inherent in the Judaic Christology as inconsequential ("trivial") in general (85–88).

1136. Ibid., 88–89. See also Sandmel, *We Jews and Jesus*, 44–45.

1137. Sandmel, *We Jews and Jesus*, 44–45.

1138. Ben-Chorin, "The Image of Jesus in Modern Judaism," 416.

1139. Ben-Chorin, *Brother Jesus*, viii.

1140. Ben-Chorin, *Bruder Jesus: Der Nazarener in jüdischer Sicht*, 3rd ed. (1970; repr., Munich: List, 1972), 231.

1141. Ibid., 232.

1142. Ibid., 234.

1143. Pinchas Lapide, "Jesus in Israeli Literature," *Journal of Theology for Southern Africa* 5 (December 1973): 54.

1144. Hagner, *The Jewish Reclamation of Jesus*, 33.

1145. Ibid., 249.

1146. Harvey Cox, "Rabbi Yeshua ben Yoseph: Reflections on Jesus' Jewishness and the Interfaith Dialogue," in *Jesus' Jewishness*, ed. James H. Charlesworth, 39–40. Ben-Chorin coined the phrase *Heimholung Jesu*, Jesus' homecoming, which became synonymous with the Jewish reclamation of Jesus.

1147. Géza Vermès, review of *Brother Jesus: The Nazarene through Jewish Eyes*, by Schalom Ben-Chorin, *Journal of Jewish Studies* 56, no. 1 (Spring 2005): 178. Here, perhaps, we have an echo of G. David Schwartz's thesis, that Liberal Jews write about Jesus in defense of Reform Judaism.

1148. Amy-Jill Levine, review of *Brother Jesus: The Nazarene through Jewish Eyes*, by Schalom Ben-Chorin, *Journal of the American Academy of Religion* 73, no. 1 (Spring 2005): 222. Levine is professor of New Testament Studies at Vanderbilt University Divinity School, Nashville. She is also New Testament Book Review Editor for *The Catholic Biblical Quarterly*.

1149. Ibid.

1150. Ibid., 223.

1151. Ibid.

1152. Ibid.

1153. Ibid.

1154. Ibid.

1155. Ibid.

1156. Ibid.

1157. Ibid., 224.

1158. Ibid.

1159. Ibid.

1160. Ibid.

1161. Ibid., with emphasis added.

1162. David Flusser with Steven R. Notley, *Jesus in Selbstzeugnissen und Bilddokumenten*, corrected and augmented 3rd ed. (Jerusalem: Hebrew University magnes Press, 2001), 13. Flusser goes on to explain that "the uneventfulness of the English translation" provided the impetus for this current text.

1163. Ibid., 15.

1164. Pinchas Lapide, "Jesus in Israeli Literature," 54.

1165. Ibid. In Lapide's conversation with Hans Küng, Küng criticizes Flusser's liberal view of Jesus, implying that both Flusser and Lapide cast a Jesus in their own liberal image. Given Jesus' stance vis-à-vis the Torah, Küng argues: "At every turn he [Jesus] acts in a way that was not foreseen in the Old Testament. And it must be admitted, I think, that it is not so easy to turn him into a Liberal Jew as, for instance, your co-religionist and theological colleague David Flusser—whom I greatly respect—has done in his book on Jesus. If he had been merely a Liberal Jew, he would have had no more difficulties than—for instance—the liberal rabbi, Hillel" (Küng in *Brother or Lord?* 28).

1166. Ben-Chorin, "The Image of Jesus in Modern Judaism," 412. Given Ben-Chorin's own assessment of his efforts in *Brother Jesus* as piecework (see n. 1145, above), as incomplete, one senses the same connotation in his description of Flusser's efforts as piecemeal. No pejorative meaning is thought to be intended.

1167. Ibid. Hagner agrees with this assessment (*The Reclamation of Jesus*, 34).

1168. Hagner, *The Jewish Reclamation of Jesus*, 78.

1169. Ibid.

1170. Ibid.

1171. Ibid.

1172. Ibid., 79.

1173. See Flusser, *Jesus*, 11 and 15, respectively.

1174. Hagner, *The Jewish Reclamation of Jesus*, 95–98.

1175. Ibid., 95.

1176. Ibid., 96. For Hagner's citation of Lapide, see Lapide, *Der Rabbi von Nazaret*, 52.

1177. Craig A. Evans, review of *Jesus*, revised 1997 edition, by David Flusser, *Mishkan* 33 (2000): 86.

1178. Ibid.

1179. Ibid., 86–87.

1180. Ibid., 87.

1181. Ibid.

1182. Ibid.

1183. Ibid.

1184. Ibid., 88–89, passim.

1185. Ibid., 89.

1186. Ibid., 90–91.

1187. Ibid., 91.

1188. Hagner, *The Jewish Reclamation of Jesus*, 34.

1189. Lapide, *Israelis, Jews, and Jesus*, ix.

1190. Ibid., ix–x.

1191. Ibid., x.

1192. David P. Scaer, review of *Ist das nicht Josephs Sohn?* by Pinchas Lapide, *Concordia Theological Quarterly* 49, no. 4 (October 1985): 311.

1193. Paul M. van Buren, "A Positive Jewish Theology of the Church," *Commonweal* 24 (October 1986): 564.

1194. Ibid.

1195. Ibid.

1196. Ibid.

1197. Ibid.

1198. Ibid., 565.

1199. Ibid.

1200. Ibid.

1201. James H. Charlesworth, in *Jesus' Jewishness*, 274. Luz acknowledges that Lapide touches upon some of these difficulties. He also believed that no authentic religious dialogue between Jew and Christian may take place until the "rubbish heaps," the historic animosities, have been acknowledged and redressed (*Jesus in Two Perspectives*, 124, 158–60). Though perhaps more nuanced, Luz shares Lapide's optimism vis-à-vis the historical reliability of sources.

1202. Lapide in *Brother or Lord?* 41. In the introduction to the 1977 English translation (*Brother or Lord?*) of *Jesus im Widerstreit*, Rabbi Hugo Gryn expresses a debt of gratitude to both Lapide and Küng "for being part of that small band of post-Holocaust theologians who want to make a deliberate change in past attitudes and to replace the misconceptions of opponents with the insights of friends." Archbishop George Appleton, who also provides an introduction in the same edition, describes the two theologians' efforts as "friendly and open-minded." Each speaks "frankly of the heart of his own faith and is ready to be probed and eager to probe in return."

1203. Cullen I. K. Story, review of *The Resurrection of Jesus*, by Pinchas Lapide, *Theology Today* 42 (January 1986): 564, http://theologytoday.ptsem.edu/jan1986/v42-4-booknotes15.htm (accessed September 29, 2007). James Dunn asks in what sense we may speak of the resurrection of Jesus as historical and posits the image of metaphor: "the phrase is saying *something which could not otherwise be said*" (878) as a viable response (*Jesus Remembered*, 876–79, esp. 878).

1204. Wendell W. Frerichs, review of *Jewish Monotheism and Christian Trinitarian Doctrine*, by Pinchas Lapide, *Word and World* 1, no. 2 (1982): 92.

1205. Gerald O'Collins, SJ, review of *The Resurrection of Jesus*, by Pinchas Lapide, *Heythrop Journal* 26 (January 1985): 58.

1206. Ibid. See also Pheme Perkins, review of *The Resurrection of Jesus*, by Pinchas Lapide, *Theological Studies* 45 (September 1984): 555–56.

1207. Joseph Sievers, "Jesus of Nazareth as Seen by Jewish Writers of the XX Century," http://www.vatican.va/jubilee_2000/magazine/documents/ju_mag_01111997_p-48_en.html (accessed September 29, 2007). This is an updated version of an article that appeared in *Nuova Umanità* 64/65 (July–October 1989): 125–36; and in an abbreviated form in *Unità e Carismi* 6 (November/December 1996): 33–38.

1208. Bennett, *In Search of Jesus*, 269.

1209. Religious News Service, *Christianity Today* 28, no. 4 (March 2, 1984): 69.

1210. *Time*, May 7, 1979, 88.

1211. Vermès, *Jesus and His Jewish Context*, 2.

1212. Ibid.

1213. Ibid.

1214. James Dunn, as we have indicated, concurs, acclaiming Vermès as the *John the Baptist of the third quest*. E. P. Sanders, in his review of Vermès's more recent book *The Changing Faces of Jesus*, while agreeing with Dunn, goes further by asserting that "in Vermès Jesus has found his best Jewish interpreter" ("In Quest of the Historical Jesus," review of *The Changing Faces of Jesus*, by Géza Vermès, *The New York Review of Books* 48, no. 18 (November 15, 2001): 8, http://www.nybooks.com/articles/article-preview?article_id=14789 (accessed September 29, 2007).

1215. Géza Vermès, "Jesus the Jew: Christian and Jewish Reactions," *Toronto Journal of Theology* 4, no. 1 (Spring 1988): 118. Both academic critique and Vermès's response to same, when available, will follow Vermès's survey. For a concise summary of three objections raised against Vermès and his brief responses, see the preface of his *Jesus and the World of Judaism* (1983), vii–x.

1216. Vermès, "Jesus the Jew: Christian and Jewish Reactions," 118.

1217. Many of the sources for the citations that follow are included in the Related Bibliography of this study.

1218. Ibid.

1219. Ibid., 118–19.

1220. Ibid., 119.

1221. Ibid.

1222. Vermès, *Jesus in His Jewish Context*, 132–33.

1223. Ibid., 133.

1224. Ibid., 133–34. See also Tessa Rajak, review of Géza Vermès, *The Religion of Jesus the Jew, Jewish Chronicle*, August 6, 1993.

1225. Ibid., 134. Vermès reports the following as evidence of the widespread import of his trilogy: "The tangible proof that the trilogy made some mark was provided by the fact that between 1977 and 1995, *Jesus the Jew* was translated into Spanish, French, Italian, Japanese, Portuguese, German and Hungarian. *Jesus and the World of Judaism*, already extant in Portuguese, reached the Hungarian market during the Budapest book week in June 1997, and *The Gospel of Jesus the Jew* has been included in *Jesus der Jude*, the German translation of *Jesus the Jew*. As for *The Religion of Jesus the Jew*, it has already appeared in Spanish, Portuguese and Hungarian, and a translation into Korean is in the making" (*Jesus in His Jewish Context*, 134). Vermès followed the trilogy with *The Changing Faces of Jesus* (2000), *Jesus in His Jewish Context* (2003)—the revised edition of *Jesus and the World of Judaism, The Authentic Gospel of Jesus* (2003), and most recently *The Passion* (2005).

1226. Vermès, *Jesus the Jew*, preface, 11.

1227. The phrase "muddling through" was meant to be indicative of Vermès's methodological style as a *true* British pragmatist. The context in which the phrase is cited occurs in a section of *The Religion of Jesus the Jew*, wherein Vermès, lightheartedly or perhaps in a self-deprecating manner, explains his approach as "guidelines" rather than methodology (*The Religion of Jesus the Jew*, 7 and n. 11).

1228. Vermès, *Jesus in His Jewish Context*, vii–viii.

1229. Meier, *A Marginal Jew*, vol. 2 (1994), 6.

1230. Ibid. Vermès's response to Meier could lead one to see in Meier's caution a self-critique vis-à-vis his reaction to Vermès's pragmatism. Or is Meier reacting to Vermès's critique of scholarly dogmatism, which follows his comments on methodology?

1231. Ibid., 14n7.

1232. Vermès, *Jesus in His Jewish Context*, 1.

1233. Meier, *A Marginal Jew*, 2:522n2.

1234. Ibid., 581.
1235. Ibid. Also see Luke Timothy Johnson, commenting upon Marcus J. Borg as influenced by Vermès and issuing a similar critique, in *The Real Jesus: The Misguided Quest for the Historical Jesus and the Truth of the Traditional Gospels* (San Francisco: Harper, 1996), 42.
1236. Meier, *A Marginal Jew*, 2:584. Freyne opens his essay by giving with one hand and taking with the other. He writes: "The 'rediscovery' of Hanina ben Dosa by Géza Vermès may not have had the same repercussions in the study of Second Temple Judaism and early Christianity as those other discoveries of our times have had, in the elucidation of which Professor Vermès has played a notable part. Nevertheless, by drawing attention to this little known 'Galilean saint' the question of the immediate context of the ministry of Jesus of Nazareth and his social role within Galilean life have been raised in a new and provocative manner. In this present essay I do not intend to directly address myself to Vermès's thesis as this has been set out in his book *Jesus the Jew*. Instead I wish to suggest an alternative approach to the evaluation of the Hanina traditions on which the argument of that study is based. . . . If Bultmann and many other New Testament scholars after him have had 'to make virtue out of necessity' and abandon the detailed quest for the historical Jesus, even a fleeting glance at the Hanina traditions must convince us that this applies with even greater force in his case." Freyne nonetheless concedes: "Fortunately this skepticism does not make our task a negative one from the outset. We do have Hanina traditions, and Vermès's study of them, though at times lacking the methodological rigor of the Neusner school, has nevertheless been extremely helpful in isolating and classifying the relevant data. Accordingly, even if the historical Hanina lies shrouded in the mists of rabbinical polemics and legendary accretions, the discovery of the different tendencies in the traditions about him has much to tell about the role of the Hasidic and/or charismatic miracle-worker within the developing Judaism of the period" (Sean Freyne, "The Charismatic," in *Ideal Figures in Ancient Judaism: Profiles and Paradigms*, ed. John J. Collins and George W. E. Nickelsburg [Chico, CA: Scholars Press, 1980], 1–2).
1237. Meier, *A Marginal Jew*, 2:584. See also Vermès, "Hanina ben Dosa: A Controversial Galilean Saint from the First Century of the Christian Era," *Journal of Jewish Studies* 23 (1972): 28–50; and 24 (1973): 51–64. Here, Meier is referencing "Hanina ben Dosa" (1973), 57–64. A summary of Vermès's position may be found in his *Jesus the Jew*, 72–78.
1238. Meier, *A Marginal Jew*, 2:586. Meier stresses "that none of the three texts in the Mishna explicitly and unambiguously present Hanina as a miracle-*worker* in the more rigorous sense of that term (i.e., a human person who directly performs a miracle by giving certain commands or using certain gestures)" (586, his emphasis).
1239. Ibid., 586–87.
1240. Ibid, 587. Meier argues: "In the last analysis, all we can say with fair probability about the 'historical' Hanina is that he was a Palestinian Jew, who lived in the 1st century A.D., that he was noted for praying over the sick, and that he enjoyed the reputation of having precognition as to the results of his prayers for

healing. That he lived in Galilee has no written attestation before the two Talmuds. Poverty and asceticism are likewise not attested in the earliest written traditions" (587).

1241. Freyne, "The Charismatic," 227. Sean Freyne also criticizes Vermès's focus upon the "deeds" of Jesus rather than the "sayings" in reconstructing a portrait of Jesus. "It is only hypercritical scholarship that ignores or rejects Jesus' teaching as unimportant in locating him within the spectrum of Galilean life of his own day" (*Galilee from Alexander the Great to Hadrian* [Wilmington: Michael Glazier, 1980], 373, 388n92). Vermès, "perplexed," does not recall indicating that Jesus' teachings were unimportant (*Jesus in His Jewish Context*, 26, 149n70). Finally on this point, Jacob Neusner, in an early review of *Jesus the Jew*, approves of Vermès's initial focus ("Jesus as Jew," 71).

1242. Freyne, "The Charismatic," 242. Meier is aware of both of these assertions (*A Marginal Jew*, 2:606n36, 607n37). Freyne argues a different trajectory for the Hanina traditions, one in which Hanina progressively evolves and is assimilated into rabbinic tradition ("The Charismatic," 241–42).

1243. Bruce Chilton, "Jesus within Judaism," in *Judaism in Late Antiquity*, ed. Jacob Neusner (Leiden: Brill, 1995), 262–84, esp. 264. Vermès takes exception to Chilton's adjective "popular" in describing his work and suggests that Chilton is implying "the opposite of scholarly" (*Jesus in His Jewish Context*, 142n8).

1244. Chilton, "Jesus within Judaism," 265.

1245. Ibid.

1246. Ibid.

1247. Ibid. Chilton is quoting Philip R. Davies, "Qumran Beginnings," in *Behind the Essenes: History and Ideology in the Dead Sea Scrolls*, Brown Judaic Studies 94 (Atlanta: Scholars Press, 1987), 15–31, esp. 15. Vermès considers Chilton's "psychoanalytical dissection of my latent motives" as "a hilarious hotchpotch of irrelevancies," such as he has "never encountered in an academic work." He offers a firm rebuttal to Chilton's explanation (*Jesus in His Jewish Context*, 141–142n7).

1248. Chilton, "Jesus within Judaism," 265–66.

1249. Ibid., 266.

1250. Ibid.

1251. Ibid.

1252. Hurtado, "A Taxonomy of Recent Historical-Jesus Work," 279.

1253. Ibid.

1254. Ibid.

1255. Ibid.

1256. Vermès, *Jesus in His Jewish Context*, vii.

1257. Ibid.

1258. Ibid.

1259. Ibid.

1260. Ibid.

1261. Ibid., viii. Continuing, Vermès points out that the method that he employs "seeks first to trace with the help of all available data the evolutionary curve of a given theme, and then to determine the precise place on that literary curve of the various examples of the theme."

1262. Ibid.
1263. Ibid., viii–ix, with his emphasis.
1264. Ibid., ix. The text in question is Vermès, "Hanina ben Dosa."
1265. Ibid., x, with his emphasis and brackets.
1266. Neusner, "Jesus as Jew," 71.
1267. Ibid. Neusner takes exception to Vermès's elevation of Jesus as "second to none in profundity of insight and grandeur of character." Providing a brief juxtaposition of Jesus and other Jewish notables, Neusner affirms the latter against Vermès's hyperbolic claim.
1268. Neusner, *Jews and Christians*, 120, with emphasis added. Neusner's position vis-à-vis the validity of the historical Jesus quest mirrors, in some measure, that of other scholars, such as Luke Timothy Johnson.
1269. Géza Vermès in a personal e-mail to me, responding to my request for a comment given Neusner's critique, September 5, 2005.
1270. Jacob Neusner in a personal e-mail to me, December 5, 2004. Reaffirmed, September 18, 2005.
1271. David Flusser, review of *Jesus and the World of Judaism*, by Géza Vermès, *Judaism* 35 (1986): 362. Though agreeing with the Hasidic typology, Flusser takes exception to Vermès's depiction of "Jesus' fresh and simple religiousness and his lack of expertise"(362)—a depiction that is consistent with the typology. Ironically Flusser, unlike Vermès, is able to hold both views of Jesus, scholar and pious Hasid, inexplicably in tandem.
1272. Vermès, *The Authentic Gospel of Jesus*, 373. With regard to his status an innovator, Vermès writes: "Thirty years ago, anyone foolhardy enough to confront the problem of the Jesus of history appeared an innovator. Since then an increasing number of scholars have ventured in that direction, first in Oxford, and more recently in the United States, too" (*Jesus in His Jewish Context*, 134).
1273. Nicholas King, review of *Jesus and the World of Judaism*, by Géza Vermès, *The Heythrop Journal* 28, no. 2 (April 1987): 202.
1274. Ibid.
1275. Ibid., 203, with added emphasis.
1276. Paula Fredriksen, review of *The Religion of Jesus the Jew*, by Géza Vermès, *Journal of Jewish Studies* 44 (Autumn 1993): 319–20.
1277. Ibid., 321.
1278. Ibid.
1279. Ibid., with added emphasis.
1280. Sanders, "In Quest of the Historical Jesus," 6.
1281. Ibid., 8, with emphasis added.
1282. Neusner, *A Rabbi Talks with Jesus* (2000), 31.
1283. Ibid., foreword, xi.
1284. Ibid.
1285. Ibid.
1286. Ibid., xii.

1287. Ibid. Gently suggesting that "Jesus (the Matthean Jesus) did not understand the Torah very well" hardly resonates with Neusner's candid assertion that Jesus got it wrong. With the exception of Akenson's foreword and online bookstore reviews, as for Blackwell, McGill-Queen's University Press, and so forth, the reviews of *A Rabbi Talks with Jesus* produced from library catalog and online bibliographical searches, such as ATLA, etc., showed only reviews of the 1993 text. Ironically, no reviews of the revised (2000) book surfaced.

1288. Jeffrey K. Salkin, review of *A Rabbi Talks with Jesus: An Intermillenial Interfaith Exchange*, by Jacob Neusner, *Theology Today* 50, no. 4 (January 1994): 664, http://theologytoday.ptsem.edu/jan1994/v50-4-booknotes8.htm (accessed September 29, 2007).

1289. Ibid.

1290. Ibid.

1291. Mark Daniel Napack, review of *A Rabbi Talks with Jesus: An Inter-millenial Interfaith Exchange*, by Jacob Neusner, *Spiritual Life* 39 (Autumn 1993): 182.

1292. Ibid.

1293. William E. Phipps, review of Neusner, *A Rabbi Talks with Jesus: An Intermillenial Interfaith Exchange*, by Jacob Neusner, *Interpretation* 49 (1995): 307.

1294. Ibid.

1295. Ibid.

1296. Philip A. Cunningham, review of *A Rabbi Talks with Jesus: An Intermillenial Interfaith Exchange*, by Jacob Neusner, *New Theology Review* 9 (February 1996): 102.

1297. Ibid. Cunningham, in referring to stage 1 and stage 3, is referencing one of two significant documents on Catholic biblical scholarship, namely, *Sancta Mater Ecclesia* (1964), which describes the gospel formation in three stages: stage 1, the ministry of Jesus; stage 2, postresurrectional preaching of the apostles; and stage 3, the time of the evangelists. The second, equally significant, document, *Bible et Christologie* (1984), translated into English as *Scripture and Christology* (1986), stresses the importance of studying Judaism for a correct understanding of the person of Jesus.

1298. Ibid.

1299. Ibid.

1300. Ibid., 102–3.

1301. Ibid., 103.

1302. Daniel J. Harrington, review of *A Rabbi Talks with Jesus: An Intermillenial Interfaith Exchange*, by Jacob Neusner, *America* 170 (March 12, 1994): 19.

1303. Ibid.

1304. Joseph Ratzinger, review of *A Rabbi Talks with Jesus: An Intermillenial Interfaith Exchange*, by Jacob Neusner. As quoted from the jacket cover of the 1993 edition. Professor Neusner recently confirmed for me the origin of the request that prompted Cardinal Ratzinger's response and the source of the quotation.

1305. Ruth Graf, review of *A Rabbi Talks with Jesus: An Intermillenial Interfaith Exchange*, by Jacob Neusner, *Review for Religious* 52 (November–December 1993): 940.

1306. Ibid.
1307. Ibid.
1308. Underlying this hope is Neusner's apologia of Judaism, "a discourse of autonomy for Judaism" vis-à-vis a Christian majority (*A Rabbi Talks with Jesus* [2000], 16).

Conclusion: "Theology's Masquerade"

1309. Meier also makes a distinction between the historical Jesus, "a modern abstraction and construct," "the Jesus whom we can 'recover' and examine by using scientific tools of modern historical research" on one hand; and on the other hand, "the real Jesus," "a reasonably complete biographical portrait" (*A Marginal Jew*, 1:22, 24).
1310. See Jacob Neusner, "Who Needs 'The Historical Jesus'? An Essay-Review," 113–26; and Craig A. Evans, "The Need for the 'Historical Jesus': A Response to Jacob Neusner's Review of Crossan and Meier," 127–34; both in *Bulletin for Biblical Research* 4 (1994). See also, Jacob Neusner, *The Rabbinic Traditions about the Pharisees before 70: Part I, The Masters* (Atlanta: Scholars Press, 1999), preface to the 1999 reprint of the 1971 text, iii–v.
1311. Klausner, *Jesus of Nazareth*, 11.
1312. Ibid.
1313. Lapide, *Israelis, Jews, and Jesus*, 8.
1314. Ibid.
1315. Shin Shalom, *Galiäisches Tagebuch* (Heidelberg: Drei Brücken, 1954), as quoted by Lapide in *Israelis, Jews, and Jesus*, 9.
1316. Meier, *A Marginal Jew*, 1:25.
1317. Dunn, *Jesus Remembered*, 125–26. See also, Meier, *A Marginal Jew*, 1:21–26; Terrence Merrigan, "The Historical Jesus in the Pluralist Theology of Religions," in *The Myriad Christ: Plurality and the Quest for Unity in Contemporary Christology*, ed. Terrence Merrigan and Jacques Haers (Louvain: Leuven University Press, 2000), 61–62. Dunn points out as well that "the Enlightenment ideal of historical objectivity also projected a false goal onto the quest for the historical Jesus," which implied that there was a "historical Jesus," objectively verifiable, "who will be different from the dogmatic Christ and the Jesus of the Gospels and who will enable us to criticize the dogmatic Christ and the Jesus of the Gospels" (*Jesus Remembered*, 125).
1318. See Martin Kähler, *The So-Called Historical Jesus and the Historic Biblical Christ*, trans., ed., and introduction, Carl E. Braaten (Philadelphia: Fortress, 1964).
1319. Dunn, *Jesus Remembered*, 126–27.
1320. Ibid., 142. Dunn affirms the usefulness of external sources in demonstrating the existence of Jesus vis-à-vis the periodic claims that he never existed.
1321. It is a curiosity of scholarship that Vermès, Dunn, and Meier find themselves in agreement while arguing the validity of the historical Jesus quest, albeit from a historian's perspective. Though this seems apparent, it is nonetheless certain that neither Meier nor Dunn endorses Vermès's use of rabbinic data to inform

his Jesus study. Nor does either seek to retrieve the *real* Jesus from the Synoptics, but rather the *historical* Jesus, the figure reconstructed from a historical-critical investigation of the sources. Meier does "doff" his exegetical hat, donning the hat of a person of faith, to affirm the benefit that Christian theology derives from the quest for the historical Jesus. In doing so, he identifies four ways in which the quest serves the interest of theology (*A Marginal Jew*, 1:199).

1322. The Aramaic we know from the time of Jesus does not attest to the usage Vermès adduces from later rabbinic texts to support his assertion.

1323. *Nostra Aetate*, 4, passim; http://www.vatican.va/archive/hist_councils/ii_vatican_council/documents/vat-ii_decl_19651028_nostra-aetate_en.html (accessed September 29, 2007). Sandmel's *We Jews and You Christians: An Inquiry into Attitudes* (1967) received its impetus from the promulgation of *Nostra Aetate* (1965).

1324. This was during the pontificate of John Paul II, whose zeal for reconciliation and deeper understanding between these two faith communities opened up a new era in relations between Catholics and Jews. For a Jewish assessment of his pontificate visit: http://www.acton.org/publications/randl/index.php?id=514 (accessed September 5, 2005).

1325. Address of His Holiness Pope Benedict XVI on the Occasion of His Visit to the Synagogue of Cologne, August 19, 2005, http://www.jcrelations.net/en/?id=2533 (accessed September 29, 2007).

1326. The title is derived from Zech 8:16: "These are the things that you are to do: Speak the truth to one another, render true and perfect justice in your gates."

1327. "*Dabru Emet:* A Jewish Statement on Christians and Christianity" appeared as a full-page advertisement in the *New York Times*, Sunday, September 10, 2000, 23, New England edition, http://www.bc.edu/bc_org/research/cjl/Documents/dabru_emet.htm (accessed September 29, 2007).

1328. For evidence of "the new trend: Jesus research," see the appendix in James H. Charlesworth, *Jesus within Judaism: New Light from Exciting Archaelogical Discoveries* (New York: Doubleday, 1988), 187–207.

1329. John P. Meier, commenting on the various "gains" inherent in the "third quest for the historical Jesus" notes that the "first gain," that which distinguishes the "third quest" from previous quests, has been its ecumenical tenor: notably, the fruitful exchange between Jewish and Christian scholars. See John P. Meier, "The Present State of the 'Third Quest' for the Historical Jesus: Loss and Gain," *Biblica* 80 (1999): 461.

1330. Vermès, *The Changing Faces of Jesus*, 282.

1331. Ibid.

1332. Ibid.

1333. Vermès, *Jesus and the World of Judaism*, 57.

1334. Ibid.

Select Bibliography

Ben-Chorin, Schalom. "Das Jesusbild im modernen Judentum." *Zeitschrift für Religions- und Geistesgeschichte* 5 (1953): 231–57.

———. *Bruder Jesus: Der Nazarener in jüdischer Sicht.* Munich: List, 1967. 3rd ed., 1970. Reprint, 1972.

———. *Jesus im Judentum.* Wuppertal: Theologischer Verlag, 1970.

———. "The Image of Jesus in Modern Judaism." *Journal of Ecumenical Studies* 11 (1974): 401–30.

———. "Fraternal Dialog." In *Brothers in Hope*, edited by J. Oesterreicher. New York: Herder & Herder, 1975.

———. "Jesus und Paulus in jüdischer Sicht." *Annual of the Swedish Theological Institute* 10. Edited by B. Knutson. Leiden: Brill, 1976.

———. Review of *Der Jude Jesus: Thesen eines Juden, Antworten eines Christen*, by Pinchas Lapide and Ulrich Luz. *Zeitschrift für Religions- und Geistesgeschichte* 33 (1981): 161–63.

———. "A Jewish View of the Mother of Jesus." In *Mary in the Churches*, edited by H. Küng and J. Moltmann, translated by T. L. Westow. New York: Seabury, 1983.

———. *Was ist der Mensch: Anthropologie des Judentums.* Tübingen: Mohr, 1986.

———. "Did God Make Anything Happen in Christianity? An Attempt at a Jewish Theology of Christianity." Translated by D. Livingstone [paper delivered to the Evangelical/Catholic Clergy Day, June 21, 1982]. In *Christian Identity*, ed. C. Duquoc and C. Floristan. Edinburgh: T&T Clark, 1988.

———. *Weil wir Brüder sind: Zum christlich-jüdischen Dialog heute.* Gerlingen: Bleicher, 1988.

———. "Der christlich-jüdische Dialog heute." In *Das Judentum*, edited by H. Flothkotter and B. Nacke. Würzburg: Echter, 1990.

———. *Brother Jesus: The Nazarene through Jewish Eyes.* Translated and edited by J. Klein and M. Reinhart. Athens: University of Georgia Press, 2001.

Borowitz, Eugene B. "Openness of Catholic Theology." *Judaism* 14 (1965): 212–19.

———. "Christkillers No More: Jewish Education and the Second Vatican Council." *Religious Education* 61 (1966): 344–48.

———. "The Legacy of Martin Buber." *Union Seminary Quarterly Review* 22 (1966): 3–17.

———. *Contemporary Christologies: A Jewish Response.* New York: Paulist Press, 1981.

————. "Recent Historic Events: Jewish and Christian Interpretations." *Theological Studies* 44 (1983): 221–40.

————. "The Challenge of Jesus the Jew for the Church." In *Proceedings of Center for Jewish-Christian Learning.* Edited by Arthur E. Zannoni. Vol. 2. St. Paul, MN: University of St. Thomas, Jay Phillips Center for Jewish-Christian Learning, Spring 1987.

————. "Jesus the Jew in the Light of the Jewish-Christian Dialogue." In *Proceedings of Center for Jewish-Christian Learning.* Edited by Arthur E. Zannoni. Vol. 2. St. Paul, MN: University of St. Thomas, Jay Phillips Center for Jewish-Christian Learning, 1987.

————. "Rethinking Our Holocaust Consciousness." *Judaism* 40 (1991): 389–406.

————. "Fully Human, Fully Jewish." In *Aus zweier Zeugen Mund*, edited by Julius Schoeps. Gerlingen: Bleicher, 1992.

————. "The Ideal Jew." In *Judaism in the Modern World*, edited by Alan Berger. New York: New York University Press, 1994.

Flusser, David. *Jesus in Selbstzeugnissen und Bilddokumenten.* Hamburg: Rowohlt, 1968.

————. *Jesus.* Translated by R. Walls. New York: Herder & Herder, 1969.

————. "Jesus und die Synagoge." In *Der Mann aus Galiläa*, edited by Erich Lessing. Freiburg: Herder & Herder, 1971.

————. "Literary Approaches to the Trial of Jesus." *Judaism* 20 (1971): 32–36.

————. "Hillel's Self-Awareness and Jesus." *Immanuel* 4 (1974): 31–36.

————. "To What Extent Is Jesus a Question for the Jews?" In *Christians and Jews*, edited by H. Küng and W. Kasper, translated by D. Livingstone. New York: Seabury, 1974.

————. "The Crucified One and the Jews." Translated by Y. Bearne. *Immanuel* 7 (1977): 25–27.

————. "Do You Prefer New Wine? [Mark 2:18–22; Matt 9:14–17; Luke 5:33–39]." *Immanuel* 9 (1979): 26–31.

————. "At the Right Hand of the Power [Luke 22:69; Qumran parallel, 1QH 3:2–18]." *Immanuel* 14 (1982): 42–46.

————. "The Jewish-Christian Schism, Part 1." *Immanuel* 16 (1983): 32–49.

————. "What Was the Original Meaning of *Ecce Homo* [John 19:5]." Translated by A. Barber [from Proceedings of the Israel Academy of Sciences and Humanities 6, no. 8 (1982): 143–51.] *Immanuel* 19 (1984–85): 30–40.

————. *Mary: Images of the Mother of Jesus in Jewish and Christian Perspective.* Philadelphia: Fortress Press, 1986.

————. Review of *Jesus and the World of Judaism* (1983), by Géza Vermès. *Judaism* 35 (1986): 361–64.

————. "Who Is It That Struck You?" *Immanuel* 20 (1986): 27–32.

————. *Jewish Sources in Early Christianity.* New York: Adama Books, 1987.

————. "The Dead Sea Sect and Pre-Pauline Christianity." In *Judaism and the Origins of Christianity.* Jerusalem: Hebrew University Magnes Press, 1988.

————. "Jesus and the Sign of the Son of Man." In *Judaism and the Origins of Christianity.* Jerusalem: Hebrew University Magnes Press, 1988.

————. "The Jewish-Christian Schism." In *Judaism and the Origins of Christianity.* Jerusalem: Hebrew University Magnes Press, 1988.

————. *Judaism and the Origins of Christianity.* Jerusalem: Hebrew University Magnes Press, 1988.

————. "Melchizedek and the Son of Man." In *Judaism and the Origins of Christianity.* Jerusalem: Hebrew University Magnes Press, 1988.

————. "A New Sensitivity in Judaism and the Christian Message." In *Judaism and the Origins of Christianity.* Jerusalem: Hebrew University Magnes Press, 1988.

————. "The Social Message from Qumran." In *Judaism and the Origins of Christianity*, 193–201. Jerusalem: Hebrew University Magnes Press, 1988.

————. *Jewish Sources in Early Christianity.* Translated by John Glucker. New York: Adama Books, 1987. Tel Aviv: Naidat Press, 1989.

————. *The Spiritual History of the Dead Sea Sect.* Translated by Carol Glucker. Tel Aviv: Naidat Press, 1989.

————. "Jesus, His Ancestry, and the Commandment of Love." in *Jesus' Jewishness: Exploring the Place of Jesus within Early Judaism*, edited by J. H. Charlesworth, 153–76. New York: Crossroad, 1991.

————. "Jesus and Judaism: Jewish Perspectives." In *Eusebius, Christianity, and Judaism*, edited by Harold Attridge and Gohei Hata. Detroit: Wayne State University Press, 1992.

————. "The Parable of the Unjust Servant: Jesus' Criticism of the Essenes." In *Jesus and the Dead Sea Scrolls*, edited by J. H. Charlesworth, 176–97. New York: Doubleday, 1992.

————. "Hillel and Jesus: Two Ways of Self-Awareness." In *Hillel and Jesus*, edited by J. Charlesworth et al. Minneapolis: Fortress, 1997.

Flusser, David, with R. Stevens. *Jesus.* Jerusalem: Hebrew University Magnes Press, 1997.

Flusser, David. *Jesus in Selbstzeugnissen und Bilddokumenten.* Corrected and augmented ed. Hamburg: Rowohlt, 1997.

Flusser, David, with R. Steven Notley. *Jesus.* Corrected and augmented 3rd ed. Jerusalem: Hebrew University Magnes Press, 2001.

Lapide, Pinchas E. *Three Popes and the Jews.* New York: Hawthorn Books, 1967.

————. "Jesus in Israeli Literature." *Christian Century* 87 (1970): 1248–53.

————. "Jesus in der israelischen Literatur." *Internationale Katholische Zeitschrift "Communio"* 2 (1973): 375–81.

————. "Jesus in Israeli Literature." *Journal of Theology for Southern Africa* 5 (1973): 47–56.

————. "Jesus in Israeli School Books." *Journal of Ecumenical Studies* 10 (1973): 515–31.

————. *Der Rabbi von Nazaret: Wandlungen des jüdischen Jesusbildes.* Trier: Spee, 1974.

―――. "Insights into Qumran into the Language of Jesus." *Revue de Qumran* 8, no. 4 (1975): 483–501.

―――. "Two Famous Rabbis." In *Annual of the Swedish Theological Institute*, vol. 10, edited by B. Knutson, 97–109. Leiden: Brill, 1976.

―――. *Hebräisch in den Kirchen: Forschungen zum judisch-christlichen Dialog.* Neurichen-Vluyn: Neukirchener Verlag, 1976.

―――. *Auferstehung: Ein jüdisches Glaubenserlebnis.* Munich: Calwer: Kösel, 1977.

―――. *Israelis, Jews, and Jesus.* Translated by Peter Heinegg. Garden City, NY: Doubleday, 1979.

―――. "Jesu Tod durch Römerhand: Zur blasphemischen These vom 'Gottesmord,' durch die Juden." In *Gottesverächter und Menschenfeinden*, edited by H. Goldstein. Düsseldorf: Patmos, 1979.

―――. *Der Jude Jesus: Thesen eines Juden, Antworten eines Christen.* Cologne: Benziger, 1979. 3rd, rev. ed., 1983.

―――. "Die Bergpredigt—Friedensutopie oder Realpolitik? Eine jüdische Auslegung." In *Christen im Streit um den Frieden: Beiträge zu einer neuen Friedensethik; Positionen und Dokumente.* Aktion Suhnezeichen / Friedensdienste [Association: Berlin]. Mainz: Matthias-Grünewald; Freiburg: Dreisam, 1982.

―――. *The Bergpredigt—Utopie oder Programm?* Mainz: Matthias-Grünewald, 1982.

―――. "What Did Jesus Ask? The Sermon on the Mount: A Jewish Reading." Translated by L. Swidler. *Christianity and Crisis* 42 (1982): 139–42.

―――. *Heil von den Juden? Ein Gespräch* [P. Lapide and K. Rahner]. Mainz: Matthias-Grünewald, 1983.

―――. *The Resurrection of Jesus: A Jewish Perspective.* Translated by Wilhelm C. Linss. Minneapolis: Augsburg, 1983.

―――. *Hebrew in the Church: The Foundations of Jewish-Christian Dialogue.* Translated by E. F. Rhodes. Grand Rapids: Eerdmans, 1984.

―――. *Jesus in Two Perspectives: A Jewish-Christian Dialog / Pinchas Lapide and Ulrich Luz.* Translated by L. W. Denef. Minneapolis: Augsburg, 1985.

―――. *The Sermon on the Mount: Utopia or Program for Action?* Translated by Arlene Swidler. Maryknoll: Orbis Books, 1986.

―――. *Encountering Jesus—Encountering Judaism: A Dialogue / Karl Rahner and Pinchas Lapide.* Translated by D. Perkins. New York: Crossroad, 1987.

―――. *Jesus: Ein gekreuzigter Pharisäer?* Gütersloher: G. Mohn, 1990.

Lapide, Pinchas E., and Hans Küng. *Brother or Lord? A Jew and a Christian Talk Together about Jesus / Hans Küng and Pinchas Lapide.* Translated by E. Quinn. London: Fount Paperbacks, 1977.

―――. "Is Jesus a Bond or Barrier? A Jewish-Christian dialogue [reprint and translation of radio broadcast]." *Journal of Ecumenical Studies* 14 (1977): 466–83.

Lapide, Pinchas E., and Juergen Moltmann. *Jewish Monotheism and Christian Trinitarian Doctrine: A Diaologue.* Translated by Leonard Swidler. Philadelphia: Fortress, 1981.

Neusner, Jacob. *The Rabbinic Traditions about the Pharisees before 70.* 3 vols. Leiden: Brill, 1971. Augmented ed., Atlanta: Scholars Press, 1999.

———. *From Politics to Piety: The Emergence of Pharisaic Judaism.* Englewood Cliffs, NJ: Prentice-Hall, 1973.

———. "Jesus as Jew." Review of *Jesus the Jew,* by Géza Vermès. *Midstream* 20 (December 1974): 70–73.

———. *Judaism in the Beginning of Christianity.* Philadelphia: Fortress Press, 1984.

———, ed. *Approaches to Ancient Judaism.* New Series, vol. 12. Atlanta: Scholars Press, 1987.

———. "Marcus' *Jesus and the Holocaust*; Cohn-Sherbok's *Crucified Jew* [review article]." In *Approaches to Ancient Judaism.* New Series, vol. 12. Edited by J. Neusner. Atlanta: Scholars Press, 1987.

Neusner, Jacob, et al., eds. *Judaisms and Their Messiahs at the Turn of the Christian Era.* Cambridge: Cambridge University Press, 1987.

Neusner, Jacob, with P. Borgen, E. S. Freichs, and R. Horsley, eds. *Religion, Literature, and Society in Ancient Israel, Formative Christianity, and Judaism: Ancient Israel and Christianity* [bibliographies]. Lanham, MD: University Press of America, 1987.

Neusner, Jacob, ed. *Approaches to Ancient Judaism.* New Series, vol. 13. Atlanta: Scholars Press, 1988.

———. "Geldwechsler im Tempel: Von der Mischna her erklärt." Translated by I. Betz. *Theologische Zeitschrift* 45 (1989): 73–80.

———. "Money-changers in the Temple: The Mishnah's Explanation." *New Testament Studies* 35 (1989): 287–90.

———. *Jews and Christians: The Myth of a Common Tradition.* London: SCM Press, 1991.

———. "Mr. Sanders' Pharisees and Mine: A Response to E. P. Sanders, Jewish Law from Jesus to the Mishnah." *Scottish Journal of Theology* 44 (1991): 73–95.

———. "There Has Never Been a Judaeo-Christian Dialogue—But There Can Be One." *CrossCurrents* 42 (1992): 3–25.

———. *A Rabbi Talks with Jesus: An Intermillennial, Interfaith Exchange.* Garden City, NY: Doubleday, 1993.

———. *Telling Tales: Making Sense of Christian and Judaic Nonsense.* Louisville: Westminster / John Knox, 1993.

———. *Rabbinic Literature and the New Testament.* Valley Forge, PA: Trinity Press, 1994.

———. *What Is Midrash? and, A Midrash Reader.* Atlanta: Scholars Press, 1994.

———, ed. *Approaches to Ancient Judaism.* New Series, vol. 7. Atlanta: Scholars Press, 1995.

———. *Judaism in Late Antiquity.* Part 2, *Historical Synthesis* [bibliographies, figures, indexes]. Edited by Jacob Neusner. Leiden: Brill, 1995.

———. "What Should We Know about the Gospels? An Outsider's View of New Testament Studies." In *Approaches to Ancient Judaism.* New Series, vol. 8. Edited by J. Neusner. Atlanta: Scholars Press, 1995.

———. Review of *Jesus and the Holocaust: Reflections on Suffering and Hope,* by Joel Marcus [New York: Doubleday, 1997]. *Books and Culture* 3 (1997): 19.

———. *Jewish-Christian Debates: God, Kingdom, Messiah.* Minneapolis: Augsburg Fortress, 1998.

———. *A Rabbi Talks with Jesus.* Montreal: McGill-Queen's University Press, 2000.

———. *Jews and Christians: The Myth of a Common Tradition.* Expanded ed., Binghamton, NY: Global Publications, 2001.

Neusner, Jacob, Bruce Chilton, and Craig Evans. *The Missing Jesus: Rabbinic Judaism and the New Testament.* Boston: Brill, 2002.

Sandmel, Samuel. *We Jews and Jesus.* New York: Oxford University Press, 1965.

———. *We Jews and You Christians: An Inquiry into Attitudes.* New York: Lippincott, 1967.

———. *The First Christian Century in Judaism and Christianity: Certainties and Uncertainties.* New York: Oxford University Press, 1969.

———. "The Trial of Jesus: Reservations." *Judaism* 20 (1971): 69–74.

———. "Christians, Their Problem of Jesus, and We Jews" [bibliographic overview of recent Christology]. In *Justice, Justice Shalt Thou Pursue,* edited by R. Sobel and S. Wallach. New York: Ktav, 1975.

———. "Jesus: A Jewish Perspective." In *The Living Light* 12 (1975): 130–41.

———. *A Jewish Understanding of the New Testament.* Augmented ed. London: SPCK, 1977.

———. "Jewishness of Jesus" [23 minutes]. *Thesis Theological Cassettes* 8, no. 1 F [sound recordings of Pittsburgh Theological Seminary theses]. 1977.

———. *Anti-Semitism in the New Testament.* Philadelphia: Fortress, 1978.

———. *Judaism and Christian Beginnings.* New York: Oxford University Press, 1978.

———. "Christology, Judaism, and Jews." In *Christological Perspectives: Essays in Honor of Harvey K. McArthur,* edited by Robert Berkley and Susan Edwards. New York: Pilgrim Press, 1982.

Vermès, Géza. *Les manuscrits du désert de Juda.* Tournai: Desclée, 1953.

———. *Scripture and Tradition in Judaism: Haggadic Studies.* Leiden: Brill, 1961.

———. *The Dead Sea Scrolls in English.* 1st ed. Harmondsworth: Penguin Books, 1962.

———. "Hanina ben Dosa: A Controversial Galilean Saint from the First Century of the Christian Era." *Journal of Jewish Studies* 23 (1972): 28–50; 24 (1973): 51–64.

———. *Jesus the Jew: A Historian's Reading of the Gospels.* London: Collins, 1973.

Vermès, Géza, and T. A. Burkill, eds. and revisers. *On The Trial of Jesus,* by Paul Winter [1st ed., 1961]. 2nd ed. Berlin: de Gruyter, 1974.

Vermès, Géza. "Impact of the Dead Sea Scrolls on the Study of the New Testament." *Journal of Jewish Studies* 27 (1976): 107–16.

———. "The Use of *bar nash / bar nasha* in Jewish Aramaic." In *An Aramaic Approach to the Gospels and Acts,* edited by M. Black, 310–28. Oxford: Clarendon, 1976.

———. *The Dead Sea Scrolls: Qumran in Perspective.* London: Collins, 1977.

———. "'The Son of Man' Debate." *Journal for the Study of the New Testament* 1 (1978): 19–32.

————. "Jesus the Jew." In *The Messiahship of Jesus: What Jews and Jewish Christian Say*, edited by Arthur W. Kac. Chicago: Moody, 1980.

————. "The Gospels without Christology." In *God Incarnate: Story and Belief*, edited by A. E. Harvey. London: SPCK, 1981.

————. *Jesus the Jew: A Historian's Reading of the Gospels.* 1973. Fortress Press ed., Minneapolis: Augsburg Fortress, 1981.

————. *Jesus and the World of Judaism.* London: SCM Press, 1983.

————. "Jewish Studies and New Testament Interpretation." *Journal of Jewish Studies* 33 (1983): 361–76.

————. "Jesus and Christianity" [reprinted]. In *Renewing the Judeo-Christian Wellsprings*, edited by Val McInnes. New York: Crossroad, 1987.

————. "The Jesus Notice of Josephus Re-examined." *Journal of Jewish Studies* 38 (1987): 1–10.

————. "Jesus the Jew" [bibliography; reprinted]. In *Renewing the Judeo-Christian Wellsprings*, edited by Val McInnes. New York: Crossroad, 1987.

————. "Jesus the Jew: Christian and Jewish Reactions." *Toronto Journal of Theology* 4 (1988): 112–23.

————. "Josephus' Portrait of Jesus Reconsidered." In *Occident and Orient*, edited by Robert Dán. Leiden: Brill, 1988.

————. "La religione di Gesu l'ebreo." In *Il "Gesu storico: Problema della modernità,"* edited by G. Pirola and F. Coppellotti, translated by E. Costa, Casale Monferrato, Provincia di Alessandria, Italy: Piemme, 1988.

————. Review of *From Jesus to Christ: The Origins of the New Testament Images of Jesus*, by Paula Fredriksen. *Times Literary Supplement* 4486 (March 24–30, 1989): 321.

————. "Jesus the Jew: Christian and Jewish Reactions." In *Jews and Christians in a Pluralistic World*, edited by Ernst-Wolfgang Böckenförde. New York: St. Martin's Press, 1991.

————. "Jesus the Jew." In *Jesus' Jewishness: Exploring the Place of Jesus in Early Judaism.* Edited by James H. Charlesworth. New York: Crossroad, 1991.

————. Review of *Jewish Law from Jesus to the Mishnah: Five Studies*, by E. P. Sanders. *Times Literary Supplement* 4580 (January 11, 1991): 19.

————. *The Religion of Jesus the Jew.* Minneapolis: Augsburg Fortress, 1993.

————. "Escape and Rescue: An Oxford Don's Peregrinations" [interview by H. Shanks]. *Bible Review* 10 (1994): 30–37.

————. "Jesus the Jew and His Religion." *Living Pulpit* 3 (1994): 22–23.

————. *The Complete Dead Sea Scrolls in English.* 7th ed. New York: Penguin Press, 1997.

————. *Providential Accidents: An Autobiography.* London: SCM Press, 1998.

————. *The Changing Faces of Jesus.* New York: Viking Compass, 2001.

————. *The Authentic Gospel of Jesus.* London: Penguin Books, 2003.

————. *Jesus in His Jewish Context.* Minneapolis: Fortress Press, 2003.

————. *The Passion.* London: Penguin Books, 2005.

————. Review of *Brother Jesus: The Nazarene through Jewish Eyes*, by Schalom Ben-Chorin. *Journal of Jewish Studies* 56 (2005): 178.

Related Bibliography

Adan-Bayewitz, David. *Common Pottery in Roman Galilee: A Study of Local Trade.* Ramath Gan: Bar-Ilan University Press, 1993.

Allen, Charlotte. *The Human Christ: The Search for the Historical Jesus.* New York: Free Press, 1998.

Arnal, William E. *Whose Historical Jesus?* Edited by W. E. Arnal and Michel Desjardins. Waterloo, ON: Wilfrid Laurier University, 1997.

Barr, James. "Abba Isn't Daddy!" *Journal of Theological Studies* 39 (1988): 28–47.

Barrett, C. K. *The New Testament Background: Selected Documents.* San Francisco: Harper & Row, 1995.

Bennett, Clinton. *In Search of Jesus: Insider and Outsider Images.* New York: Continuum, 2001.

Betz, Otto, and Rainer Riesner. *Jesus, Qumran, and the Vatican: Clarifications.* New York: Crossroad, 1994.

Blinzler, Josef. *Die Brüder und Schwestern Jesu.* Stuttgart: Katholisches Bibelwerk, 1967.

Bornkamm, Günther. *Jesus of Nazareth.* Translated by I. and F. McLuskey, with J. M. Robinson. Minneapolis: Fortress, 1995.

Bouttier, Michel. Review of *Jesus the Jew: A Historian's Reading of the Gospels*, by Géza Vermès. *Études théologiques et religieuses* 176 (1978): 88.

Broshi, Magen. Review of *Jesus the Jew: A Historian's Reading of the Gospels*, by Géza Vermès. *Jerusalem Post*, December 7, 1984.

Brown, Raymond. *The Birth of the Messiah.* Garden City, NY: Doubleday, 1979.

———. *The Death of the Messiah.* 2 vols. New York: Doubleday, 1994.

———. *Jesus, God and Man: Modern Biblical Reflections.* New York: Macmillan, 1967.

Buber, Martin. *Two Types of Faith.* Translated by Norman P. Goldhawk. New York: Macmillan, 1951. Reprint, New York: Harper & Row, 1961.

Büchler, Adolf. *Types of Jewish-Palestinian Piety from 70 B.C.E. to 70 C.E.* London: Jews' College, 1922.

Bultmann, Rudolf. *Jesus and the Word.* London: Scribner, 1934.

Charlesworth, James H., ed. *L'ebraicità di Gesù.* Translated by Teresa Franzosi. Torino: Claudiana Editrice, 2002.

———. "The Foreground of Christian Origins and the Commencement of Jesus Research." In *Jesus' Jewishness*, edited by J. H. Charlesworth. New York: Crossroad, 1991.

————, ed. *Jesus and the Dead Sea Scrolls.* New York: Doubleday, 1992.

————, ed. *Jesus' Jewishness: Exploring the Place of Jesus in Early Judaism.* New York: Crossroad, 1991.

————. *Jesus within Judaism: New Light from Exciting Archaeological Discoveries.* New York: Doubleday, 1988.

Charlesworth, James H., and Loren L. Johns, eds. *Hillel and Jesus.* Minneapolis: Fortress, 1997.

Charlesworth, James H., and Walter P. Weaver, eds. *Images of Jesus Today.* Valley Forge, PA: Trinity Press, 1994.

————, eds. *Jesus Two Thousand Years Later.* Harrisburg, PA: Trinity Press, 2000.

Chilton, Bruce. *A Galilean Rabbi and His Bible: Jesus' Use of the Interpreted Scripture of His Time.* Wilmington, DE: Michael Glazier, 1984.

————. "Jesus within Judaism." In *Judaism in Late Antiquity*, ed. Jacob Neusner, 262–84. Leiden: Brill, 1995.

Chilton, Bruce, and C. A. Evans, eds. *Studying the Historical Jesus.* Leiden: Brill, 1994.

Corbishley, Thomas. Review of *Jesus the Jew: A Historian's Reading of the Gospels*, by Géza Vermès. *The Tablet*, December 3, 1974, 1179.

Crossan, John Dominic. *The Historical Jesus: The Life of a Mediterranean Jewish Peasant.* San Francisco: HarperSanFrancisco, 1991.

Cunningham, Philip A. Review of *A Rabbi Talks with Jesus: An Intermillennial Interfaith Exchange*, by Jacob Neusner. *New Theology Review* 9 (1996): 101–3.

Cupitt, Don. Review of *The Religion of Jesus the Jew*, by Géza Vermès. *Guardian*, March 27, 1993.

Daube, David. Review of *Jesus the Jew: A Historian's Reading of the Gospels*, by Géza Vermès. *Journal of Jewish Studies* 25 (1975): 332–36.

Davies, Philip R. "Qumran Beginnings." In *Behind the Essenes: History and Ideology in the Dead Sea Scrolls*, 15–31. Brown Judaic Studies 94. Atlanta: Scholars Press, 1987.

DiSanto, C. Review of *Fratello Gesu: Un punto di vista ebraico sul Nazareno*, by Schalom Ben-Chorin. *SIDIC: Service International de Documentation Judeo-Chretienne* 19 (1987): 33.

Donnelly, Doris, ed. *Jesus: A Colloquium in the Holy Land.* New York: Continuum, 2001.

Dunn, James D. G. "Altering the Default Setting: Re-envisaging the Early Transmission of the Jesus Tradition." *New Testament Studies* 49 (April 2003): 139–75.

————. "Jesus and Factionalism in Early Judaism." In *Hillel and Jesus*, edited by J. H. Charlesworth and L. L. Johns, 156–75. Minneapolis: Fortress, 1997.

————. *Jesus Remembered.* Vol. 1 of *Christianity in the Making.* Grand Rapids: Eerdmans, 2003.

————. *The Parting of the Ways between Christianity and Judaism and Their Significance for the Character of Christianity.* London: SCM Press, 1991.

Evans, Craig A. "Jesus in Non-Christian Sources." In *Studying the Historical Jesus*, edited by Bruce Chilton and C. A. Evans, 443–78. Leiden: Brill, 1994.

————. *Life of Jesus Research: An Annotated Bibliography.* Leiden: Brill, 1989.

————. Review of *Entdeckungen im Neuen Testament*, vol. 2, *Jesus-Qumran-Urchristentum*, by David Flusser [Neukirchen-Vluyn: Neukirchener Verlag, 1999]. *Dead Sea Discoveries* 9 (2002): 253–54.

————. Review of *Jesus*, by David Flusser [rev. ed., Jerusalem: Hebrew University Magnes Press, 1997]. *Mishkan* 33 (2000): 86–91; and (an abridged version) *Dead Sea Discoveries* 7 (2000): 110–15.

Falk, Harvey. *Jesus the Pharisee: A New Look at the Jewishness of Jesus*. New York: Paulist Press, 1979.

Fitzmyer, Joseph A. "Another View of 'the Son of Man' Debate." *Journal for the Study of the New Testament* 4 (1979): 58–68.

————. "The Aramaic Language and the Study of the New Testament." *Journal of Biblical Literature* 99 (1980): 5–21.

————. "The Qumran Scrolls and the New Testament after Forty Years." *Revue de Qumran* 13 (1988): 609–20.

————. *A Wandering Aramean: Collected Aramaic Essays*. Missoula, MT: Scholars Press, 1979.

Fredriksen, Paula. *From Jesus to Christ: The Origins of the New Testament Images of Jesus*. New Haven: Yale University Press, 2000.

————. *Jesus of Nazareth, King of the Jews: A Jewish Life and the Emergence of Christianity*. New York: Knopf, 1999.

————. Review of *The Religion of Jesus the Jew*, by Géza Vermès. *Journal of Jewish Studies* 44 (1993): 319–22.

————. "Who He Was." *The New Republic*, October 15, 2001, 51.

Frerichs, Wendell W. Review of *Jewish Monotheism and Christian Trinitarian Doctrine*, by Pinchas Lapide. *Word and World* 1 (1982): 92.

Freyne, Seán. "Archaeology and the Historical Jesus." In *Archaeology and Biblical Interpretation*, edited by John R. Bartlett, 117–44. London: Routledge, 1997.

————. "The Charismatic." In *Ideal Figures in Ancient Judaism: Profiles and Paradigms*, edited by John J. Collins and George W. E. Nickelsburg, 223–58. SBLSCS 12. Chico, CA: Scholars Press, 1980.

————. "Galilean Questions to Crossan's Mediterranean Jesus." In *Whose Historical Jesus?* edited by W. E. Arnal and M. Desjardins, 62–91. Waterloo, ON: Wilfrid Laurier University, 1997.

————. *Galilee from Alexander the Great to Hadrian, 323 B.C.E. to 145 C.E.: A Study of Second Temple Judaism*. Wilmington, DE: Michael Glazier, 1980.

————. *Galilee, Jesus, and the Gospels: Literary Approaches and Historical Investigations*. Philadelphia: Fortress, 1988.

————. "Urban-Rural Relations in First-Century Galilee." In *The Galilee in Late Antiquity*, edited by Lee I. Levine, 75–91. New York: Jewish Theological Seminary of America, 1992.

Frymer-Kensky, Tikva, et al., eds. *Christianity in Jewish Terms*. Boulder, CO: Westview, 2000.

Gager, John G. "Scholarship as Moral Vision: David Flusser on Jesus, Paul, and the Birth of Christianity." *Jewish Quarterly Review* 95 (2005).

Goodman, Martin. *The Ruling Class of Judea*. Cambridge: Cambridge University Press, 1987.

Graf, Ruth. Review of *A Rabbi Talks with Jesus: An Intermillennial Interfaith Exchange*, by Jacob Neusner. *Review for Religious* 52 (1993): 939–40.

Hagner, Donald, A. *The Jewish Reclamation of Jesus: An Analysis and Critique of the Modern Jewish Study of Jesus*. Eugene, OR: Wipf & Stock, 1997.

Harrington, Daniel J. "The Jewishness of Jesus: Facing Some Problems." *Catholic Biblical Quarterly* 49 (1987): 1–13.

———. Review of *A Rabbi Talk with Jesus*, by Jacob Neusner. *America* 170 (1994): 19.

Harvey, Anthony. Review of *The Religion of Jesus the Jew*, by Géza Vermès. *The Times Literary Supplement*, April 9, 1993.

———. Review of *Jesus the Jew: A Historian's Reading of the Gospels*, by Géza Vermès. *The Times Literary Supplement*, February 24, 1984.

Hedrick, Charles W. "Introduction: The Tyranny of the Synoptic Jesus." *Semeia* 44 (1988): 1–8.

Henaut, Barry W. "Is the 'Historical Jesus' a Christological Construct?" In *Whose Historical Jesus?* edited by W. E. Arnal and M. Desjardins, 241–68. Waterloo, ON: Wilfrid Laurier University, 1997.

Hengel, Martin. *The Charismatic Leader and His Followers*. Translated by J. C. G. Greig. Studies of the New Testament and Its World. Edinburgh: T&T Clark, 1981.

———. *Judaism and Hellenism*. London: SCM, 1974.

Heschel, Susannah. *Abraham Geiger and the Jewish Jesus*. Chicago: University of Chicago Press, 1998.

Heyer, C. J. den. *Jesus Matters: 150 Years of Research*. Translated by John Bowden. Valley Forge, PA: Trinity Press, 1996.

———. *Opnieuw: Wie is Jezus? Balans van 150 jaar onderzoek naar Jezus*. Zoetermeer: Meinema, 1996.

Horbury, William. Review of *Jesus the Jew: A Historian's Reading of the Gospels*, by Géza Vermès. *Theology* 77 (1974): 277.

Horsley, Richard. *Jesus and the Spiral of Violence: Popular Jewish Resistance in Roman Palestine*. Philadelphia: Fortress, 1987.

Hurtado, Larry W. *Lord Jesus Christ: Devotion to Jesus in Earliest Christianity*. Grand Rapids: Eerdmans, 2003.

———. *One God, One Lord: Early Christian Devotion and Ancient Jewish Monotheism*. Philadelphia: Fortress, 1988.

———. "A Taxonomy of Recent Historical-Jesus Work." In *Whose Historical Jesus?* edited by W. E. Arnal and M. Desjardins, 272–95. Waterloo, ON: Wilfrid Laurier University, 1997.

Jacob, Isaac. Review of *We Jews and Jesus*, by Samuel Sandmel. *Journal of Ecumenical Studies* 3 (1966): 168–70.

Jeremias, Joachim. *Jerusalem in the Time of Jesus*. London: SCM Press, 1969.

Johnson, Luke Timothy. "A Historiographical Response to Wright's Jesus." In *Jesus and the Restoration of Israel: A Critical Assessment of N. T. Wright's Jesus and the Victory of God*, edited by Carey C. Newman, 206–24. Downers Grove, IL: InterVarsity Press, 1999.

———. *The Real Jesus: The Misguided Quest for the Historical Jesus and the Truth of the Traditional Gospels.* San Francisco: Harper, 1996.

Judant, Denise. Review of *Jesus the Jew: A Historian's Reading of the Gospels*, by Géza Vermès. *La pensée catholique* 176 (1978): 88.

Kähler, Martin. *The So-Called Historical Jesus and the Historic Biblical Christ.* [German, 1896.] Translated and edited by Carl E. Braaten. Philadelphia: Fortress, 1988.

Käsemann, Ernest. "The Problem of the Historical Jesus." In *Essays on New Testament Themes*, translated by W. J. Montague, 15–47. London: SCM Press, 1964.

King, Nicholas. Review of *Jesus and the World of Judaism*, by Géza Vermès. *The Heythrop Journal* 28 (1987): 202–3.

Klausner, Joseph. *Jesus of Nazareth: His Life, Times and Teaching.* London: George Allen & Unwin, 1925.

Leaney, A. R. C. Review of *Jesus the Jew: A Historian's Reading of the Gospels*, by Géza Vermès. *Journal of Theological Studies* 25 (1974): 489.

Lee, Bernard J. *The Galilean Jewishness of Jesus: Retrieving the Jewish Origins of Christianity.* New York: Paulist Press, 1988.

Levine, Amy-Jill. Review of *Brother Jesus: The Nazarene through Jewish Eyes*, by Schalom Ben-Chorin. *Journal of the American Academy of Religion* 73 (2005): 222–24.

Lieu, Judith. Review of *The Changing Faces of Jesus*, by Géza Vermès. *Journal of Jewish Studies* 52 (2001): 375–76.

Lightfoot, John. *Horae Hebraicae et Talmudicae.* 6 vols. Cambridge: Johannes Field, 1658–78.

Lindeskog, Gösta. *Die Jesusfrage im neuzeitlichen Judentum: Ein Beitrag zur Geschichte der Leben-Jesu-Forschung.* Leipzig, 1938. Reprint, Darmstadt: Wissenschaftliche Buchgesellschaft, 1973.

Lindsey, Robert. *A Hebrew Translation of the Gospel of Mark.* Jerusalem: Dugith, 1969.

———. "A Modified Two-Document Theory of the Synoptic Dependence and Inter-dependence." *Novum Testamentum* 6 (1963).

Martola, Nils. "Vermès' *Jesus the Jew* after Twenty-five Years." Review of *Jesus the Jew*, by Géza Vermès. *Approaches to Ancient Judaism* 7 (1995).

Meier, John P. "From Elijah-like Prophet to the Royal Davidic Messiah." *Jesus: A Colloquium in the Holy Land*, edited by Doris Donnelly, 45–83. New York: Continuum, 2001.

———. *A Marginal Jew.* Vol. 1, *The Roots of the Problem and the Person.* Vol. 2, *Mentor, Message, and Miracles.* Vol. 3, *Companions and Competitors.* New York: Doubleday, 1991, 1994, 2001.

———. "The Present State of the 'Third Quest' for the Historical Jesus: Loss and Gain." *Biblica* 80 (1999): 459–87.

———. "Reflections on Jesus-of-History Research Today." In *Jesus' Jewishness*, edited by James H. Charlesworth, 84–107. New York: Crossroad, 1991.

Merleau-Ponty, Maurice. *Phenomenology of Perception.* Translated by Colin Smith. New York: Routledge, 1962.

Merrigan, Terrence. "The Historical Jesus in the Pluralist Theology of Religions." In *The Myriad Christ: Plurality and the Quest for Unity in Contemporary Christology,* edited by T. Merrigan and J. Haers, 61–82. Louvain: Leuven University Press, 2000.

Moltmann, Jürgen. *The Church in the Power of the Spirit.* New York: Harper & Row, 1977.

Montefiore, C. G. *The Synoptic Gospels.* 1927. Reprint, New York: Ktav, 1968.

Musholt, Silas. Review of *We Jews and Jesus,* by Samuel Sandmel. *Catholic Biblical Quarterly* 27 (1965): 289–91.

Napack, Mark D. Review of *A Rabbi Talks with Jesus,* by Jacob Neusner. *Spiritual Life* 39 (1993): 181–82.

O'Collins, Gerald. Review of *The Resurrection of Jesus,* by Pinchas Lapide. *Heythrop Journal* 26 (1985): 58.

Perkins, Pheme. Review of *The Resurrection of Jesus,* by Pinchas Lapide. *Theological Studies* 45 (1984): 555–56.

Perrin, Norman. *Rediscovering the Teaching of Jesus.* New York: Harper & Row, 1967.

Phipps, William E. Review of *A Rabbi Talks with Jesus,* by Jacob Neusner. *Interpretation* 49 (1995): 306–7.

Polkow, Dennis. "Method and Criteria for Historical Jesus Research." In *Society of Biblical Literature 1987 Seminar Papers,* edited by Kent H. Richards, 336–56. Altanta: Scholars Press, 1987.

Rajak, Tessa. Review of *The Religion of Jesus the Jew,* by Géza Vermès. *Jewish Chronicle,* August 6, 1993.

Ratzinger, Joseph. Review of *A Rabbi Talks with Jesus: An Intermillennial Interfaith Exchange,* by Jacob Neusner. As quoted from the jacket cover of the 1993 edition.

Ricoeur, Paul. *Time and Narrative.* Translated by K. McLaughlin and D. Pellauer. 3 vols. Chicago: University of Chicago Press, 1984–88.

Rosenzweig, Franz. *The Star of Redemption.* Translated by Barbara E. Galli. Madison: University of Wisconsin Press, 2005.

Salkin, Jeffrey K. Review of *A Rabbi Talks with Jesus: An Intermillennial Interfaith Exchange,* by Jacob Neusner. *Theology Today* 50 (1994): 664.

Sanders, E. P. *The Historical Figure of Jesus.* London: Penguin Press, 1993.

———. *Jesus and Judaism.* London: SCM Press, 1985.

———. "In Quest of the Historical Jesus." Review of *The Changing Faces of Jesus,* by Géza Vermès. *New York Review of Books,* November 15, 2001, 48.

Sarfatti, G. B. "Pious Men, Men of Deeds, and the Early Prophets." *Tarbiz* 26 (1956–57).

Scaer, David P. Review of *Ist das nicht Josephs Sohn?* by Pinchas Lapide. *Concordia Theological Quarterly* 49 (1985): 310.

Schürer, Emil. *The History of the Jewish People in the Age of Jesus Christ (175 B.C.–A.D. 135).* A new English version, revised and edited by Géza Vermès and Fergus Millar. Edinburgh: T&T Clark, 1973.

Schwartz, G. David. "Explorations and Responses: Is There a Jewish Reclamation of Jesus?" *Journal of Ecumenical Studies* 24 (1987): 104–9.

Schweitzer, Albert. *The Quest for the Historical Jesus: A Critical Study of Its Progress from Reimarus to Wrede.* [German, 1906.] Translated by W. Montgomery. New York: Macmillan, 1968.

Sievers, Joseph. "Jesus of Nazareth as Seen by Jewish Writers of the XX Century." http://www.vatican.va/jubilee_2000/magazine/documents/ju_mag_01111997_p-48_en.html. This is an updated version of an article that appeared in *Nuova Umanità* 64/65 (July–October 1989): 125–36; and in an abbreviated form in *Unità e Carismi* 6 (November/December 1996): 33–38.

———. "Who Were the Pharisees?" In *Hillel and Jesus*, edited by James H. Charlesworth and L. L. Johns, 137–55. Minneapolis: Fortress, 1997.

Story, Cullen I. K. Review of *The Resurrection of Jesus*, by Pinchas Lapide. *Theology Today* 42 (1986): 564, http://theologytoday.ptsem.edu/jan1986/v42-4-booknotes15.htm.

Strack, Hermann, and Paul Billerbeck. *Kommentar zum Neuen Testament aus Talmud und Midrasch.* 4 vols. in 5. Munich: Beck, 1922–28.

Swidler, Leonard. *Yeshua: A Model for Moderns.* Kansas City, MO: Sheed & Ward, 1988.

Theissen, Gerd. *The Gospels in Context: Social and Political History in the Synoptic Tradition.* Translated by Linda M. Maloney. Minneapolis: Fortress, 1991.

Thoma, Clemens. *A Christian Theology of Judaism.* New York: Paulist Press, 1980.

Van Buren, Paul. "A Positive Jewish Theology of the Church." Review of works of Pinchas Lapide. *Commonweal* 24 (1986): 564–65.

Weaver, Walter P. *The Historical Jesus in the Twentieth Century: 1900–1950.* Harrisburg, PA: Trinity Press, 1999.

Webb, Robert L. "John the Baptist and His Relationship to Jesus." In *Studying the Historical Jesus*, edited by Bruce Chilton and C. A. Evans, 179–230. Leiden: Brill, 1994.

———. *John the Baptizer and Prophet: A Socio-Historical Study.* Sheffield: JSOT, 1991.

Wilson, A. N. Review of *The Religion of Jesus the Jew*, by Géza Vermès. *Evening Standard*, March 2, 1993.

Winter, Paul. *On the Trial of Jesus.* Berlin: de Gruyter, 1961.

———. "The Person of Jesus." Review of *We Jews and Jesus*, by Samuel Sandmel. *Commentary,* September 1965, 107–10.

Witherington, Ben. *The Christology of Jesus.* Minneapolis: Fortress, 1990.

———. *The Jesus Quest: The Third Search for the Jew of Nazareth.* Downers Grove, IL: InterVarsity Press, 1995. 2nd ed., 1997.

———. *Women in the Ministry of Jesus.* Cambridge: Cambridge University Press, 1984.

Wright, N.T. *Jesus and the Victory of God.* Minneapolis: Fortress, 1996.

———. *The New Testament and the People of God.* Minneapolis: Fortress, 1992.

———. *The Resurrection of the Son of God.* Minneapolis: Fortress Press, 2003.

Young, Brad. "Jewish Scholarship and Jesus." Review of *The Jewish Reclamation of Jesus*, by Donald Hagner. *Immanuel* 19 (1984/85): 103–6.

Index

Akenson, Donald H., 231–32
Aron, Robert, 71
Authentic Gospel of John, The (Vermès)

Baal Shem Tov. *See* Besht
baptism:
    of Essenes, 93;
    of Jesus, 93–94, 106, 157
Baeck, Leo, 13, 18, 72
Ben-Chorin, Schalom, 3, 10–13;
    on Flusser, 212–13;
    on Jesus, 11–13, 154–69;
    Lapide on, 209;
    on the Messiah, 155;
    method of, 11, 71–74, 210–11;
    on the New Testament, 72–73;
    reviews of, 208–12;
    on Sandmel, 206;
    on son of Man, 162–63;
    Vermès on, 210
ben Dosa, Hanina. *See* Hanina ben Dosa
Benedict XVI. *See* Ratzinger, Joseph
Bennett, Clinton, 206, 219
Besht, the, Jesus and, 172–73
Bornkamm, Günther, 31
Borowitz, Eugene, 5, 28–30;
    on Jesus, 29–30, 198–201;
    method of, 28–29, 81–82
Braaten, Carl E., 2, 75, 76
*Brother Jesus: The Nazarene Through Jewish
    Eyes* (Ben-Chorin), 10–11, 20–29
Brown, Raymond E., 2–3
Buber, Martin, 3, 10, 11, 15, 17, 18, 165
Bultmann, Rudolf, 3, 22, 31, 72–73;
    school of, 3, 31

"Challenge of Jesus the Jew for the Church,
    The" (Borowitz), 28
Changing Faces of Jesus, The (Vermès), 22
Charlesworth, J. H., 6, 32, 59, 204, 218, 236
Chilton, Bruce, 70, 224–25

Christ:
    Jesus as, 10, 21, 39–41, 86
Cox, Harvey, 209
Crossman, John Dominic, 236
Cunningham, Philip A., 233

Dabru Emet, 243, 245
Daniel, Book of:
    Son of Man in, 12, 132–33, 162–63
Dead Sea Scrolls, 2, 13, 22;
    Flusser on, 52–53, 214–15;
    Sandmel on, 38;
    Vermès on, 62–63
Didache, The, 68
Dunn, James D. G., 1, 83, 236, 241–42

Elijah, Jesus compared to, 12, 141–43
Elisha, Jesus compared to, 12
Essenes:
    baptism of, 93;
    Flusser on, 52–53, 95, 96–97;
    Jesus and, 53, 93, 96;
    and love, 96–97, 151–52;
    Vermès on, 63, 151–52
Evans, Craig A., 214–15

Flusser, David, 13–17, 238–39;
    Ben-Chorin on, 212–13;
    on the Dead Sea Scrolls, 52–53, 214–15;
    on Essenes, 52–53, 95, 96–97;
    on the Gospels, 14, 48, 55–56;
    on Jesus, 15–17, 56, 90–110;
    Lapide on, 212;
    on the Messiah, 51, 108–9;
    method of, 2, 13–16, 47–56, 214–15;
    on Pauline letters, 54;
    and rabbinic literature, 49–52, 214–15;
    reviews of, 207, 209, 212–15;
    on Son of Man, 107–8
Fredriksen, Paula, 230
Frerichs, Wendell W., 218–19
Freyne, Sean, 223, 224

Galilee:
    Jesus and, 124–27, 129;
    Judaism in, 124–27, 129
Geiger, Abraham, 87–88
God:
    as Father, 104, 118–20;
    Jesus' relation to, 16, 101–4, 106, 118–20,
       199
Goodman, Martin, 31
Gospels:
    Flusser on, 14, 48, 55–56;
    Hebrew origins of, 48, 56, 75–77,
       266n354;
    as midrash, 43;
    Sandmel on, 8–9, 41–47, 84–86;
    Synoptic Problem and, 14, 48;
    Vermès on, 33, 57–58, 59, 66–68. *See also*
       individual Gospels
Graf, Ruth, 234
Graves, Robert, 72
Gryn, Hugo, 299n1202

Hagner, Donald A., 206–7, 209, 213, 216
Hanina ben Dosa:
    Flusser on, 103;
    Jesus compared to, 24, 103, 138, 146–48,
       223, 301n1236;
    Vermès on, 24, 138, 146–48, 223
Harrington, Daniel J., 233–34
Hasidim:
    Ben-Chorin on, 12;
    Flusser on, 102–5;
    Jesus compared to, 12, 22, 23–25, 64,
       102–5, 138, 144–49, 152, 223–25;
    Vermès on, 22, 24, 144–49
Heimholung Jesu:
    Ben-Chorin and, 11, 75–76;
    and Vermès, 22
Heschel, Susannah, 206
Hillel, Jesus compared to, 16, 88–89
historical Jesus:
    Borowitz on, 28–29;
    Flusser on, 13–15;
    quests for, 5–6, 13–15, 22–23, 31–33,
       41–43, 83–84, 241–43;
    Sandmel on, 8–9, 41–43. *See also* Jesus
       scholarship
Holocaust, Jesus scholarship after, 2, 18,
    238–39
Honi the Circle-Drawer:
    Ben-Chorin on, 12;
    Flusser on, 103;

    Jesus compared to, 12, 24, 103, 138,
       145–46, 223;
    Vermès on, 22, 138, 145–46, 223
Hurtado, Larry W., 3, 225–26

Isaiah, Servant Song in, 94
Israel ben Eliezer. *See* Besht

Jacob, Isaac, 206
Jesus:
    baptism of, 93–94, 106, 157;
    Ben-Chorin on, 11–13, 154–69;
    and the Besht, 172–73;
    Borowitz on, 29–30, 198–201;
    as Christ, 10, 21, 39–41, 57, 86;
    death of, 109–10, 129–31, 164–69;
    and Elijah, 12, 141–43;
    and Essenes, 53, 93, 96, 151–52;
    as exorcist, 113–14, 157–58;
    family of, 93, 127–28, 156–57;
    Flusser on, 15–17, 56, 90–110;
    and Galilee, 124–27, 129;
    and God, 16, 101–4, 106, 118–20, 199;
    and Hanina ben Dosa, 12, 22, 23–25, 64,
       102–5, 138, 144–49, 152, 223–25;
    and Hasidim, 12, 22, 23–25, 64, 102–5,
       138, 144–49, 152, 223–25;
    and Hillel, 16, 88–89, 101–2;
    historical, 5–6, 13–15, 22–23, 31–33,
       41–43, 83–84, 241–43;
    and Honi the Circle-Drawer, 12, 24, 103,
       138, 145–46, 223;
    humanity/divinity of, 2–3;
    and John the Baptist, 93–94, 127, 157;
    in Josephus, 61;
    and kingdom of God, 17, 100–1, 109–10,
       120–24, 152, 168, 195–97;
    Lapide on, 18–21, 169–85, 239–40;
    and the law, 12, 15–17, 97–98, 116–18,
       155–56, 174–77;
    as lord, 139–40;
    on love ethic, 99–100, 176;
    marital status of, 144, 149, 161–62;
    as messiah, 9, 17, 20–21, 40–41, 51, 86,
       108–9, 134–37, 144, 155, 184;
    Neusner on, 26–27, 80, 185–98;
    parables of, 20, 158–59, 199;
    and Pharisees, 12, 16, 20, 104–5, 128–29,
       156, 174–75, 196–97;
    prayer of, 104, 119–20, 160;
    as prophet, 12, 106–7, 140–43, 155;
    as rabbi, 12, 89–90, 92, 172–73;
    resurrection of, 179–83, 218–20;

and Sadducees, 128, 167–68, 174, 177;
    Sandmel on, 8–10, 84–90;
    self-awareness of, 12–13, 16–17, 101–2,
        106–10, 162–63, 199;
    as son of God, 137–39;
    as son of Man, 11–12, 107–8, 144, 162–63;
    sonship of, 101–2, 106;
    as teacher, 20, 114–16, 158–59, 174–77;
    and Torah, 26–27, 78–80, 185–98,
        266n358;
    Vermès on, 23–25, 64, 110–52, 246–47;
    as wonderworker, 12, 22, 23–25, 64,
        102–5, 113–14;
    and women, 160–61;
    and Zealots, 176–77
Jesus (Flusser), 13, 15
Jesus, God and Man (Brown), 2–3
Jesus scholarship:;
    and *Heimholung Jesu*, 11, 22;
    after the Holocaust;
    and historical Jesus quest, 5–6, 13–15,
        22–23, 31–33, 41–43, 83–84, 241–43;
    Vermès on, 31–32
Jesus the Jew (Vermès), 1, 22, 111
"Jesus the Jew in the Light of the Jewish-
    Christian Dialogue" (Borowitz), 28
John, Gospel of, 55
John the Baptist, Jesus and, 93–94, 127, 157
Josephus:
    Flusser on, 52, 92;
    Jesus in, 61;
    Sandmel on, 37;
    Vermès on, 61–62
Judaism:
    Galilean, 124–27, 129

Kähler, Martin, 241
Käsemann, Ernst, 31, 118
King, Nicholas, 229–30
kingdom of God, Jesus and, 17, 100–1, 109–10,
    120–24, 152, 168, 195–97
Klausner, Joseph, 18, 237
Küng, Hans, 76, 77, 218, 288n910, 297n1165

Lapide, Pinchas, 1, 2, 17–21, 238;
    on Ben-Chorin, 209;
    on Flusser, 212;
    on Jesus, 18–21, 169–85, 239–40;
    on messiah, 17, 20–21;
    method of, 19, 74–77;
    on resurrection, 179–83, 218–20;
    reviews of, 215–20;
    on Sandmel, 206;

    Sandmel on, 216
law, Mosaic:
    Jesus and, 12, 15–17, 97–98, 116–18,
        155–56, 174–77;
    and love, 12, 95–96, 155–56. *See also* Torah
Leil-Shimmurim, of Jesus, 165–67
Levine, Amy-Jill, 210–11
Lindsey, Robert L., 14, 48
lord, Jesus as, 139–40
Lord's Prayer, 104, 119–20, 160
love:
    Essenes and, 96–97;
    Jesus on, 99–100, 176;
    and Mosaic law, 12, 95–96, 155–56;
    and Pharisees, 95–96
Luke, Gospel of, 14, 16–17, 48
Luz, Ulrich, 77, 218

Maimonides, Moses, 182, 183–84
Matthew, Gospel of, 27, 79–80, 185–88
Meier, John P., 221–24, 226–27, 236, 280n710
Merleau-Ponty, Maurice, 204
messiah:
    Ben-Chorin on, 155;
    Flusser on, 51, 108–9;
    Jesus as, 9, 17, 20–21, 40–41, 51, 86,
        108–9, 134–37, 144, 155, 184;
    Lapide on, 17, 20–21;
    Sandmel on, 9, 40–41, 86;
    in Second Temple Judaism, 50–51;
    Vermès on, 134–37, 144
methodology:
    of Ben-Chorin, 11, 71–74, 210–11;
    of Borowitz, 28–29, 81–82;
    of Flusser, 2, 13–16, 47–56, 214–15;
    of Lapide, 19, 74–77;
    of Neusner, 26–27, 78–80;
    of Sandmel, 8–9, 34–47;
    of Vermès, 22–23, 56–68, 111, 131–32,
        222–27
midrash, 43, 259n195. *See also* rabbinic
    literature
Mishnah. *See* rabbinic literature
Moltmann, Jürgen, 2, 181, 182, 184
Musholt, Silas, 205

Napack, Mark Daniel, 232–33
Neusner, Jacob, 6, 25–27;
    on Jesus, 26–27, 80, 185–98;
    method of, 26–27, 78–80;
    reviews of, 231–34;
    on Sandmel, 208;
    on Vermès, 227–29

New Testament:
    Ben-Chorin on, 72–73;
    Flusser on, 53–56;
    Sandmel on, 38–47;
    Vermès on, 65–68. *See also* Gospels
Nostra Aetate (Vatican II), 243, 244, 250n14
Notley, R. Steven, 14–15

O'Collins, Gerald, 219
Outler, Albert, 219

parables, Jesus' use of, 20, 158–59, 199
Paul, letters of:
    Flusser on, 54;
    Sandmel on, 39–41
Perl, Josef, 15, 252n65
Pharisees:
    Jesus and, 12, 16, 20, 104–5, 128–29, 156,
        174–75, 196–97;
    love and, 95–96
Philo of Alexandria, 40
Phipps, William E., 233
prayer, of Jesus, 104, 119–20, 160
prophet, Jesus as, 12, 106–7, 140–43, 155

Qumran scrolls. *See* Dead Sea Scrolls

Rabbi Talks with Jesus, A (Neusner), 26–27
rabbinic literature:
    Flusser and, 49–52, 214–15;
    Lapide and, 171;
    Sandmel and, 37–38;
    Vermès and, 59, 60–61, 63–65, 223–24
Rahner, Karl, 77
Rajak, Tessa, 222
Ratzinger, Joseph, 234, 244–45, 248
Renan, Ernst, 87–88
resurrection, of Jesus, 179–83, 218–20;
    Lapide on, 179–83, 218–20
Rosenthal, Friedrich. *See* Ben-Chorin, Schalom
Rosenzweig, Franz, 206

Sadducees, Jesus and, 128, 167–68, 174, 177
Salkin, Jeffrey, 232
Sanders, E.P., 230–31, 236
Sandmel, Samuel, 7–10;
    Ben-Chorin on, 206;
    on the Gospels, 8–9, 41–47, 84–86;
    on historical Jesus quests, 8–9, 41–43;
    on Jesus, 8–10, 84–90;
    on Lapide, 216;
    Lapide on, 206;
    on messiah, 9, 40–41, 86;
    method of, 8–9, 34–47;

Neusner on, 208;
    on Pauline letters, 39–41;
    and rabbinic literature, 37–38;
    reviews of, 205–8
Scaer, David P., 216–17
Schwartz, G. David, 207–8
Scripture and Christologie, 243
Sermon on the Mount:
    Ben-Chorin on, 158–59;
    Lapide on, 175
Shalom, Shin, 240
Sievers, Joseph, 219
son of God:
    Jesus as, 137–39
son of Man:
    Ben-Chorin on, 162–63;
    Flusser on, 107–8;
    Jesus as, 11–12, 107–8, 132–34, 144,
        162–63;
    Vermès on, 132–34, 144
Story, Cullen I.K., 218

Talmud. *See* rabbinic literature
Ten Commandments, Neusner on, 189–95
Thoma, Clemens, 245
Torah, Jesus and, 26–27, 78–80, 185–98,
    266n358. *See also* law

van Buren, Paul M., 217
van der Vaart Smit, H.W., 170
van Ranke, Leopold, 268n396
Vermès, Géza, 1, 21–25;
    on Ben-Chorin, 210;
    on the Dead Sea Scrolls, 62–63;
    on the Gospels, 33, 57–58, 59, 66–68;
    on Hasidim, 22, 24, 144–49;
    on Jesus, 23–25, 64, 110–52, 246–47;
    and Josephus, 61–62;
    on Messiah, 134–37;
    method of, 22–23, 56–68, 111, 131–32,
        222–27;
    Neusner on, 227–29;
    and rabbinic literature, 59, 60–61, 63–65,
        223–24;
    reviews of, 220–31;
    on Son of Man, 132–34

We Jews and Jesus (Sandmel), 8, 34–35, 84–85
Winter, Paul, 130, 205–
women, Jesus and, 160–61

Zealots, Jesus and, 176–77